Ancient Rhetorical Theory

MW01167170

Contributions to Biblical Exegesis and Theology, 17
Edited by Tj. Baarda (Amsterdam), A. van der Kooij (Leiden), and A.S. van der Woude (Groningen).

Advisory Board: C. Breytenbach (Berlin), R. Collins (Washington), M.A. Knibb (London), P. van Boxtel (London).

1. J.A. Loader, *A Tale of Two Coties, Sodom and Gomorrah in the Old Testament, early Jewish and early Christian Traditions*, Kampen 1990
2. P.W. Van der Horst, *Ancient Jewish Epitaphs. An Introductory Survey of a Millennium of Jewish Funerary Epigraphy (300 BCB-700 CE)*, Kampen, 1991
3. E. Talstra, *Solomon"s Prayer. Synchrony and Diachrony in the Composition of I Kings 8, 14-61*, Kampen, 1993
4. R. Stahl, *Von Weltengagement zu Weltüberwindung: Theologische Positionen im Danielbuch*, Kampen, 1994
5. J.N. Bremmer, *Sacret History and Sacred Texts in early Judaism. A Symposium in Honour of A.S. van der Woude*, Kampen, 1992
6. K. Larkin, *The Eschatology of Second Zechariah: A Study of the Formation of a Mantological Wisdom Anthology*, Kampen, 1994
7. B. Aland, *New Testament Textual Criticism, Exegesis and Church History: A Discussion of Methods*, Kampen, 1994
8. P.W. Van der Horst, *Hellenism-Judaism-Christianity: Essays on their Interaction*, Kampen, 1994
9. C. Houtman, *Der Pentateuch: die Geschichte seiner Erforschung neben einer Auswertung*, Kampen, 1994
10. J. Van Seters, *The Life of Moses. The Yahwist as Historian in Exodus-Numbers*, Kampen, 1994
11. Tj. Baarda, *Essays on the Diatessaron*, Kampen, 1994
12. Gert J. Steyn, *Septuagint Quotations in the Context of the Petrine and Pauline Speeches of the Acta Apotolorum*, Kampen, 1995
13. D.V. Edelman, *The Triumph of Elohim, From Yahwisms to Judaisms*, Kampen, 1995
14. J.E. Revell, *The Designation of the Individual. Expessive Usage in Biblical Narrative*, Kampen, 1996
15. M. Menken, *Old Testament Quotations in the Fourth Gospel* (in preparation)
16. V. Koperski, *The Knowledge of Christ Jesus my Lord. The High Christology of Philippians 3:7-11*, Kampen, 1996
17. M.C. De Boer, *Johannine Perspectives on the Death of Jesus*, Kampen, 1996
18. R.D. Anderson, *Ancient Rhetorical Theory and Paul*, Kampen, 1996

R. Dean Anderson Jr.

Ancient Rhetorical Theory and Paul

Pharos

CIP-GEGEVENS KONINKLIJKE BIBLIOTHEEK, DEN HAAG

© 1996, Kok Pharos Publishing House
P.O. Box 5016, 8260 GA, Kampen, The Netherlands
Cover Design By Karel van Laar
ISBN 90 390 0142 1
NUGI 632

Table of Contents

Preface

This book is the product of my doctoral studies at the Theological University of Kampen (Broederweg), the Netherlands. It has been a pleasure for me, after so many years studying theology both in Canada and the Netherlands, to return to the field of classics where a number of my years were spent in New Zealand. The separation of the two disciplines, classics and New Testament studies, has not always led to the most happy results in either field. It is to be hoped that communication between the two may be increased in the coming years.

The present study was born out of the conviction that a union between these two fields is essential for a responsible approach to the vexed question of the applicability of ancient rhetorical theory to the New Testament. "Rhetorical" studies in many fields have been blossoming over the last two decades and New Testament studies have not remained isolated from this trend. Given the ancient character of the New Testament documents, this has naturally also meant that many scholars have sought to use *ancient* rhetorical theory in this respect, although, as will be shown below, there is quite some confusion as to how this ought to be accomplished.

The scope of this book is restricted to the question of the application of ancient rhetorical theory to certain letters of the apostle Paul. Upon detailing something of the background of studies in this area, particularly over the last two and a half decades (chapter one), a fairly extensive overview is given of the relevant sources for ancient rhetorical theory from Anaximenes to Quintilian (chapter two). Given the distinct weakness of many New Testament studies in effectively coming to grips with ancient rhetorical theory and the problem of the various sources, this has been viewed as an important desideratum. In this chapter, apart from providing an overview of the sources themselves and their respective editions and commentaries, I attempt to show which sources may be considered most applicable to a Greek author such as Paul in the first century AD, and also which *aspects* of such ancient rhetorical theory may be most suitably used. Chapter three addresses the question of the relationship between ancient rhetorical theory and epistolography. From there we are able to proceed, in the ensuing chapters, to an investigation of Paul's letters to the Galatians, Romans and the first letter to the Corinthians. In each case a discussion of much of the recent literature in this field is provided. On the basis of the analysis of these letters certain general conclusions are then drawn in chapter seven with respect to the applicability of ancient rhetorical theory to Paul and the question of the viability and methodology of further research in this area.

I would like to extend thanks to my supervisor Prof. Jakob van Bruggen for his unfailing guidance throughout my work on this project. With respect to the material on ancient rhetorical theory, my gratitude is extended to Prof. Michael Winterbottom for his critical reading of my manuscript at various stages, and for his gracious encouragement, particularly at the time of our meeting in Oxford in the Spring of 1995. Special thanks are also due to Dr. Jakob Wisse for his painstaking assistance and critical comment, especially with respect to the second chapter. Of course, there are many others who deserve mention for their help in respect of this project. I name only Dr. Janet Fairweather for her critical reading of chapters four and six, Drs. Frits Vrij for his stimulation in my reading of the church fathers, and Mr. Pieter Boon for his careful proof-reading of the entire dissertation.

Thanks are also due to the various agencies and persons which have offered me the necessary financial support during my studies in the Netherlands, in particular, the Reformed Churches of Silverstream and Masterton (New Zealand) who also supported me financially and spiritually for the greater part of my theological studies in Canada. Mention must also be made of the Stichting 'HBS' (Foundation for Assisting Foreign Students) for their financial support, and to the Stichting 'Afbouw' for underwriting publication expenses. Last but not least, thanks must be offered to my parents in New Zealand for their support during all my various studies over the last 13 years, and also to my "surrogate parents" here in the Netherlands, Mr and Mrs. A. de Mooij of Rijnsburg, for all their support and encouragement over the last three and a half years.

May the result of this labour redound to the glory of God.

List of Abbreviations

a) Primary Sources

Abbreviations of pagan Greek authors follow the lexicon of Liddell/ Scott/ Jones. Note that the unfortunate authorial indications for *Anonymous Seguerianus* (Corn.) and Anaximenes (Arist.) have been placed in square brackets, as have several other clearly pseudonymous works. A number of works (e.g. Arist. *Rh.*) have been cited by section number rather than by the page number of a certain edition. [Aristid.] *Rh.* is cited by section number from the edition of G. Schmid (BSGRT; Leipzig: B. G. Teubner, 1926), not by Spengel's edition (as LSJ). Philo's works have been itemised according to the abbreviations in the *Theological Dictionary of the New Testament* (ed. G. Kittel; trans. G. W. Bromiley; Grand Rapids: W. B. Eerdmans, 1964), vol. 1. Latin authors are abbreviated according to the *Oxford Latin Dictionary* and Greek Patristic authors according to the *Patristic Greek Lexicon* of Lampe. The books of the New Testament and Septuagint are cited as in LSJ. Citations from the Old Testament in general (not specifically the Septuagint) use the same abbreviations as in LSJ but are prefaced by "OT" instead of "LXX." For ease of reference the abbreviations for the main rhetorical treatises discussed in this book are listed here:

Arist. *Rh.*	Aristotle, *Rhetoric*
[Arist.] *Rh.Al.*	(Anaximenes) *Rhetorica ad Alexandrum*
Cic.	Cicero
de Inv.	*de Inventione*
de Orat.	*de Oratore*
Orat.	*Orator*
Part.	*Partitiones Oratoriae*
Top.	*Topica*
Demetr. *Eloc.*	Demetrius, *de Elocutione*
D.H.	Dionysius of Halicarnassus
Amm.	*Epistula ad Ammaeum*
Comp.	*de Compositione Verborum*
Dem.	*de Demosthene*

Din.	*de Dinarcho*
Isoc.	*de Isocrate*
Lys.	*de Lysia*
Orat. Vett.	*de Oratoribus Veteribus*
Th.	*de Thucydide*
[Longin.]	Ps.-Longinus, *de Sublimitate*
Phld. *Rh.*	Philodemus, *Rhetorica*
Quint. *Inst.*	Quintilian, *Institutio Oratoria*
Rhet.Her.	*Rhetorica ad Herennium*
Rut.Lup.	P. Rutilius Lupus, *Schemata Dianoeas et Lexeos*
Theon *Prog.*	Theon, *Progymnasmata*

In addition, the following abbreviations have been used for authors not listed in the above-mentioned reference works:

Anon. *Excerpt.*   *Excerpta Rhetorica e cod. Parisino n.7530 edita* (ed. C. Halm, *Rhetores Latini Minores* [Leipzig: B. G. Teubner, 1913])

Aug. *Doct.*   Aurelius Augustinus, *De Doctrina Christiana* (ed. J. Martin, CCL 32 [1962])

Aug. *Rhet.*   (Ps.?) Aurelius Augustinus, *Liber de Rhetorica* (ed. C. Halm, *Rhetores Latini Minores*, [Leipzig: B. G. Teubner, 1913]).

Bion Borys.   Bion of Borysthenes (ed. J. F. Kindstrand, *Bion of Borysthenes: A Collection of the Fragments with Introduction and Commentary* [Uppsala, 1976]).

[Demetr.] *Typ.*   Ps.-Demetrius, Τύποι Ἐπιστολικοί (ed. V. Weichert [BSGRT; Leipzig: B. G. Teubner, 1910]).

Empor. *Eth.*   Emporius, *De Ethopoeia* (ed. C. Halm, *Rhetores Latini Minores* [Leipzig: B. G. Teubner, 1913]).

Iul.Rufin.   Iulius Rufinianus, *De Figuris Sententiarum et Elocutionis Liber* (ed. C. Halm, *Rhetores Latini Minores* [Leipzig: B. G. Teubner, 1913]).

[Iul.Rufin.] *Schem.L.* Ps.-Iulius Rufinianus, *De Schematis Lexeos* (ed. C. Halm, *Rhetores Latini Minores* [Leipzig: B. G. Teubner, 1913]).

Iul.Vict. *Rhet.*   Iulius Victor, *Ars Rhetorica* (ed. R. Giomini & M. S. Celentano [BSGRT; Leipzig: B. G. Teubner, 1980]).

[Lib.] *Ep.Char.*   Ps.-Libanius, Ἐπιστολιμαῖοι Χαρακτῆρες (ed. R. Förster, *Libanii Opera* [BSGRT; Leipzig: B. G. Teubner, 1927] vol.9).

LXX *PsSal.*	*Psalmi Salomonis* (an addition to the list in LSJ).
Philo of Larissa	Fragments ed. H. J. Mette (see bibliography).
Vict. *Gal.*	Marius Victorinus, *Commentarius in Epistulam Pauli ad Galatas* (ed. A. Locher [BSGRT; Leipzig: B. G. Teubner, 1972]). Cited by page number in Migne, PL 8.

b) Reference Works and other Abbreviations

BAGD	W. Bauer/ W. F. Arndt/ F. W. Gingrich/ F. W. Danker, *A Greek-English Lexicon of the New Testament and Other Early Christian Literature* (2nd ed.; Chicago: University Press, 1958)
BSGRT	Bibliotheca Scriptorum Graecorum et Romanorum Teubneriana
Denniston, *Part.*	J. D. Denniston, *The Greek Particles* (2nd ed.; Oxford: Clarendon Press, 1954)
K.-G., *Gram.*	R. Kühner/ B. Gerth, *Ausführliche Grammatik der griechischen Sprache* (3rd ed.; Hannover, 1890-1904; reprint, 1955)
LCL	The Loeb Classical Library
LSJ	H. G. Liddell/ R. Scott/ H. S. Jones/ R. McKenzie, *A Greek-English Lexicon with a Supplement* (Oxford: Clarendon Press, 1968).
M.-T., *Gram.*	J. H. Moulton/ N. Turner, *A Grammar of New Testament Greek* (3rd ed.; Edinburgh: T & T Clark, 1908-76; reprint, 1980-6)
Mayser, *Gram. Pap.*	E. Mayser, *Grammatik der griechischen Papyri aus der Ptolemäerzeit mit Einschluss der gleichzeitigen Ostraka und der in Ägypten verfassten Inschriften* (Berlin and Leipzig: de Gruyter, 1970)
OCT	Oxford Classical Texts
SBLDS	Society of Biblical Literature Dissertation Series
Str.-B.	H. L. Strack/ P. Billerbeck, *Kommentar zum Neuen Testament aus Talmud und Midrasch* (München: C. H. Beck, 1924-61; reprint, 1985-9)
SWC	Sammlung wissenschaftlicher Commentare

Secondary literature appearing in the select bibliography is cited by date and short title.

I. Modern Rhetorical Criticism and New Testament Scholarship

1 Background

Whilst the occasion for this book lies in the resurgence of interest in applying ancient rhetorical theory to the letters of Paul which has arisen particularly since the 1970's, we ought not to proceed blinded to the fact that a rhetorical approach to the Bible has many precursors in history. The following brief notations can be nothing more than a few snapshots taken from this history. By highlighting a few authors it is hoped that the reader will be averted from thinking that the recent interest in the application of rhetorical theory to the Bible is some kind of new discovery.

It seems appropriate to begin with the early church. Despite the rhetorical training of many of the church fathers, both Greek and Latin, as far as I am aware the only person to systematically treat the Bible in relation to rhetorical theory was Augustine. In his pre-Christian days Augustine had been a professor of rhetoric and there is even an extant rhetorical treatise under his name (the genuineness of which is disputed). Late in his life (AD 426/27) Augustine finally came to writing the fourth and final book of his *de Doctrina Christiana*. His primary aim was to discuss the eloquence appropriate to a Christian teacher, but it is here that he also addresses the question of the Bible's presentation of its contents. Augustine's piety leads him to assert at the outset that the authors of the inspired Scriptures combined their wisdom with eloquence (*Doct.* 4.6.9). Foremost in Augustine's mind in terms of *eloquentia* is clarity (cf. *Doct.* 4.11.26), which, as we shall see, is indeed one of the virtues of speech in rhetorical theory. Thus where Augustine feels able to understand the Scriptures, he is emboldened to say that just as there is nothing more wise, so is there nothing more eloquent. Yet even where Augustine cannot fathom the meaning of the Scriptures, he presumes that their eloquence must be of the same kind. Such obscurity is, for Augustine, by definition *utilis* and *salubris* (*Doct.* 4.8.22), and various reasons for it are offered.

At *Doct.* 4.7.11 Augustine uses Paul as an example of what he is talking about. Although surely no one would contend that Paul knew any rhetorical theory, nevertheless Paul's writings evidence the kind of eloquence taught there. Augustine points to the figure of κλῖμαξ in *Ep.Rom.* 5.3-5 and cites (unconvincingly) v.5 as an example of a περίοδος.[1] Next, an analysis into περίοδοι, κῶλα and κόμματα is provided for 2 *Ep.Cor.* 11.16-30.

At *Doct.* 4.20 Augustine illustrates the three types of style (taken from Cic. *Orat.*) with various passages from Paul's letters. Whilst interesting, Augustine does not, however, discuss *why* he thinks any given passage belongs to one or other of the types of style. We do learn that Augustine notices the distinct lack of prose rhythm in the Scriptures, at least in their Latin translation (*Doct.* 4.20.41). He suspects, although he confesses that he does not know for certain, that such lack of prose rhythm is also apparent in the original Greek.

It is important to note that Augustine's approach is apologetic. He is defending the eloquence of Paul (and the Bible in general) against certain unnamed men (apparently Christian) who had criticised the eloquence of the Bible (cf. *Doct.* 4.6.10; 4.7.14).

The next person I should like to briefly comment upon is Philip Melanchthon. This immediately takes us to the period of the renaissance and Reformation.[2] Although many of the reformers utilised rhetorical theory in their explanations of the Scriptures, none were so systematic or dedicated in their rhetorical approach as Melanchthon. The renaissance had brought with it a renewed interest in rhetorical theory among the scholars of the day.[3] Melanchthon, however, not only studied rhetorical theory, but also lectured and wrote extensively on it. A list of the titles of his rhetorical works gives some idea of his preoccupation with this subject:

---

[1]   Augustine appears to define the περίοδος somewhat unusually in terms of a sentence wherein the clauses are suspended by means of the tone (voice) of the speaker, and not syntax: *ambitus siue circuitus, quem περίοδον illi* [*sc. Graeci*] *appellant, cuius membra suspenduntur uoce dicentis, donec ultimo finiatur.* Augustine goes on to cite *Ep.Rom.* 5.5 as a three-membered period: *spes autem non confundit, quoniam caritas dei diffusa est in cordibus nostris, per spiritum sanctum qui datus est nobis.* This cannot be defined as a περίοδος in the commonly accepted sense. There is no real circuit, or syntactical connection between the beginning and the end. The same point may be made with respect to the "περίοδοι" Augustine notes in 2 *Ep.Cor.* 11 (*Doct.* 4.7.13). Any complete sentence appears to be able to be categorised as a περίοδος.

[2]   An examination of the use of rhetorical theory in medieval exegesis would make an interesting study. Unfortunately, I am not in a position to comment on this myself. See, however, C. J. Classen (1995, "Analyse") for a brief comment on H. Bebel's *Commentaria Epistolarum Conficiendarum* (Strassburg, 1503). Bebel was, though, more concerned with ancient epistolary theory, or rather the lack thereof.

[3]   One of the standard textbooks was apparently R. Agricola's *de Inventione Dialectica* (see D. C. Parker, 1989, "Introduction," 17).

1519, *De Rhetorica Libri Tres* (reprinted four times between 1519 and 1529)
1521, *Institutiones Rhetoricae* (lecture notes published, with approval, by students. Revised in 1531 and printed as *Elementorum Rhetorices Libri II* which edition was often reprinted and revised again in 1542)
1523, *Encomium Eloquentiae*

In addition he wrote several treatises on the related discipline of dialectics. C. J. Classen has recently shown that Melanchthon's rhetorical theory, whilst founded to a large extent upon classical rhetorical theory, often departs from it. Melanchthon appears to have developed his own division of genres and frequently to have invented his own technical terminology.[4] Melanchthon's rhetorical analysis of Paul's letters is thus *not* the historical discipline of applying ancient rhetorical theory, but the modern discipline of using and adapting rhetorical theory to clarify the letters.

That interest in a rhetorical approach to the Bible did not wane in the succeeding centuries is clear from a number of works published in this period.[5] During the nineteenth century it was particularly German scholarship which paid attention to Paul and rhetorical theory. In 1843 C. G. Wilke published *Die neutestamentliche Rhetorik: Ein Seitenstuck zur Grammatik des neutestamentlichen Sprachidioms* (Dresden/ Leipzig: Arnold), a work which looks especially at the tropes and figures in the New Testament.[6] In 1887 C. F. G. Heinrici published the first edition of his commentary on Paul's second letter to the Corinthians (1887, *Sendschreiben*), in which he paid particular attention to Paul's relationship to rhetorical theory. Ten years later J. Weiss (1897, "Beiträge"), referring to Wilke and Heinrici, decided that it was time for a more detailed examination of Paul's "rhetoric." Weiss produced an interesting study of Paul's use of parallelism, antithesis and symmetry in general, analysing in particular Paul's letter to the Romans and portions of the first letter to the Corinthians. Weiss estimated that Paul had possessed a singular practice and ability in the symmetrical construction of language (194). He also demonstrated that whilst to some degree there is an

---

4   1993, "Epistles," 271-80. Classen briefly discusses Melanchthon's approach to both the letter to the Galatians and that to the Romans. A glimpse at Melanchthon's structural rhetorical analysis of Paul's letter to the Colossians, as summarised by D. C. Parker (1989, "Introduction," 20-21), confirms Classen's comments. It is of course possible that some or even many of the differences between Melanchthon's rhetorical theory and classical theory may be attributable to some work(s) published in the intervening period.
5   See, for example, John Prideaux, *Sacred Eloquence: The Art of Rhetoric as it is Laid Down in Scripture* (London: George Sawbridge, 1659); C. L. Bauer, *Logica Paullina* (Halle/ Magdeburg, 1774) and *Rhetorica Paullina* (2 vols; Halle, 1782).
6   I have not seen this book myself, but rely upon the report of J. Weiss, 1897, "Beiträge," 166n.

influence from Semitic parallelism, this cannot account for the many particularly Greek forms of parallelism evident in Paul's language.[7] Weiss' analysis, however, did not apply specifically *ancient* rhetorical theory, although he saw this as a desideratum for someone versed in this area (247). The reader should take care not to interpret his frequent comments on "rhythm" and "music" as if they refer to ancient conceptions of prose rhythm or harmony.

Controversy over the application of rhetorical theory to Paul's letters was aroused a year later when E. Norden reacted strongly to C. F. G. Heinrici's above-mentioned commentary.[8] Norden was particularly unimpressed with Heinrici's comments relating 2 *Ep.Cor.* 10 - 12 to rhetorical theory, and its practice in, for example, Demosthenes. To Norden such analogies are rather far-fetched. Whilst Norden's critique was, at least partially, based on a misunderstanding of Heinrici, it must be admitted that Heinrici had not expressed himself very carefully. In the second edition of his commentary, Heinrici devoted a lengthy appendix to defending himself against Norden's criticism.[9] There he made it clear that he in no way intended to suggest that Paul's letters showed any direct influence of school rhetoric, but merely that various rhetorical effects can be traced in his letters, effects that were generally current within the Hellenistic culture of the time. Nevertheless, when discussing the relationship of rhetorical theory to Paul's letters on pages 38-41 of his second edition, Heinrici does suggest a close relationship to rhetorical theory, even going so far as to state that the *partes orationis* (i.e., the various sections of a formal speech) may be detected in the letters.[10] Norden apologised for his tone in the second edition of his *Kunstprosa* and made one small retraction.[11] Norden's own discussion of Paul's style is generally quite perceptive.[12] He also takes into account the various rhetorical figures used by Paul, although he attributes them not to knowledge of school rhetoric, but to the Asianist style (in his view) so preponderant in

---

[7]   It is, perhaps, worth mentioning that this point appears to have escaped E. von Dobschütz in his otherwise interesting study on Paul's style in the letter to the Romans (1934, "Wortschatz"). Dobschütz' study is more linguistically orientated, although he rather all too briefly passes off the "rhetoric" in Paul's style as rooted in Old Testament forms (64-65).

[8]   1898, *Kunstprosa*, 2.492-98.

[9]   1900, *Brief*, 436-57.

[10]   In a later book (1908, *Charakter*, 66-69), Heinrici speaks generally of Paul's style, relating it especially to the so-called *diatribe* (a comparison also made earlier in his commentaries on the Corinthian correspondence). In terms of rhetorical theory he cites Aug. *Doct.* 4, and also goes on to speak of "die zahlreichen rhythmischen Anklänge" (p.68, cf. 1900, *Brief*, 314) in Paul's language, but no proof is offered.

[11]   1915, *Kunstprosa*, Nachträge pp.3-4.

[12]   1898, *Kunstprosa*, 492-510.

the contemporary world. Norden also provides a very interesting summary of comments from the church fathers on Paul's style.[13]

The beginning of the twentieth century saw a decline in the general teaching of rhetorical theory in schools and universities. Already in 1913 F. H. Colson complained that ancient rhetoric was a subject "forgotten and ignored by the average classical scholar."[14] Studies applying ancient rhetorical theory to the Bible during the first part of this century are therefore few. We may note, however, two articles by American classical scholars. T. S. Duncan in 1926 published an article entitled "The Style and Language of Saint Paul in his First Letter to the Corinthians." Duncan first treats Paul's style in general, largely basing his discussion upon Norden. He then provides a listing of various figures found in 1 *Ep.Cor.*. This list of figures is used to support Norden's contention that Paul's rhetoric is influenced by Asianism. In fact he goes so far as to say that "it seems most likely that his [*sc.* Paul's] rhetorical training was received from the Asianic schools" (143). In the 1948/49 issue of *The Classical Journal*, W. A. Jennrich published a short article on "Classical Rhetoric in the New Testament." Jennrich's article is basically a plea for more appreciation of the rhetorical element in the New Testament, particularly in the letters of Paul. He supports this plea by arguing that the New Testament language must be viewed within the context of a tradition of literary *koine* in the first century AD, and not against the background of the lacklustre papyri. Interestingly, the editor of the journal notes that "the rhetorical aspects of the New Testament have been one of his [*sc.* Jennrich's] special interests." Unfortunately, I am unaware of anything else Jennrich may have written on this subject. In any event, his plea appears to have fallen on deaf ears among the New Testament scholars of the time. Not until the late 1960's does it appear that interest in rhetoric among Bible scholars underwent a revival.

2 The "Muilenburg School"

In 1968 the retired, but still active, Old Testament professor James Muilenburg delivered what was to be a very influential, even programmatic, address to the Society of Biblical Literature. It was subsequently published in 1969 as "Form Criticism and Beyond" and contained a plea for a new direction in scholarly research, namely, what Muilenburg called "rhetorical criticism." He began by voicing his discontent with the

---

13   *Op. cit.*, 501-506.
14   1913, Τάξει, 62.

emphasis in Old Testament scholarship on form criticism.[15] Not that Muilenburg was opposed to form criticism as such. As a student of Gunkel, he had great praise for the achievements of form criticism and *Gattungsforschung*.[16] But Muilenburg had also been led to see certain limitations in the approach. Firstly, form criticism tends to define a general *Gattung* without dealing with the stylistic and rhetorical uniqueness of *various* examples of the same *Gattung*. Thus "the individual, personal, and unique features of the particular pericope are all but lost to view" (5). Secondly, form criticism often disregards the concrete historical context, and doesn't allow "biographical or psychological interpretations" (5). This can be explained "in part as a natural, even inevitable, consequence of its disregard of literary criticism" (6).

Muilenburg went on to discuss with approval the emphasis by some on what has been called stylistics, a form of literary criticism.[17] He went on to formulate his new proposed approach, adding:

> What I am interested in, above all, is in understanding the nature of Hebrew literary composition, in exhibiting the structural patterns that are employed for the fashioning of a literary unit, whether in poetry or in prose, and in discerning the many and various devices by which the predications are formulated and ordered into a unified whole. Such an enterprise I should describe as rhetoric and the methodology as rhetorical criticism. (8)

With these words Muilenburg verbalised a concern and a challenge to direct biblical (particularly Old Testament) studies in a new way. That is not to say that studies engaging in this sort of approach did not exist before then, but from that time on many scholars consciously began to work with this new perspective, seeing themselves as engaging in what Muilenburg had coined "rhetorical criticism." A number of scholars who began to show this emphasis in their studies are referred to as "the Muilenburg (or Berkeley) school."[18]

But the influence of Muilenburg's address was by no means limited to Old Testament scholars, for many New Testament scholars saw application to their own field of study as well, particularly in relation to the form criticism of the Gospels. The new "method" of rhetorical criticism as such was also eventually applied even to the letters

---

[15]   Also known as *Formgeschichte*, i.e., the discipline whereby various irreducible units (forms) in a literary or oral tradition are isolated and classified. Such conventional "forms" are considered to have had their origin in various concrete sociological contexts.

[16]   Muilenburg spent his sabbatical of 1929-1930 at Marburg, Germany, where he had much contact with Gunkel.

[17]   For example, the work of L. Alonzo-Schökel.

[18]   Scholars such as W. Wuellner, W. J. Brandt and E. P. J. Corbett.

of Paul, and Pauline scholars interested in this method continue to acknowledge the address of Muilenburg as programmatic for their discipline.

It ought to be noticed, however, that what is termed "rhetorical criticism" by New Testament scholars today, is slightly different from what Muilenburg himself envisaged. Muilenburg saw rhetorical criticism as a form of literary criticism that dealt with stylistics, whilst New Testament scholars, as we shall see, have tended to emphasise rhetoric in terms of argumentation. Another work published (in translation) in 1969 significantly helped to bring about this new emphasis, for New Testament scholars anyway.

3 The "New Rhetoric"

In 1969 there appeared an (American) English translation of Ch. Perelman and L. Olbrechts-Tyteca's book *La Nouvelle Rhétorique: Traité de l'Argumentation* ("The New Rhetoric: A Treatise on Argumentation"), first published in Belgium in 1958. This translation was to prove very influential in areas probably never envisaged by its authors, as it gave great impetus to the development of the movement of rhetorical criticism in biblical studies.

Yet the book itself is not written as a guide to rhetorical or literary criticism, whether ancient or modern. It is rather a philosophical work on argumentation; its structure, premises, and techniques. Perelman and Olbrechts-Tyteca place themselves in the tradition of Aristotle's *Rhetorica*.[19]

Aristotle's *Rhetorica* was, in large part, also a work on argumentation conceived philosophically. This was probably a contributory factor in its neglect in ancient schools of rhetoric. Particularly important for Perelman and Olbrechts-Tyteca is the way in which Aristotle set his work on rhetoric apart from his work on formal logic by arguing that rhetoric deals with probabilities and not with certitudes. It is precisely within this context that Perelman and Olbrechts-Tyteca conceive their work.

They argue that the history of philosophy, especially since Descartes, has tended to embrace the science of formal logic and neglect and even look down upon rhetoric. In fact formal logic with its mathematical precision and certainties has been considered the only foundation for true philosophy. "A rational science cannot indeed be content with more or less probable opinions; it must elaborate a system of necessary propositions which will impose itself on every rational being" (2). Beginning from so-called

---

[19]   Cf. F. H. van Eemeren/ R. Grootendorst, 1993, "Invloeden," 176-78.

self-evident premises, a philosophical system can be built up that, if properly based upon the rules of formal logic, *must* be accepted. This emphasis upon formal logic has only increased in our century, but this concentration upon purely formal logic, a logic with mathematical certainty, has resulted in a great restriction and reduction to the scope of philosophy. Such logic is restricted to those things that can be determined with mathematical precision, leaving out "questions of a moral, social, political, philosophical, or religious order" (512). This Perelman and Olbrechts-Tyteca term "*a perfectly unjustified and unwarranted limitation of the domain of action of our faculty of reasoning and proving*" (italics theirs, 3). They thus part ways here with this emphasis in modern philosophy. Their re-emphasis upon informal logic/ argumentation, or rhetoric as classically conceived, marks for them a "break with a concept of reason and reasoning due to Descartes" (1).

Perelman and Olbrechts-Tyteca make it quite clear that they are supporting a philosophy of reasoning or argumentation that is by nature relative, without absolutes. "We do not believe in definitive, unalterable revelations, whatever their nature or their origin. And we exclude from our philosophic arsenal all immediate, absolute data, be they termed sensations, rational self-evidence, or mystical intuitions." (510) Rhetoric is the art of inducing or increasing the mind's adherence to the theses presented for its assent (4). As such, in the line of Aristotle, it has inherently to do with probabilities, not certainties.

Now Perelman and Olbrechts-Tyteca do not mean to deny that argumentation always begins with premises assumed to be held in common. In fact this question forms an important part of the book's discussion (pp.63-114). But as with ancient rhetoric, so also here, argumentation is closely related to the audience at which it is directed (a central concern of the first section of the book). In fact "*it is in terms of an audience that an argumentation develops*" (italics theirs, 5). They show that various audiences can be shown to hold different "agreements" in common. Even a "universal audience" as conceived by one person or group will differ from that as conceived by others (i.e., when one believes he is presenting arguments acceptable not just to his particular audience, but to anyone). Herein lies their relativism. But it is just this relativism which they extol as giving "meaning to human freedom" which they define as "a state in which a reasonable choice can be exercised." (514)

Having described the philosophical context and approach of their work on argumentation, something should be said of its relation to classical rhetoric. Unlike most of classical rhetoric, they do not restrict themselves to oral discourse, but their work aims to analyse verbal argumentation wherever it occurs, and thus also literary argumentation. In their terms, they do not restrict their audience to a crowd gathered in a public square. In this sense their scope is broader. But at the same time they limit themselves as well, in that, unlike ancient rhetoric, they do not discuss *memoria* or delivery. This different scope is much like the scope of biblical rhetorical criticism, which in the nature of the case must also deal with literary documents.

In their analysis of argumentation Perelman and Olbrechts-Tyteca frequently take a different approach than ancient rhetoric. They reject the basic division of rhetoric into three broad genres: forensic, deliberative, and epideictic (21). Yet they do discuss the epideictic genre, viewing it as the most significant (in stark contrast to ancient rhetorical theory). Whilst ancient rhetorical theory tended to define the epideictic genre in terms of a speech for the enjoyment of an audience consisting of praise or blame, Perelman and Olbrechts-Tyteca insist that there is much more to it than this. It is also argument designed to strengthen "the disposition toward action by increasing adherence to the values it lauds" (50).[20] It is thus "educative," which they define as supporting traditional values. Thus "the purpose of an epidictic [sic] speech is to increase the intensity of adherence to values held in common by the audience and the speaker" (52). This (re-)definition of the epideictic genre is important, as it has tended to function in the discussion and analysis of Paul's letters in relation to ancient rhetoric.

Yet on the whole Perelman and Olbrechts-Tyteca are not concerned with rhetorical form or genre (structural rhetoric). They are rather concerned with techniques of argumentation and their effectiveness. It is also in this respect that they deal with stylistics. In their words:

> "We refuse ... to study stylistic structures and figures independently of the purpose they must achieve in the argumentation." (142)

As such they explicitly add that their work is not concerned with forms of expression solely designed to produce an aesthetic effect (142-43).

It should be noticed at this point that terminology designating different aspects of rhetorical analysis is not standardised. A distinction is frequently made between i)

---

[20]   "Unlike deliberative and legal speeches, which aim at obtaining a decision to act, the educational and epidictic speeches create a mere disposition toward action, which makes them comparable to philosophical thought." (54) Here, despite their rejection of rhetorical genres on p.21, they reason as if these genres are accepted. Perhaps their ambivalence at this point explains why biblical scholars using the Perelman/ Olbrechts-Tyteca approach still see the need to categorise Paul's letters in terms of one of these three genres, cf., for example, F. Siegert, 1985, *Argumentation*, 111-12.

structural rhetoric (concerned with form or genre and its formal division into parts), and ii) textual rhetoric (concerned with stylistics and the progression and analysis of argumentation). This distinction is sometimes indicated by the terms macro- and micro-rhetoric, or architectonic and stylistic rhetoric.

4 The Influence of the "New Rhetoric"

The influence of this book on biblical rhetorical criticism has been considerable. In the first place, it dove-tailed well with the desires outlined by James Muilenburg's presidential address to the Society of Biblical Literature in 1968 discussed above. Muilenburg wanted an analysis of the structural patterns, the stylistics of various pericopes or literary forms (*Gattungen*). The work of Perelman and Olbrechts-Tyteca gave biblical scholarship a new approach in dealing with these phenomena, namely, setting them within the framework of *argumentation*.

New Testament scholarship, frequently also influenced by Muilenburg's programmatic address, has seized upon this work, and begun to utilise it for its own rhetorical criticism. A dedicated example of this is F. Siegert's dissertation *Argumentation bei Paulus*, 1985. After giving a lengthy précis of Perelman and Olbrechts-Tyteca's book, illustrated from the Septuagint, he analyses the argumentation of *Ep.Rom.* 9 - 11. He then uses this as a basis upon which to draw more general conclusions as to the nature of Paul's argumentation. It is a striking fact that this work hardly utilises ancient rhetoric at all. It is true that Siegert is of the opinion that the letter to the Romans is an epideictic speech (111), and he notes formal divisions of this letter made on that basis (113-14), but as his interest is in textual rhetoric these are only introductory questions for him. Siegert's analysis of the textual rhetoric of *Ep.Rom.* 9 - 11 is based thoroughly upon Perelman and Olbrechts-Tyteca, and he does not analyse textual rhetoric from the perspective of ancient rhetoric.[21]

But such a *pure* "new rhetoric" approach has been unusual in biblical studies. Many studies concerned with rhetorical criticism have combined the new approach of Perelman and Olbrechts-Tyteca with the study of ancient rhetoric.[22] It is thought that

---

[21]   A similarly based analysis of *Ep.Rom.* 1 - 8 is provided by G. Bouwman, 1980, *Paulus*. A modern rhetorical analysis of *Ep.Gal.* is worked out by G. W. Hansen, 1989, *Abraham*, 79-93. For other studies based on a modern rhetorical approach see: D. Fraikin, 1986, "Function"; A. H. Snyman, 1988, "Style"; N. Elliott, 1990, *Rhetoric*; J. N. Vorster, 1993, "Strategies"; K. A. Plank, 1987, *Paul*; W. Wuellner, 1986, "Paul."

[22]   Cf. G. A. Kennedy, 1984, *New Testament*; B. L. Mack, 1990, *Rhetoric*; J. D. Hester, 1986, "Use"; W. Wuellner, 1976, "Rhetoric."

ancient rhetoric itself could not really be neglected, since the literature under considera-tion belonged to ancient society. The claims for ancient rhetoric will be examined briefly below (chapter one, § 6).

The fact that rhetorical criticism has proceeded to work upon the New Testament from both the perspective of ancient rhetoric *and* the new rhetoric, has also meant that there has been an emphasis on evaluation of argumentation. (Of course that is not to say that ancient rhetoric did not also wish to evaluate argumentation.) But rhetorical criticism seems to have concentrated not on the historical discipline of evaluating New Testament argumentation within its own time framework, but on evaluating it for our-selves today. Of course we no longer have access to the original audiences of the New Testament documents, so it is impossible to survey their reactions. Yet modern evalua-tion is quite possible. The only problem here is that modern evaluation all too fre-quently uses modern canons of acceptability determined by modern philosophy. Thus, for example, B. L. Mack's evaluation of New Testament rhetoric in general (particu-larly Paul) is quite negative, primarily because of the use of harsh rhetoric based on non-negotiable claims to authority.[23] This appears to reflect the philosophical back-ground of Perelman and Olbrechts-Tyteca (by whom Mack is heavily influenced).

5 Kennedy's Methodology and Approach

It was some time before a work finally appeared that was once again to direct New Testament rhetorical criticism in a definitive way. Such direction was eventually provided in 1984 with the publication of *New Testament Interpretation Through Rhetorical Criticism* by the classicist specialising in rhetoric, G. A. Kennedy. Kennedy had experienced a line of students of biblical literature who wished to study ancient rhetoric under him, and much as a result of this experience he produced this book. Having come into contact with biblical, and particularly New Testament, rhetorical criticism, he noticed the lack of a "rigorous methodology" and sought to supply such in his book.[24]

Kennedy's methodology is in fact quite simple, although it has proved difficult to outline (33-38). Subsequent scholars have sought to summarise it in five steps, but the

---

23   Cf. B. L. Mack, 1990, *Rhetoric*, 102.
24   For another (modern) methodology see E. Schüssler Fiorenza, 1987, "Situation."

division into five seems to differ with each attempt.[25] Without numeration, the basic steps are:

- Determination of the *rhetorical unit* which must have a beginning, middle, and end. The unit should not be too large. Understanding of a large rhetorical unit (e.g., lengthy epistle) should be "built up from an understanding of the rhetoric of smaller units" (33).
- Determination of the *rhetorical situation*. What situation invited the utterance? Examine the persons (esp. audience), events, objects, relations, time, place.
- Determination of the overriding *rhetorical problem* (e.g., ill-disposed audience), of *stasis* (in the classical sense), and of the *species of rhetoric*.
- Determination of the *arrangement of material*, i.e., division into parts and their working together towards some unified purpose. In short an analysis of the argumentation, including stylistics, keeping in mind the principle of linear development.
- Review of the success of the argumentation in meeting its (historical) goal. What are the implications for the audience?

Such a method seems virtually self-explanatory, but one thing is startlingly lacking. There appears to be no distinction made between the study of the rhetoric or argumentation of a unit in general, and the relationship or contribution of *ancient* rhetoric to the unit. This fact has to do with Kennedy's understanding of the discipline of rhetorical criticism as a whole, and with the part that classical rhetoric plays in it.

Kennedy sets out to define rhetorical criticism by setting it off from form criticism and redaction criticism (which, he rightly observes, has more to do with the work of an editor, especially his theological intent). He then proceeds to contrast rhetorical criticism with literary criticism (meaning what is generally known as *new criticism*).[26] This is done in two ways. Firstly, he notes that literary criticism, whilst also concerned with rhetoric (at least stylistics), is generally more concerned with the text's interaction with the *modern* reader and not with its effect upon the *ancient* audience. Rhetorical criticism is then concerned with:

... reading the Bible as it would be read by an early Christian, by an inhabitant of the Greek-speaking world in which rhetoric was the core subject of formal education and in which even

---

[25]   Contrast for example W. Wuellner, 1987, "Criticism," 455-58; and D. F. Watson, 1992, "Criticism," 699. Compare also A. H. Snyman, 1988, "Style," 218 who summarises the method in four steps, and C. C. Black, 1989, "Criticism," 254-55 who outlines six steps!

[26]   "Literary criticism" is, unfortunately, a rather vague term. In older works this term is used in a very general sense, which would mean that *rhetorical criticism* would be a sub-discipline of *literary criticism*. More recent scholarship has developed *literary criticism* in two directions, namely, (literary) structuralism, and what is known as the *new criticism*. In some ways the attempt to classify all argumentation into one of three species (forensic, deliberative, and epideictic), each with a characteristic division into parts, can be considered as a form of (rhetorical) structuralism, cf. G. Bouwman, 1980, *Paulus*, 23-24.

those without formal education necessarily developed cultural preconceptions about appropriate discourse. (5)

What he means here by "Bible" as opposed to New Testament is not immediately clear, but this will become more obvious below.

Secondly, Kennedy states that even though we are concerned with texts and not oral communication (as is literary criticism), nevertheless, the New Testament documents were conceived orally and thus "the Bible retained an oral and linear quality for its audience" (5). This linear quality is important for Kennedy. He admits that Christian communities heard (and read) the same documents over and over again and thus were eventually able to easily recall what had gone before and what was to come. But his emphasis is on the impact of these documents upon their *first* hearing, and this was completely *linear*. The letters of Paul, for example, were read out loud to their audiences. This means analysis must bear in mind the linear nature of the argumentation. The audience could not flip back and forth between pages, as it were (and rolling a scroll back and forth is not that simple). They heard the argumentation in a straight line. This further distinguishes rhetorical criticism from literary criticism.

Kennedy's justification for rhetorical criticism of biblical literature in general is twofold. There is, firstly, for the New Testament in particular, an *historical* justification. Here arguments such as the following are presented: the extent of the Hellenisation of Jewish culture by the first century AD; the fact that rhetoric was "universally taught throughout the Roman empire"; that in fact several important rhetoricians came from Syria and Palestine; and that Paul must have had some exposure to rhetoric, even *if* he didn't have a rhetorical education (8-10). The New Testament documents were orally (and thus rhetorically) conceived.

Secondly, he approaches the discipline from a more *philosophical* viewpoint. As Aristotle argued, rhetoric is a universal phenomenon applicable to all ages and societies. Aristotle's *Rhetorica* was meant to describe this universal phenomenon of rhetoric, *not* Greek rhetoric (though it uses Greek examples). Specific to Greek rhetoric is its arrangement and style (as opposed to "basic devices of invention") (8), the structured system which the theoreticians put together and which was taught and learned (11). In fact, Kennedy defines classical rhetorical theory as the "structured system which describes the universal phenomenon of rhetoric in Greek terms" (11). As far as the Old Testament is concerned, although no theory of rhetoric existed in those times (just as for early Greek history), yet "the importance of speech among them is everywhere evident" (11). They learned rhetoric by imitation. He concludes: "In understanding how their rhetoric worked we have little choice but to employ the concepts and terms of the Greeks."

Kennedy clearly views ancient (Greek) rhetoric not just as something we may use to illucidate aspects of the rhetoric of its time, but as a universal system, in theory appropriate for analysing the rhetoric of any age or culture (10-11).

6 The Place of Ancient Rhetorical Theory

This brings us to the question of the place of ancient rhetoric in rhetorical criticism. Kennedy's approach to this discipline is unsatisfactory. He is sensitive to the criticism that his approach sets up classical rhetoric as a standard by which the Bible is to be judged. But he argues that when rhetoric is seen as more than just stylistics, and when due account is taken of traditions, for example, of Jewish speech (e.g., chiasm), then this criticism disappears (11-12).

Yet Kennedy does not address what seems to me to be a more pertinent problem, namely, whether classical rhetoric as a system is really sufficient to use as a universal tool for analysing rhetoric in various cultures and times (which is what is implied). Would we not then be better off refining that system and using the benefits of modern research in creating a universal grammar of rhetoric? Is not this in fact what Perelman and Olbrechts-Tyteca have attempted in their *New Rhetoric*? This would seem to be a much better *universal* tool than a Greek system written *c.* 2,000 years ago. If we are only interested in an ahistorical rhetorical framework for the Bible (or New Testament), then something like the *New Rhetoric* is probably a far better tool. The work of F. Siegert (1985, *Argumentation*) noted above has shown how this can be used with good sensitivity to the historical context and situation of the original audience, and this is precisely the interest of Kennedy: "The ultimate goal of rhetorical analysis, briefly put, is the discovery of the author's intent and of how that is transmitted through a text to an audience" (12). Although verbalised differently, this is virtually identical to the goal of Perelman and Olbrechts-Tyteca.[27]

What then is the place of *ancient* rhetoric in biblical studies? Here I believe B. L. Mack (1990, *Rhetoric*) has a better approach. Mack is a hearty supporter of the direction of thinking shown by Perelman and Olbrechts-Tyteca, and thus a proponent of the use of their work in terms of biblical rhetorical criticism. Yet Mack also sees an impor-

---

[27]   Kennedy is not unaware of their work, although it is not used in his text. He lists it in his bibliography of books "likely to be of interest to the practitioner of rhetorical criticism" (162).

tant place for the study of classical rhetoric. For him the classical tradition provides the cultural context for a rhetorical study of the New Testament. He gives three reasons for the usefulness of a knowledge of classical rhetoric:

> First, one needs some sense of the place of rhetoric, its importance, and its pervasive influence in first-century society and culture. This is important in order to understand how early Christian authors came into contact with rhetorical practice. Second, one needs some knowledge of the forms of rhetorical speech and their several patterns of argumentation. This is important in order to discern units of rhetorical composition in the New Testament. Third, it is necessary to grasp the principles of rhetorical proof (in distinction from philosophical demonstration). This is important in order to evaluate the New Testament use of maxims, metaphors, examples, and scriptural citations as proofs that count in a pattern of argumentation. (25)

Although not entirely clear, the context of Mack's remarks would seem to imply that what he means by "the forms of rhetorical speech," "patterns of argumentation" and "principles of rhetorical proof" are those forms, patterns, and proofs specific to *ancient* rhetoric, and not necessarily utilised or viewed in the same way by modern society.

Such a historically conditioned application of ancient rhetorical theory would indeed be a valid and significant contribution to biblical studies. Does ancient rhetoric supply us with specific forms, patterns of argumentation, and proofs that show up in the New Testament and therefore help us understand its rhetoric in its own historical setting? This to my mind is the question that application of ancient rhetoric should answer, and it is precisely this question that a universal rhetoric cannot be expected to satisfy. Despite the fact that all societies to some extent engage in "rhetoric," use metaphors, similies, etc., our interest here must be not in these general phenomena themselves, but in the specific ways in which they are used and applied in ancient rhetoric.[28]

Yet even apart from the need to distinguish between modern and ancient rhetoric, Kennedy's methodology has not proved to be a sufficient guide to biblical scholars. As we shall see when reviewing the secondary literature on certain letters of Paul, there are several major methodological problems which occur time and again.

A fundamental question concerns the most appropriate sources for determining the kind of school rhetoric taught in the first century AD. Here, as we shall see in the following chapter, it is important to clearly distinguish between philosophical rhetorical theory and school rhetoric. In this respect, for example, it will be shown that a treatise such as Aristotle's is *not* a helpful source for our purposes.

---

28   The distinction, for example, between the use of figures anyone (even untrained in rhetoric) might use by nature and the more methodical, continual and vibrant use of a trained rhetorician was correctly recognised even in ancient rhetorical theory, cf. Caecilius of Calacte, *Fr.* 103 Ofenloch.

There is also the question as to how the rhetorical treatises were to be used in terms of writing a speech. An understanding of this can go a long way towards ensuring an appropriate use of the various elements of the theory itself. All too often biblical scholars have been pulling concepts out of treatises (for example, the "three" rhetorical genres) without properly understanding how they functioned in the theory itself, and how they were used as *aids* when writing specific speeches.

Coupled with these questions is the need to discern which aspects of rhetorical theory might be most applicable to Paul. The nature of Paul's writings (i.e., *letters*) as well as the subject matter need to be borne in mind.

In the following chapter an attempt will be made to answer the questions concerning the rhetorical sources themselves. The relation between epistolography and rhetoric will be more fully discussed in chapter three. Thereupon, after a review of the relevant secondary literature, a cautious application of ancient rhetorical theory will be made to Paul's letters to the Galatians and Romans, and a discussion on certain themes from the first letter to the Corinthians.

We cannot, however, just assume that Paul used ancient rhetorical theory. The approach taken, therefore, will be to apply rhetorical theory to certain letters from the perspective of a contemporary professor of rhetoric. How might a contemporary, who was well-versed in rhetorical theory, have looked at Paul's letters? The results gained from this analysis will enable us to make certain comments on the question of Paul's own consciousness of rhetorical theory (or not) in the final concluding chapter, as well as an assessment of the value of the approach.

II. The Sources for Ancient Rhetorical Theory

We turn now to look at the sources of ancient rhetorical theory itself. It is at this point that we encounter a number of complexities.

Firstly, we must understand that "ancient rhetorical theory" is an inexact concept. There was no uniform systematic set of dogmata in antiquity. Rhetorical theory developed over the centuries in various ways. The rhetorical theorists often differed from each other, sometimes even forming rival schools propagating their own peculiar doctrines. Therefore someone wishing to apply ancient rhetorical theory needs to have some grasp of the kind of variation possible within theoretical doctrine. It is thus quite insufficient to restrict oneself to one or two theorists alone. An important consideration here is the distinction between school rhetoric and rhetoric as found in the philosophers. Whilst there are a number of sources of rhetorical theory which exhibit the influence of philosophical rhetoric, such philosophical rhetoric was hardly popular in the rhetorical schools, nor does it appear to have had much influence on regular rhetorical practice. It is therefore important that we understand this distinction, and also some of the most important ways in which school rhetoric *differed* from philosophical rhetoric. Not only are we then able to lay specifically philosophical treatises aside, but we are also in a better position to judge what is and is not relevant to school rhetoric in a hybrid treatise such as Quintilian's *Institutio*.

Secondly, there is also the question as to how far the theoretical doctrine was actually applied in practice. Rhetorical theory often tended to supply seemingly endless rules and distinctions. Actual rhetorical practice, however, was frequently more supple - a fact sometimes admitted by the theorists themselves. Whilst this book is primarily concerned with the (possible) application of rhetorical *theory* to the letters of Paul, certain comments with regard to the relation of theory to practice are made where pertinent.

Thirdly, there is the unfortunate fact that there are very few sources of Greek rhetorical theory extant from the Hellenistic period through to the end of the first century AD. Our knowledge of Hellenistic rhetorical theory is largely dependent on Latin rhetorical theorists from the first centuries BC and AD.

Particularly in view of the first and third considerations, a review of possibly relevant sources of rhetorical theory is a desideratum.

As will be seen in our evaluation of recent scholarship with respect to Paul and ancient rhetorical theory, this is an area where New Testament scholars have paid precious little attention, although some have noted the problem. In short the question is: Where is suitable rhetorical theory to be found for application to a writer of Greek in the mid first century AD?

Due to the dearth of Hellenistic sources we are forced to make a fairly wide sweep of rhetorical theory throughout some 500 years. The following presentation is a limited overview.[29] The detail and kind of discussion given is based on three factors: i) relevancy to the kind of school rhetoric taught in the first century AD and possibly applicable to the writings of Paul, ii) helpfulness in terms of understanding a background against which either school rhetoric, or Paul's writings, may be contrasted, iii) attentiveness to treatises which, whilst less helpful, have been (mistakenly) extensively used in recent scholarship.[30]

We begin with the first extant rhetorical treatises at the close of the classical era, namely, Anaximenes and Aristotle. These treatises may be separated from later Hellenistic rhetorical theory which, as we shall see, developed in a way quite different to Aristotle, and much more complex than Anaximenes. We then take a brief look at philosophical rhetorical theory as well as the outlook of the main philosophical schools on rhetoric. This outlook, and the controversy between philosophy and school rhetoric, is important background to much recent literature concerning Paul's own statements about his "rhetoric" (particularly in the Corinthian correspondence). We then proceed to look at various Hellenistic rhetorical treatises, before finally dealing separately with some of the later works of Cicero as well as the mammoth *Institutio* of Quintilian.

What follows is *not* intended as a history of rhetorical theory in this period. An overview of such history may be found in the books of G. A. Kennedy, *The Art of Persuasion in Greece* (Princeton, N.J.: University Press/ London: Routledge & Kegan Paul, 1963); *The Art of Rhetoric in the Roman World* (Princeton, N.J.: University

---

[29]   The various fragments of treatises no longer completely extant (e.g., the lost rhetorical works of Aristotle, *Fr.* 68-69, 125-41 Rose; Theophrastus, *Fr.* 666-713 FHS&G; Hermagoras, ed. D. Matthes; Caecilius of Calacte, the attributed fragments in ed. E. Ofenloch; Apollodorus and Theodorus, ed. R. Granatelli) have been read in order to determine relevancy, but have proven of little value for the purposes of this book.

[30]   In the discussion below I have attempted to utilise the most important literature on the subject, however it ought to be realised that there has been a veritable explosion of research on many aspects of ancient rhetorical theory in recent years, both in America and Europe. The literature has become extremely vast. An overview of some of this literature (including relevant reviews) can be found in the volumes of *L'Année Philologique: Bibliographie Critique et Analytique de l'Antiquité Gréco-Latine* (Paris: Les Belles Lettres).

Press, 1972); and more recently, a revised and abridged overview, *A New History of Classical Rhetoric* (Princeton, N.J.: University Press, 1994). Our purpose is to provide a review and evaluation of relevant sources, particularly with respect to the areas most applicable to the letters of Paul, namely, general theory of argumentation and style.[31] Each source is briefly placed within its own context and comments are made on its specific trends and approach. Relevant textual editions and commentaries on the various treatises are also noted. It is hoped that this overview may prove helpful to New Testament scholars seeking a brief orientation in the rhetorical sources.

1 The End of the Classical Age
1.1 *Rhetorica ad Alexandrum*

> Editions: The standard critical edition is M. Fuhrmann (ed.) *Anaximenis Ars Rhetorica* (BSGRT; Leipzig: B. G. Teubner, 1966). A companion volume is *Untersuchungen zur Textgeschichte der pseudo-aristotelischen Alexander-Rhetorik (der Τέχνη des Anaximenes von Lampsakos)* (Akademie der Wissenschaften und der Literatur: Abhandlungen der geistes- und sozialwissenschaftlichen Klasse 7, 1964). Translation (not always accurate) by H. Rackham in *Works of Aristotle* (vol. 16; LCL; London: Heinemann, 1937).

The *Rhetorica ad Alexandrum* is the sole surviving rhetorical treatise before Aristotle.[32] That this tract in its original form dates to the last part of the fourth century

---

[31] For a justification of this restriction, see the discussion on rhetorical method at the end of this chapter (§ 5). In addition, it should be noted that prose rhythm has not been dealt with in this study. The complexity of the subject (which really requires a separate investigation) combined with the unlikelihood that the apostle Paul engaged in it (see the comments in chapter three on his careless language), is sufficient cause for omission. Particularly with respect to *Greek* prose rhythm, scholarship still confronts a number of difficult problems relating to the conflicting and not always very lucid views expressed in our sources. Although most rhetorical treatises treat briefly of prose rhythm with respect to the ends of clauses, Dionysius of Halicarnassus developed a (not always consistent) theory embracing the "rhythm" of whole sentences. A knowledge of contemporary music theory is an important prerequisite to serious study of his rhythmic theory (see below § 3.4 for a few brief comments on it). It should be remembered that the ancient notion of rhythm depended on relative syllable *length*, a fact not always taken into account by New Testament scholars venturing comments on Paul's use of "rhythm."
   The modern trend of syllable *counting* in exegesis has really nothing to do with ancient rhetorical theory, despite claims to the contrary (cf. J. Smit Sibinga, *Literair Handwerk in Handelingen* [Leiden: E. J. Brill, 1970] 14-16). Smit Sibinga's pupil, M. J. J. Menken (*Numerical Literary Techniques in John* [Leiden: E. J. Brill, 1985] 13-16), although referring to the same sources as his mentor, rightly notes that syllable counting in ancient rhetorical theory is restricted to the figure of ἰσόκωλον, applied only to a series of successive short clauses. Even then, an identical number of syllables per clause is not required, cf. *Rhetorica ad Herennium* 4.27-28 who also brings the matter of syllable *length* to bear on this figure. (In this respect, note that Menken cites Alexander, *de Figuris* 2.26 incorrectly. Alexander's example does *not* contain equal numbers of syllables. Furthermore, Menken [14-15] overlooks the textual problem caused by ἀλλά γε which seems to suggest that the original text allowed for an unequal number. See the *critical notes* in Spengel's edition.)
[32] There were of course many treatises written on the subject before then. For the collected fragments of these works (there are 38 of whom the author is known!) see: L. Radermacher, 1951, *Artium*.

BC is now undisputed.[33] However, its present form and authorship have been debated. The tract as we have it is supplied with a cover letter purportedly from Aristotle who dedicates the work to Alexander the Great (his former pupil). There is, however, no doubt that this letter is a forgery,[34] and the work is probably to be attributed to Anaximenes of Lampsacus.

> The case for attribution is complex and in itself not very important, yet it points to an important problem with the treatise, namely, the poor state of the textual tradition. Briefly put, the forged letter is known to have existed as early as the second century AD (Athen. 508a) which explains the fact that Syrianus in the fifth century AD thought that the treatise came from the hand of Aristotle. Although clearly referring to this treatise at *in Hermog.* 2, p.11 R. (Syrianus gives a direct quotation at p.11,24 - 12,2 R.), yet he states that it taught *two* γένη as well as the seven εἴδη. The later mss of this treatise (the earliest is 14th century) speak of *three* γένη and seven εἴδη. A third γένος would appear to have been added sometime after the fifth century to bring the work more into line with the genuine *Rhetoric* of Aristotle. That the treatise before this time only spoke of *two* γένη is confirmed by a striking parallel in Quint. *Inst.* 3.4.9. Quintilian says that *Anaximenes* (of Lampsacus) distinguished seven species (εἴδη), and he goes on to list them. The list and its order is identical to *Rh.Al.* 1.1. He then adds that Anaximenes distinguished two general parts of rhetoric, judicial and public.[35] Given the unique nature of this genre analysis there must be little doubt that Quintilian is referring to our treatise. On his authority, therefore, the treatise may reasonably be attributed to Anaximenes.

The textual state of the treatise as we have it is unfortunately quite poor. Some grasp of the nature of this problem is necessary so as to alert the reader to exercise appropriate caution with the text.

Fuhrmann has shown that all our codices, of which the earliest date from the 14th century, go back to one medieval archetype.[36] Earlier suspicions that this textual tradition had been variously tampered with were finally confirmed with the discovery of substantial fragments of the tract on papyrus dating to the first half of the third century BC. Although it contains just less than 10 percent of the entire work, the papyrus evidence has adequately shown just how poor the textual condition of the codices is (omissions, additions, disturbed word order, etc.). For example, at *Rh.Al.* 4.1 the papyrus

---

[33]   A *terminus post quem* is provided in *Rh.Al.* 8.8 by the mention of the Corinthian aid rendered to Syracuse against the Carthaginians in 341 BC.

[34]   Apart from the consideration that the style and content of the tract itself are not reminiscent of Aristotle, there is also the fact that the letter reflects a student/ teacher relationship that was no longer operative at the time when it was supposed to have been written.

[35]   Quintilian adds concerning the list of seven species: *quarum duae primae deliberativi, duae sequentes demonstrativi, tres ultimae iudicialis generis sunt partes.* This appears to be his own comment based on the later (Aristotelian) division of rhetoric into three broad genres. *Rh.Al.* (1.1; 37.1) in fact states that the last species (ἐξεταστικόν) can stand either on its own or in combination with another.

[36]   1966, *Anaximenis,* xxxviii.

shows how a reference to rhetorical genres has been added to the later mss tradition.[37] From this Fuhrmann rightly argues that many other such terms or even sentences referring to rhetorical genres may be later additions.[38] There is no escaping the conclusion that there are interpolations in the codices, and we have already noted one such example above in the discussion on the attribution to Anaximenes. Fuhrmann concludes that since we do not really know what the author actually wrote, it is best not to attempt to emend the text.[39] We therefore need to be cautious when reading this tract. In sections where there is no testimony from the papyri, there is no guarantee that the text we have has not been altered in some way.[40]

That Anaximenes' work was still consulted and used in the first century and later is clear from the citations noted above in Quintilian, Athenaeus and Syrianus. The probable additions and changes to the text also bear witness to its popularity in later times.[41]

The treatise is divided into three main sections (1-5, 6-28, 29-38). The first undertakes general definitions of the seven εἴδη of rhetoric. It is the second section that should be of most interest to scholars wishing to apply rhetorical theory to the letters of Paul. Here we find a description of arguments and figures common to all the forms of rhetoric (although Anaximenes notes that some are more common in certain forms than others). He mentions seven topics to be used in conjunction with the protreptic and apotreptic species (that the matter be shown to be just, lawful, beneficial, etc., fully discussed at § 1.4-24). Such topics as these became standard for deliberative rhetoric in later treatises. Next come seven methods of magnifying or diminishing one's topic (αὔξησις and ταπείνωσις, fully discussed at § 3.6-14).[42] Such methods are also a standard part of later treatises. Anaximenes then provides a discussion of the various kinds of proofs (πίστεις, §§ 7-17) divided into two groups (later called ἔντεχνοι and

---

[37] 1964b, *Untersuchungen*, 150.

[38] A suggested list is supplied in, 1966, *Anaximenis*, xli; cf. 1964b, *Untersuchungen*, 150-52.

[39] The only emendation he has accepted is that of the corrupt number at § 17.3 already noted by Spengel (cf. 1964b, *Untersuchungen*, 153-54, 158). It should also be noted that Fuhrmann demonstrates that a number of terms in the tract are quite late and thus evidence of later alteration (1964b, *Untersuchungen*, 158-71).

[40] The papyrus contains (with some *lacunae*) sections 1.13 - 2.3; 2.15 - 2.28; and fragments from 3.8 - 4.4.

[41] Marginal notes could be responsible for some of the additions/ alterations. Other reasons may have been the desire to keep it up to date or bring it into line with the (later) supposed authorship of Aristotle.

[42] Anaximenes seems to have had a particular penchant for the number 7, and possibly also the number 3.

ἄτεχνοι).[43] There follows a discussion of προκαταλήψεις (anticipating the arguments of an opponent, § 18, cf. 1-2), αἰτήματα (requests the speaker can make of the audience, § 19), various ways of recapitulating (both at the end of a line of argument and at the end of a speech, §§ 20-21), and several comments on prolonging or shortening one's speech and other matters of style and expression (§§ 22-25). Finally, several Gorgianic figures are discussed (though they are not called such, §§ 26-28). The third part of the treatise discusses the seven εἴδη according to the parts of a speech, and is of less interest to the Pauline scholar.

In general, Anaximenes is not afraid of teaching what we might call sophistic argumentation. He quite blatantly shows how one might argue for or against any given matter, and how various kinds of arguments can be both effectively used and refuted. Further, although the treatise is much simpler than later school rhetoric, many of the concepts and τόποι (see select glossary s.v.) did not undergo serious change in later times. Anaximenes is, however, unfortunately often rather brief, merely describing a particular figure or way of reasoning without suggesting why or when one might use this.[44] This is less helpful for our application of rhetorical theory to Paul. It is very easy to label a particular passage or argument in Paul's writings by some Greek technical term, but unless rhetorical theory enables us to say something relevant concerning its *use* and *function* at that point, our analysis is pretty worthless. This does not mean to say Anaximenes never says something valuable regarding function, and the relevant portions of his treatise are well worth studying.

1.2 Aristotle, *Rhetorica*

> Editions: Greek text editions and translations abound. The most recent edition is R. Kassel (ed.) *Aristotelis Ars Rhetorica* (Berlin/ New York: de Gruyter, 1976).[45] An older but still helpful commentary is that of E. M. Cope, *The Rhetoric of Aristotle with a Commentary* (Revised & ed. J. E. Sandys; 3 vols; Cambridge: University Press, 1877; repr. Dubuque, Iowa: Wm. C. Brown, n.d.,

---

[43]   The first group consists of εἰκότα, παραδείγματα, τεκμήρια, ἐνθυμήματα, γνῶμαι, σημεῖα, and ἔλεγχοι. A couple of points are worth noticing here. Firstly, he defines εἰκότα as statements of which the audience know examples in their minds. That is why the statement is "probable" to them. When this is not the case, the orator must provide examples (παραδείγματα) himself. Secondly, it becomes clear throughout the treatise that ἐνθυμήματα (short considerations) and γνῶμαι are considered to be the standard kinds of arguments used when bringing a line of argument to a close.

[44]   Note that Dionysius of Halicarnassus (*Is.* 19) did not think much of any of the writings of Anaximenes.

[45]   This is based on his study, *Der Text der aristotelischen Rhetorik: Prolegomena zu einer kritischen Ausgabe* (Berlin/ New York: de Gruyter, 1971). D. C. Innes in her positive review noted that Kassel has for the first time provided a reliable stemma of the Greek mss of this work (1976, *Review*). Kassel is also quite critical of previous text editions.

and Hildesheim: Olms, 1970). A more recent commentary on books one and two of the treatise is W. M. A. Grimaldi, *Aristotle, Rhetoric: A Commentary* (2 vols; New York: Fordham University Press, 1980/88).[46] G. A. Kennedy has provided a recent translation (with extensive notes) maintaining Aristotle's technical terminology (Aristotle, *On Rhetoric: A Theory of Civic Discourse* [New York/ Oxford: Oxford University Press, 1991]).

Apart from Anaximenes, Aristotle's treatise is the only comprehensive rhetorical treatise extant in Greek in the period examined in this chapter (i.e., up to the end of the first century AD).[47] Nevertheless, as we shall see, both the inherent difficulty of this work and its completely different approach to the subject made it of little value to later rhetorical theorists. Hence the value of this treatise is severely limited for those wishing to apply ancient rhetorical theory to the apostle Paul. Despite this fact, the popularity of this treatise among New Testament scholars demands a somewhat fuller presentation of its contents if only to show more clearly how the work *differs* from later school rhetoric.

We ought to bear in mind that the *Rhetoric* was almost certainly never prepared for publication. It belongs to that group of works known as esoteric. The original function of these works is open to question. The *Rhetoric*, just as the other esoteric works, is written in very elliptical, almost shorthand, language, which makes it often rather difficult to ascertain precisely what Aristotle is trying to say.[48] It has been surmised that they were either lecture notes or perhaps summaries of lectures for students who may have missed classes.

The notorious difficulty of the *Rhetoric* combined with the apparent existence of a number of contradictions has meant that its essential unity has not always been accepted. For this reason it had been popular towards the end of last century to view the *Rhetoric* as having been altered by subsequent editors. Later F. Solmsen, following the approach of W. Jaeger, postulated that a development of Aristotle's thought could be seen in the treatise.[49] Despite the influence this theory has had, modern scholarship is inclined to accept the general unity of the work.[50]

---

[46] Due to Grimaldi's early death, an added volume on book three is not to be expected. This commentary propagates the controversial views on the *Rhetoric* propounded in Grimaldi's earlier work, 1972, *Studies*.
[47] Aristotle's interest in rhetoric is shown by the number of works he devoted to this subject (e.g., συναγωγὴ τεχνῶν - a collection and explanation of earlier treatises on rhetoric, *Gryllus*, *Theodectea*), but our treatise is unfortunately his only work extant on the subject.
[48] One may sympathise with A. D. Leeman's comment, even if it is somewhat overstated (A. D. Leeman/ A. C. Braet, 1987, *retorica*, 10): "Het werk is vol onduidelijkheden, herhalingen en tegenspraken en stelt de moderne verklaarder voor een aantal vrijwel onoverkomelijke moeilijkheden."
[49] *Die Entwicklung der aristotelischen Logik und Rhetorik* (Neue philologische Untersuchungen 4; Berlin: Weidmann, 1929).
[50] E.g., W. M. A. Grimaldi, 1972, *Studies*, 49-52. For a short summary of approaches to the *Rhetoric*, see J. Wisse, 1989, *Ethos*, 9-13. Wisse also accepts the general unity of the *Rhetoric*, although

In any event, by the first century BC the *Rhetoric* was clearly approached as a unity, although book three may also have been available separately (see below). For our purposes, we must also attempt to read it as such.

Aristotle's treatise is divided into three books in which the structure is organised according to what were later called the *officia oratoris*, namely, the duties of the orator. Aristotle discusses three such duties: εὕρεσις (the invention and arrangement of material, bks 1 and 2), λέξις (style, bk. 3.1-12) and τάξις (the arrangement of the parts of the speech, bk. 3.13-19).[51]

Aristotle's fondness for analytical classification clearly shows through in the treatise as a whole. After the introduction and general definitions (*Rh.* 1.1-2) where he lays out his views on the various means of persuasion and their classification, he launches into the main subject of books one and two, namely, the means of persuasion. The organisation of *Rh.* 1.3 - 2.26 is essentially constructed around Aristotle's conception of ἐνθυμήματα.

In *Rh.* 1.2.20-21 Aristotle distinguishes between two kinds of ἐνθυμήματα, namely, those whose προτάσεις (premises) are founded upon established views or facts and those which rely on particular methods of argumentation (τόποι). Only the latter are proper rhetorical syllogisms (ἐνθυμήματα). The former actually engage one in other disciplines to establish the necessary προτάσεις.[52] Nevertheless, Aristotle deals with these first (*Rh.* 1.3 - 2.17), distributing them under three headings; those concerned with the matter itself (τὸ πρᾶγμα), those concerned with the trustworthiness of the speaker's character (ἦθος), and those concerned with the emotional swaying of the audience (πάθος).[53] Those relating to the matter (τὸ πρᾶγμα) are discussed under the

---

not in the same way as Grimaldi.

[51]   This arrangement is very similar to that of Anaximenes (rhetorical genres 1-5; proofs 6-21; λέξις 22-28; τάξις 29-38), even though Anaximenes' own identification of his structure is a little different. He considers sections 6 through 28 to form one whole consisting of matters common to all the rhetorical genres and does not identify λέξις as a separate structural portion of his treatise. Yet the basic idea of first dealing with matters particular to the various genres and then with those common to them all is also the structural principle behind Aristotle's arrangement of the means of persuasion. It is noteworthy that Aristotle has relegated the ἄτεχνοι πίστεις to the discussion of the δικανικὸν γένος.

[52]   W. M. A. Grimaldi (1972, *Studies*, cf. 1980, *Aristotle*, on 1.2.20-21) argues that Aristotle means to say that the specific material for ἐνθυμήματα will be discussed first, and then the forms of inference in which this material may be cast. On his interpretation there are not two distinct kinds of ἐνθυμήματα. Whilst this interpretation seems attractive, for my part, I cannot but think that Aristotle is indeed distinguishing two kinds of ἐνθυμήματα here.

[53]   Note that the three terms πρᾶγμα, ἦθος and πάθος retain their regular meanings (matter, character, emotion) in Aristotle (and most later treatises) and are not used as technical terms describing the kinds of proofs with which they are associated, see J. Wisse (1989, *Ethos*, 60-61).

heads of three kinds of rhetoric (συμβουλευτικόν, ἐπιδεικτικόν, and δικανικόν), *Rh.* 1.3-15. Then follows the material needed for persuasion in respect of the trustworthiness of the speaker's character (*Rh.* 2.1.5-7) and that needed for the emotional swaying of the audience or judge (*Rh.* 2.1.8 - 2.11.7).[54] An appendix analysing the various characters of people is added (*Rh.* 2.12-17).[55]

At *Rh.* 2.18-26 Aristotle finally comes to the rhetorical proofs proper (παραδείγματα and ἐνθυμήματα, i.e., inductive and deductive proofs). After an introductory chapter (*Rh.* 2.18) he first, however, separates out three κοινά, i.e., "necessary preconditions to all rhetorical discourse."[56]

Thereupon he deals with παραδείγματα (as inductive reasoning, *Rh.* 2.20.2-9) and rhetorical ἐνθυμήματα (*Rh.* 2.21-25 - the γνῶμαι of 2.21 are treated as a part of ἐνθυμήματα).

It is well known that Aristotle developed his own theory concerning the ἐνθύμημα by basing himself on an analogy to his *Analytics*. It is not necessary to describe the theory in full here, suffice it to say that at *Rh.* 1.2 an ἐνθύμημα is described as the rhetorical equivalent of the συλλογισμός (syllogism) in dialectics just as the παράδειγμα (example) is equivalent to the ἐπαγωγή (induction) (*Rh.* 1.2.8). The ἐνθύμημα is thus a deductive process of reasoning, a version of the three step syllogism (major premise, minor premise, conclusion). Παράδειγμα and ἐνθύμημα are the two kinds of logical proofs (πίστεις) available to the orator. The rhetorical

---

54   There is some tension with the opening paragraph of the *Rhetoric*. Aristotle accuses his predecessors of not paying proper attention to the central matter of proof/ means of persuasion (σῶμα τῆς πίστεως), namely, what he calls ἐνθυμήματα (rhetorical syllogisms, *Rh.* 1.1.3, 9-11). Those considerations relating to the audience or the speaker, being ἔξω τοῦ πράγματος are manifestly not the main point (i.e., what he later speaks of as inciting πάθη in the audience and displaying the appropriate ἦθος in the speaker).
    W. M. A. Grimaldi (1972, *Studies*) has attempted to overcome this tension by a not entirely successful reinterpretation of the text. A better discussion is provided by J. Wisse (1989, *Ethos*, 13-29). Wisse cogently argues that Aristotle's opening discussion should be viewed as polemical overstatement. A solution in terms of Aristotle's proposed developing thought is offered by W. W. Fortenbaugh (1992, "Aristotle," 232-40).
55   J. Wisse (1989, *Ethos*, 36-43) in discussing the place of *Rh.* 2.12-17 (an analysis of the various ἤθη of people) conjectures that this section may have been Aristotle's initial attempt at fulfilling the programme of ψυχαγωγία laid out in Plato's *Phaedrus* (cf. 271a4 - b5; 271c10 - 272b4; 277b5 - c6). The analysis of various ἤθη may have been retained by Aristotle as a sort of appendix to a later discussion of persuasion through character and emotion (*Rh.* 2.1.5 - 2.11). W. W. Fortenbaugh (1992, "Aristotle," 238) has recently suggested that *Rh.* 2.2-11 (on emotions) be read against the background of Plato's *Philebus*. Wisse (46-47) has shown how easily the whole arrangement here may have been misread by later readers in antiquity (as also moderns), who probably overlooked the very short section on persuasion through character at *Rh.* 2.1.5-7 and considered *Rh.* 2.12-17 as *the* section on this matter.
56   The description comes from W. M. A. Grimaldi (1980, *Aristotle*, 1.349). I follow Grimaldi's interpretation of Aristotle's terminology here. Cope incorrectly called the three κοινά, the κοινοὶ τόποι. But the κοινοὶ τόποι are quite clearly those τόποι of *Rh.* 2.23. The three κοινά are common aspects necessary to any argumentation, namely, that one must know 1) whether something is possible or impossible, 2) whether something did/ will occur, and 3) whether it is great or small.
    Grimaldi's view is, however, not universal. Contrast, for example, A. D. Leeman/ A. C. Braet, 1987, *retorica*, 73-74.

ἐνθύμημα, however, is not a συλλογισμός in the technical sense. An orator hardly ever spells out a formal syllogism, but the elements should all be present or at least clearly implied. With this definition Aristotle is able to effectively organise various kinds of proofs (which in rhetorical theory are usually treated separately) under the head of the ἐνθύμημα. Thus probabilities (εἰκότα), signs (σημεῖα), evidences (τεκμήρια, i.e., necessary signs) are all materials of ἐνθυμήματα. At *Rh.* 2.21 even γνῶμαι are classified as parts of ἐνθυμήματα. At *Rh.* 2.23 Aristotle discusses 28 different τόποι or στοιχεῖα, by which he means the forms of argumentation which an ἐνθύμημα may take, e.g., arguing from opposites (if x is good, the opposite of x is bad). This is followed in *Rh.* 2.24 by 10 fallacious τόποι and finally in *Rh.* 2.25 by some remarks on refutation.

In all of the detailed argumentative analysis of these sections, however, virtually nothing is said about the *function* and *placement* of various arguments. This fact, apart from the distinctly philosophical nature of this approach (see below), makes Aristotle's analysis of little value for historical rhetorical analysis.[57]

The third book, after an introduction, deals firstly with λέξις (*Rh.* 3.2-12). Here Aristotle deals with many subjects which would become traditional in rhetorical treatises though his terminology is often idiomatic. He begins with the ἀρετή of speech (clarity and propriety, *Rh.* 3.2-4),[58] then comes the ἀρχή of speech, which amounts to a proper (and especially clear) use of language (*Rh.* 3.5), the ὄγκος of speech (by which he means expansiveness, *Rh.* 3.6), propriety (*Rh.* 3.7), and the σχῆμα of speech (by which he means rhythmical form, *Rh.* 3.8). This section closes with a discussion of paratactic (εἰρομένη λέξις) and periodic (κατεστραμμένη λέξις) sentence structure (*Rh.* 3.9).

The final section of the treatise deals with τάξις (*Rh.* 3.13-19). It is interesting to note that Aristotle, in evident opposition to others, maintained that the only essential parts of a speech were the πρόθεσις and the πίστεις, although Aristotle does not hereby mean to say that a normal speech ought only to contain these two parts.

Having outlined the contents of the treatise, a few words on its availability and use in the first centuries BC and AD are in order. Despite the ancient story of the loss and eventual recovery of Aristotle's esoteric works culminating in their republication by Andronicus (*c.* 40 BC), modern scholarship is virtually unanimous that many of

---

[57]   Logical analysis of the forms of argumentation can be better approached from modern rhetorical theory. The prime use of ancient theory is to help us understand what may have been historically conditioned ways of using various argumentative forms. But it is this that is lacking in the treatise. *Rh.* 2.21 on γνῶμαι is, however, an exception.

[58]   I accept the view that Aristotle only distinguishes one ἀρετή of speech, even if it does have multiple characteristics, cf. D. C. Innes, "Theophrastus and the Theory of Style," in *Rutgers University Studies in Classical Humanities* 2 (New Brunswick, N.J.: Transaction Publishers, 1985) 255-56; and 1995, "Demetrius," 326; *contra* F. Solmsen, 1941, "Tradition," 43.

these works must, to some extent, have been available during the Hellenistic period.[59] In any case, the situation for each work must be considered on its own merits. In the case of the *Rhetoric* there are reasonable grounds for supposing that it was generally available before Andronicus (even if it was not commonly read), cf. Cic. *Inv.* 2.7; *de Orat.* 2.160.[60] From the two related catalogues of Aristotle's works which seem to go back to the third century BC we may conclude that the *Rhetoric* may have been known in two ways, either as two works, namely, books one and two together and book three separately, or as one work containing the three books together.[61] Given that books one and two are the most removed from later rhetorical theory (see below), the availability of book three separately *may* have been more attractive to later readers.

The question in how far the *Rhetoric* was actually read is more difficult. Scholarship, influenced by questions on its availability, has tended to doubt that the *Rhetoric* was widely read, and has frequently (in many cases probably correctly) attributed allusions to the *Rhetoric* to secondary sources. Recently, J. Wisse has made a probable case for the hypothesis that Cicero had read the *Rhetoric* by 55 BC (the date of the *de Oratore*).[62]

However, a more pertinent question for us concerns the relevance of the *Rhetoric* for rhetorical theorists of the first centuries BC and AD. Compared with what we know of the school rhetoric of this period, Aristotle's treatise must have seemed rather strange and out of step with tradition in many respects. On three important counts readers would have had a sense of familiarity, namely, the division of the genres of

---

[59]   The following story is told in a number of ancient sources (Str. 13.1.54; Plu. *Sull.* 26; cf. D.L. 5.52; Porph. *Plot.* 24; Ath. 214d; Luc. *Ind.* 4; Suid. *s.v.* Σύλλας). Many of Aristotle's works together with those of Theophrastus were lost to the world after his death. These manuscripts passed into the family of Neleus in Scepsis where they were eventually significantly damaged by moisture and moths (otherwise Ath. 3ab). This collection was purchased by Apellicon of Teos (died 84 BC) who brought it to Athens and had it edited and published with the lacunae conjecturally emended. But this edition was apparently of very poor scholarly quality. When Sulla took Athens in 84 BC he brought the library of Apellicon back to Rome with him. This library was later worked upon by Tyrannio (the elder), who arrived in Rome in 67 BC. Tyrannio edited most of Aristotle's (and Theophrastus') works. His edition was obtained by Andronicus of Rhodes, who published it (probably *c.* 40 BC) and wrote a tract of five books concerning the cataloguing of Aristotle's works.
  On the difficult question of the transmission of Aristotle's works see O. Regenbogen, 1940, "Theophrastos," 1370-79; I. Düring, 1950, "Notes," 37-70; and C. Lord, 1986, "History," 137-61 and other literature cited there.
[60]   See discussion in J. Wisse, 1989, *Ethos*, 155-56.
[61]   Books one and two, D.L. 5.24 *title* 78; book three, D.L. 5.24 *title* 87 (the two books mentioned would be the λέξις and the τάξις), cf. *Vita Menagiana* # 79; books one, two and three together, *Vita Menagiana* # 72 (though this may be an emendation, cf. D.H. *Comp.* 25.198; *Amm.* 1, 8; Quint. *Inst.* 2.17.14).
[62]   1989, *Ethos*, 105-89.

rhetoric into the three standard classes, the broad structure of the treatise according to the *officia oratoris* (although by the Hellenistic period it had become customary to deal with five such *officia* in place of Aristotle's three), and the distinction between ἄτεχνοι and ἔντεχνοι proofs.

Apart from such points of recognition, the treatise must indeed have appeared quite strange, particularly the set-up of the first two books. A number of important differences (by no means comprehensive) are itemised below:

First, Hellenistic rhetoric did not take up Aristotle's view of the ἐνθύμημα. Certain aspects of syllogistic reasoning were incorporated into Hellenistic treatments of the ἐπιχείρημα, but discussion of this matter was generally brief - a stark contrast to the pride of place which the ἐνθύμημα takes in Aristotle's *Rhetoric*.

Second, Aristotle's triad of proofs through emotion, through character, and through the matter itself, is not reflected in later tradition. Considerations related to proof through character were found as comments appropriate to the προοίμιον of a speech, and exciting emotion was similarly dealt with in respect of the ἐπίλογος.

Third, Aristotle's separation of the three κοινά (*Rh.* 2.19) from the other τόποι is not found elsewhere. Furthermore, his provision of κοινοὶ τόποι in the sense of abstract argumentative patterns was only taken up in philosophical rhetorical treatises (*Rh.* 2.23). School rhetoric generally ignored such abstract τόποι in favour of specific τόποι (specific arguments on particular matters) or generalised τόποι (e.g., on virtues and vices).

Fourth, Aristotle's treatment of εὕρεσις lacks two important items invariably found in Hellenistic treatises, namely, a treatment of στάσις theory (which became important after Hermagoras' work in the second century BC), and the treatment of the parts of a speech.[63] The latter consideration leads us to the next difference:

Fifth, Aristotle deals with the parts of a speech not under εὕρεσις, but under τάξις. Later school treatises would often discuss these parts under εὕρεσις and reserve the section on τάξις for a short discussion on the ordering of arguments.

Sixth, with respect to λέξις, Aristotle's classification of only one ἀρετὴ λέξεως was not accepted by later tradition. Theophrastus' division into four virtues became popular, but there were also other variants of multiple virtues. Such virtues were frequently used as an organising principle for the discussion of λέξις.

---

[63]   See below, § 3 on Hellenistic rhetoricians, and also the entry for στάσις in the select glossary at the end of this book.

From the above list we can see that even in the unlikely event that a Hellenistic teacher of rhetoric would take the trouble to read Aristotle, the books on εὕρεσις in particular would have had quite limited value.[64] At the most, he may have used such a work for information on proofs through character or emotion, or on any of the other εἴδη or specific topics. Further, he may have gleaned some relevant information on particular kinds of proofs, e.g., παραδείγματα or especially the helpful section on γνῶμαι. But all this information would have been much easier to obtain from other contemporary treatises. The book on λέξις and τάξις, apart from its structure, would probably have been of more value. It shows less deviation from later theory and may therefore be useful as a supplementary source in applying rhetorical theory to Paul.[65] But our conclusion must be that Aristotle's treatise as a whole should be used with extreme caution, and is probably better just left aside.

2 Hellenistic Philosophers

2.1 Peripatetics

Whilst Aristotle's treatise may not have had much direct impact on later rhetoric, yet its influence *was* felt indirectly, particularly through his most famous student Theophrastus. Theophrastus is known to have written many rhetorical works, however only a few fragments remain.[66] It is clear that Theophrastus expanded and developed

---

[64]   The general neglect of Aristotle by professors of rhetoric is echoed in Cicero, *Topica* 3. It is true that Dionysius of Halicarnassus had read Aristotle and was to a certain extent influenced by him, but C. Wooten (1994, "Tradition") has shown that this influence is diminished in the more mature works of Dionysius.

[65]   Certain comments on style may profitably be compared with Paul, cf. the warning at *Rh.* 3.5.2 against inserting too many intermediate clauses before completing one's main thought, transgressed especially at the beginning of *Ep.Eph.* 2 and again in *Ep.Eph.* 3. On a more positive note, with respect to propriety, Aristotle argues that appropriate language also makes the matter persuasive (*Rh.* 3.7.4). For example, if dealing with matters that are ἀσεβῆ καὶ αἰσχρά then the language ought to be of someone indignant and cautious even to speak of these things (δυσχεραίνοντος καὶ εὐλαβουμένου καὶ λέγειν, *Rh.* 3.7.3), cf. *Ep.Eph.* 5.12. Another example is Aristotle's notice of how orators, if they were about to exaggerate, would first reprove themselves for this: δοκεῖ γὰρ ἀληθὲς εἶναι, ἐπεὶ οὐ λανθάνει γε ὃ ποιεῖ τὸν λέγοντα (*Rh.* 3.7.9), cf. (*Theodectea*) *Fr.* 131 Rose, which sums the matter up: ἡ γὰρ ὑποτίμησις ἰᾶται τὰ τολμηρά. Compare 2 *Ep.Cor.* 10.13-18. But these are all elements also to be found in later rhetorical theory.

One ought to remain wary of aspects specific to Aristotle or Aristotelianism, cf. Aristotle's latent ideas on the argumentative value of the μεταφορά, and his negative assessment of ὑπερβολή (see the respective entries in my forthcoming *Glossary*).

[66]   For the rhetorical fragments see *Theophrastus of Eresus: Sources for his Life, Writings Thought and Influence*, ed. W. W. Fortenbaugh, P. M. Huby, R. W. Sharples and D. Gutas (Leiden: E. J. Brill, 1992) *Fr.* 666-713. Older attempts to reconstruct the treatise περὶ λέξεως have not been successful, e. g. H. Rabe, *De Theophrasti Libris Περὶ Λέξεως* (Bonn, 1890); A. Mayer, *Περὶ Λέξεως Libri Fragmenta* (BSGRT; Leipzig: B. G. Teubner, 1910). Although a number of fragments concerning style are extant, the title of this work is only mentioned by Diogenes Laertius and Dionysius of Halicarnassus (Thphr. *Fr.* 666 [17a], 688, 692).

the systematic arrangement of λέξις as found in Aristotle's third book on *Rhetoric*. He appears to have distinguished three ἰδέαι of speech, namely, τὸ σαφές, τὸ μεγαλοπρεπές, τὸ ἡδὺ καὶ πιθανόν (*Fr.* 683 FHS&G = Simp. *in Cat.* p.10 K.). Further, J. Stroux showed that Theophrastus also spoke of four ἀρεταὶ λέξεως as opposed to Aristotle's one, namely, ἑλληνισμός, σαφές, πρέπον and κατασκευή (*Fr.* 684 FHS&G = Cic. *Orat.* 79).[67] The fourth virtue very probably dealt with ἐκλογή, ἀρμονία and σχήματα.[68] This structural division into four virtues was later revived by Cicero who influenced Quintilian (Cic. *de Orat.* 3.37-212; Quint. *Inst.* 8 - 11.1), but does not appear to have been influential in Greek rhetorical theory.[69] In many respects, however, it seems clear from the rhetorical fragments that Theophrastus, although having restructured matters and sometimes disagreeing with Aristotle (cf. Quint. *Inst.* 3.8.62), often simply handed down his mentor's doctrines. Although insufficient material from Theophrastus' work is available to be of help in terms of analysing Paul's rhetoric, we at least learn of an important mediator of Aristotle's views on λέξις.

It is fairly clear that the Peripatetics continued to write on rhetoric down through to the beginning of the second century BC (cf. Quint. *Inst.* 3.1.15).[70] At that time the great controversy between philosophy and rhetoric flared up and the Peripatetic school, under the leadership of Critolaus of Phaselis, took sides with philosophy against rhetoric.[71] This anti-rhetorical stance was continued by Critolaus' pupils Ariston the younger and Diodorus of Tyrus.[72] Even so, we do possess a later treatise on rhetorical style which is at least under Peripatetic influence (cf. Demetrius below).[73] Peripatetics

---

[67]   1912, *Theophrasti*, 9-13. F. Solmsen (1931, "Demetrios," 241-42) preferred the term κεκοσμημένον to κατασκευή. A more recent discussion is D. C. Innes, "Theophrastus and the Theory of Style," in *Rutgers University Studies in Classical Humanities* 2 (New Brunswick, N.J.: Transaction Publishers, 1985) 251-67, although I have not seen this myself, cf. 1995, "Demetrius," 326.

[68]   J. Stroux, 1912, *Theophrasti*, 18-28, esp. 19, cf. *Fr.* 691 FHS&G.

[69]   See F. Solmsen, 1941, *Tradition*, 181-86.

[70]   See also J. M. van Ophuijsen, 1994, "Topics," 131-34. The fragments of Demetrius of Phalerum (another pupil of Aristotle) on rhetoric are collected and commented upon in Wehrli (*Fr.* 156-73). There is, however, little here of interest to this investigation. Eudemus (*Fr.* 25-29, Wehrli) and Hieronymus of Rhodes (*Fr.* 50-52, Wehrli) also *appear* to have written on style.

[71]   Critolaus, *Fr.* 25-39 (Wehrli).

[72]   Ariston, *Fr.* 1-5; Diodorus, *Fr.* 6 (Wehrli).

[73]   The practice in θέσεις (treatments *pro* and *contra* on general subjects) said to have begun with Aristotle (Cic. *Orat.* 46; *de Orat.* 3.80; D.L. 5.3), clearly remained an important part of their activities (Str. 13.1.54, see also J. M. van Ophuijsen, 1994, "Topics," 148-57 who also cites evidence from Alex.Aphr. *in Top.*). Such θέσεις, however, were more distinctly philosophical than rhetorical. The ὑποθέσεις on (relevant) concrete subjects were the province of rhetoric. Cicero attributes Aristotle's use of θέσεις to a rhetorical rather than philosophical purpose, but this seems more to reflect his own view on the usefulness of the tradition of θέσεις for a rhetor (*Orat.* 46; cf. Cic. *Orat.* 12). Diogenes Laertius quite properly distinguishes exercise in θέσεις from rhetorical practice: καὶ πρὸς θέσιν συνεγύμναζε [*sc.* Ἀριστοτέλης] τοὺς μαθητάς, ἅμα καὶ ῥητορικῶς ἐπασκῶν (5.3).

J. M. van Ophuijsen presumes that rhetoricians (in Athens at least) from the period following

probably continued to write treatises on τόποι (in the Aristotelian sense of abstract argumentative patterns), and in this context we may consider the *Topica* of Cicero.[74]

2.1.1 Cicero, *Topica*

Editions: A. S. Wilkins in Cicero, *Rhetorica* (vol. 2; OCT; Oxford: Clarendon, 1903). A new edition by G. Di Maria is now available, *Topica* (Bibliotheca Philologica 1; Palermo: L'epos, 1994). Translation by H. M. Hubbell in *Cicero* (LCL; vol.2; Cambridge, Mass.: Harvard University Press, 1949).

Cicero's *Topica* is a work, composed in 44 BC, professedly explaining Aristotle's *disciplina* (§ 2) of τόποι. The work is certainly not a translation either of Aristotle's *Topica* or of the appropriate section of his *Rhetorica*. Nevertheless, it does present a detailed analysis of those kinds of τόποι which Aristotle presented, namely, abstract patterns of argumentation. However, the classification upon which the work is based differs from Aristotle. The work divides its *loci* into those which are intrinsic to the matter in hand (containing the Aristotelian kind of *loci*) and those which are extrinsic (containing specific *loci* based on the ἄτεχνοι proofs), a distinction already known from Cicero's treatises *de Oratore* 2.164-73 (55 BC) and *Partitiones Oratoriae* 5-8 (54-52 BC).[75] In fact the list of *loci* is identical to that contained in *de Orat.* and related to the *loci* in *Part.*.[76] Furthermore, the presentation of *loci* in these three treatises is also related to the τόπος theory of Themistius (most likely independent of Cicero), a fourth century AD Aristotelian commentator and rhetor.[77] The philosophical origin of the abstract argumentative patterns (which form the bulk of the work) is confirmed at § 3 where Cicero notes that the rhetorical teacher whom his friend Trebatius consulted was

---

Aristotle's death had great interest in θέσεις and on this basis contends that Peripatetic interest in θέσεις also had important rhetorical application (*loc. cit.*). Apart from the highly questionable interest of rhetoricians in θέσεις at that time (see my discussion below, pp.49-50), such a phenomenon could hardly be decisive for the question as to whether Peripatetic exercise in θέσεις was rhetorically motivated or not.

[74]   We at least hear of third century BC activity in this area, e.g., Theophrastus (D.L. 5.45, *title* 92; 5.50 *title* 294), and Straton (D.L. 5.59, *title* 35, cf. *Fr.* 19-31 Wehrli)

[75]   On the dating of the *Partitiones* see below. A relationship between the *Topica* and the *Partitiones* is also apparent in the discussion of *quaestiones* closing the treatise.

[76]   *Part.* 7 clearly contains two interpolations (bracketed text in most editions) listing *loci* identical to those in *Top.* and *de Orat.* (the first interpolation containing the first four *loci*, and then a complete list). After the interpolations a third list is presented which, although clearly related to the list from *Top.* and *de Orat.*, is not identical. We may assume that this is the list originally belonging to the treatise.

[77]   Themistius' τόπος theory is explained in the second book of Boethius' *de Topicis Differentiis*, see J. M. van Ophuijsen, 1994, "Topics," 146-47.

ignorant of "these Aristotelian matters" (*haec Aristotelia*). Indeed, such abstract *loci* do not figure anywhere in the rhetorical school treatises extant. The evidence may suggest a Peripatetic origin for Cicero's system of abstract *loci*, although the *Partitiones* show that such *loci* were also used in the Academy.[78]

Following the detailed analysis of the *loci*, the treatise includes a short section, very similar to Cic. *Part.* 61-138, on the various kinds of inquiries (*quaestiones*).[79]

Apart from the fact that the tradition of *loci* in terms of abstract argumentative patterns is a philosophical phenomenon, we should also note that such abstract *loci* do not easily lend themselves to an historically based rhetorical analysis. For this reason they are of little value for this investigation.

2.1.2 Demetrius, *de Elocutione*

> Editions: The two standard editions are L. Radermacher (ed.), *Demetrii Phalerei Qui Dicitur de Elocutione Libellus* (SWC; Leipzig: B. G. Teubner, 1901; repr. Stuttgart, 1966) with (Latin) notes, and W. R. Roberts (ed.), *Demetrius on Style: The Greek Text of Demetrius de Elocutione Edited After the Paris Manuscript* (Cambridge, 1902; repr. Hildesheim: Olms, 1969) with translation and commentary.[80] A synthetic commentary is provided by D. M. Schenkeveld, *Studies in Demetrius "On Style"* (Amsterdam: A. Hakkert, 1964). The text used here is that of Radermacher. The Loeb edition has recently been revised by D. C. Innes, who also provides an excellent introductory essay, in *Aristotle* (LCL; vol. 23; London: Heinemann, 1995).

The last extant rhetorically related treatise associated with the Peripatetics (within our time frame) is this work on style by Demetrius. Although the treatise is clearly under Peripatetic influence, it is not certain that Demetrius himself belonged to this school.[81] Equally uncertain is the vexed question of date. Scholarship has reached no unanimity on this question, although a date somewhere between the second century BC and first century AD seems most probable.[82]

---

[78]   For a good brief discussion of the *Topica* and its relationship to the other treatises mentioned here, see J. Wisse, 1989, *Ethos*, 133-42.

[79]   As in the *Partitiones*, *quaestiones* are separated into two groups, those concerned with a general inquiry (θέσεις), and those concerned with a specific inquiry (i.e., concerning specific person(s), place, time, etc., known as ὑπόθεσεις). The θέσεις are further divided into those which are *cognitionis* and those which are *actionis*, two categories which are again subdivided. In *Top.* 87-90, however, Cicero goes beyond what is treated in the *Partitiones* by suggesting which *loci* are most suited to the three kinds of θέσεις *cognitionis* (contrast *Part.* 68). See further, § 2.2.1 below.

[80]   Roberts' edition, and particularly his translation, received a very critical review from W. G. Rutherford (1903, "Roberts"), to which Roberts replied (1903b, "Roberts").

[81]   See D. C. Innes, 1995, "Demetrius," 316.

[82]   Note that LSJ list the treatise as authored by "Demetrius Phalereus" and date it to the fourth century BC despite the fact that Roberts' edition is used for citation (of whose dating see below). Yet *nota bene* a separate entry is given for the (genuine) historical fragments of Demetrius Phalereus. No modification is suggested in the supplement.

Both Radermacher and Roberts, arguing primarily from considerations of language, postulated a late date in their respective editions. This essentially agreed with the consensus of late nineteenth century scholarship.[83] Radermacher postulated a date after Dionysius of Halicarnassus, i.e., first century AD or thereafter, and Roberts eventually agreed.[84] A first century AD date has not, however, been the unanimous opinion of scholars. F. Boll argued, against Radermacher, that the date of the treatise does not *have* to be late, and W. Kroll, assessing the research on the matter up to his time, considered it still conceivable that the author could be Demetrius of Phalerum, despite the odd indication that might suggest a later school rhetoric.[85] More recently G. M. A. Grube has made an interesting, but not conclusive, case for a date in the third century BC, although in his view the work is probably not to be attributed to Demetrius of Phalerum (on grounds of language).[86] This dating is maintained by Grube against critics, and was at first accepted by Kennedy[87] who now, however, tentatively mentions a first century BC date.[88] D. M. Schenkeveld has also provided a refutation of Grube, arguing for a date in the first century AD.[89] D. C. Innes tentatively argues for the second century BC.[90]

Demetrius' tract is concerned with ἑρμηνεία in the sense of literary expression. His work is not restricted to ἑρμηνεία in oratory and thus not directly concerned with rhetoric, although it overlaps in the treatment rhetorical writers gave to style. The work begins with an introductory section on the various constituents of prose expression, namely, κῶλα, κόμματα, and περίοδοι. Demetrius then moves to the burden of his treatise, the explanation of the four "simple" or, perhaps better, "basic" characters or styles. This discussion is introduced in §§ 36-37. Demetrius indicates that knowledge of these basic styles is essential for a proper analysis of the style of both prose and poetry. Of course style is often rather complex and cannot always simply be put into one of four categories, but according to Demetrius style is often a mixture of these four components (of which *nota bene* certain mixes are not possible).[91] Demetrius opposes those who reduce the number of simple components to two (cf. Cic. *Brut.* 201).

---

[83]   For an annotated bibliography on this point for that period see G. M. A. Grube, 1961, *Greek*, 22-23n.

[84]   Radermacher, 1901, *Demetrii*, 77; Roberts, 1927, "Demetrius," 270-77.

[85]   Boll, 1917/18, "Demetrius," 25-33; Kroll, 1940, "Rhetorik," 1079-80.

[86]   1961, *Greek*.

[87]   Grube, 1964, "Date"; Kennedy, 1963, *Art*, 285-86; 1972, *Art*, 120n.
Grube's appeal to the so-called "late" terminology in the text of the *Rhetorica ad Alexandrum* (firmly dated as early as the late fourth century BC) has, however, been greatly weakened by the research of M. Fuhrmann into its textual tradition (see Grube, 1961, *Greek*, 47, 156-63; Fuhrmann, 1964b, *Untersuchungen*, 158-64).

[88]   1994, *History*, 88

[89]   1964, *Studies*, 135-48

[90]   1995, "Demetrius." In 1972 ("Demetrius," 172) she had suggested a century earlier.

[91]   The words ὁρῶμεν ... πάντας μιγνυμένους πᾶσιν at § 37 should not be taken to mean that style is *invariably* a mixture of these components, but only that any kind of mixture may take place (apart from the exceptions). This interpretation is supported by the opening sentence of § 36, which enumerates the four basic types of style and then adds mixtures as a continuation of the enumeration.

The early origin and development of the division of style into several character-istics is controversial. In any case, Aristotle himself would appear to have opposed such an analysis (*Rh.* 3.12.6). Demetrius' organisation into four χαρακτῆρες does not, however, really reflect either earlier or later rhetorical theory. Later rhetorical theory often spoke of three χαρακτῆρες λέξεως (types of style), not infrequently classifying various writers by them (plain, ornate/ grand and middle styles). But Demetrius does not necessarily intend his χαρακτῆρες to be used as categories with which to classify various authors. Rather, they are four basic styles which often appear in literature in various mixed forms.[92]

He describes his four styles (in order: ἑρμηνεία μεγαλοπρεπής, γλαφυρά, ἰσχνή, and δεινή, i.e., the grand, elegant/ smooth, plain, and forceful style) by discuss-ing the appropriate figures and methods to use in each of three traditional areas,[93] namely, σύνθεσις (composition), λέξις (word-choice), and πράγματα or διάνοια (sub-ject matter). A digression here or there is not infrequently added. The treatment of each style is completed by a brief description of its adverse counterpart.[94]

Demetrius' descriptions and definitions are quite short and yet they can also be quite helpful in that he often tries to show (with examples) how certain figures or methods are appropriate to certain contexts. He realises that the same kinds of figures can often be used in various different contexts and to various different effects; however we look here in vain for an in-depth analysis of why this is so.

It seems clear that Demetrius relied heavily on secondary sources to write his work. This much is clear from § 179 where he admits difficulty with his subject *because* he could find no earlier treatment of it. Literary citations are frequently bor-rowed from other treatises. Many of them, for instance, clearly derive from Arist. *Rh.*

---

[92] It has been not infrequently noted that this makes Demetrius' χαρακτῆρες seem somewhat more akin to ἀρεταί (virtues), cf. F. Solmsen, 1931, "Demetrios," 242. Yet I believe this statement goes too far. Demetrius is clearly dealing with stylistic analysis in the same sense as other writers, but simply takes a different approach. That the concern addressed in his approach was not unique is clear from Dionysius of Halicarnassus who seems to have been aware of similar criticism of literary analysts (like himself) who classified authors according to various styles. Yet at *de Demosthene* 37 Dionysius also admits that no author uses any one style (χαρακτήρ) completely purely. There are always mixtures. It is rather a matter of the dominance of one particular style. Similarly Cicero, whilst agreeing that whole ora-tions could be classified in one or other style, also stated that it was often necessary for several styles to be used within one oration (*Orat.* 74). See my further comments in the section on Cicero's *Orator* (§ 4.1). Similarly, Quint. *Inst.* 12.10.66-72.

[93] Cf. D. C. Innes, 1995, "Demetrius," 323n.

[94] See F. Solmsen, 1931, "Demetrios," for a helpful article in understanding the organisation of the treatise and a good analysis of its sources and in particular the relation to Aristotle's rhetoric (even if secondary).

3. Yet it is not certain that he knew Aristotle's work first hand.[95] Among his sources are most probably Arist. *Rh.* 3 (probably via some other source); a work of Archedemus (possibly just the preface to his edition of Aristotle's letters);[96] and perhaps the third century BC Peripatetic grammarian Praxiphanes (cf. §§ 56ff). But it could be, as F. Solmsen suggests, that Demetrius took these three sources in quotation from some later work.[97]

Despite the fact that this tract appears to have been little used by later rhetorical theorists (according to D. C. Innes it is cited in Syrianus, Ammonius and Phoebammon),[98] it shows much in common with traditional rhetorical theory. The strong Peripatetic influence is, in Innes' words, "often adapted and supplemented to fit standard later theory."[99] For this reason the treatise may be considered quite useful for rhetorical analysis of Paul.

2.2 Academicians

As was to be expected from Plato's own attitude, Academic philosophy did not contribute much to rhetoric. Although with the turn to scepticism in the third century BC it came into vogue to be able to debate both sides of an issue, this must not be considered in terms of rhetorical practice.[100] The Academy only seems to have taken up the

---

[95] Demetrius never explicitly indicates which book any given citation comes from. Furthermore, his citations not infrequently vary from what we find in Aristotle's *Rhetoric*. Grube, however, in line with his theory on the dating, disagrees. He argues that Demetrius at times deliberately disagreed with Aristotle and altered what he taught. For Grube, Demetrius although thoroughly Peripatetic, wrote at a time before Aristotle was virtually canonised by his followers. See, however, my comments on the ἐνθύμημα in Demetrius in the select glossary appended to this book, where Demetrius' discussion is traceable to a post-Aristotelian source used in common with Quintilian (*Inst.* 5.14.1-4).

[96] An unidentified Peripatetic whose edition of Aristotle's letters is also mentioned in Andronicus' list of Aristotle's works (first century BC). Roberts would identify him with a Stoic philosopher of Tarsus who probably lived around 130 BC, author of περὶ φωνῆς and περὶ στοιχείων (cf. D.L. 7.40, 55, 68, 84, 88, 134, 136). Was he also the common source of Demetrius, *de Elocutione* 30-33 and Quintilian, *Institutio Oratoria* 5.14.1-4 (cf. Demetr. *Eloc.* 281 and Quint. *Inst.* 9.2.92)?

[97] 1931, "Demetrios," 265. He points to L. Radermacher's comment on § 34 (1901, *Demetrii*, 75-76) as evidence that Demetrius probably did not himself read Aristotle's treatise.

[98] 1995, "Demetrius," 312-13n.

[99] 1995, "Demetrius," 320. Innes refers to traditional elements of rhetorical theory throughout her introductory essay.

[100] This is not to say that a later orator such as Cicero could not find the practice helpful for the training of an orator (cf. Cic. *Orat.* 12; *N.D.* 2.168). Certain rhetorical implications were later seen in the visit of Carneades (214-129 BC) to Rome in 155 BC as member of a political embassy on behalf of Athens. Carneades achieved notoriety by delivering a public speech on justice and then the following day another speech against justice (Lact. *Inst.* 5.15; cf. Plu. *Cat.Ma.* 22). At this time, however, the Academy was still negatively disposed to rhetoric (cf. Cic. *de Orat.* 1.45-46).

teaching of rhetoric under Philo of Larissa (*c.*159/58-84/83 BC)[101], head from 110/109 BC.[102] In 88 BC Philo fled to Rome where he continued teaching both rhetoric and philosophy (cf. Cic. *Tusc.* 2.9). Here Cicero became one of his pupils. In the *Partitiones Oratoriae* Cicero provides us with what is essentially an Academic rhetorical treatise.[103]

But the Academy's surprising turn to rhetoric under Philo (was it only Philo?) seems to have been somewhat controversial. We know at least that Philo's contemporary Charmadas disparaged rhetoric as mere aptitude and practice (cf. *de Orat.* 1.84-93, esp. § 90, and S.E. *M.* 2.20).[104] In addition, Antiochus, Philo of Larissa's rival, does not appear to have taught rhetoric (cf. Cic. *Brut.* 315).[105]

2.2.1 Cicero, *Partitiones Oratoriae*

> Edition: The standard text is still that of A. S. Wilkins in Cicero, *Rhetorica* (vol. 2; OCT; Oxford: Clarendon, 1903). The translation by H. Rackham (*Cicero* [vol.4; LCL; London: Heinemann, 1942]) is based on an older Latin text.

The *Partitiones Oratoriae* is a very simple short treatise in catechism form embracing the whole system of rhetoric. The two *personae* of the dialogue are Cicero and his young son Marcus Tullius. At the opening we are told that what follows is a Latin translation of what Marcus has learned in Greek. At the end we learn that what has been taught comes from the Academy. In fact Cicero even adds that rhetoric cannot

---

[101]   See J. Glucker, 1978, *Antiochus*, 100n.

[102]   The scanty fragments extant preserve virtually nothing of specifically rhetorical teaching (see H. J. Mette, 1986/87, "Philon," 14-20).

[103]   At *de Orat.* 3.75 Cicero mentions a certain Metrodorus with whom he studied in Asia. This Metrodorus is said to be *ex Academia rhetor*, but we learn elsewhere that he *transferred* from the philosophical to the political life, although he mostly *wrote* speeches (Str. 13.1.55).

[104]   Charmadas' critique at Cic. *de Orat.* 1.87 seems to be couched in terms reminiscent of Plato, *Phaedrus* 271a ff, cf. 277bc. J. Wisse (1989, *Ethos*, 165-75) has cogently argued that the allusion to reputable character and swaying of the emotions here is deliberately worded in such a way as to reflect Cicero's own discussion of these matters later in the treatise. It should not be taken to mean that Charmadas was influenced by Aristotelian doctrine on this point. Charmadas' claim that the rhetors lacked the necessary knowledge concerning character and emotion is meant as an argument *against* rhetoric *per se*. It cannot be interpreted (against the rest of our evidence as to his views) to mean that he accepted a philosophical kind of rhetoric. Of course Cicero uses this point to *bolster* his own synthesis of philosophy and rhetoric.

[105]   See also J. Wisse, 1989, *Ethos*, 170-71

be understood or applied without the Academy.[106] The treatise is to be dated 54-52 BC, when Marcus was 11-13 years old.[107]

The *Partitiones* are divided into three separate sections, the first dealing with the ἔργα τοῦ ῥήτορος (so briefly as to be of little value for this study). The second is organised according to the parts of a speech with a natural emphasis on the *confirmatio*, which is, however, oriented towards judicial rhetoric and structured according to the στάσεις. The final section analyses the *quaestiones*, distinguishing between θέσεις (abstract questions) and ὑποθέσεις (concrete questions) (similarly, Cic. *Top.* 79-99), a distinction which has been used by scholars discussing Pauline rhetoric, particularly in connection with the letter to the Romans. The somewhat expanded treatment of the θέσεις may reflect the philosophical background of this treatise.

Certain Hellenistic rhetorical theorists since Hermagoras had incorporated θέσεις into their systems, but there is evidence that θέσεις were sometimes little more than mentioned (cf. Cic. *Inv.* 1.8; *de Orat.* 2.78).[108] Rhetorical theory was more concerned with ὑποθέσεις. Cicero, in accordance with the attempt to synthesize rhetoric and philosophy in his later rhetorical treatises, championed the value of θέσεις for the training of the orator. He also incorporated a discussion of the analysis of θέσεις into *Part.* 61-68 (similarly, *de Orat.* 3.109-19).[109] He rightly pointed out that θέσεις had a long tradition in the Peripatetic and (especially since the turn to scepticism) Academic schools.[110] The inclusion of θέσεις into rhetorical theory from the second century BC on was probably to deliberately incorporate philosophy into the scope of rhetorical education.

Although we cannot be sure how school rhetoric dealt with θέσεις in the first or second centuries BC (did they do anything more than mention them?), by the first century AD we find the θέσις grouped among the various preliminary exercises commonly known as προγυμνάσματα.[111] That θέσεις became a standard exercise among the προγυμνάσματα is clear from Quint. *Inst.* 2.4.24-32 and Theon *Prog.* 12. Theon's treatment of θέσεις is quite clearly very rhetorical, and

---

[106] See also O. Angermann (1904, *Aristotele*, 4-5) and W. Kroll (1940, "Rhetorik," 1088 where other studies are cited) who argue that it is simply a translation (possibly reworked) of a Greek work from "Middle Platonism." That is not to say that Cicero may not have included here and there something gleaned from his own Roman experience, cf. § 118.

[107] See B. B. Gilleland, 1961, "Date."

[108] Cicero, *de Inventione* 1.8 is itself evidence that this trend of incorporating θέσεις was not universal. He denies that θέσεις have a place in rhetorical theory. Apollodorus (*c.* 104-22 BC), who taught at Rome, is also known to have criticised Hermagoras on this point, arguing against the distinction ὑπόθεσις/ θέσις altogether (*Fr.* 2 Gran., = Aug. *Rhet.* 5). On the other hand, we know that Athenaeus (second century BC, a rival of Hermagoras) emphasised the close connection between the ὑπόθεσις and θέσις by calling it *pars causae* (cited in Quint. *Inst.* 3.5.5). Theodorus of Gadara (fl. 33 BC) called the θέσις, κεφάλαιον ἐν ὑποθέσει (*Fr.* 9 Gran., cited in, e.g., Theon *Prog.* ii, p.120,19 Sp.). This is probably to be connected with Theodorus' στάσις theory (see *Fr.* 4 Gran., = Quint. *Inst.* 3.6.2; 3.11.3 [cf. 3.11.27]; Aug. *Rhet.* 12; J. Adamietz, 1966, *Quintiliani*, 113).

On the place of the θέσις in the rhetorical education of the Roman republic, see M. L. Clarke (1951, "Thesis") who provides a good discussion of many of the sources.

[109] Cicero's discussion in *de Oratore* differs in one respect, in that he asserts that his analysis applies to both *consultationes* (θέσεις) and *causae* (ὑποθέσεις), *de Orat.* 3.111-12.

[110] See further, H. Throm, 1932, *Thesis*, 171-83.

[111] On these exercises see § 3.3 of this chapter.

also polemical against philosophy. He divides θέσεις into those which are θεωρητικαί and those which are πρακτικαί (*Prog.* ii, p.121,6-17 Sp.). Although this seems to reflect the division in Cic. *Part.* 62 into the θέσις *cognitionis* and *actionis*, the analysis is quite different. Theon refers to the θεωρητικαί as philosophical and the πρακτικαί as rhetorical. However, he goes on to argue that rhetoric is just as able to treat of philosophical as rhetorical θέσεις. He provides a detailed list of τόποι for dealing with θέσεις and adds remarks on the ordering of material, αὔξησις, and other typical rhetorical methods. The *Partitiones*, on the other hand, deal with the θέσις *cognitionis* in terms of a simple application of στάσις doctrine. The θέσις *actionis* is divided into that concerning instruction in duty (e.g., to parents) and that concerning the calming or arousing of emotions (explained as incorporating various kinds of consolation or exhortation in Cic. *de Orat.* 3.118).[112] Clearly both kinds of θέσεις in the *Partitiones* are philosophical in origin.

The *Partitiones* go on to discuss the ὑποθέσεις according to the three rhetorical genres (cf. Cic. *de Orat.* 3.109; *Top.* 91-99), by far the most space being given to judicial rhetoric where στάσις doctrine (precise analysis of the kind of case) is more fully explained. An interesting passage in the discussion of deliberative rhetoric (§§ 89-97) seems to be an attempt to follow through the programme of ψυχαγωγία outlined in Plato's *Phaedrus* 271a4 - b5; 271c10 - 272b4; 277b5 - c6.[113]

The structural arrangement of the treatise is not mirrored in the extant rhetorical treatises, and may be peculiar to Academic rhetoric.

The brevity and simplicity of this rhetorical catechism, coupled with its distinct philosophical emphases (e.g., arrangement of τόποι §§ 6-7,[114] more detailed handling of θέσεις §§ 62-68), renders it rather less useful for our purposes, as also its (typical) concentration upon judicial rhetoric in connection with στάσις doctrine.

2.3 Epicureans

2.3.1 Philodemus

Our knowledge of Epicurean attitudes to rhetoric is largely based on the significant papyrus fragments of Philodemus' περὶ ῥητορικῆς.[115] Philodemus, an avid

---

[112]   Compare Sen. *Ep.* 94-95.

[113]   The subordination of all the arguments listed under the στάσις *coniectura* to the principle of probability (§§ 34-40) may also be influenced by Pl. *Phdr.* 272e1 - 273a1.

[114]   For the τόποι see above pp.43-44.

[115]   Extensive fragments from this work were found during the excavations at Herculaneum in the eighteenth century. The treatise, in seven books, concerns itself more with a critical discussion of various views on rhetoric, rather than a positive presentation of rhetorical theory. The fragments were gathered and published by S. Sudhaus, *Volumina Rhetorica* (3 vols; BSGRT; B. G. Teubner; Leipzig, 1892-96). Sudhaus' ordering of the books is, however, out of date. For the structure of the treatise see T. Dorandi, 1990, "ricomposizione." A new edition of books one and two (with Italian translation) was published in 1977, ΦΙΛΟΔΗΜΟΥ ΠΕΡΙ ΡΗΤΟΡΙΚΗΣ *Libros Primum et Secundum* (F. L. Auricchio ed.; Ricerche sui papiri Ercolanesi 3; Naples: Giannini, 1977). For other recent textual emendations and edited portions of the text see the bibliography on Philodemus' *De Rhetorica* in D. Obbink (ed.), *Philodemus and Poetry: Poetic Theory and Practice in Lucretius, Philodemus, and Horace* (Oxford: University Press, 1995) 276-78. A synopsis of the work in English was published by H. M. Hubbell in 1920, "The

Epicurean of the first century BC, sought to follow his mentors, the great fathers of Epicureanism, namely, Epicurus himself, Metrodorus and Hermarchus, all of whom had written on rhetoric. From Philodemus we learn of a dispute among Epicureans of his day concerning the views of Epicurus *et al* on rhetoric. Philodemus maintains that Epicurus in his περὶ ῥητορικῆς had restricted the notion of rhetoric as a τέχνη to *writing* (as opposed to speaking) speeches and producing epideictic. This rhetoric is termed sophistic (τέχνην [εἶν]αι τὴν σοφιστικὴν τ[οῦ λ]όγους συγγράφειν καὶ ἐπ[ιδε]ίξεις ποιεῖσθαι, [τοῦ δὲ] δίκας λέγειν καὶ δη[μη]γορεῖν οὐκ εἶναι τέ[χνη]ν, *Rh.* p.95,1-7 Auricchio). Deliberative and forensic rhetoric was thus *not* considered a τέχνη.[116] This restrictive view of rhetoric represents general Epicurean antipathy to rhetoric in public life.[117] Yet we learn of other Epicureans who went even further and argued that Epicurus had denied that any form of rhetoric could be considered a τέχνη.[118] Philodemus' work is also helpful in terms of his critique of the ideas of Peripatetics and Stoics, thereby adding to what little we know of these schools during Hellenistic times.

Philodemus himself favoured a simple and natural style (τὸ κατὰ φύσιν ὂν εὔσχημον, *Rh.* 1.163 S.) instead of ὁμοιοτέλευτα, ὁμοιόπτωτα, etc..[119] In terms of style, he clearly accused the rhetorical theorists of being overly interested in classification. In his view they do not properly define cases when certain figures (in a general sense) may or may not be used, but rely on subjective criteria (e.g., if it sounds good to the ear, e.g., *Rh.* 1.163 [hiatus], 172-73 [metaphors], 176 [τὰ εὖ λελεκμένα]).

Rhetorica of Philodemus: Translation and Commentary" in *Transactions of the Connecticut Academy of Arts and Sciences* 23 (1920) 243-382. The title is somewhat misleading as no running commentary is given. The "translation" is more of a précis. Hubbell's presentation is, nevertheless, very helpful, the more due to the very confusing nature of Sudhaus' arrangement of the fragments and their inherent difficulty. Nevertheless, Hubbell's "translation" is inadequate for scholarly citation and recourse to the Greek is essential for any serious consideration of what Philodemus says.

[116] According to Ammianus Marcellinus (30.4.3), Epicurus called forensic oratory a κακοτεχνία. We learn elsewhere that Epicurus apparently made σαφήνεια the sole requisite (ἀρετή?) of rhetoric (D.L. 10.13), and also that he condemned the use of εἰρωνεία (Cic. *Brut.* 292).

[117] It would seem that Epicurus was reacting against the views of his teacher Nausiphanes, a philosopher who also taught rhetoric and held that the study of natural philosophy (φυσιολογία) was necessary for training in rhetoric. Nausiphanes also held that the philosopher should engage in the political life (contrast Epicurus). For discussion of Nausiphanes' views see H. von Arnim, 1898, "Sophistik," 43-62, and for discussion of Epicurus, pp.73-77.

[118] Of the views of Epicureans: *Rh.* p.21,9-29 Auricchio (cf. Suppl. p.8,5-13 S.): τοῖς δ' ἡμετέροις μεμπτέον ἂν εἴη καὶ περιττότε[ρ]ον τοῖ[ς] γέ τοι τοιού[το]ις, ὅσοι καὶ τὴν σοφισ[τ]ικὴν ῥητορικὴν οὐ[κ] εἶναι τέχνην διειλήφασι καὶ τούτου συστατικοὺς λόγους πεποιήκασι. εἰ γὰρ Ἐπί[ί]κουρος καὶ Μητρό-δωρος ἔτι δ' Ἕρμαρχος ἀποφαίνονται τέχνην ὑπάρχειν τὴν τοιαύτη[ν] ὡς ἐν τοῖς ἑξῆς ὑπομνήσομεν, οἱ τούτοις ἀντιγράφοντες οὐ πάνυ τι μακρὰν τῆς τῶν πατραλοιῶν καταδίκης ἀφεστήκασιν. Cf. Quint. *Inst.* 2.17.15.

[119] A not uncommon sentiment among philosophers generally, cf. Sen. *Ep.* 40.

Philodemus surely has a point here and it is to be regretted that we do not possess treatises with more in-depth explanations in this regard. What is left of Philodemus' work does not provide us much help in this respect either.[120]

2.4 Stoics

Despite evidence that Stoics included rhetoric into their philosophical system (D.L. 7.41; Quint. *Inst.* 3.1.15), there is unfortunately very little on this subject extant.[121] They seem to have paid no attention to θέσεις and ὑποθέσεις nor to abstract τόποι (as the Peripatetics and later Academics did, Cic. *Fin.* 4.7; *Top.* 6; Cic. *de Orat.* 2.159), and rejected the use of emotions in attempting to sway the judge(s) (*SVF* 3, *Fr.* 451; cf. Quint. *Inst.* 6.1.7; 11.1.33). Although we hear of the odd Roman influenced by such Stoic theory (*de Orat.* 1.227-30; *Brut.* 113-17), it cannot be said that the Stoics influenced rhetorical theory in these respects. From Diogenes Laertius we also learn of a number of books devoted to λέξις (probably, "style"), e.g., περὶ λέξεως εἰσαγωγή (*Fr.* 44 EK) of Posidonius (of whose writings on literature and rhetoric, see Sen. *Ep.* 95.65-66 and Quint. *Inst.* 3.6.37). It is fairly clear that with respect to style they distinguished five ἀρεταὶ λόγου (virtues of speech): ἑλληνισμός, σαφήνεια, συντομία, πρέπον, κατασκευή (i.e., correct language, clarity, brevity, suitability, ornamentation, D.L. 7.59).[122] Whilst the number of items classified as ἀρεταί is peculiarly Stoic, none of the items themselves are especially surprising. All of them can be found in the third book of Aristotle's *Rhetoric*.[123]

Their main interest, however, seems to have been dialectics, not rhetoric (cf. e.g., Cic. *Brut.* 119). Rhetorical theorists generally recognised that Stoic dialectics had

---

[120]   For an attempt to read a positive theory of εὕρεσις into Philodemus' text see, R. N. Gaines, 1985, "Philodemus."

[121]   The rhetorical fragments of the Stoics are meagre and do not offer much of help to our investigation. See H. von Arnim, *Stoicorum Veterum Fragmenta*, Zeno, vol. 1, *Fr.* 74-84; Cleanthes, vol. 1, *Fr.* 491-92; Chrysippus & Stoicism generally, vol. 2, *Fr.* 288-98; Diogenes of Babylon, vol. 3, *Fr.* 91-126, and the discussion in von Arnim, 1898, "Sophistik," 77-80. We do learn that Diogenes of Babylon (*c.* 240-152 BC) taught that only (Stoic) philosophers could be real rhetors, i.e., men able successfully to advise the state, since only philosophers mastered the truth and were fit to fill all the offices of the statesman. Furthermore, only Stoicism made good citizens (*Fr.* 125). On Stoic rhetorical theory (especially as regards style) see C. Atherton, "Hand Over Fist: The Failure of Stoic Rhetoric," *Classical Quarterly* 38 (1988) 392-427.

[122]   On the last, see J. Stroux (1912, *Theophrasti*, 35-36) for a clear interpretation. Stroux (37) sees the influence of Theophrastus in this enumeration of ἀρεταί.

[123]   K. Barwick (1957, *Probleme*) has researched several elements related to Stoic rhetoric, especially word-coinage and tropes. He, however, rightly admits that for the Stoics such matters had more bearing on poetry than prose (p.93, cf. Quint. *Inst.* 10.1.84).

little to offer them (cf. Cic. *de Orat.* 2.157-59; D.H. *Comp.* 4 [pp.21-23 U.-R.]), nor was Cicero impressed with Stoic rhetorical theory (*Fin.* 4.7).

2.5 The Controversy Between Philosophy and Rhetoric

We have now briefly reviewed the extant sources of rhetorical theory which have their provenance in the philosophical schools. Along the way we have noted a varying attitude to rhetoric. It is, therefore, appropriate to briefly sketch the relationship between philosophy and rhetoric, as far as our sources allow us to reconstruct this.[124] Some understanding of this relationship is important for the discussion which has taken place around Paul's own understanding of his preaching in the letters to the Corinthians.

Both rhetorical and philosophical training in the fourth century BC were generally concerned to prepare their students for public life, which included public speaking. The common conception of φιλοσοφία at this time included rhetoric and general education for public life. It was here that Plato objected, desiring to reserve philosophy for abstract research into the truth. Plato's concept, however, did not catch on in his own time, but it was furthered in the work of Aristotle. From the third century BC on philosophy was generally distinguished from rhetoric. Von Arnim (68) makes the point that the practical result of this change was that rhetorical and philosophical education no longer rivaled each other in the strict sense, in that they no longer had the same aims. Rhetorical education prepared students for public life. Philosophical schools became institutions of research where students later became researchers, remaining in the school to continue the quest for true knowledge. Although von Arnim describes the change which took place in the philosophical schools in quite anachronistic terminology, his main point is valid, namely, that they generally became more interested in theoretical problems than in the provision of an education directed to public life. He concludes that in this new scenario, rhetorical education would really only have rivaled the training in rhetoric which was possibly still provided by a few Peripatetics.[125] Von Arnim (80-81) goes on to argue that the status of the philosophical schools (particularly

---

[124]   Although in some respects dated, an important essay on this subject is still the first chapter of H. von Arnim's *Leben und Werke des Dio von Prusa* (1898, "Sophistik").

[125]   See above, p.42.

in Athens) was very high in the early Hellenistic period, and contrasts this to the little we hear of rhetorical schools and tutors.[126]

From the second century BC on we find Roman interest in the Greek schools.[127] Von Arnim posits that it is this Roman interest that provoked rivalry between the philosophical and rhetorical schools. Further rivalry between rhetorical and philosophical schools was probably engendered by Hermagoras' inclusion of θέσεις into his rhetorical system (cf. Cic. *Inv.* 1.8; *de Orat.* 2.65-66; Plu. *Pomp.* 42.5). Rhetorical theory was thereby encroaching upon the domain of philosophy.[128] A controversy was hereby born. Added fuel for the controversy was provided by the question, already posed by Plato, as to whether rhetoric was a τέχνη or not.[129] It is at the advent (around the beginning of the second century BC) of this controversy, centering around the respective domains of rhetoric and philosophy, that we have noted that the Peripatetics seem to have dropped their direct associations with rhetoric. The Stoics naturally maintained that only a Stoic sage could ever be a true rhetor. The animosity to rhetorical schools was, therefore, maintained right across the philosophical spectrum. Only in the first century BC Academy, under Philo of Larissa, do we hear of a return to general rhetorical theory. Philo, however, seems to have been alone in this reversal. In addition, he appears to have kept the two disciplines apart, teaching philosophy and rhetoric at separate times (Cic. *Tusc.* 2.9).[130] He may well have been motivated by the desire to

---

[126] Nevertheless, anyone interested in a public career would have likely elected for rhetorical training. Only those interested in the rather ascetic life of research would take training in a philosophical school instead. Of course, there was always the possibility that someone trained for public life (i.e., in rhetoric) could later broaden his education in the field of philosophy. Such a step become common later on for wealthy Romans who were inevitably first trained in rhetoric.

[127] S. F. Bonner, 1977, *Education*, 65-66, cf. 90-96.

[128] J. Wisse (1989, *Ethos*, 80n) argues that Quint. *Inst.* 3.1.15-16 suggests that Hermagoras was the first significant rhetorician after the dominance of the philosophical schools in the third century, and therefore suggests a date around 150 BC or even earlier (answering the arguments of D. Matthes, 1958, *Hermagoras*, for a later date). Elsewhere (A. D. Leeman *et al*, 1981-96, *Tullius*, 4.96) he notes Phld. *Rh.* 1.201, xxᵃ12 - 225,11 S. as further evidence that rhetorical theory was claiming a very broad territory. We may note Theon (see above, pp.49-50) as a late (probably first century AD) reflection of this trend (without necessarily implying an active controversy in his time).

It should, perhaps, be noted, e.g., that H. Throm (1932, *Thesis*, 89-104) argued on the basis of Hermagoras' definition of rhetoric in terms of the πολιτικὸν ζήτημα, that Hermagoras' θέσεις were restricted to those elsewhere labelled πρακτικαί, and that therefore Cicero's critique of Hermagoras' position was unfair (*Inv.* 1.8). He further suggests that the work mentioned by Quint. *Inst.* 3.5.14 may have concerned Hermagoras' contention that θεωρητικαὶ θέσεις do not belong to rhetoric. This latter view is speculative, but interesting.

[129] For a discussion of these arguments see H. Hubbell, 1920, "Rhetorica," 364-82.

[130] We may assume that Cicero's *Partitiones* represents the kind of rhetorical teaching he gave (whether or not this treatise depends directly on him). Although it is uniquely structured and shows definite philosophical influences, it still follows the broad outlines of school rhetoric.

cater to more students and to the popularity of rhetorical training among Romans. Romans, at least from the first century BC on, considered a rhetorical education highly desirable and generally preferred Greek tutors.

We should briefly note the differences between Roman and Hellenistic Greek "pre-tertiary" education. M. P. Nilsson (1955, *Schule*) has shown, mostly from inscriptional evidence, that Hellenistic Greek schooling often divided the children into three broad groups (frequently with their own gymnasia): παῖδες (up to 14 years), ἔφηβοι (15-17, not to be confused with the more specific Athenian ἔφηβοι), and οἱ νέοι (18 years old and higher, probably till about 21-22). The education offered in these schools emphasised physical exercises and music. Tutors in language and literature were often of inferior quality and probably only provided the elements of reading and writing. Homer was, of course, a standard text. There is, however, evidence that schools not infrequently made use of itinerant experts by paying them to give courses to their students for a set period. One interesting inscription mentions the engagement of both a rhetor and a heavy-weapons expert to teach their respective disciplines to all the age groups.[131] Only wealthy Greeks could have afforded to send their νέοι out of town to any of the famous schools for a more dedicated "tertiary" education (e.g., in philosophy, rhetoric or medicine), or perhaps to the famous *Epheby* at Athens, which by the first century AD was an all-round finishing school, teaching philosophy (from various schools), grammar, geometry, rhetoric and music.[132]
Roman education was more directly literary and rhetorical. One attended the *grammaticus* from about 12-15 years and then the *rhetor* from about 16 and above, but arrangements were private and much depended on the wealth and desires of the family concerned. Further higher education could be attained abroad (e.g., Athens, Rhodes or Asia Minor), whether in rhetoric or philosophy.

J. Wisse has suggested that the controversy between rhetoric and philosophy must have lasted until the 40's of the first century BC and thus forms the backdrop for Cicero's attempted synthesis of philosophy and rhetoric in the *de Oratore*.[133] The controversy does not appear to have functioned after that time, a development, in Wisse's view, connected with the general demise of philosophical schools.[134] This fact may also

---

[131] IG. 12.9.234,8-12. καὶ παρέσχεν (sc. ὁ γυμνασίαρχος) ἐκ τοῦ ἰδίου ῥήτορά τε καὶ ὁπλομάχον, οἵτινες ἐσχόλαζον ἐν τῷ γυμνασίῳ τοῖς τε παισὶν καὶ ἐφήβοις καὶ τοῖς ἄλλοις τοῖς βουλομένοις τὴν ἀπὸ τῶν τοιούτων ὠφελίαν ἐπιδέχεσθαι.
[132] See M. P. Nilsson, 1955, *Schule*, 26-27 (esp. the inscriptional evidence cited on p.26 note 2) and also Plutarch, *Moralia* 736d. An eclectic philosophical education seems to have become more popular in this age. An inscription (tentatively dated to 122/1 BC) shows the ἔφηβοι engaged in philosophical courses from various different philosophers and schools: IG. 2.2.1006,19-20, προσεκαρτ[έ]ρησαν δὲ καὶ Ζηνοδότωι σχολ[ά ζ]οντε[ς ἐν τ]ε τῶι Πτολεμαίωι καὶ | ἐν Λυκείωι, ὁμοίως δὲ καὶ τοῖς ἄλλοις [φιλο]σόφοις ἅπασι[ν] τοῖς τε ἐν Λυκείωι καὶ ἐν ᾿Ακαδημ[ίαι δὶ ὅλου τοῦ ἐ]νιαυτοῦ·. One is reminded of the later stories of varied philosophical education told of Apollonius of Tyana (Philostr. *VA* 1.7), Galen (*Anim.Pass.* 1.8, §§ 41-42), Justin Martyr (*dial.* 2), and Hermogenes of Pontus (Him. 14,23-24). Compare also Josephus (*Vit.* 10).
[133] In A. D. Leeman *et al*, 1981-96, *Tullius*, 4.96; cf. 1994, *Welsprekendheid*, 14-17.
[134] 1994, *Welsprekendheid*, 17. On pp.16-17 (cf. A. D. Leeman *et al*, 1996, *Tullius*, 4.96) he argues that the controversy must have been over by the time that Dionysius of Halicarnassus had written the preface to his work on the ancient orators (*Orat.Vett.*, c. 25 BC). We may add that D.H. *Th.* 50 also implies that little fundamental discord was felt between the schools of rhetoric and philosophy by Dionysius. He writes concerning those men who have come διὰ τῶν ἐγκυκλίων μαθημάτων ἐπὶ ῥητορικήν τε < καὶ > φιλοσοφίαν.

explain the absence of the controversy in the first century AD. If this is correct, then we should be cautious against all too easily referring Paul's negative comments on persuasion to a contemporary *philosophical* animosity to rhetoric.

> According to Eunapius (455) the period of philosophy from Plato onwards eventually experienced a rupture or break due to certain public calamities (an evident reference to the disruptions during the late Roman republic). A new period began with the influx of philosophers in the time of Claudius and Nero.[135] The demise of philosophy towards the end of the first century BC is reflected in the general languishing of the once famous schools of philosophy in Athens. The Academy seems to have become defunct after Philo of Larissa, who spent his last years in Rome (died *c.* 84/83 BC)[136]. The rival "Old Academy" of Antiochus of Ascalon seems to have ceased after the death of his successor (and brother) Aristus. The Peripatetic school also appears to have closed about the time of Sulla's siege of Athens.[137]

2.6 Overview

Our survey of rhetorical theory among the philosophers has shown that although we have Peripatetic and Academic sources of rhetorical theory, we need to carefully note the differences these sources exhibit from school rhetoric (e.g., the use of $\theta\acute{\epsilon}\sigma\epsilon\iota\varsigma$, abstract $\tau\acute{o}\pi o\iota$, Aristotle's views on portrayal of characters and swaying of emotion, etc.).[138] Given that school rhetoric did not generally incorporate these aspects of philosophical rhetorical theory into their teaching, and also the fact that the philosophical schools no longer appear to have taught rhetoric in the first century AD (nor do they appear to have been very important in and of themselves), we should be very reticent in applying any of their rhetorical theory to the writings of Paul. Effectively,

---

[135] Eun. 454 mentions Ammonius of Egypt (Plutarch's teacher); Plutarch; Euphrates of Egypt; Dio Chrysostom; Apollonius of Tyana; the Cynics Carneades, Musonius, Demetrius and Menippus; and Demonax.

[136] See J. Glucker, *Antiochus*, 100n.

[137] See J. P. Lynch, *Aristotle*, 163-207, and J. Glucker, 1978, *Antiochus*. Glucker (364-73) goes on to argue that the Stoic school also ceased to exist in this period, and makes further suggestions concerning the evidence of Epicurean succession. He attributes the decline of philosophy in Athens to the trend for foreign philosophers (who traditionally trained in Athens and tended to remain there) to remain in the East (or at least return after study). The centre of philosophical learning thus shifted from Athens to Asia in particular (see pp.373-79).

After the close of the famous Athenian schools, the most common form of higher education in philosophy was to hire a philosopher as tutor, or at least attach oneself to a philosopher as a fee-paying student. This new scenario seems to have led (in some instances at least) to philosophers being at the beck and call of their students (cf. A. Gellius 1.9.8-11).

[138] Although as far as the Academy is concerned, probably the only figure interested in rhetoric was Philo of Larissa, I use the broader term "Academic" with reference to Cic. *Part.* (cf. § 139).

this means that works such as Aristotle's *Rhetoric* should be avoided. Of course where such theory seems not to have been too different from school rhetoric (e.g., many aspects of the third book of Aristotle's *Rhetoric*), it may be used, but with caution. A non-philosophical treatise such as Demetrius' *de Elocutione* may also be helpful, although the reader needs to keep an open eye for the author's Peripatetic leanings. Furthermore, knowledge of the distinctive characteristics of Peripatetic rhetorical theory will help the reader to rightly discern where aspects from such Peripatetic rhetoric have influenced Cicero's later rhetorical treatises, and how, in turn, elements from Cicero's later treatises have found their way into the *Institutio* of Quintilian. In this way, elements foreign to school rhetoric in these later treatises may be properly identified and set aside when attempting to apply rhetorical theory appropriate to the apostle Paul.

3 Hellenistic Rhetoricians

The general layout of a typical Greek rhetorical treatise became somewhat standardised during Hellenistic times. Two forms of layout appear to have been used: that organised according to the parts of a speech, and that organised according to the five duties of the orator (the most common form, cf. Quint. *Inst.* 3.3.1). Only the latter kind of treatise is extant in our period.[139] A summary view of such a treatise is given in

---

[139]   On these two forms, see K. Barwick, 1922, "Gliederung," 1-11. That treatises organised according to the parts of a speech must have existed is clear from the existence of such a treatise as the *Ars Rhetorica* of Apsines and Ps.-Hermogenes' *de Inventione*. One might compare [Corn.] *Rh.* (= *Anonymous Seguerianus*) and Rufus Rhetor, but these treatises are relatively short and not as comprehensive. Consequently they may only have been intended as specialised treatises on the parts of speech within the broader scope of an *ars rhetorica* in general. [Corn.] *Rh.*, for example, is quite clearly aware of the importance of στάσις doctrine (§ 170, 214), but this subject is nowhere discussed in the treatise. Apsines, on the other hand, whilst telling us that στάσις doctrine will not be discussed because it has been sufficiently dealt with by predecessors, by virtue of this remark shows us the point at which such a discussion belonged in his (rather comprehensive) treatise (*Rh.* p.291,4-5 Ham.). Ps.-Hermogenes clearly refers the reader to his (lost) treatise on the division of the στάσεις (*Inv.* 3.4, this reference shows by its description of the treatise on στάσεις that it *cannot* be referring to extant treatise on this subject by Hermogenes).

J. Wisse (1989, *Ethos*, 89-90) has argued for the contemporaneous existence (at least until the first half of the first century BC) of treatises organised according to the five duties of the orator where the section on τάξις deals with the parts of the speech (as in the case of Aristotle's *Rhetoric*). He refers to A. D. Leeman and H. Pinkster's interpretation of *de Orat.* 1.138-45, that the parts of the speech discussed in 1.143 refer to the *ordo* of 1.142 (see 1981-96, *Tullius*, 1.232-33 for arguments). Leeman and Pinkster, however, consider the organisation here (on their interpretation) to be Cicero's own. Wisse (correctly I think) argues that Cicero is merely describing traditional school rhetoric.

The merging of the five *officia oratoris* and the *partes orationis* did naturally cause a problem as to where to place the *partes orationis*. It seems as if there may also have been treatises which solved this problem by expounding six *officia oratoris*. In Philo we find the departments of rhetoric listed as: εὕρεσις, φράσις, τάξις, οἰκονομία, μνήμη and ὑπόκρισις (*Som.* 1.205). In later rhetorical treatises οἰκονομία is a synonym for τάξις. Here, οἰκονομία would appear to concern the right ordering of argu-

Cic. *de Orat.* 2.78-80. It tended to begin by dividing the whole subject into θέσεις (generalised subjects) and ὑποθέσεις (subjects with concrete particulars). A treatise is then divided into five branches: εὕρεσις (discovery of appropriate arguments), τάξις (putting the arguments in an acceptable order), λέξις (style), μνήμη (memory) and ὑπόκρισις (delivery). By far the most emphasis was laid upon εὕρεσις and λέξις.

Since Hermagoras (mid second century BC), an important part of the section on εὕρεσις concerned στάσις theory, an intricate way of analysing the differences between various forms of judicial disputes. Each kind of judicial controversy (στάσις) was provided with a list of appropriate τόποι (i.e., ready-made arguments). Whilst this general approach became standard, the nature of such lists, their organisation within a treatise, and the classification of the στάσεις themselves varied.[140] Given that the kind of τόποι provided for the στάσεις are related to typical judicial disputes, they are not actually very relevant to an analysis of Paul's letters. For this reason no extended analysis of στάσις doctrine has been included in the following discussion, nor are the significant fragments concerning the work of Hermagoras of Temnos (fl. *c.* 150 BC) dealt with. These fragments almost all pertain to the section of his rhetorical work dealing with εὕρεσις and expound his detailed systematic analysis of the kinds of controversies (commonly called στάσεις, though Hermagoras uses the term in a more restricted way).[141]

Within a typical treatise the division of a speech into its parts would also be discussed. This division (such as outlined below) was often made the organising principle within the section of the treatise on εὕρεσις. In such an arrangment, each part of the speech would be discussed in turn with respect to the discovery of arguments appropriate to it. The precise number of parts belonging to a speech was a controversial subject, but a fairly typical division is summed up in Cic. *de Orat.* 2.80 as follows:

> *exordium* (προοίμιον) - to win goodwill and make the listener receptive and attentive
> *narratio* (διήγησις) - a statement of the case
> *propositio* (πρόθεσις) and *divisio* - proposition and heads
> *confirmatio* (πίστεις) - proofs
> *refutatio* (ἔλεγχος) - refutation of the opponent

---

ments, whilst τάξις probably refers to the *partes orationis*.
[140]   For an extensive discussion on alternate views of στάσις classification see Quint. *Inst.* 3.4.29-62. Even the classifications in the *Rhetorica ad Herennium* and Cicero's *de Inventione* vary considerably, although they probably represent modified versions of the same ultimate source. For discussion on the organisation of the proof section of the treatises see the discussion on rhetorical method below (§ 5).
[141]   Fragments ed. D. Matthes (*Hermagoras Fragmenta* [BSGRT; Leipzig; B. G. Teubner, 1962]), discussed by M. Fuhrmann, 1964a, "Review."

[possibly a *digressio* (παράβασις) for the sake of embellishment and elaboration]
peroratio (ἐπίλογος) - [summing up, final swaying of the emotions or plea for mercy]

Unfortunately no general *Greek* Hellenistic rhetorical treatises are extant. We rely, therefore, on a number of Latin treatises which are essentially adaptations from Greek works and several Greek treatises on more specialised subjects.

3.1 Cicero, *de Inventione*, and the *Rhetorica ad Herennium*

Editions: The standard edition of Cicero's *de Inventione* is still that of E. Ströbel, *Rhetorici libri duo* (BSGRT; Leipzig: B. G. Teubner, 1915; repr. 1991). The text is slightly modified in the Loeb edition of H. M. Hubbell *Cicero* (vol. 2; LCL; London: Heinemann, 1949).
The standard edition of the *Rhetorica ad Herennium* is still that of F. Marx, *Rhetorica ad Herennium* (BSGRT; Leipzig: B. G. Teubner, 1923; 2nd ed., corrected *cum addendis* by W. Trillitzsch, 1964; repr. 1993). This text is slightly modified in the Loeb edition of H. Caplan *Cicero* (vol. 1; LCL; London: Heinemann, 1954). Caplan supplies helpful notes.[142] A more recent edition with (Italian) commentary by G. Calboli is *Cornifici Rhetorica ad C. Herennium* (2nd ed.; Bologna: Pàtron, 1993).

Cicero's *de Inventione* and the *Rhetorica ad Herennium* are the two earliest extant rhetorical treatises preserving Hellenistic rhetorical theory. That there is a distinct relationship between these two works and that they both ultimately go back to a Greek tradition is not doubted. The *precise* relationship between them has, however, been a matter of some debate. It is now generally accepted that the *de Inventione* of Cicero predates the *Rhetorica ad Herennium*, but that the latter is not directly dependent upon the former despite the close (often verbal) relationship. It seems most probable that they have some Latin (as opposed to Greek) source in common. This would explain the *verbal* identity between the two in several places and the not infrequent use of the same *Roman* examples. D. Matthes argues for a Latin source common to the respective teachers of Cicero and the anonymous author of *Rhet.Her.*.[143] This Latin source appears to have been in essence a translation of a Greek work probably originating at Rhodes (given the various Rhodian examples present in our two works).[144] The source was clearly influenced by, but also at times critical of, Hermagoras. Matthes concludes that Cicero gives a more faithful picture of this Latin source than the *Rhet.Her.* (a con-

---

[142] Caplan's suggestion of Greek equivalents for the Latin terminology, however, is not always demonstrable from extant sources. For a list of reviews see G. Calboli's edition, p.442.
[143] 1958, "Hermagoras," 96. See his whole discussion on this point, pp.81-100. For an alternative reconstruction of the sources see G. A. Kennedy, 1972, *Art*, 126-38.
[144] That one simple Latin source common to both treatises cannot explain the diversification was already recognised by F. Marx (*Proleg.*) and reiterated by H. Caplan (1954, *Cicero*, xxviii).

troversial point), although he also appropriately notes that it is not really feasible to attempt a reconstruction.

Marcus Tullius Cicero (106 - 43 BC), who went on to become Rome's greatest orator, received as a youth a thorough education in rhetoric. It was at this youthful period in his life, by his own confession, that he wrote the *de Inventione* (properly, *Rhetorici libri duo*). The work can be dated sometime between 91 and 88 BC.[145] Cicero himself later characterised the treatise as youthful and lacking practical experience. We learn that it basically consists of his school notes written up for publication (cf. *de Orat.* 1.5; Quint. *Inst.* 3.6.59). Although the original plan was for a work structured upon the five ἔργα τοῦ ῥήτορος (tasks of the orator, see below on *Rhet.Her.*), only the section on εὕρεσις (invention) was completed (hence the popular title *de Inventione*). Cicero's emphasis is clearly upon judicial rhetoric. In fact deliberative and epideictic rhetoric receive only a few short (and insignificant) sections at the end of book two. Book one, after a short introduction, takes up εὕρεσις in general terms. After a general discussion of στάσεις, the rest of the book deals with general argumentation ordered according to the divisions of a speech (cf. *Rhet.Her.*). Book two analyses argumentation in more detail, this time ordered according to the various στάσεις and their subdivisions.

A valuable analysis of Cicero's earliest speech, the *pro Quinctio*, in relation to the *de Inventione* is to be found in G. A. Kennedy, 1972, *Art*, 138-48. Kennedy shows something of the limitations of the rhetorical theory, and where it is and is not most applicable.[146] Despite some helpful comments in book one regarding general argumentation, the strong judicial emphasis of this work and its alignment to στάσις doctrine do not render it particularly suitable for application to the writings of the apostle Paul.

The *Rhetorica ad Herennium* (probably to be dated between 86-82 BC)[147] is the first extant rhetorical work organised according to the five ἔργα τοῦ ῥήτορος (εὕρεσις, τάξις, ὑπόκρισις, μνήμη, λέξις). However, what goes by the name of τάξις in Aristotle (namely, the division of the speech) is here the organising principle within the

---

[145] Cf. G. A. Kennedy, 1972, *Art*, 106-110.
[146] See also the studies of F. Rohde (*Cicero, quae de inventione praeceperit, quatenus secutus sit in orationibus generis iudicialis* [Diss.; Königsberg, 1903]) and R. Preiswerk (*De inventione orationum Ciceronianarum* [Basel, 1905]).
[147] D. Matthes, 1958, "Hermagoras," 82n.

section on εὕρεσις. For *Rhet.Her.*, τάξις concerns the proper order of argumentation. The discussion on εὕρεσις devotes by far most attention to the judicial genre of rhetoric (*Rhet.Her.* maintains the typical threefold division of rhetorical genres). Of this discussion most space is devoted to the analysis of the στάσεις. There is also an interesting discussion on argumentative method (i.e., ἐπιχείρημα).[148] The sections on delivery and memory are naturally of little interest for someone wishing to analyse written documents.

The last and longest of the four books is devoted to the section on λέξις (style). It begins with a short description of the three kinds of style (*gravis, mediocris* and *adtenuata,* i.e., grand, middle, and plain)[149] and their faulty counterparts. The rest of the book is structurally organised under three ἀρεταί of speech, a modification of the four ἀρεταί of Theophrastus. Of these "virtues," the last (*dignitas*) receives by far the most space. It is in fact a lengthy listing of the various figures of speech (including tropes). Each figure is briefly described and illustrated with examples. There is often a helpful comment on the effect(s) of any given figure, though little is said in relation to argumentative method.[150] This last section is the first extant theoretical discussion of figures of speech. Treatises περὶ σχημάτων (*On Figures*) and περὶ τρόπων (*On Tropes*) abound in the later literature, and there is evidence that it was a popular form even in Hellenistic times.

3.2 P. Rutilius Lupus, *Schemata Dianoeas et Lexeos*

Edition: G. Barabino, *P. Rutilii Lupi Schemata Dianoeas et Lexeos* (Genova: Istituto di Filologia Classica e Medioevale, 1967). This edition contains an Italian translation and an extensive introduction amounting to a commentary on the work. Barabino discusses both the figures and the exemplary citations.[151]

---

[148] W. Kroll (1940, "Rhetorik," 1101) speaks of the "arg verballhornte Lehre vom Epicheirema" in this treatise. The discussion in this treatise is not representative of discussions of the ἐπιχείρημα which largely replaced that of Aristotle's ἐνθύμημα in later rhetorical theory.

[149] This is incidentally the first extant mention of this threefold division which became a commonplace in rhetorical theory.

[150] In terms of the stylistic and argumentative analysis of ancient documents we need to be careful not to fall into the trap common to so many of the ancient theorists in thinking that it is sufficient to identify and label various figures. It is the *effect* of such figures, both stylistically and argumentatively, that is important. It is unfortunate that no extant treatise deals with this aspect in any great detail. We are left to glean suggestive comments here and there. In this respect we may be thankful that the *Rhet.Her.* does offer some suggestions in this regard.

[151] The edition by E. Brooks Jr. (*P. Rutilii Lupi de Figuris Sententiarum et Elocutionis* [Leiden: Brill, 1970]) can, unfortunately, not be recommended. See the review by M. E. Welsh (1972, "Review").

This treatise, according to the title in the mss, is a Latin translation of Gorgias the Younger's περὶ σχημάτων (*On Figures*). This is confirmed by Quintilian's statement that Rutilius (a contemporary of Gorgias) incorporated the four books of Gorgias' work into one of his own (*Inst.* 9.2.102). Quintilian's knowledge and use of Rutilius' translation is evident from *Inst.* 9.2.101-106 (see also the references in the *index nominum* of Winterbottom's OCT ed. of Quint. *Inst.*). Rutilius refers to Gorgias' work at 2.12 for a more detailed treatment of a particular point.

Of Gorgias himself we know little. In 44 BC he was a tutor (in Greek rhetoric) of Cicero's son at Athens, but upon Cicero's instructions was dismissed for leading his son into a dissolute lifestyle (Plu. *Cic.* 24; Cic. *Fam.* 16.21.6).

The treatise as we have it is unfortunately not complete.[152] It is extant in two books which present the various figures in no particular order. Each figure is briefly defined and examples are given from the Greek orators (mostly, but not exclusively, Attic). Little or nothing is said concerning the function or value of the various figures, which effectively limits the value of the work (for our purposes) to determining contemporary terminology.

3.3 Theon, *Progymnasmata*

Edition: L. Spengel (ed.), *Rhetores Graeci* (3 vols; Leipzig: B. G. Teubner, 1853-6) ii, pp.59-130. More recent is the work of James R. Butts, *The Progymnasmata of Theon. A New Text with Translation and Commentary* (Diss.; Claremont Graduate School, 1987) to which I unfortunately did not have access.[153]

From the Suda we learn of the rhetor Aelius Theon from Alexandria who wrote a number of rhetorical works including a περὶ προγυμνασμάτων.[154] His dates are difficult to determine, but he must have lived either in the first or in the second century AD.[155] If he is to be identified with Theon the Stoic mentioned by Quintilian (*Inst.*

---

[152] There is also disagreement among scholars as to whether the text which we do have is an epitome of the original work or not, cf. E. Brooks, 1970, *Rutilii*, xiv.

[153] An in-depth study of the transmission of the text has been provided by I. Lana, *I Progimnasmi de Elio Teone: Vol. 1, La Storia del Testo* (Torino: Università di Torino, 1959). A fourth to fifth century AD papyrus fragment has been published by M. Groenewald, 1977, "Fragment." The papyrus shows no major deviations from Spengel's text.

[154] The entry reads: Θέων, Ἀλεξανδρεύς, σοφιστής, ὃς ἐχρημάτισεν Αἴλιος, ἔγραψε Τέχνην, Περὶ προγυμασμάτων, Ὑπόμνημα εἰς Ξενοφῶντα, εἰς τὸν Ἰσοκράτην, εἰς Δημοσθένην, Ῥητορικὰς ὑποθέσεις· καὶ Ζητήματα περὶ συντάξεως λόγου, καὶ ἄλλα πλείονα.

[155] For a summary of older views on the dating of this treatise, see W. Stegemann, 1934b, "Theon," 2037-38.

9.3.76; cf. 3.6.48), then he must be placed within the first century.[156] This would also seem to fit with Theon's comments against Asianism (*Prog.* ii, p.71 Sp.), if they are taken to be relevant to his own time. Asianism as a stylistic trend was radically opposed by the so-called Atticists, who strove for a simple, economical style modelled after the great Attic masters. Atticism arose in Roman circles during the first century BC (D.H. *Orat. Vett.* 2-3) and continued to exist until at least the end of the first century AD, although there does not appear to have been much left of it (cf. Quint. *Inst.* 12.10.14-15).[157]

The προγυμνάσματα were rhetorical exercises set at the beginning of one's rhetorical training, graded according to difficulty.[158] Although our first extant treatise on these exercises (i.e., Theon) dates from the first century AD at the earliest, we know from references in Roman authors that such exercises must have been a regular part of the Greek rhetorical curriculum by the beginning of the first century BC. Cic. *Inv.* 1.27 and *Rhet.Her.* 1.12-13 deal with the *narratio* as a rhetorical exercise, subdivided into the *fabula*, *historia* and *argumentum*. Further, in Cic. *Inv.* 1.76 exercises on ἐπιχειρήματα (rhetorical syllogisms) are mentioned, cf. Cic. *de Orat.* 1.154 which mentions both paraphrasing of poets and translation from Greek to Latin. In addition both Quintilian and Suetonius provide us with lists of exercises (προγυμνάσματα) (to be) used by the grammarian and rhetorician respectively. The lists are as follows:[159]

Grammar:		Rhetoric:	
Quint. (*Inst.* 1.9)	**Suet.** (*Gram.* 4)	**Quint.** (*Inst.* 2.4)	**Suet.** (*Rhet.* 1)
paraphrasis of	*problemata* (θέσεις?)	*narratio*	*dicta* (χρεῖαι)
Aesop's fables	*paraphrasis*	- *fabula*	*apologi* (fables)
sententiae	*allocutiones* (ἠθο-	- *argumentum*	*narrationes*
chriae	ποιΐα)	- *historia*	*Graecorum scripta*
aetiologiae	*aetiologiae*	- ἀνα-/κατασκευή	*convertere*
narratiunculae	*(atque alia)*	*laudare/ vituperare*	θέσεις (*pro* and
a poetis		*comparatio*	*contra*)
		communes loci	*laudare/ vituperare*
		theses	ἀνα-/κατασκευαί of
		legum laus ac	*fabulae*
		vituperatio	

---

[156] The words *Theon Stoicus* at Quint. *Inst.* 9.3.76 (text: Winterbottom) are a generally accepted conjecture first suggested by Halm (in the form *Theo Stoicus*). The text tradition (A) reads *cheostolcus*. Certain expressions from Stoic philosophy have been detected in Theon's work, cf. W. von Christ, 1920-4, *Geschichte*, 2.1 p.461.

[157] Cf. J. M. Crossett/ J. A. Arieti, 1975, *Dating*, 41-42, and the excursus below, pp.66-67.

[158] For a good introductory discussion of the προγυμνάσματα and how they functioned in the education system, see S. F. Bonner, 1977, *Education*, 250-76.

[159] The following should be noted regarding the listed προγυμνάσματα:

Re: Quint. *Inst.* 1.9, *paraphrasis* of Aesop's fables: F. H. Colson (1924, *Fabii*, 116-17) separates the paraphrasing of poetry as a distinct exercise. See also the comments of S. F. Bonner, 1977, *Education*, 255-56. Others view this as an elaboration of (a poetical version of) Aesop's fables.

Re: Suet. *Gram.* 4, *problemata*: These *problemata* may be simple forms of θέσεις. Compare the θέσις-like character of the subjects called προβλήματα in Plutarch's *Quaestiones Convivales* (specifically called a [rhetorical] θέσις at 2.741d). Note also the comment of Alexander Aphrodisiensis (early third century AD) *in Top.* p.82,19-23 W. τοὺς γοῦν εἰς προβλήματα λέγοντας εἰς θέσιν λέγειν φασίν. ἤδη δέ

The lists of both authors are quite obviously not comprehensive. Elsewhere Quintilian mentions several other items used as school exercises: προσωποποιΐα (*Inst.* 3.8.49); ἤθη (*Inst.* 6.2.17)¹⁶⁰; θέσεις, *destructio et confirmatio sententiarum* and *loci communes* (*Inst.* 10.5.11-12). Neither do the lists agree in all particulars. The placement of both χρεΐαι and θέσεις varies.¹⁶¹ Suetonius' reported placement of προβλήματα (if they are a form of θέσεις) and ἠθοποιΐα in the hands of the grammarians seems strange. Both exercises are rather advanced. Among the Greeks the προγυμνάσματα appear to have remained a standard part of *rhetorical* education, but it is clear from Quintilian and Suetonius that by the first century AD it was not uncommon in Roman education for some or even all of these exercises to be handled by the grammarians (the preceding phase of a boy's education).¹⁶² Quintilian bemoans this fact at the beginning of book two of his *Institutio* and then comes with his recommendation as listed above. It is interesting to note that Suetonius (*Gram.* 4), writing at the beginning of the second century AD, states that, due to the sloth and inarticulateness of certain teachers, the use of προγυμνάσματα by grammarians and rhetoricians had mostly been given up in his time.¹⁶³ Nevertheless, the προγυμνάσματα remained a popular educational tool in antiquity.¹⁶⁴

When the students had completed their course in προγυμνάσματα, they proceeded to declamations (Theon *Prog.* ii, p.59,8-10, 13-5 Sp.; Quint. *Inst.* 2.10.1). Declamation was thus the goal to which the προγυμνάσματα were designed to lead. As a rhetorical exercise, declamations were traced all the way back to Demetrius of Phalerum (cf. Quint. *Inst.* 2.3.41-42) or even Aeschines (Philostr. *VS* 481), and became very popular (cf. Quint. *Inst.* 10.5.14-23).¹⁶⁵

τινες θέσεις καὶ τὰ ῥητορικὰ καλοῦσι προβλήματα, ἐφ᾽ ὧν τὸ τῆς ὑποθέσεως ὄνομα συνηθέστερον τῷ δοκεῖν τὰ τοιαῦτα ἐπὶ ὑποκειμένοις τισὶ καὶ ὡρισμένοις συνίστασθαι· κοινότερα γὰρ τὰ διαλεκτικὰ καὶ καθολικώτερα. However, given that the exercise falls under the domain of the grammarian, the term may have a more general meaning.
Re: Suet. *Rhet.* 1: The translation of J. C. Rolfe (1914, *Suetonius*) is quite plainly incorrect at this point. I have followed R. A. Kaster's text (1995, *Suetonius*). This edition is also provided with a better translation.
¹⁶⁰ The term seems to be used in the sense of abstract ἠθοποιΐαι (characterisation of kinds of people, e.g., the miser), see my forthcoming *Glossary, s.v.* ἠθοποιΐα II.
¹⁶¹ It is interesting to note that the order χρεΐα, μῦθος, διήγημα evidenced in Suet. *Rhet.* 1 is identical to the original order (see below) of the first three προγυμνάσματα of Theon. This is the more striking because of the fact that all the later treatises on προγυμνάσματα present the order: μῦθος, διήγημα, χρεΐα. R. F. Hock/ E. N. O'Neil's claim (1986, *Chreia*, 66) that Theon's ordering of these three exercises may have been an innovation fails to account for the evidence of Suetonius (not noted by them).
¹⁶² Note that M. L. Clarke (1951, "Thesis," 164-65) has reasonably argued that Suet. *Rhet.* 1.5 only means to say that the προγυμνάσματα have disappeared from the rhetorical schools (and thus been transferred to the grammatical schools), cf. R. A. Kaster (1995, *Suetonius*, 280).
¹⁶³ Compare Theon (*Prog.* ii, p.59,8-10 Sp.) who complains of students rushing off to declamations before having been exercised in the προγυμνάσματα.
Concerning Suet. *Gram.* 4, R. A. Kaster (1995, *Suetonius*, 103) has cogently argued that the words: *quae quidem omitti iam video desidia quorundam et infantia* refer to teachers and not to pupils (*contra* J. C. Rolfe's translation [1914, *Suetonius*]). Suetonius' comment refers to Roman schools, and for all we know Theon may have been a Greek tutor to Romans.
¹⁶⁴ Witness the number of works extant from late antiquity on this subject: [Hermog.] *Prog.*; Aphth. *Prog.*; Lib. *Progymnasmata* (in vol. 8, ed. Förster); Nicol. *Prog.*; Priscianus, *Praeexercitamina ex Hermogene Versa*; Emporius, *de Ethopoeia; de Loco Communi*. For further works, consult the first two volumes of C. Walz, *Rhetores Graeci* (9 vols; Stuttgart: J. G. Cottae, 1832-6).
¹⁶⁵ Plb 12.25a.5 compares the way Timaeus composed speeches for his *History* to the method used in school (ἐν διατριβῇ) for attempting to argue for some policy (ὑπόθεσις). Whilst the term ὑπόθεσις is probably not used in the technical sense of a declamation here, one may well see an allusion to the composition of speeches in schools. The idea that declamations only became common in Roman rhetorical education after Cicero, and that they replaced earlier exercises in θέσεις (based on Sen. *Con.* 1, *pr.* 12; Quint. *Inst.* 2.1.9; and Suet. *Rhet.* 1.5) is quite properly refuted by M. L. Clarke, 1951 "Thesis," cf.

Apart from these scattered references, Theon's work is the first extant treatise on προγυμνάσματα. That the tradition of such works goes back much earlier is stated by Theon himself (*Prog.* ii, p.59,15-16, 18 Sp.).[166]

Theon's treatise is clearly intended as a handbook for teachers (cf. *Prog.* ii, pp.70-72 Sp.). His are the only extant treatise on προγυμνάσματα to contain an extended introduction in which he sets out his views on the literary education of youth.

The treatise as we have it, however, is not quite in its original form. The order of the sections has evidently been disturbed.[167] There is a significant *lacuna* at the end where the section on νόμος is broken off and several further sections seem to be missing (ἀνάγνωσις[168], ἀκρόασις, παράφρασις, ἐξεργασία, ἀντίρρησις). Extant are the general introduction and the sections on μῦθος, διήγημα, χρεία[169], τόπος (a discussion of methods of αὔξησις),[170] ἐγκώμιον καὶ ψόγος[171], σύγκρισις, προσωποποιΐα, ἔκφρασις, θέσις and νόμος.[172]

Such exercises formed practice in the building blocks of speeches generally (of whatever genre) and such material (e.g., instances of χρεῖαι, προσωποποιΐαι, or extended comparisons - συγκρίσεις) can, not infrequently, be found built into the speeches and other forms of literature of the time. In this respect a knowledge of the προγυμνάσματα may be helpful in terms of the analysis of literary letters.

Quint. *Inst.* 2.4.42 re: Plotius and Crassus.

[166] [Arist.] *Rh.Al.* 28.2 mentions προγυμνάσματα but this is suspect, cf. critical apparatus (ed. Fuhrmann) and M. Fuhrmann, 1964b, *Untersuchungen*, 162. Philostr. *VS* 481 attributes the beginning of κοινοὶ τόποι to Aeschines.

[167] This is clear from the list of examples from the ancients which Theon provides for his exercises (*Prog.* 2). The order of the examples here differs from that of the exercises themselves. For example, in the catalogue of examples from the ancients the χρεία is dealt with first. Yet the first exercise described is the μῦθος, although this description presupposes that the description of the χρεία (the third exercise in the current arrangement) has already been read (cf. *Prog.* ii, p.74,8-9 Sp.). It is commonly supposed that the rearrangement of the sections was to bring the treatise in line with the order of (Ps.) Hermogenes' *Progymnasmata* (written sometime between the second and fourth century AD, cf. H. Rabe, 1913, "Praefatio," iv-vi). For a probable reconstruction of the original order, cf. W. Stegemann, 1934b, "Theon," 2042.

[168] For this exercise see O. Schissel, "Synesios von Kyrene ergänzt den Ailios Theon," *Berliner Philologische Wochenschrift* 52 (1932) 1117-20.

[169] A critical text and translation with notes (taken from the preliminary work of Butts, see above) for this exercise is printed (not without typographical errors) in R. F. Hock/ E. N. O'Neil, 1986, *Chreia*, 82-112.

[170] This contrasts with the two kinds of *loci* discussed by Quintilian under the προγυμνάσματα. Quint. *Inst.* 2.4.22-23 concerns the *loci* of virtues and vices, whereas *Inst.* 2.4.27 concerns *loci* pro and contra the ἄτεχνοι proofs which are discussed under θέσεις.

[171] That exercises in ἐγκώμια and ψόγοι were common and considered generally helpful is due to the fact that short ἐγκώμιοι were often used within a deliberative or forensic speech (cf. D.H. *Isoc.* 17). For examples of such exercises see Lib. *Enc.*.

[172] For definition and brief discussion of these terms see my forthcoming *Glossary*.

3.4 Dionysius of Halicarnassus

Editions: The standard edition of Dionysius' rhetorical writings is H. Usener, L. Radermacher (ed.), *Opuscula* (2 vols; BSGRT; Leipzig: B. G. Teubner, 1899-1929; repr. 1985). Editions with commentary are provided by W. Rhys Roberts, *Dionysius of Halicarnassus, The Three Literary Letters* (London, 1901); *Dionysius of Halicarnassus, On Literary Composition* (London, 1910). These works are also available in the Loeb series, S. Usher (transl.) *The Critical Essays* (2 vols; LCL; London: Heinemann, 1974/85). A good overview and analysis of these works is provided by S. F. Bonner, *The Literary Treatises of Dionysius of Halicarnassus: A Study in the Development of Critical Method* (Cambridge: University Press, 1939).

Dionysius of Halicarnassus was a rhetor and historian who lived and worked at Rome from *c.* 30 BC. He was author of a number of rhetorical works of which the most important for our purposes are those on the ancient orators, and the *de Compositione Verborum*. The *Ars Rhetorica* going under his name is, however, falsely ascribed and probably to be dated to the beginning of the third century AD.

We learn from the preface to his works on the orators (*de Oratoribus Veteribus*) that Dionysius was a convinced Atticist and as such strongly opposed the Asianist style which he argues took over after the death of Alexander the Great. Asianism is vaguely described in the sources as a rather overdone flamboyant sing-song style known particularly for its emphasis on certain prose rhythms. Dionysius refers to Atticism as something that had come about in his own times and now held the upper hand. This turn of events is attributed to the world domination of Rome.

That Atticism as a movement began in Rome during the first century BC becomes clear from Cicero's works (cf. *Opt. Gen.*; *Brut.* 284-91; *Orat.* 23-32, 75ff). Its roots *may*, perhaps, be attributed to Greek tutors favouring a return to a more Attic style.[173] In Cicero's works we learn of a brand of Atticism which appears to have arisen in Rome during Cicero's later life, a brand of Atticism which extolled the plainness of Lysias' language as its ideal.[174] We also learn that Cicero himself was criticised for exhibiting Asian qualities (cf. Quint. *Inst.* 12.10.12 where he is specifically said to have been called "Asian"). Against this Cicero wrote in favour of the "*Atticism*" of Demosthenes. In *Brut.* 325 he also distinguished two forms (*genera*) of Asianism common in his day, namely, that which is *sententiosum et argutum, sententiis non tam gravibus et severis quam concinnis et venustis*; and that which is *non tam sententiis frequentatum quam verbis volucre atque*

---

[173] Cf. T. Gelzer, 1978, "Klassizismus," 18-19; G. W. Bowersock, 1978, "Problems," 63. See, however, J. Wisse, 1995, "Greeks," 74-81 who provides several important considerations for viewing Atticism as a "movement" (the term is used in a loose sense) begun by Calvus in Rome which eventually influenced Greek rhetoricians.

[174] I do not go into the modern controversy here as to the size, background and history of this Roman "Atticism." See J. Wisse, 1995, "Greeks," 67-69; G. W. Bowersock, 1978 "Problems"; A. E. Douglas, 1973, "Background" 119-31, and for a summary of scholarship on this issue in the first half of this century: S. F. Bonner, 1954, "Oratory," 363-68.

incitatum, and has an *admirabilis orationis cursus* (rush/ running of admirable speech). He notes that both kinds were more suitable for youth than the dignity appropriate to older men. This rather positive analysis of Asianism should be balanced by his harsh criticism of the style of Hegesias of Magnesia *et al* (*Brut.* 287; *Orat.* 230-31). Hegesias is often singled out in the sources as the foremost (negative) example of Asianism.

Asianists are generally negatively portrayed in the sources and often associated with a profligate lifestyle. A good example is Plutarch's description of Antony (*Ant.* 2.5). Quintilian also speaks of the difference between the Atticist and Asianic schools, but he introduces the controversy as a past phenomenon and no longer current (*Inst.* 12.10.16-26). Following Cicero he favours a broad Atticism, despising those dry Atticists who stick rigidly to the ultra plain style of Lysias (*Inst.* 12.10.14-15). He thus adopts the Ciceronian vision of a broadly defined Atticism including the famous Greek orators of fourth century BC. Asianism is criticised for its bombast, and a kind of middle form in the Rhodian orators is also noted.[175] Of interest is Quintilian's citation of Santra (a contemporary of Cicero) who apparently argued that Asianists overused periphrasis. U. von Wilamowitz has, however, argued that the increased use of periphrasis was common to κοινή Greek as a whole.[176] As Wilamowitz (41) rightly stated, Atticism's enemy really ended up being, not Asianism, but normal everyday Hellenistic language.

Dionysius' works on the various ancient orators must be seen in the light of his emphasis on the importance of μίμησις, i.e., imitation of the great Attic orators. This was the central thrust of his rhetorical teaching method. Those treatises that survive (*de Lysia, de Isocrate, de Isaeo, de Demosthene*) occasionally provide us with insights into the application of certain forms of rhetorical argumentation. The *de Demosthene* is important for the fact that Dionysius sets out his stylistic theory there.

In terms of style Dionysius developed two threefold analytical schemes, both of which are presented in his work on Demosthenes. In terms of language (λέξις), and particularly word-choice, he held on to the common division into the plain, grand, and mixed styles.[177] This division is summarised in *Dem.* 33 (p.203,8-10 U.-R.): διελόμενος μὲν τὴν λέξιν εἰς τρεῖς χαρακτῆρας τοὺς γενικωτάτους τόν τε ἰσχνὸν καὶ τὸν ὑψηλὸν καὶ τὸν μεταξὺ τούτων. The plain style is described in terms of bare and simple language which seems to have the elaboration and vigour of everyday speech (ἡ λέξις ἡ λιτὴ καὶ ἀφελὴς καὶ δοκοῦσα κατασκευήν τε καὶ ἰσχὺν τὴν πρὸς ἰδιώτην ἔχειν λόγον καὶ ὁμοιότητα, *Dem.* 2, p.130,6-8 U.-R.). Its prime representative is Lysias. The grand style is further described as lofty, extravagant and varied language (ὑψηλὴ καὶ περιττὴ καὶ ἐξηλλαγμένη λέξις, *Dem.* 34, p.204,6-7 U.-R.). Thucydides is the main representative here. The middle style is described as a combination of the other two (ἡ μικτή τε καὶ σύνθετος ἐκ τούτων τῶν δυεῖν, *Dem.* 3, p.132,3-4 U.-R.). It is

---

175 But contrast the remark on Rhodian orators in D.H. *Din.* 8 (p.308,5-10 U.-R.).
176 1900, *Asianismus*, 4.
177 Already noted in *Rhet.Her.* 4.11-16, cf. also p.46.

represented by Plato and Isocrates, though the representative *par excellence* is Demosthenes.[178]

At § 36, however, Dionysius turns to a new question concerning Demosthenes' style. He asks: τίς δὲ ὁ τῆς ἁρμονίας αὐτοῦ χαρακτήρ? By ἁρμονία Dionysius is clearly thinking of the musical quality in terms of the linear progression of the text.[179] His analysis centres around a discussion of the juxtaposition of harsh or smooth combinations of letters and syllables, and of rhythms and metres. For this discussion Dionysius uses a different threefold analytical scheme. Whereas the division into plain, grand and middle styles centred on the question of language (λέξις)[180], in terms of ἁρμονία Dionysius speaks of the rough, smooth and mixed style. The discussion of these harmonic styles in the treatise on Demosthenes is similarly presented in his treatise on composition (§§ 21-24).

The rough style (*Dem.* 38-39; *Comp.* 22, represented by, e.g., Pindar, Aeschylus, Thucydides) is characterised as αὐστηρά (rough), ἀκόμψευτος (unrefined) and φιλάρχαιος (old-fashioned), having the qualities σεμνότης (solemnity), βάρος (gravity) and τόνος (intensity). It uses ordinary language often with clashing sounds (letters) and simple uneven periods without the more flashy figures or fullness of particles. Its figures are described as τὰ ἀρχαιοπρεπέστερα σχήματα (old-fashioned) and as οἱ γενναῖοι καὶ ἀξιωματικοὶ σχηματισμοί (noble and dignified). Its rhythms are described as ὑψηλοί (lofty), ἀνδρώδεις (masculine) and μεγαλοπρεπεῖς (grand). At *Dem.* 47 its τέλος is said to be τὸ καλόν.

The smooth style (*Dem.* 40; *Comp.* 23, represented by e.g., Hesiod, Sappho, Euripides, Isocrates) is described as γλαφυρά (smooth/ polished) and θεατρική (showy), preferring τὸ κομψόν (refinement) to τὸ σεμνόν (solemnity). It strives to be smooth (avoiding hiatus), uses many particles, carefully balanced periods, rhythmic clausulae and the more showy, poetical figures, e.g., ἀντίθεσις, παρομοίωσις, παρίσωσις, παρονομασία, ἀντιστροφή, ἐπαναφορά (i.e., those suited to epideictic rhetoric, *Comp.* 23).[181] Its rhythms are not ἀξιωματικοί (dignified) but χαριέστατοι (most graceful), and its τέλος is τὸ ἡδύ (*Dem.* 47).

The mixed style (*Dem.* 41-42; *Comp.* 24, represented by, e.g., Homer, Sophocles, Herodotus, Demosthenes and Plato) is termed εὔκρατος (well-blended) and

---

178   Compare Ps.-Plu. *Vit.Hom.* 72 who categorises Thucydides, Lysias and Demosthenes in precisely the same way.
179   Musical harmony in the ancient world was always thought of in terms of linear progression. Music was always monophonic.
180   But the word λέξις can easily have a wider meaning in Dionysius, cf. *Amm.* 2, 2 (p.425,8 U.-R.) where it appears to include all aspects of style.
181   On these figures, see my forthcoming *Glossary*.

said to be the best kind of style. It is thus a mixture of the best qualities of the other two.

In introducing his discussion of the harmonic styles at *Dem.* 37, Dionysius makes an important concession with respect to his analytical treatment. He admits that no one style is to be found in any one given author in pure form. There is always some mixture. This reminds one of the comments of Demetrius prefacing his fourfold analysis of style (Demetr. *Eloc.* 36).

Connected to the question of harmonic styles is another important aspect of Dionysius' work which surfaces in his treatise *de Compositione Verborum*. At the beginning of this work, Dionysius explains how he classifies the study of literature. He divides it into two main classes, περὶ νοήματα and περὶ ὀνόματα, of which the latter is further divided into περὶ τῆς ἐκλογῆς τῶν ὀνομάτων and περὶ τῆς συνθέσεως ὀνομάτων. We see here once again the three elements which formed the basis for Demetrius' discussion of ἑρμηνεία, namely, subject matter (διάνοια or πράγματα), word choice (λέξις), and composition (σύνθεσις). Dionysius' treatment of composition differs from that of Demetrius however. Dionysius is mostly concerned with σύνθεσις in terms of ἁρμονία.[182] In this respect he provides us with a very interesting discussion on the qualities of the various letters and how they can be combined to provide smoother or rougher combinations. This is an important building block for his later classification of various harmonic styles. Prose rhythm also forms an important part of this process - a subject that is unfortunately still problematic for modern scholarship.[183] Dionysius' harmonic theory, whilst highly interesting, did not, however, catch on.[184] Nevertheless, a cursory knowledge of the literary concerns which his theory attempted to address may function as a backdrop to our analysis of Paul's style. Demonstration of the contrast between such highly developed literary concerns and Paul's style helps us to place Paul in an appropriate context.

One final aspect of Dionysius' literary theory deserves comment, namely, his analysis of the virtues (ἀρεταί) of style (to be found in *Pomp.* 3.16-20). Dionysius shows an idiomatic approach to this subject as well. Whilst prior discussion often seems to have been based upon the four ἀρεταί probably going back to Theophrastus

---

[182] Note that at *Dem.* 37 the harmonic styles are called τρεῖς συνθέσεως σπουδαίας χαρακτῆρες.

[183] On Dionysius' seemingly arbitrary analysis of prose rhythm, see S. F. Bonner, *Treatises*, 73-74.

[184] Quintilian shows some knowledge of Dionysius' works (*Inst.* 3.1.16; 9.3.89; 9.4.88), but does not appear to use them in any meaningful way. The one exception may be Dionyius' περὶ μιμήσεως. A relationship between this work and book 10 of the *Institutio* has long been recognised, although the exact nature of the relationship is disputed (do they have, for example, a common source or did Quintilian rely on Dionysius?), cf. S. F. Bonner, 1939, *Treatises*, 39.

(ἑλληνισμός, σαφές, πρέπον and κατασκευή), sometimes slightly modified, Dionysius developed a new system of multiple virtues. He distinguishes between necessary and supplementary virtues (αἱ ἀναγκαῖαι and αἱ ἐπίθετοι ἀρεταί, cf. *Th.* 22, p.358,19-22 U.-R.). There are three necessary virtues, ἡ καθαρὰ διάλεκτος, σαφήνεια, and συντομία. The supplementary virtues are manifold, but it should be noted that they include both πρέπον and what Dionysius calls αἱ τῆς κατασκευῆς ἀρεταί (i.e., those producing τὸ μέγα καὶ θαυμαστόν).

In none of his extant works does Dionysius provide us with an analytical discussion of rhetorical argumentation, nor does he ever discuss the matter of rhetorical figures in any detail, although according to Quint. *Inst.* 9.3.89 Dionysius did write a book on this subject.[185] In these respects the works of Dionysius are not so helpful for our investigation.

3.5 Ps.-Longinus, *de Sublimitate*

Editions: The standard edition is that of D. A. Russell, *Longinus* (OCT; Oxford: Clarendon, 1968); translation *On Sublimity*, 1965. The edition of O. Jahn (*Dionysii vel Longini de Sublimitate Libellus* [4th ed. rev. by J. Vahlen; SWC; Leipzig: B. G. Teubner, 1910; repr. Stuttgart, 1967]) contains a running commentary of helpful citations from ancient authors. Textual commentaries (among others) have been published by W. Rhys Roberts (*Longinus on the Sublime*, [2nd ed.; Cambridge, England, 1907]); J. P. Hoogland (*Longinus "over Het Verhevene": Vertaling met Inleiding en Opmerkingen* [Groningen: M. de Waal, 1936]) and D. A. Russell (*Longinus on the Sublime* [Oxford: Clarendon, 1964]). A commentary on §§ 33-36 may be found in U. von Wilamowitz-Moellendorff, *Griechisches Lesebuch* (vol. 2 "Erläuterungen" pp.237-41; Berlin: Weidmann, 1902). The commentary of J. A. Arieti and J. M. Crossett (*Longinus on the Sublime* [Texts and Studies in Religion 21; New York: Edwin Mellen, 1985]) is designed for non-Greek readers and more concerned with modern literary application. Their translation is the most literal available and generally very good, though suffering occasionally from idiosyncratic terminology.[186] A new Loeb edition is also now available, revised by D. A. Russell, in *Aristotle* (LCL; vol. 23; London: Heinemann, 1995).

This little treatise of which about two thirds has come down to us has been popular in critical literary circles since the end of the seventeenth century. The author sets out in his work to provide a set of notes (ὑπομνήματα, 1.2) on ὕψος, sublimity. The *raison d'être* is the dissatisfaction felt upon reading the tract περὶ ὕψους of Caecilius. It is addressed to the author's friend Terentianus (otherwise unknown) with whom he had originally read Caecilius' work.

The authorship of the work is unfortunately unknown. Certain medieval mss suggest Dionysius (*sc.* of Halicarnassus) or Longinus (*sc.* Cassius), but modern scholarship

---

185   See H. Usener/ L. Radermacher, *Dionysius*, 2.252.
186   For example, the insistence on "development" as a translation for αὔξησις.

is virtually unanimous that neither of these suppositions can be correct.[187] Scholarly consensus has settled upon a date somewhere in the first century AD.[188]

The mss handed down to us are all based upon one 10th century ms (Parisinus 2036) which is itself, unfortunately, of poor textual quality and contains a number of significant lacunae (about a third of treatise is missing). Attempts at scholarly emendations abound and it is imperative that the reader have an edition with a good textual apparatus (if not textual commentary).[189]

The work is cast in the common form which M. L. Stirewalt termed the Greek letter-essay,[190] but Ps.-Longinus typifies it himself as ὑπομνήματα (1.2) or "notes." After an introduction (1-2) and a brief description of various styles to be avoided (3-6) he proceeds to outline the main subject of his work at § 8 where he states that he will discuss five sources of ὑψηγορία (τὸ περὶ τὰς νοήσεις ἀδρεπήβολον, τὸ σφοδρὸν καὶ ἐνθουσιαστικὸν πάθος, ἡ ποιὰ τῶν σχημάτων πλάσις, ἡ γενναία φράσις, ἡ ἐν ἀξιώματι καὶ διάρσει σύνθεσις).[191] His discussion is often insightful, particularly with regard to the effects of various figures, yet unhelpfully subjective.

---

[187] G. M. A. Grube, *On Great Writing* (The Library of Liberal Arts Press: Bobbs-Merrill, 1957), has argued for the authorship of Cassius Longinus, but his thesis has not gained general acceptance.

[188] J. M. Crossett and J. A. Arieti (1975, *Dating*) argue for a probable date around the middle of the century under Nero. They place especial weight on situating § 44 (on reasons for the decline in sublime oratory) in its most likely historical context, a consideration also deemed important by D. A. Russell (1964, *Longinus*, xxv; 1995, "Longinus," 146-47).

[189] For an overview of some of the extensive literature see, *Bibliography of the "Essay on the Sublime"* (ΠΕΡΙ ΥΨΟΥΣ) compiled by D. St. Marin (privately printed: Netherlands, 1967).

[190] See 1991, "Form." Stirewalt gives several examples from the first century BC and AD, analysing each. J. A. Arieti/ J. M. Crossett's structural analysis of the work as a speech, divided into exordium, narrative, proof, and peroration is rather forced to say the least (1985, *Longinus*, xi-xv).

[191] Despite this clear outline, the structure of the treatise can be confusing to readers, and is controversial. Due to the second lacuna of six folia it is not entirely clear where (or even if) Ps.-Longinus begins discussion of the second source. D. A. Russell (1964, *Longinus*, xii-xiv), primarily on the basis of § 44.12 has suggested that Longinus did not include a separate discussion of the second source. He has even suggested that the treatise as a whole has somewhat of a hidden agenda outside of these five sources (see discussion in 1981, "Longinus"). Recently, J. A. Arieti/ J. M. Crossett (1985, *Longinus*) have argued that the second source begins at § 10 and that this is indicated by ἕτερος which they explain as "the other of two" indicating the other of the first two sections which concern natural talent as opposed to skill that can be learned. Several considerations tell against this analysis, however, and in favour of positing the beginning of the discussion on the second source in the lacuna: 1) Ps.-Longinus says: εἴ τι καὶ ἕτερον ἔχοιμεν ὑψηλοὺς ποιεῖν τοὺς λόγους δυνάμενον, ἐπισκεψώμεθα ("Let us examine if we might also have some other means able to make writings sublime"). Arieti ignores the effect of the τι καί both in his reasoning and in his translation. The statement more suitably introduces the beginning of a new *sub*section. 2) The point of the row of examples from 9.4 through 9.15 would seem to fit quite well with τὸ σφοδρὸν καὶ ἐνθουσιαστικὸν πάθος (the title given at § 8 to the second source). In 9.11 Homer is described as experiencing madness as he writes of the Trojan war, at 9.13 ἐν ἀκμῇ πνεύματος. Ps.-Longinus then goes on to note that the composition of the Odyssey by contrast is more narrative-like, yet concludes that it may be said of Homer that δίχα τῆς σφοδρότητος παραμένει τὸ μέγεθος (9.13). 3) In addition it should perhaps be noted that ἕτερος, especially in later Greek, may quite simply substitute for δεύτερος, not necessarily implying one or the other of *two* things. This is certainly the sense at the opening of 4.1.

Ps.-Longinus couples the term ὕψος with τὸ μέγεθος, a connection also known from D.H. *Lys.* 13. This causes one to think of the grand style, known from the common classification of literary style into three groups (grand, mixed, simple), although his discussion sometimes transcends purely stylistic considerations. His own various definitions of ὕψος within this treatise remain rather vague and lofty. This could characterise his work as a whole, and although the treatise may remain stimulating reading, this fact makes it less useful as a source for pinpointing concrete argumentative or stylistic rules and traits in rhetoric.[192] The author correctly realised that style cannot be reduced to a set of rules, and, further, gave attention to the psychological reactions to literature in the audience.[193] His own literary style is rather verbose if not bombastic, although quite varied. He deliberately seeks variety of expression and carefully crafted composition. At many places he is clearly attempting by his own style to emulate the stylistic effects he is describing. This does not make the tract easier to read and in fact points to a departure from the accepted stylistic norm in technical treatises. Most Greek treatises are deliberately written in simple, clear language, without attempts at carefully crafted periods.

Despite the fact that this tract has had considerable influence in modern Western literary thought, it is *never* cited in the extant ancient literature until John of Sicily (*c.* eleventh century AD).

4 Roman Rhetorical Theory

As may be deduced from the Latin adaptations of Greek rhetorical works already handled above, Roman rhetorical theory leaned heavily upon the Greeks. Greek teachers of rhetoric flourished in Rome and Roman teachers of rhetoric really only began to arise by the first century BC. Even then they were generally considered second rate. Wealthy Romans would normally employ Greek tutors for the education of their sons, including rhetorical tutors for more advanced training. Good students would often go on to complete higher education in Athens itself, or perhaps Rhodes or Asia Minor. But in this matter of dependency upon earlier (Greek) treatises, Roman rhetoric did not really differ from contemporary Greek rhetoric which also relied heavily on earlier works.

---

[192] This does not mean that no concrete advice is given at all, cf. especially the third section on figures (§§ 16-29).
[193] Certainly a contributing factor to his popularity among moderns.

Roman rhetorical theory is, therefore, often no more than an adaptation of Greek rhetorical theory. Differences tend to emerge only in terms of the different Roman situation. Romans were generally not interested in rules for epideictic oratory (cf. Quint. *Inst.* 2.1.2). In fact Roman rhetorical theory maintained the Greek trend of laying great stress upon judicial rhetoric.[194]

Roman adaptations in terms of judicial rhetoric naturally had to do with the different way Roman law courts functioned. One of the most obvious factors was that in the Roman situation, orators were generally advocates leading a defence or prosecution *on behalf* of a client. In the Greek system one was expected to make one's own defence or prosecution, though even then the parties involved often employed orators to write their speeches for them.[195]

Under the emperors, Roman rhetoric changed somewhat. The great political trials of the late republic were a thing of the past, though judicial rhetoric remained important. A tradition of fictitious declaiming became very popular not only among students but among rhetors in general. Certain rhetorical teachers even seem to have gone so far as to have only taught via *declamationes*, abandoning the dry theory, cf. Quint. *Inst.* 2.10.2; 2.11.[196]

One final influential factor in the development of Roman rhetorical tradition was the importance and standing given to the orator Cicero. His speeches became models and even his rhetorical writings were to become standard works for later Roman rhetorical tradition.[197] Later theory, however, tended to prefer the *de Inventione* to the more difficult *de Oratore*. Perhaps even Quintilian did not always rightly understand the latter work.

The treatises to be discussed in this section are those Latin works which cannot be said to be *direct* adaptations of Greek treatises, namely, certain later works of Cicero and Quintilian's *Institutio*. The reader should be warned, however, that these works *cannot* be said to be typical of Roman rhetorical theory. In the *de Oratore* and *Orator* Cicero developed his rhetorical theory in ways quite different from the school rhetoric

---

194 Greek rhetors teaching in Rome also evidenced this trend. Quintilian, for example, reports that Apollodorus (*c.* 104-22 BC) restricted himself to judicial oratory (*Inst.* 3.1.1, = *Fr.* 1b Gran.).
195 On this whole matter see G. A. Kennedy, 1968, "Rhetoric of Advocacy." Kennedy traces the differences between the situation in ancient Greece and Rome, discussing how this affected contemporary speeches. In addition he notes how the rhetoric of advocacy is accounted for in Cicero's *de Oratore* and Quintilian's *Institutio*.
196 The popularity of *declamationes* under the empire (in both the Greek and Roman situation) meant that rhetorical theory also began to address itself to this (cf. Quint. *Inst.* 2.10; 10.5.14-23).
197 For Cicero's prevailing influence among Romans after his death, see M. Winterbottom, 1982b, "Cicero."

of the time. These works, in turn, influenced Quintilian to some extent. But the sheer scope of Quintilian's mammoth-sized treatise puts it outside regular school rhetoric to begin with. Unfortunately, no other Latin rhetorical treatises are extant from this period.

4.1 Cicero, *de Oratore* and *Orator*

Editions: *De Oratore*: The standard text edition is that of K. F. Kumaniecki (*Ciceronis de Oratore* [BSGRT; Leipzig: B. G. Teubner, 1969; repr. 1995]). Note that the Loeb text (trans. by E. W. Sutton and H. Rackham, *Cicero* [vols 3 & 4; LCL; London: Heinemann, 1942]) is based on the antiquated Latin edition of Bétolaud (1845). The translation unfortunately leaves much to be desired.[198] Commentaries are available by K. W. Piderit (German), *Cicero, de Oratore* (3 vols; 6th ed. rev. by O. Harnecker; Leipzig: B. G. Teubner, 1886-90; repr. Amsterdam: A. M. Hakkert, 1965); by A. S. Wilkins (English), *De Oratore Libri III* (Cambridge, 1892; repr. Amsterdam: A. M. Hakkert, 1962). A good new commentary by Dutch scholars (in progress, written in German) is *M. Tullius Cicero, De Oratore Libri III: Kommentar* by A. D. Leeman, H. Pinkster, H. L. W. Nelson, E. Rabbie and J. Wisse (4 vols to date; Heidelberg: Carl Winter, 1981-96).[199] *Orator*: The standard edition is that of R. Westman (*M. Tullius Cicero: Orator* [BSGRT; Leipzig: B. G. Teubner, 1980]). Commentaries by J. E. Sandys (English), *Orator* (rev. text with introductory essays and critical and explanatory notes; Cambridge, 1885; repr. Hildesheim: Olms, 1973); and W. Kroll (German), *M. Tullii Ciceronis Orator* (Berlin: Weidmann, 1913; repr. 1961).

Those rhetorical works of Cicero which appear to be adaptations of Greek treatises have been discussed above, i.e., the youthful *de Inventione* and the more mature *Partitiones* and *Topica*. Cicero's other mature rhetorical works are reviewed here. By the time these mature works were written Cicero had become somewhat embarrassed by his youthful work, no longer desiring to present a technical treatise compounded with lengthy lists of rules. In this sense, as A. E. Douglas has correctly noted, none of the three late rhetorical works of Cicero is a rhetorical treatise in the traditional sense.[200]

---

[198]   The Loeb edition is discussed by B. L. Ullman, 1943, "Review." The translation appears to be based on a more current text, cf. 3.202 where the older reading (*huic contraria saepe*) *praecisio* is printed, but the translation (without explanation) follows the more modern reading *percursio*. The translation itself is not always accurate.

[199]   The first three volumes are discussed by M. Winterbottom, 1983, 1986 and 1991, "Review."

[200]   1973, "Background," 122. Only the *de Oratore* and the *Orator* are dealt with here. The *de Optimo Genere Oratorum*, written in 46 BC, is a short introduction to a proposed translation of speeches by Demosthenes and Aeschines (not extant and probably never completed). The *Brutus*, also written in 46 BC, is a work giving a brief historical review of Roman orators from the beginning of Roman oratory down to the time of Cicero. There is little of importance in either of these works for our investigation, although they are both of interest for the development of Atticism in Rome.

For our purposes it is the *de Oratore* and the *Orator* which are important. The *de Oratore* is a dialogue in three books written in 55 BC (cf. *Att.* 4.13.2; *Fam.* 1.9.23).[201] According to the latter reference it was written *Aristotelio more*. This phrase has generally been interpreted as a reference to the method of Aristotle's dialogues. His dialogues are believed to have differed from Plato's by allowing the interlocuters to expound developed dogma instead of seeking for the truth by question and answer.[202] In any case, this difference from Platonic dialogue is apparent in those of Cicero. But this is not the only Aristotelian feature of this treatise, which seeks to present a synthesis of rhetoric and philosophy, two disciplines which, as we have seen, had been at loggerheads since early in the second century. It was especially by taking up what he considered Aristotelian principles that Cicero sought both to distance himself from the typical school rhetoric of his day, and provide a truly practical philosophical approach.[203] Several other Aristotelian features not generally traceable to typical Hellenistic theory thus appear.

Firstly, there is the division of the means of persuasion into rational argument, self-recommendation (character portrayal), and the arousal of the emotions.[204] School rhetoric had generally relegated considerations of character portrayal and arousal of the emotions to the προοίμιον and ἐπίλογος (respectively) of a speech. But although Cicero once again took up Aristotle's threefold division of the means of persuasion, his definition of persuasion by character portrayal and persuasion by arousal of emotions is slightly different. Following the trend of school rhetoric, he defined persuasion by character portrayal in terms of the effecting of those *mild* emotions which produce *benevolentia* (goodwill or sympathy) in the audience with respect to either the character of the orator or his client (reflecting the Roman practice of advocacy). Persuasion by arousal of emotions refers to the effecting of the *violent* emotions. Note, however, that Cicero studiously avoids the use of technical terms in this treatise, and never even specifically uses the terms ἦθος or πάθος or any *technical* Latin equivalent.

Secondly, in his discussion of *loci* for rational argumentation (*de Orat.* 2.130-77) Cicero provided a list of *loci* which reflect the κοινοὶ τόποι of Aristotle, i.e., set *patterns* of argumentation (2.163-73), instead of the specific *loci* of school rhetoric.

---

201 For an interesting discussion of the dating see A. D. Leeman *et al.*, 1981-96, *Tullius*, 1.17-21.
202 Cf. R. Y. Tyrrell and C. C. Purser, 1885-1901, *Correspondence*, 2.179, and D. R. Shackleton Bailey, 1977, *Cicero*, 1.315. An alternative explanation has been offered by A. D. Leeman *et al* (1981-96, *Tullius*, 1.67-69) to the effect that *Aristotelio more* should be interpreted here as referring to "die aristotelische Unterrichtsmethode," that is, the exercise of *in utramque partem disputare* (debating both sides of the argument).
203 There are also other differences from school rhetoric, e.g., the incorporation of a discussion on wit (*de Orat.* 2.216ff).
204 For an expanded discussion of this point see J. Wisse, 1989, *Ethos*.

Thirdly, we may also note that Cicero chose to discuss the parts of a speech under the heading *dispositio* (τάξις) where Aristotle had discussed them (*de Orat.* 2.315-32), instead of using the parts of a speech as an organising principle for the section on *inventio*. But Cicero also discusses the order of arguments here (which was the regular treatment of *dispositio* in Hellenistic rhetorical theory, *de Orat.* 2.307-314).[205]

Apart from these specifically Aristotelian features, the treatise also differs from typical Hellenistic rhetoric in its fundamental concern that the true orator be a man of vast learning and experience. Cicero's emphasis is somewhat reminiscent of the old ideal of Isocrates. The thrust of this work is to get away from the hackneyed rules of school rhetoric and to see the orator as an experienced wise man, knowledgeable in many areas, who can speak well. In fact, Cicero attributed the greatest influence on his formation as an orator to the Academy (*Orat.* 12). Greek rhetorical theory is at times roundly ridiculed for its overdose of rules and classifications formulated by men who have no real experience in the law courts, although the rules themselves are not considered to be totally without value (cf. 1.145-46; 2.74-84).

The thrust of this work being as it is, the kind of detailed discussion on argumentation and style which would be helpful for our purposes is quite lacking: this despite the fact that ultimately all the five duties of the orator (*officia oratoris*) discussed in a typical Hellenistic treatise are dealt with. In his discussion of *loci* (κοινοὶ τόποι) the speaker, Antonius, is quite brief and does not go beyond the kind of skeletal definitions with examples we have seen elsewhere (2.130ff). Relation of the arguments to their function and place within any given speech is neglected deliberately as something which even a mediocre mind may judge for itself (2.175; cf. 3.119).

Figures of thought and speech are dealt with at the end of book three (3.200-208), but we unfortunately only find a *list* of figures with little or no comment. The dry definitions provided in typical Hellenistic treatises were precisely the kind of thing Cicero wanted to avoid in this treatise. Comparison with the equally meagre list of figures in *Orat.* 135-39 shows that these lists were probably based upon the same (presumably Greek) treatise. With few exceptions the order of figures is identical in both works, although the *Orator* (139) provides a more select list and adds a separate short-list not present in *de Oratore* (already noted by Quint. *Inst.* 9.1.36). A careful analysis of these may show us the kind of figures generally recognised in Greek treatises of his day, but they do not much further our knowledge of their definition or application.[206]

---

[205] A more detailed analysis of similarities and differences between Arist. *Rhet.* and Cic. *de Orat.* is provided by J. Wisse, 1989, *Ethos*, 105-45.
[206] For Cicero's treatment of θέσεις in book three, see pp.49-50 above.

The *Orator* was written in 46 BC, some years after the *de Oratore*, as a letter-essay in reply to Brutus who desired to learn from Cicero which *genus eloquentiae* he most approved (3). Cicero replied with a tract on the ideal orator, centering his discussion on style, although not neglecting to speak on other duties of the orator as well. Cicero's disapproval of the rigorous form of Atticism (which was opposed to his own rhetorical style) is evident, and the treatise is a defence of his own views. Much attention is paid to the difficult problem of prose rhythm.

Of particular interest is Cicero's discussion of style. At § 69 he appears to connect the three Aristotelian modes of proof (rational argumentation, self-recommendation, arousal of emotions), with three types of style (plain, middle, grand). Yet the terms *probare*, *delectare*, *flectere* (to prove, to charm, to influence) are here defined not as modes of proof for persuading which come under *invention*, but as the tasks of the orator (*officia oratoris*) in connection with *style*.[207] *Probare* should be done in the plain style, *delectare* in the middle style, and *flectere* in the vigorous style. Although it may be that Cicero does not really intend to associate the three modes of proof with the three styles here,[208] Quintilian certainly made this connection later on (Quint. *Inst.* 12.10.59-61, 69-70).[209]

Cicero goes on to make a connection between the three kinds of style and three kinds of subject matter (*Orat.* 100-101). Here the plain style is connected with lowly subject matter, the grand style with lofty subject matter, and the middle style with moderate subject matter. At *Orat.* 102 he gives examples of how he has composed several of his speeches in one or other of the three styles, but in the ensuing sections his concern is to advocate a varied use of style, even within the confines of one speech. Demosthenes in particular is extolled for his ability to use and alternate the various styles in an appropriate way.

---

[207] These three tasks also appear in *Brut.* 185, 187-88, 198, 276, 279, 322.

[208] For objections to this identification see, J. Wisse, 1989, *Ethos*, 212-20.

[209] In this respect it is also interesting to note what D.H. *Dem.* 4 (p.135,12-18 U.-R.) states. In a discussion of the middle style of Isocrates, Dionysius notes that Isocrates takes elements from the plain style of Lysias and the grand style of Thucydides and Gorgias. He then adds a description as to how Isocrates uses these elements: καὶ εἰς μὲν τὸ διδάξαι τὸν ἀκροατὴν σαφέστατα, ὅ τι βούλοιτο, τὴν ἁπλῆν καὶ ἀκόσμητον ἑρμηνείαν ἐπιτηδεύει τὴν Λυσίου, εἰς δὲ τὸ καταπλήξασθαι τῷ κάλλει τῶν ὀνομάτων σεμνότητά τε καὶ μεγαληγορίαν περιθεῖναι τοῖς πράγμασι τὴν ἐπίθετον καὶ κατεσκευασμένην φράσιν τῶν περὶ Γοργίαν ἐκμέμακται. ("And in order to teach the hearer most plainly whatever he wishes, he uses the plain and unadorned style of Lysias, but in order to astound him by the beauty of the words and to bestow solemnity and grandiloquence upon the matter he has moulded the artificial and elaborate speech of the followers of Gorgias.")

In general, we must conclude that, in spite of Cicero's achievements in these treatises, for our purposes they are of less value than his earlier work. Some knowledge of their idiosyncracies is, however, necessary in order to use Quintilian's *Institutio* with discernment. As we shall see, when reading the *Institutio* we need to be able to determine when Quintilian is following Cicero instead of traditional Hellenistic rhetorical theory.

4.2 Quintilian, *Institutio Oratoria*

Editions: The standard edition is by M. Winterbottom (*Quintilian: Institutio Oratoria* [2 vols; OCT; Oxford: University Press, 1970]). A companion textual commentary is M. Winterbottom, *Problems in Quintilian* (University of London Institute of Classical Studies; Bulletin Supplement 25, 1970). A translation (based on the text of Halm, 1868) is provided by H. E. Butler, *Quintilian: Institutio Oratoria* (4 vols; LCL; London: Heinemann, 1920-22).
Commentaries: F. H. Colson, *M. Fabii Quintiliani Institutionis Oratoriae Liber I* (Cambridge: University Press, 1924); J. Adamietz, *M. F. Quintiliani Institutionis Oratoriae Liber III: Mit einem Kommentar* (München: Wilhelm Funk, 1966); W. Peterson, *Quintilianus, Institutionis Oratoriae Liber X* (Oxford: Clarendon Press, 1891; reprint Hildesheim: Olms, 1967); H. S. Frieze on books 10 and 12 (2nd ed.; New York, 1888);[210] R. G. Austin, *Institutionis Oratoriae Liber XII* (3rd ed.; Oxford: Clarendon Press, 1965).

Quintilian, born in Spain in the late 30's of the first century AD, received a rhetorical education at Rome, having chosen the orator Domitius Afer as his mentor. At some point he returned to Spain, but came back to Rome with the new emperor Galba in AD 68 at about which time he began a highly successful teaching career in rhetoric. After twenty years dedicated to this profession he retired and was persuaded to begin work on a rhetorical treatise.

Quintilian's massive work on the education of the orator, *Institutio Oratoria*, represents the zenith of Roman rhetorical theory. Quintilian sought to discuss how the orator ought to be educated in a most comprehensive way, from the cradle to maturity. His *Institutio* was published in 12 books towards the end of AD 94 or early 95.[211] Book one takes the reader through the preliminary education of the budding orator, whilst book two discusses the choice of a rhetorical tutor, preliminary rhetorical exercises, and the elements and essence of rhetoric. Both these books contain brief but helpful comments on various preliminary exercises known as προγυμνάσματα.[212] Books three to eleven take the reader through the well-known five-fold division of a rhetorical

---

[210]   I have not seen this work.

[211]   G. A. Kennedy, 1972, *Art*, 493.

[212]   On the προγυμνάσματα and their usefulness see § 3.3 above.

treatise: *inventio* (bks 3-6); *dispositio* (bk. 7); *elocutio* (bks 8-11.1); *memoria* (bk. 11.2); and *pronuntiatio* (bk. 11.3). The final book (12) deals with a discussion of the perfect orator, relying heavily on the concept as presented in Cicero's *de Oratore* and *Orator*.

Quintilian wrote this work whilst in retirement, taking out two years for research and writing (*the introductory letter to Trypho*, 1). The work is thus based both on this research in various Greek and Latin treatises as well as on the material he had used in his teaching career as professor of rhetoric in Rome. What helps to make the work interesting (as well as bulky) is Quintilian's frequent citation of the views of his predecessors, often with critical comment. In addition, whilst the treatise covers all the normal departments of rhetoric (and more), Quintilian constantly attempts to give a practical bent to his advice. The work is thus not the dry highly technical treatise so common in his age. This is, however, not to say that there is no technical discussion. The familiar emphasis on forensic oratory pervades the treatise, as does the typical emphasis on στάσις doctrine. Epideictic and deliberative rhetoric are briefly dismissed in two chapters (3.7 and 3.8). The rest of the treatment of *inventio* is devoted to judicial rhetoric (3.10 - 6.5), essentially organised under the various parts of a speech. Here, of special interest to us, is his discussion of proofs in book five. They are divided into the common categories of ἄτεχνοι (5.2-7) and ἔντεχνοι (5.8-12). Under the section *refutatio* Quintilian discusses the use of the ἐνθύμημα and ἐπιχείρημα (5.13-14), that is, rhetorical syllogistic reasoning.

The arrangement of the section on *inventio* reflects Quintilian's special partiality towards Cicero, in particular his later works. Quintilian, however, did not wish to abandon the regular methods of rhetorical theory to quite the extent which Cicero did. What we have, therefore, is an attempt to combine traditional rhetorical theory with the (philosophically influenced) ideas of Cicero's *de Oratore*. The result is an organisational mélange. Quintilian's basic organising principle for *inventio* is the parts of a speech. Like Cicero's *de Inventione* (book one), his plan does not incorporate a discussion of στάσεις and their relevant *loci*. Instead, the various proofs are discussed and the typical rhetorical *loci* are listed. But Quintilian adds to these *loci* of school rhetoric, a list of *loci communes* in the philosophical sense (argumentative patterns), a list clearly dependent upon Cicero's later work. Quintilian is left with the problem of where to place a discussion of the στάσεις and their *loci*. Unlike Cic. *Inv.*, he does not place them in a separate chapter under *inventio*, but curiously inserts them into the section on *dispositio*, after the regular discussion on the order of arguments.

Under the influence of the *de Oratore* is also the extended treatment given to self-recommendation and arousal of emotions (where the terms ἦθος and πάθος come up for discussion), although the content of this treatment differs.[213] Quintilian's placement of these two concepts under the ἐπίλογος is due to the influence of traditional rhetorical theory. The Aristotelian idea, taken up by Cicero, of three means of persuasion (rational, self-recommendation and arousal of emotion) is abandoned.[214] As in Cicero's *de Oratore*, Quintilian appends a discussion on jesting to his treatment of self-recommendation and arousal of emotions.

The books concerning *elocutio* are organised around the four virtues *Latinitas* (8.1), *perspicuitas* (8.2), *ornatus* (8.3 - 9.4), and *dicere apte* (11.1), which probably go back to Theophrastus, although Quintilian himself is following Cicero here. *Ornatus* receives by far the most extended treatment, with a lengthy discussion of tropes and figures. Book ten, occurring between the discussion of the third and fourth virtues of style, discusses the *facilitas* of the orator. This *facilitas* is developed by imitating the great writers of the past (chapter 10.1 is famous for its review of Greek and Latin literature) and by well organised writing practice, thought, and the ability to improvise.

Another way in which Quintilian's organisation reflects that of Cicero's *de Oratore* is in the placement of the discussion of *amplificatio* (*Inst.* 8.4).[215] Both *Rhet.Her.* and (with different terminology) Cic. *Inv.* discuss *amplificatio* as a method belonging to the ἐπίλογος. Here it concerns the stirring up of the audience. Cicero in the *de Oratore*, however, introduces a discussion of *amplificatio* in book three under *elocutio* (3.104-108), and it is precisely in this context that Quintilian addresses *amplificatio*. Cicero's placement of *amplificatio* here has to do with a complex digression and should not be interpreted to mean that he viewed *amplificatio* as a stylistic phenomenon. Quintilian, however, deals here with amplification by means of style (*Inst.* 8.3.90). He does note that there is also amplification in terms of matters (*res*) and states that he has already covered this (*Inst.* 8.3.89-90). It is true that Quintilian

---

[213] Quintilian appears to go one step further than Cicero in terms of definition by defining πάθος and ἦθος as violent and mild emotions respectively, without any further delimitation (*Inst.* 6.2.9). He adds that some authorities (unnamed) further define ἦθος as continual and πάθος as temporary (*Inst.* 6.2.10). Quintilian also mentions the common definition of ἦθη as *mores*, and at times seems to combine this with his definition of ἦθη as mild emotions (cf. *Inst.* 6.2.8-9, 17-18).

[214] Quintilian knew of Aristotle's *Rhetoric*, but does not appear to have used it systematically. Quint. *Inst.* 2.17.14 mentions both the *Gryllus* and the *Rhetoric* in three books, noting information from *Rh.* 1.1. Quint. *Inst.* 4.2.32 appears to refer to *Rh.* 3.16.4, and Quintilian (or his source) clearly refers to the third book at 3.8.8-9, although in a confused way. He refers comments Aristotle makes about epideictic speeches to demonstrative rhetoric. However, he does not appear to have used this treatise in his treatment of ἦθος and πάθος in 6.2. These terms are there defined quite differently, although at 6.2.25 he intimates that he has discussed *everything* contained in the treatises he has read.

[215] The content of Quintilian's discussion, however, is unrelated to any extant treatise prior to his work.

has discussed the stirring up of the audience under the ἐπίλογος when he deals with appeals to the emotions (*Inst.* 6.1.14-18). However, amplification is nowhere separately dealt with there or elsewhere.

The final book on the perfect orator sums up Quintilian's vision of rhetoric as speaking well (cf. *Inst.* 2.15) and the perfect orator as being a virtuous man with a well-rounded education (*Inst.* 12.1-4).[216] It is also within this final book that Quintilian comes to a discussion of *kinds* of style (*Inst.* 12.10). He mentions two forms of a threefold division of style (*Inst.* 12.10.58-59). Both included the plain style (ἰσχνόν - suited for teaching) and the grand style (ἁδρόν - suited for moving). He then adds that some teach a middle style (for conciliating), whilst others teach a flowery style (ἀνθηρόν - for charming). These comments are interesting in that they show that the threefold division of style into plain, grand, and middle was perhaps not so widely accepted as scholarship sometimes likes to think.[217] Quintilian (*Inst.* 12.10.59, 70) connects the use of these three styles with the concepts of proving (plain style), conciliating (middle style), and stirring emotions (forceful style). But like Demetr. *Eloc.* 36-37, Quintilian realised that in practice there are many mixed or intermediate forms of style (*Inst.* 12.10.66-68).

In general, Quintilian's work shows a deep respect for and not infrequent reliance upon Cicero. Equally important, however, (particularly for the sections on *elocutio*, style and rhetorical syllogisms) is his clear reliance upon Greek rhetorical theory. Quintilian remains, therefore, an important source in these areas for our consideration of the application of ancient rhetorical theory to Greek writings of the first century AD. The reader of the *Institutio* must, however, exercise discernment in order to distinguish philosophically influenced discussions (usually taken from Cicero) from those parts which more properly rely upon Hellenistic rhetorical theory.

5 Overview and Rhetorical Method

Our review of rhetorical theorists over a period of some 500 years leads us, perhaps, to consider how much we are missing more than what is still extant. We have seen that some rhetorical theorists are not as relevant for our purposes as others. We

---

[216] For the background to this emphasis see M. Winterbottom, 1964, "Quintilian."

[217] It is interesting to compare the theory of style in Ps.Plu. *Vit.Hom.* 73-74 (second century AD). The first half of this work is dedicated to an analysis of the language of Homer using rhetorical categories. At § 73 Ps.-Plutarch speaks of three χαρακτῆρες, the ἁδρόν, ἰσχνόν and μέσον represented by Thucydides, Lysias and Demosthenes respectively. However, at § 74 he goes on to speak of τὸ ἀνθηρὸν εἶδος.

began our survey with the treatises of Anaximenes and Aristotle. Due to ease of access, and also probably to the fact that it is the only major complete rhetorical treatise extant in Greek, many New Testament scholars have made use of Aristotle in attempting to apply rhetorical theory to the New Testament. The analysis of Aristotle's work, therefore, received considerable attention in section 1.2, as did the question as to how much this treatise was actually read in later times. This was necessary in order to show just how much Aristotle's approach *differs* from later Hellenistic rhetorical theory. His treatise was not generally read in later times, perhaps partially because of its scarcity and inherent difficulty, but no doubt also because it was quite out of date (for the reasons we have outlined above).

Typical Hellenistic rhetorical theory is best represented in two treatises, the *Rhetorica ad Herennium* and Cicero's *de Inventione*, although the latter is not complete (treating only *inventio*) and concentrates on judicial rhetoric. Despite the fact that there are obvious connections to earlier rhetorical treatises, Hellenistic rhetorical theory was structured and approached quite differently. Cicero's later rhetorical treatises are not really representative of the typical school rhetoric of his times. In this respect, the mammoth work of Quintilian can be of more help. Despite its unusual size, its coverage of a whole educational life, and its special devotion to Cicero, it is structured along more traditional lines. In addition, Quintilian provides a wealth of information on the views of earlier (mostly Hellenistic) rhetorical theorists. With regard to matters of style we are better provided for by a number of additional Hellenistic treatises devoted to this subject, though once again several of them are not really typical of the period (e.g., Ps.-Longinus' approach, or Dionysius' theory of harmony).

At this point some comment on the matter of rhetorical genres is warranted, particularly given the use made of them by recent Pauline scholarship. The classification and definition of rhetorical genres among the theorists is not as uniform as is sometimes thought. Although Aristotle's threefold classification (deliberative, judicial and epideictic) seems to have dominated rhetorical theory, there is evidence of alternative classifications.[218] Even this popular threefold classification is not free of problems. The

---

[218] Roughly contemporary with Aristotle is the treatise of Anaximenes which still seems to have been circulating in the first century AD. Anaximenes appears to have distinguished only two genres (cf. Pl., *R.* 365d referring to πειθοῦς διδάσκαλοι σοφίαν δημηγορικήν τε καὶ δικανικὴν διδόντες, and *Phdr.* 261d-e), organising them into seven species (Quint. *Inst.* 3.4.9, see discussion above and M. Fuhrmann, *Untersuchungen*, 154-56). After Aristotle, his pupil Demetrius of Phalerum argued for four genres: δημηγορικόν, δικανικόν, σοφιστικόν (= epideictic) and ἐντευκτικόν (petitionary genre), *Fr.* 157 (Wehrli). Max.Tyr. 31.6 also speaks of four genres: ἐν ἐκκλησίαις, ἐν δικαστηρίοις, ἐν πανηγύρεσιν, ἐν παιδείᾳ, as does Ruf.Rh. 2 (p.399 Sp.-H.) adding ἱστορικόν to the three generally accepted genres. For general comment on the classification of genres see Quint. *Inst.* 3.4.

three genres lent themselves to various methods of definition. Aristotle chose to define them according to the task of the audience (to deliberate about the future, judge the past, or be a spectator). Alternatively they could be defined by the occasion (in court, in a political assembly, at a festival). One could even, at least partially, attempt to distinguish them in terms of style. Hence Dionysius of Halicarnassus terms Isocrates' speeches fit only for the epideictic genre or private study (*Isoc.* 2; *Dem.* 4), although he admits that Isocrates composed many as deliberative or forensic (*Isoc.* 3). The three ways of defining the genres are more or less reflected in the variant terminology for the epideictic genre: ἐγκωμιαστικόν (of praising), πανηγυρικόν (a festival speech), ἐπιδεικτικόν (demonstrative - i.e., a rhetorical display). The variation in definition gave certain problems in terms of genre classification. For example, it was popular among some in classical Athens to present deliberative speeches (i.e., speeches offering advice on the political situation) at the festivals (cf. Lys. 33 and D.H. *Lys.* 29). The scope of the epideictic genre also varied. It could be defined narrowly, inclusive only of orations in the form of ἐγκώμια or ψόγοι (i.e., encomia or their opposite). Alternatively, it could be used as a catch-all to include whatever did not fit into the other two genres, whether in terms of oratory, or even in terms of history and poetry (cf. Cic. *Orat.* 37; *de Orat.* 2.43-64; Hermog. *Id.* 2.10, p.389,7-9 R.).

The question before us is the possible usefulness of classification according to rhetorical genres.[219] It is pretty pointless to say that such and such an oration is deliberative or epideictic and leave it at that. Such classification must be coupled with an investigation of the argumentative techniques specific to each genre. It is here that the threefold genre classification has its value. Rhetorical theory provided a distinct methodology for dealing with the respective genres. Ultimately, it all came down to certain kinds of τόποι (*loci*) which were specific to the various genres. In the treatises these τόποι are generally discussed in connection with the proof section of the speech (in a sense, the heart of the matter).

---

[219] It should be remembered that the genre classification of rhetorical theory was not the only kind of classification available. Cic. *de Orat.* 2.104 gives a fivefold classification of *causae* (judicial is divided in two, and the philosophical *disputatio* is added). In addition, philosophical theory generally adopted its own forms of genre classification, cf. for example, Sen. *Ep.* 95.65-66 (genres accepted by Posidonius); Philo of Larissa, *Fr.* 2 Mette (= Stob. 2.7.2); Arr. *Epict.* 3.23.33-38. Prose was sometimes classified in a threefold way (cf. Cic. *Orat.* 180; Ps.-Plu. *Vit.Hom.* 74-174): *genus narrandi* (ὁ ἱστορικὸς λόγος), *genus persuadendi* (ὁ πολιτικὸς λόγος - includes both forensic and deliberative), and *genus docendi* (ὁ θεωρητικὸς λόγος = philosophy). The genre classification of epistolary theory will be dealt with below (chapter three, § 2).

How then did the ancient orators approach writing the proof section of a speech? We shall begin with a consideration of judicial rhetoric, since it is here that the treatises generally devote systematic discussion to argumentation.

Going by the varied structure of our extant treatises, there appear to have been certain methodological problems. A major structural problem seems to have been caused by the advent of the importance of στάσις theory (systematised and popularised by Hermagoras in the second century BC).[220] If we may take Anaximenes as somewhat representative of pre-Aristotelian rhetorical theory, then we may suggest that school rhetoric before this time generally listed relevant τόποι in the form of both subject areas for concern and set arguments. Thereupon various *forms* of argumentation were discussed (e.g., παραδείγματα, ἐνθυμήματα, σημεῖα etc.).[221] The procedure presupposed by this structure is quite clear. The orator, having scanned the various τόποι for useful material for his speech, would then work this material out according to the relevant forms of argumentation.[222] Such a procedure is also reflected in Cic. *Inv.* 1.34-96, which probably gives us a good idea of what the section on proofs of a pre-στάσις orientated Hellenistic rhetorical treatise looked like. First of all, a list of τόποι indicating relevant subject areas is given (*materia omnium argumentationum*) divided into τόποι concerning πρόσωπα (*Inv.* 1.34-36, e.g., the name of the person[s] involved, their nature, situation in life) and those concerning πράγματα (*Inv.* 1.37-43, e.g., place, opportunity, time, occasion). Next the various forms of argumentation are discussed (*Inv.* 1.44-50), and divided into necessary and probable forms of argumentation.[223] Finally, Cicero deals with the *treatment* of argumentation (*Inv.* 1.51ff) which he divides into argument by induction (i.e., leading to a conclusion via examples or analogies) and argument by rhetorical syllogism (*ratiocinatio* = ἐπιχείρημα). Here it is envisaged that the various forms of argumentation be put together into a structured (in the case of the *ratiocinatio*, semi-syllogistic) whole, forming a carefully constructed piece of argumentation.

---

[220]   I do not touch upon the similar problem concerning treatises which attempted to integrate two quite separate structural principles, namely, the *partes orationis* and the *officia oratoris*. This problem is less relevant to the question of the applicability of rhetorical theory to the apostle Paul in that the whole treatment of *partes orationis* is of little relevance to an analysis of his letters.

[221]   Note that the term ἐνθύμημα is not used here in the sense of a rhetorical syllogism.

[222]   Such procedure is, of course, only a rough sketch. The forms of argumentation would often have suggested new material for one's argumentation, whether specific παραδείγματα or various forms of ἄτεχνοι proofs.

[223]   An example of a necessary form of argumentation would be the *enumeratio* which occurs when several possibilities are listed and all but one are eliminated (cf. select glossary *s.v.* διαίρεσις). Probable forms of argumentation include examples, comparisons, signs (e.g., traces of blood), etc..

However, the advent of στάσις theory (see select glossary *s.v.*) meant that the various στάσεις also had to be discussed, and it is clear that it very quickly became popular to list relevant τόποι (in the form of set arguments) under each of the στάσεις (cf. Cic. *Brut.* 263). The procedure for the orator presupposed here was that he first analyse the proposition to be debated and determine which στάσις it belonged to. Thereupon he could look up the checklist of specific arguments (τόποι) able to be used with that particular στάσις, choose what suited his case, and set to work.[224] This procedure is to be found in book two of Cicero's *de Inventione*. Cicero, in this treatise, has evidently set the two methods side by side.[225]

The treatise *Rhetorica ad Herennium*, whilst ultimately based upon the same source, provides a different approach. Here, an integration of the two methods is attempted (*Rhet.Her.* 2.3-46). The section on argumentation is organised according to the various στάσεις, but instead of just listing specific τόποι, the various forms of argumentation also find a place here (especially within the discussion on the στάσις *coniecturalis*).[226] In addition, a separate discussion is added on the treatment of argumentation (*Rhet.Her.* 2.27ff), i.e., a discussion of the ἐπιχείρημα (rhetorical syllogism), for which the author does not appear to have found a place midst the various στάσεις.

One may well question how successful such an integrated approach could have been. The organisation here tends to be somewhat confusing as respects considerations touching the forms of argumentation. Nevertheless, we find another example of such an attempted integration in the treatise based upon Academic rhetorical theory, namely, Cicero's *Partitiones Oratoriae*. Again it is the στάσις called *coniectura* which is used to integrate the various forms of argumentation (*Part.* 34-40). Another reflection of this method may be deduced from the brief description provided in Cic. *Orat.* 45. Here the

---

[224] For example, the στάσις termed στοχασμός (*constitutio coniecturalis*) concerned the factuality of the matter, e.g., did the person actually commit the murder? Cicero begins his treatment here by discussing arguments (*loci*) arising from the cause, i.e., possible motives for the crime. The options open to both the prosecutor and the counsel for the defence are discussed as well as considerations they may bring into play in order to support their position. Similar arguments are discussed related to the person of the accused, and the alleged crime. Finally a short list of common *loci* which are often applicable to this στάσις is provided (e.g., whether or not one should believe suspicions). These *loci* are, however, not detailed. It is assumed that the reader can refer to an appropriate list of them elsewhere.

[225] Cicero indicates, however, that his more specific treatment of arguments related to the στάσεις in book two belongs with the more general discussion of argumentation in book one §§ 34ff (cf. *Inv.* 1.34; 1.49; 2.11).

[226] *Rhet.Her.* 2.3-12 uses forms of argumentation (e.g., probability, comparison, sign) as his organising principle for the specific τόποι listed under *coniectura* (στοχασμός).

main concern of *coniectura* (indicated by the words *sitne*) is described as the *signum* (a form of argumentation).[227]

The argumentative method of the *Partitiones* is, however, also in other respects a hybrid. Apart from the integrated treatment of στάσεις and forms of argumentation, the treatise also provides a separate chapter on the *officia oratoris*. Here, the section on *inventio* lists the two kinds of τόποι which we have also found elsewhere in philosophically influenced treatises,[228] the extrinsic (ἄτεχνοι) and intrinsic τόποι (argumentative patterns, e.g., argument by similarity, dissimilarity, antecedents, consequents, etc.).[229]

This philosophical tradition of τόποι is also found in the *de Oratore* where Cicero makes his method explicit (*de Orat.* 2.132ff). Upon determining the proposition and its στάσις, the orator, instead of going to specific τόποι listed under the appropriate στάσις, should take note of the abstract question underlying his proposition and go to the intrinsic τόποι consisting of abstract argumentative patterns. The use of στάσις doctrine is thus effectively restricted to helping one pinpoint the issue at stake in his case.

Finally, we must address the method presupposed in Quintilian's *Institutio*. Quintilian's approach reflects both his background in school rhetoric and his predilection for the works of Cicero. As noted above, Quintilian does not integrate στάσις theory with forms of argumentation, but like Cicero's *de Inventione* keeps the two quite separate. However, his discussion of argumentation is set up rather differently. Instead of the progression: τόποι (*materia*); forms of argumentation (example, comparison, etc.); treatment of argumentation (induction vs ἐπιχειρήματα), Quintilian (in the context of the *probatio* of a speech, *Inst.* 5) isolates three kinds of proofs which he discusses in order: *signa* (signs, *Inst.* 5.9), *argumenta* (rhetorical syllogisms, e.g., ἐπιχείρημα, *Inst.* 5.10), and *exempla* (kinds of examples, *Inst.* 5.11). Quintilian's structure, therefore, does not make the distinction between *forms* of argument which are then used in the *treatment* of argumentation. For Quintilian, the use of various kinds of signs and examples are co-ordinate with the use of rhetorical syllogisms. The material for rhetorical syllogisms is supplied by the τόποι which are incorporated *within* the discussion on *argumenta*. Quintilian begins by listing the kind of τόποι found in

---

[227] That the *signum* is chosen as the main form of argumentation appropriate to this στάσις is reflected in its importance in *Rhet.Her.* 2.6-8 where *signum, argumentum* and *consecutio* are all related to that form of argumentation traditionally known as the σημεῖον.

[228] See above § 2.1.1.

[229] Such argumentative patterns go back to the kind of κοινοὶ τόποι discussed by Aristotle in *Rh.* 2.23. In practice there is some overlap between *forms* of argumentation (example, comparison, etc.) and *patterns* of argumentation. For example, the διαίρεσις (see select glossary *s.v.*) is discussed as a form of argumentation in Cic. *Inv.* 1.45 and as a pattern of argumentation in Arist. *Rh.* 2.23.10; Cic. *Top.* 10, 33-34; and *de Orat.* 2.165. In *Rhet.Her.* 4.40-41 it is treated as a figure of speech!

Cic. *Inv.* 1.34-43, making the same subdivision into those concerning *persona* (*Inst.* 5.10.23-31) and those concerning *res* (*Inst.* 5.10.32-52). Whilst Cicero had called such τόποι the *materia argumentationum* (*Inv.* 1.34), Quintilian terms them the *sedes argumentorum* (*Inst.* 5.10.20). At this point, however, he does not stop at providing a list of the τόποι concerned with possible relevant subject areas (the *sedes argumentorum*). He also adds a list of abstract τόποι based on the intrinsic τόποι familiar from Cicero's *de Oratore* and *Topica* (*Inst.* 5.10.53-93). Both the presence of such abstract τόποι and the general structure of his section on rhetorical syllogistic reasoning *may* be attributable to (indirect) Aristotelian influence.[230]

A discussion of the στάσεις together with their specific τόποι is provided later under the treatment of *dispositio*. This is rather a strange place to locate such specific τόποι, for methodologically one would assume that by the time the orator came to a consideration of *dispositio*, he had already worked out his proposed lines of argumentation. Nevertheless, Quintilian strives to provide some justification for placing these τόποι here by emphasising considerations concerning the disposition (i.e., order) of arguments within his discussion.

These methodological aspects of tackling the proof section of a judicial speech in our extant treatises are summarised in the table on the following page.

---

[230] Quintilian's subordination of both specific and abstract τόποι under rhetorical syllogistic reasoning reminds one of Grimaldi's interpretation of the broad setup of Aristotle's *Rhetoric*, see above, footnote 52. Although I do not agree with Grimaldi's interpretation at this point, it is possible that one of Quintilian's sources understood Aristotle in this way and hereby influenced Quintilian.

**Aspects of Rhetorical Method
for Proofs**

Pre-στάσις Method
(Cic. *Inv.* 1, cf. [Arist.] *Rh.Al.*)

Στάσις Method
(Cic. *Inv.* 2)

1) selection of τόποι from relevant subject areas
2) working out of selected τόποι according to forms of argumentation
3) putting the forms of argumentation into a structured whole (treatment of argumentation: by induction or rhetorical syllogism)

1) determination of στάσις
2) selection of τόποι belonging to selected στάσις

Integrated Method
(*Rhet.Her.*, cf. Cic. *Part.*, *Orat.*)

1) determination of στάσις
2) selection of τόποι and/or forms of argumentation belonging to selected στάσις
3) putting the forms of argumentation into a structured whole (treatment of argumentation)

Philosophically Influenced Method
(Cic. *de Orat.*)

1) determination of proposition and στάσις, and thus the θέσις underlying the proposition (ὑπόθεσις)
2) knowledge of abstract argumentative patterns (τόποι) as prerequisite to working out the proofs

Hybrid Method
(Quint. *Inst.*)

1) selection of *signa* (signs)
2) selection of *argumenta* (rhetorical syllogisms)
   i) τόποι from relevant subject areas
   ii) abstract τόποι (argumentative patterns)
3) selection of *exempla* (examples)

(τόποι for specific στάσεις are provided under *dispositio* [ordering of argumentation])

Having reviewed the rather complex methodology with respect to the proof section of a speech, we are in a position to make some comments relevant to application to the letters of the apostle Paul. In the first place, as already noted, the intricate details of στάσις doctrine and its use to pinpoint the precise issue at stake is of little relevance to Paul's letters. Discussion of στάσις doctrine in the treatises is invariably specifically related to the kind of complex (legal) questions arising in the courts. In this respect, the lists of specific τόποι which are provided for the various στάσεις are also of little help.

Such τόποι are directly related to judicial disputes and have little in common with the kinds of subjects dealt with in the letters of Paul.[231]

Secondly, the philosophical tradition of abstract τόποι of argumentative patterns is not very helpful for our purposes either. Paul's argumentation may certainly be analysed in terms of abstract argumentative patterns, but because ancient rhetorical theory generally did not discuss how, when or where these τόποι were to be used in specific instances, an analysis based on such ancient abstract τόποι will not tell us much about the relation of ancient theory to practice. For this reason such analysis of argumentative patterns is probably better approached via modern rhetorical theory. Modern rhetorical textbooks will often provide a better system for analysing argumentative patterns than those of ancient rhetorical theory.

Respecting proofs, we are therefore left with those aspects of school rhetoric common to the pre-στασις method, namely, τόποι from relevant subject areas (materia/ sedes), forms of argumentation, and treatment of argumentation. The τόποι may be dismissed for the same reason as the τόποι for στάσις doctrine. There is little in common between them and the kind of subjects dealt with in Paul's letters. We are then left with forms (examples, comparisons, etc.) and treatment (induction vs rhetorical syllogism) of argumentation. It is here that the treatises provide hints on how to use these various forms and methods which may then be applied and tested with respect to written works. For our purposes, therefore, the non-integrated approach of both Cicero's de Inventione and Quintilian's Institutio provides the most promising source of relevant information, namely, Cic. Inv. 1.44-96 and Quint. Inst. 5.[232]

We may be more brief in consideration of the methodology employed with respect to deliberative or epideictic speeches. The treatises are quite simple in their approach to these forms of rhetoric. Each genre is provided with a list of appropriate τόποι to which the orator could turn. In the case of deliberative speeches the τόποι were organised under the so-called τελικὰ κεφάλαια (arguments related to such concepts as justice, legality, advantage, etc.).[233] The respective sections of the extant

---

[231] Good examples of the direct use of these στάσις-related loci are to be found in the Minor Declamations of (Ps.?) Quintilian. See M. Winterbottom, 1982a, "Schoolroom," 65-66.

[232] The treatise of Anaximenes may, of course, also be helpful, although its arrangement and discussion is less complex than the school rhetoric of later times.

[233] As to be expected, many of the suasoriae (deliberative speeches produced in the schools) organised their presentation of arguments around these τελικὰ κεφάλαια, cf. S. F. Bonner, 1977, Education, 281.

treatises are, however, generally quite brief in their discussions.[234] The τόποι provided
are quite specifically related to the standard kinds of speeches occurring within these
genres and are not generally applicable to the letters of the apostle Paul.

Given that the specific τόποι allocated to the three genres of rhetoric have little in
common with the arguments and τόποι used in the letters of Paul (a fact mainly due to
the entirely different subjects dealt with), we must conclude that rhetorical genre analysis of Paul's letters has little value. Nevertheless, as noted above, the work of the
orator was not complete once he had selected suitable τόποι, and it is in the task of
selecting and using suitable forms of argumentation that the proof sections of the
treatises may be of use to us. We should, however, realise that the usefulness of such
portions of ancient treatises will still be limited. The treatises were written in order to
aid an orator in the *preparation* of speeches, and were *not* designed as an *analytical*
tool for speeches already written. This fact is important, for we are confronted with the
difficult problem of attempting to read a given text with a view to *re*constructing the
argumentative processes with which the author may have been at work. Such processes
will really only be evident to us in such cases where rhetorical theory is quite explicit
and where this theory has been carefully followed by the author of the writing under
examination. Even then we need to ask whether the argumentative process(es) followed
might not be attributable to common sense. This *caveat* naturally also applies to the following steps in the production of a speech.

Having a general picture of the proofs to be used in his case, the orator would
next need to turn to the question of τάξις, namely, the order in which the various arguments should be presented. Rhetorical theory actually gives very little advice on this
question and these sections of the treatises are generally very short. Typical advice
would be to place one's strongest arguments at the beginning and end, and those of
medium force in the middle (cf. *Rhet.Her.* 3.18; Cic. *de Orat.* 2.307-314; *Orat.* 50;
Quint. *Inst.* 5.12.14). In writing up the proof section attention would also be paid to
ways in which arguments could be expanded (αὔξησις) and to the use of γνῶμαι and
short considerations (the specific sense of ἐνθύμημα) at appropriate places (e.g., at the
end of a round of argumentation). Use of such methodology may often be detected in

---

[234] Cf. Cic. *Part.* 70-97; *Inv.* 2.157-78; *Rhet.Her.* 3.3-7, 10-11; Quint. *Inst.* 3.7.7-28 for epideictic
τόποι which he terms *materia* and *Inst.* 3.8.22-25 for the τελικὰ κεφάλαια of deliberative rhetoric which
he calls *partes suadendi* and out of which *loci* arise, cf. 3.8.27. In addition, τόποι for epideictic rhetoric
are provided by Theon *Prog.* ii, pp.109,28 - 111,11 Sp..

various writings, and in cases where reliance upon rhetorical theory is demonstrable, one may even make a reasonable conjecture as to how the writer may have weighed his arguments (based upon their order).

Of course the orator would also need to be pay attention to style. Hellenistic rhetorical theory began to pay considerable attention to matters of style. The whole question of style was often handled in separate treatises. Broadly speaking there were two approaches. One could organise his discussion under a number of ἀρεταί (e.g., the Theophrastian four), briefly addressing general matters such as correct language, clarity and appropriateness and then dealing with tropes and figures under the ἀρετή of embellishment (cf. *Rhet.Her.* 4; Quint. *Inst.* 8 - 11.1).[235] It is this approach which also encouraged the separate publication of treatises defining and illustrating tropes and figures (Rut.Lup., Caecilius, and many later treatises).

A second approach was to organise one's whole discussion of style around a set number of stylistic types (e.g., Demetr. *Eloc.*; [Longin.] who discusses one type of style only, i.e., ὕψος; the general approach in the rhetorical works of Dionysius of Halicarnassus). These types would be defined and then frequently discussed in terms of their word choice (ἐκλογὴ ὀνομάτων), matter (τὰ πράγματα) and word combination (σύνθεσις ὀνομάτων). Within this discussion the tropes and figures appropriate to each kind of style would be addressed.

Sometimes treatises principally based on the first approach (organised according to various virtues) added an extra section defining the various types of style (e.g., *Rhet.Her.* 4.11-16; cf. Quint. *Inst.* 12.10).

Ancient rhetorical theory, however, did not really develop any uniform approach to the analysis of types of style. We have already noted considerable variation. *Rhet.Her.* and Cicero speak of the three-fold plain, grand and middle styles; Demetrius of the four-fold grand, elegant, plain and forceful styles; Dionysius of Halicarnassus proposed a double threefold analysis, the plain, grand and middle styles of speech in general, and the smooth, rough and mixed styles of harmony (i.e., styles relating to σύνθεσις); Demetrius mentions those who advocate a twofold style (cf. Cic. *Brut.* 201); and Quintilian mentions those who speak of a three-fold style in terms of plain, grand and flowery.

---

[235] Cic. *de Orat.* 3.19-212 on *elocutio* is also broadly organised around the four Theophrastian virtues (cf. *Latine dicere* § 38, *plane dicere* § 49, *ornatus* § 53, *aptum* § 210). However, the discussion is highly discursive and the internal organisation is quite complex. Whilst Cic. *Part.* 16-24 gives an important place to the discussion of virtues of style, they are not the organising principle here.

The lack of a standard stylistic gauge in antiquity shows us that comments on types of style could also in antiquity be rather subjective. Nevertheless, many of the specific points mentioned in the treatises may be of help in judging how rhetorical theorists generally viewed various specific uses of language. It is particularly helpful for us when the theorists themselves rewrite various literary passages they are discussing in order to illustrate their point.[236] Of course, our approach is rather more complex than that of the ancient critic. An ancient critic could reasonably apply his own theory to various writings and be satisfied. An analysis of ancient writings from the perspective of ancient rhetorical theory is confronted with the much more difficult question as to whether the writing under examination shows any influence of one or other stylistic theory. We need to be very cautious in making judgements in this area.[237] However, another approach is to ask how the ancients may have applied their own theories to any given writing (e.g., the letters of Paul). When the question is put in this way, we do not need to assume that the writer (Paul, in this case) had any knowledge of the theory concerned. Our conclusions, then, tell us more about how ancient critics might have viewed Paul's literary abilities, than about what Paul himself may have thought.

A general *caveat* needs to be sounded, however, in discussing style. In isolating forms of argumentation and figures, rhetorical theory attempted to cover every possible form of expression. This fact makes it a rather simple process to analyse and label an extant speech or letter by these various terms. Such labelling, however, does not really help us much unless we can say something about the *use* and *function* of such arguments or figures. But it is precisely at this point that the extant treatises are weakest. Discussions of style and figures often seem divorced from considerations of persuasive effect. This is not to say, however, that the treatises never make any suggestions in this area and it is important that we not neglect those suggestions which are indeed made.[238]

---

[236] Such a method was especially popular with Dionysius of Halicarnassus, but also among the other theorists specialising in style. We even find an example in Quint. *Inst.* 4.1.67. A good illustration of the method is to be found in [Longin.] 20-21. Here he first explains how (among other figures) ἀσύνδετον contributes to the ὕψος in a passage from Demosthenes. He cites it as follows: πολλὰ γὰρ ἂν ποιήσειεν ὁ τύπτων, ὧν ὁ παθὼν ἔνια οὐδ᾽ ἂν ἀπαγγεῖλαι δύναιτο ἑτέρῳ, τῷ σχήματι, τῷ βλέμματι, τῇ φωνῇ. Having explained the effect of the passage he goes on to show how an Isocratean might ruin its effect by adding conjunctions as follows: καὶ μὴν οὐδὲ τοῦτο χρὴ παραλιπεῖν, ὡς πολλὰ ἂν ποιήσειεν ὁ τύπτων, πρῶτον μὲν τῷ σχήματι, εἶτα δὲ τῷ βλέμματι, εἶτά γε μὴν αὐτῇ τῇ φωνῇ.

[237] G. M. A. Grube (1967, *Greeks*, 15) makes some pertinent comments. The Greek theorists tended to be too theoretical "in that they state their theories of style and then apply their formulae to particular authors (as Dionysius does) or, worse, use their authors merely to illustrate their theories and categories. Even Aristotle does this in his *Rhetoric*." He reiterates this on p.17 where he adds that the ancient critics "were at times inclined to approach literature as a treasure house of illustrations of their own theories."

[238] Definitions and comments on devices of argumentation and style by the ancient rhetorical theorists dealt with here are generally taken up in my forthcoming *Glossary*. An appendix at the end of this book contains several select entries from this glossary relevant to the analysis of Paul's letters below.

III. RELATION OF RHETORIC TO EPISTOLOGRAPHY

Before proceeding to actual letters of Paul it is incumbent upon us to address, albeit briefly, ancient epistolary theory. We also need to address the possible relation of both ancient letters and epistolary theory to rhetoric. Rhetorical theory was, after all, developed to aid the writing of *speeches* and not letters. We begin with the nature of letters in antiquity.

1 Letters or Epistles?

G. A. Deissmann, in his deservedly celebrated book *Licht vom Osten* (4th ed., 1923), argued for a basic distinction between two kinds of letters which he called the letter and the epistle respectively.[239] By "letter" he meant a non-literary document with a particular real addressee. Letters are "geschaffen nicht von der Kunst, sondern vom Leben, bestimmt nicht für die Öffentlichkeit und die Nachwelt, sondern für den Augenblick und den Alltag" (118). By epistle he meant a "literarische Kunstform, eine Gattung der Literatur, wie zum Beispiel Dialog, Rede, Drama." (195) An epistle is thus a piece of literature written for a wider public cast in the form of a letter. Deissmann recognised that there could be inbetween forms, and suggested the "epistolary letter" (196), i.e., a real letter, but written with an eye to publication. Yet to Deissmann such letters were simply "schlechte Briefe und können uns mit ihrer Frostigkeit, Geziertheit oder eitelen Unwahrhaftigkeit lehren, wie ein wirklicher Brief nicht sein soll." His definition of "Literatur" on p.118 gives us the two elements that in his view separate an epistle from a letter. Literature is "das für die Öffentlichkeit (oder für eine Öffentlichkeit) und in einer bestimmten Kunstform abgefaßte Schrifttum." Thus for Deissmann the term "literary" not only has to do with artistic or stylised language, but also with intended audience.

It was Deissmann's research into the papyrus letters found in the rubbish tips of ancient villages in Egypt that led him to define this distinction between letter and epistle in the way that he did (212). However, he classifies more than just papyrus let-

---

239   Deissmann had already pleaded for this distinction in 1895, "Prolegomena."

ters as "letters" proper. Deissmann also considered the letters of Aristotle, the genuine letters of Isocrates and Plato, certain (fragmentary) letters of Epicurus and those of Cicero to be "letters" in the proper sense. "Epistles" he termed those of Dionysius of Halicarnassus, Plutarch, Seneca and Pliny the Younger. These were not *real* letters, but publications dressed in letter form. He went on to classify the letters of Paul, and the second and third letters of John as "letters" in the proper sense (the rest of the New Testament letters being cast in the literary form of "epistles").

But Deissmann's schema was never totally followed and has met with criticism ever since its publication.[240] His division into two kinds of letters does not really work. It is clear that the basic intention was to separate letters intended for publication (and thus unreal) from letters genuinely written and sent as such, and only preserved for us because of extraordinary circumstances. His definition of "Literatur" also reflects this, but is it helpful? When, for example, Cicero's letters are classified as "letters," does this mean that their language can never have an "abgefaßte Kunstform"? Herein lies the problem. It is one thing to separate genuine letters from literary fictions, but it is quite another to suggest that genuine letters cannot be written in affected or literary style (or that if they are, then they are a mixed form and must be written with an eye to publication). The correspondence of Cicero, a well known orator, (especially that to Atticus) is a prime example of private correspondence from someone of high social standing (and thus literary abilities) who was at least *careful* in the way he wrote.[241] But this in

---

[240]   See W. G. Doty, 1969, "Classification," 189.

My criticism here is narrowly focused on those elements affecting a possible relationship between rhetoric and epistolography. A more general three point critique is offered by S. K. Stowers (1986, *Letter*, 18-20). He argues; i) we need to remember that the papyri come from small provincial towns in Egypt and would not necessarily be representative (in terms of epistolography) of what might have been found in a trash heap of large cities like Ephesus or Corinth (this was a point made earlier by H. Koskenniemi, 1956, *Studien*, 12); ii) the distinction made between private letters and public epistles ignores the importance of friendship and family in ancient politics, and is thus more appropriate to a modern situation than an ancient one; iii) "the distinction between warm, personal, spontaneous, artless, common-private-friendly letters and impersonal, conventional artificial literary letters ... was typical of nineteenth- and early twentieth-century Romanticism." Modern theorists of literature and culture see a conventional dimension to all intelligible human behavior.

For an excellent review and critique of Deissmann's approach see W. G. Doty, *op. cit.*, 183-92. Doty sets Deissmann's letter/ epistle distinction against the background of Deissmann's general struggle against i) the theological dogmaticism of his day, ii) the classicists who tended to compare Paul's language against Attic (literary) models, and iii) the dogmatic notion of inspiration and canon.

[241]   Cicero says of his letters (*Fam.* 3.11.5): *Sed si, ut scribis, eae litterae non fuerunt disertae, scito meas non fuisse.* In *Fam.* 16.17.1 he writes to Tiro admonishing him for his incorrect use of language: *Sed heus tu, qui κανών esse meorum scriptorum soles, unde illud tam ἄκυρον, "valetudini fideliter inserviendo"?* Yet in *Fam.* 9.21.1 he writes: *Quid tibi ego in epistulis videor? nonne plebeio sermone agere tecum? nec enim semper eodem modo: quid enim simile habet epistula aut iudicio aut contioni? ... epistulas vero cottidianis verbis texere solemus.* Remember that already by the first century AD, Cicero's letters had become models of literary form!

It should be noted that Deissmann's article in *Bibelstudien* (1895, "Prolegomena") is more careful on this question of literary style, cf. pp.218 (on Isocrates), 221 (on Cicero).

no way implies that Cicero ever wrote his letters with a view to eventual publication.[242]

The fact that some letters in antiquity *may* have been written with a view to publication, or even as complete literary fiction, does not necessarily make them any different from many a private letter written by a person well-educated in letters. In the first place, the literary published letter as a prose form was generally used as a substitute for another form that would have required much stricter adherence to literary conventions.[243] A letter, even as a published literary form, was *supposed* to be written in plain, simple style.[244] And in the second place, supposed literary fictions were often written in such a way as to suggest that they were real correspondence.[245]

Deissmann's characterisation of the fresh, living character of the (real) papyrus letters also needs to be qualified. In 1956 Heikki Koskenniemi published a study on the notion and phraseology of Greek letters (1956, *Studien*). His major focus was upon the papyrus letters.[246] Koskenniemi showed how there were quite a number of formulae

---

[242] Cicero himself would have liked to correct his letters before publication (*Att.* 16.5.5), but it is uncertain whether he ever did revise any at all.

[243] Cf. Sykutris, 1931, "Epistolographie," 200.

[244] This rule was a commonplace expressed by many in antiquity, cf. H. Koskenniemi, 1956, *Studien*, 27-30. It seems related to the idea that a letter was merely one half of a conversation (which definition also became a commonplace in ancient thought, cf. [Demetr.] *Typ.* 223-235; [Lib.] *Ep. Char.* 2; Philostr. *Dial.* 1). Of course this was not always the case. Seneca for example certainly *claims* that his style was plain and simple: *quae veritati operam dat oratio, inconposita esse debet et simplex* (*Ep.* 40.4); *Oratio certam regulam non habet* (*Ep.* 114.13); *qualis sermo meus esset, si una sederemus aut ambularemus, inlaboratus et facilis, tales esse epistulas meas volo, quae nihil habent accersitum nec fictum* (*Ep.* 75.1, cf. 1-4). But his style was hardly plain, and received considerable criticism even by the ancients, cf. Quint. *Inst.* 10.1.125-31 who criticises his style, e.g., for unnatural expressions, cf. also the discussion in E. Norden, 1898, *Kunstprosa*, 306-13.

Pliny the Younger makes a similar claim: *pressus sermo purusque ex epistulis petitur* (*Ep.* 7.9.8). Commenting on this, S. K. Stowers (1986, *Letter*, 35) remarks: "The paradox is that Pliny employs elaborate structure and studied prose rhythm in order to achieve this simplicity and directness." It should be noted that Pliny adds elsewhere *est mihi cum Cicerone aemulatio, nec sum contentus eloquentia saeculi nostri* (*Ep.* 1.5.12) and describes his letter writing as *curatius* (*Ep.* 1.1).

[245] This fact, of course, makes it difficult to distinguish literary fiction from real letters. See the discussion of Sykutris, 1931, "Epistolographie," 212-13. Seneca's letters to Lucilius are usually (though not universally) considered literary fiction, yet his letters are full of comments suggesting a real letter exchange. There is a tendency among contemporary biblical scholars to take a less critical view with respect to the authorship of letter collections in antiquity than classical scholars have traditionally done. They are more often considered to be real letters in the first place, even if written with an eye to publication. Cf. M. L. Sirewalt Jr. (1991, "Form," 147-71) who accepts as real the three doctrinal letters of Epicurus, those of Dionysius of Halicarnassus, and of Plutarch; Stowers (1986, *Letter*, 19) appears to accept the letters of Seneca as real, though perhaps edited for publication, although he is elsewhere ambivalent (40). On pp.99-100 he appears to be saying that if scholars considered Seneca's letters in the light of "the paraenetic letter tradition," they would be more likely to be judged authentic.

[246] Incidentally, Koskenniemi also found reason to critique Deissmann's distinction between *Brief* and *Epistel*, cf. pp.89-91.

(fixed expressions) in use for the opening and closing of Greek letters.[247] The terminology and formulae are often so common and rigid that they lose much of their original
meaning. Occasionally such formulae are expanded or substituted to avoid this problem, but at this point a letter writer often succumbs to a degree of rhetorical flourish (at
least in terms of style). Koskenniemi noted that the (published) letters of philosophers
and orators tended to avoid the kind of fixed expressions found in the papyrus letters.
But he also noted the existence of two papyrus letters that are profoundly rhetorical in
their language (57-59). These letters (*UPZ* 144 and 145) were shown by U. Wilcken to
be most probably excerpted school copies of real letters (for exercise).[248] Their language is characterised as striving for carefully crafted periods and avoidance of hiatus
(623-24). The sentences are lengthy and complex and the vocabulary is rather florid.
Interestingly, Deissmann published the first of these among his sample collection of
papyrus letters in the "Prolegomena" of 1895, yet omitted it in *Licht vom Osten*
(1923). Their evidence, again, belies an oversimplified characterisation of real letters.

How do the letters of Paul fit into all this? Given that Paul's letters do not reflect
an "Atticising" or "Asianising" literary style, nevertheless their style and language is
still a far cry from the vulgar language of many of the papyrus examples Deissmann
himself provides. Further, whilst the basic structure of Paul's letters is in conformity
with Greek tradition as shown by Koskenniemi, and whilst traces of various epistolary
formulae are also to be found, Paul has frequently expanded and varied them. His
expansions, at least on a stylistic level, often show some degree of rhetorical flourish.[249]

Another interesting comparison of Paul's letters with those letters preserved in the
literary tradition on the one hand and the papyrus letters on the other is found in the
dissertation of E. R. Richards midst an appendix on 'The "Literary or Non-Literary"
(Deissmann) Debate.'[250] He provides a simple comparison based on *length*:

> In the approximately 14,000 private letters from Greco-Roman antiquity, the average length was
> about 87 words, ranging in length from about 18 to 209 words. ... Cicero averaged 295 words per
> letter, ranging from 22 to 2,530 words, and Seneca averaged 995, ranging from 149 to 4134. By

---

[247]   Cf. chapters four to seven. For example, formulae regarding: longing for letter-correspondence
when such is lacking, prayer for a letter response, motivations for wishing a letter, comments on the
reception of a letter, motivation for one's own letter, etc..
[248]   1927, *Urkunden*, 622-24.
[249]   Paul's expansion of such fixed formulae is certainly more than stylistic. Apart from the christianis-
ing of many formulae, the very fact that he expanded or modified them means that the expressions were
no longer in danger of losing semantic content because of a fixed formulaic character.
[250]   1991, *Secretary*, 213.

both standards, though, Paul's letters were quite long. The thirteen letters bearing his name average 2,495 words, ranging from 335 (Philemon) to 7,114 (Romans).

Whilst this fact appears to bring Paul closer to "literary" letters, yet at the same time it shows that Paul thereby flaunted one of the cardinal literary rules for writing letters, namely, that letters should be brief (cf. Isoc. *Ep.* 2.13; Demetr. *Eloc.* 228; [Lib.] *Ep. Char.* 50) - a rule closely followed, for example, by Pliny (cf. *Ep.* 2.5.13; 2.11.25).

The question of intended audience is not so simple either. In the first place, did Paul really never intend his letters to be copied and distributed? Was this only a function of the canonical work of the early church (cf. 1 *Ep. Thess.* 5.27; *Ep. Col.* 4.16; 2 *Ep. Pet.* 3.16 - implying that Paul's letters were widely read, cf. v.1)?[251] We may note that it was normal practice in Roman society to copy private letters received, in order to share them around (especially from well known or important persons).[252]

The basic point is that the characterisation "literary" is relative - in both its aspects. There is a great spectrum of possibility between the unpolished (and ungrammatical) style of many of the papyrus letters, and literary letters written in polished poetry.[253] In fact some of the examples of real letters cited by Deissmann were already in 1919 shown to be highly rhetorical and conforming to a definite rhetorical genre.[254]

---

[251] Deissmann, 1923, *Licht*, 205.

[252] Cf. E. R. Richards, 1991, *Secretary*, 4-5, 79 note 45. A friendly letter by a high society Roman was at the same time a very political (or at least potentially political) document (cf. S. K. Stowers, 1986, *Letter*, 28-31).

[253] This thought was written before I read the nearly identical conclusion of E. R. Richards, 1991, *Secretary*, 215 (based on W. G. Doty, 1973, *Letters*, 26). Yet despite this, Richards still speaks of Paul's letters as "hybrids," a "metamorphosis." This language seems to imply that Paul was stuck between two basic forms, literary and non literary (or "occasional") letters. We are led to suppose that Paul, brave as he then was, forced himself out of this mold to forge new *Gattungen*, to metamorphise a new hybrid. To suppose that someone wishing to write a letter in the first century was really placed in such a form-critical dilemma if he wished to write a real letter containing some "literary characteristics" is hardly realistic. See my discussion below, § 2.

[254] I am thinking of the work of J. Klek (1919, *Symbuleutici*) discussed below (§ 4). Klek deemed Plato, *Ep.* 7 and 8, Isocrates, *Ep.* 1, 3, 6 and 9 (although Deissmann denied the authenticity of 3 and 9. 1895, "Prolegomena," 219) and *Q.fr.* 1.1 of Cicero to be examples of deliberative rhetoric. It should be admitted that Klek does in fact seem to be somewhat influenced by Deissmann (on p.39 Deissmann's "Prolegomena" is cited), but instead of making a distinction between letters that are published ("epistle") and those that are real and not for publication ("letter"), he only distinguishes private letters: "*Tales epistulae privatae a rhetorica forma distant privatoque quasi stilo compositae sunt.*" (39) For Klek, only (non-private?) letters conforming to rhetorical rules count, but this does not make them any less real letters with real concrete situations - a point Klek emphasises greatly in connection with his definition of the deliberative genre (cf. 41). He appears to be thinking primarily of letters to prominent public persons.

2 The Question of *Gattungen*

Modern research on ancient epistolography tends to classify ancient letters into various forms or *Gattungen*, e.g., amtliche Brief, Lehrbrief, Zauberbrief, etc.[255] This is indeed a very handy way of presenting an overview of the different forms ancient letters could take. But it must be realised that these kind of *Gattungen* were generally *not* discussed (or distinguished) by the ancients themselves. That is not to say that there were no ancient epistolary theorists, nor that these theorists did not attempt to categorise letters into various *Gattungen*. Yet they did so in a very different way than moderns. Ancient epistolary theorists were not concerned with the structural form of a letter, nor with appropriate formulaic expressions. Rather, they categorised letter types into what we would today call various "rhetorical situations."[256]

There are two such handbooks of epistolary theory extant which attempt to categorise various letter types, namely, the τύποι ἐπιστολικοί of Ps.-Demetrius (*c.* first century BC) and the ἐπιστολιμαῖοι χαρακτῆρες of Ps.-Libanius (fifth century AD). Ps.-Demetrius isolates 21 types (γένη) of letters, and Ps.-Libanius 41 kinds (προσαγορίαι).[257] Ps.-Libanius appears not to have known of Ps.-Demetrius.[258] That there

---

255 Sykutris (1931, "Epistolographie") discussing "literary letters," for example, lists: der amtliche Brief, literarische Privatbrief, publizistische Brief, Lehrbrief, wissenschaftliche Literatur in Briefform, Widmungsbrief, Himmelsbrief, Zauberbrief, poetische Brief, fingierte Brief (divided in various subcategories). Recent research by biblical scholars has come up with more, e.g., the Greek letter-essay (M. L. Stirewalt, 1991, "Form"), the ambassadorial letter (R. Jewett, 1982, "Romans").

256 Most (but not all) of the relevant texts have been handily gathered together with an English translation in A. Malherbe, *Ancient Epistolary Theorists* (Atlanta, Georgia: Scholars Press, 1988).

257 Ps.-Demetrius: φιλικός, συστατικός, μεμπτικός, ὀνειδιστικός, παραμυθητικός, ἐπιτιμητικός, νουθετητικός, ἀπειλητικός, ψεκτικός, ἐπαινετικός, συμβουλευτικός, ἀξιωματικός, ἐρωτηματικός, ἀποφαντικός, ἀλληγορικός, αἰτιολογικός, κατηγορικός, ἀπολογητικός, συγχαρητικός, εἰρωνικός, ἀπευχαριστικός. Ps.-Demetrius adds: ἄλλος δὲ τῶν καθ' ἡμᾶς οὐδεὶς ἐπίκαιρος εἰς ἐπιστολικὸν τρόπον ἀνήκων τύπος (p.2,11-13 W.). Nevertheless, Ps.-Libanius managed to find 20 more! He lists: παραινετική, μεμπτική, παρακλητική, συστατική, εἰρωνική, εὐχαριστική, φιλική, εὐκτική, ἀπειλητική, ἀπαρνητική, παραγγελματική, μεταμελητική, ὀνειδιστική, συμπαθητική, θεραπευτική, συγχαρητική, παραλογιστική, ἀντεγκληματική, ἀντεπισταλτική, παροξυντική, παραμυθητική, ὑβριστική, ἀπαγγελτική, σχετλιαστική, πρεσβευτική, ἐπαινετική, διδασκαλική, ἐλεγκτική, διαβλητική, ἐπιτιμητική, ἐρωτηματική, παραθαρρυντική, ἀναθετική, ἀποφαντική, σκωπτική, μετριαστική, αἰνιγματική, ὑπομνηστική, λυπητική, ἐρωτική, μικτή.

258 R. Förster (1927, "Libanii," esp. pp.1-3) argues that this work, whilst it shows no knowledge of Ps.-Demetrius' kindred tract, does show acquaintance with the letters of Philostratus to Aspasius; Gregory of Nazianzus, *ep.* 51 to Nicobulus; and with Syrianus' commentary on Hermogenes' *de Statibus*. He concludes that the work was written in the mid fifth century by a Christian author. It should be noted, however, that the author has no scruples against speaking of pagan gods, cf. § 75 (in a sample letter): κρεῖττον γὰρ ἡμῖν τῷ Πλούτωνι ξυντυχεῖν ἢ τῷ τοῖς θεοῖς ἐχθρῷ.

were more Greek epistolary theorists in antiquity is clear.[259]

Underlying this kind of categorisation is the basic sentiment that a letter should confine itself to one theme only (although Ps.-Libanius adds a mixed form). Such a literary letter rule is followed closely by Pliny the Younger. It is interesting to note how many of the short papyrus letters also confine themselves to one theme, and many can thus be categorised.[260] Perhaps this is attributable to letter training in schools (for professional secretaries?). We may note that the treatise of Ps.-Demetrius (and probably that of Ps.-Libanius) were intended as textbooks for secretaries.[261] It is further notable that this classification into "rhetorical situations" is similar to the basic criteria involved in the division of rhetoric into three classes, namely, forensic, deliberative, and epideictic. Ps.-Demetrius, in fact, includes the deliberative type (συμβουλευτικός) among his 21fold epistolary classification. That this is related to the rhetorical genre of the same name is clear from his division of it into προτροπή (exhortation) and ἀποτροπή (dissuasion), the standard division for the equivalent rhetorical genre (cf. [Arist.] *Rh.Al.* 1; Arist. *Rh.* 1.3.3; *Rhet.Her.* 1.2.2; Cic. *Part.* 91; Quint. *Inst.* 3.8.15). Although Ps.-Demetrius does not mention the epideictic genre as such, he lists its two main divisions according to rhetorical theory as separate types (praise and blame). Ps.-Libanius also includes praise and blame in his classification into 41 letter types. This relationship to rhetorical genres shows that epistolary theorists did not feel themselves bound to the three broad categories of rhetorical theory. It would seem that whilst rhetorical theory early on developed a standardised threefold categorisation, such was not the case for epistolary theory which does not appear to have reached any standardisation of genre classification at all. Many of the types separated by Ps.-Demetrius and Ps.-Libanius are mentioned as sub-divisions in rhetorical theory. Further, as we might expect, a distinct forensic type is missing among the epistolary classifications. Finally, we should note that the epistolary theorists never prescribe a strict argumentative order or divide any genre into various parts (contrast the *partes orationis*

---

[259]   The excursus of Demetr. *Eloc.* 223-35 on epistolary style was clearly based on the work of someone else (probably Artemon's introduction to his edition of Aristotle's letters, cf. *Eloc.* 223). Demetrius is extremely cautious when he writes about a subject without reliance on other sources, cf. § 179, 186. See in addition Philostratus (third century AD), *Dial.* 1, who alludes to seven types of letters (also in terms of "rhetorical situations"). Ps.-Libanius refers to other theoreticians at § 5 when he notes that some wrongly confuse παραινετική with συμβουλευτική: ταύτην δέ τινες καὶ συμβουλευτικὴν εἶπον οὐκ εὖ, παραίνεσις γὰρ συμβουλῆς διαφέρει.

[260]   Cf. S. K. Stowers, 1986, *Letter*, 49-173.

[261]   Ps.-Demetrius writes in his introduction that he has written his work because in his view letters ought to be written ὡς τεχνικώτατα. Yet he has noticed that "those who undertake services for men appointed to office" tend to write indifferently (ὡς ἔτυχεν).

in rhetorical theory). The fact that many of the epistolary types (or "rhetorical situations") do not really correspond with rhetorical theory plainly indicates that a rhetorical situation for the presentation of a speech is quite a different scenario to that of writing a letter. We may at this point already tentatively suggest that it is vain to attempt to strictly apply a scheme of classification designed for speeches, to letters. Whilst there may be a relationship and some degree of overlap, the general picture is quite different. This warning needs to be sounded as there has been a tendency in Pauline scholarship to want to classify Paul's letters in terms of one of the three established genres from rhetorical theory.[262]

The fact that there was no standard classification in ancient epistolary theory also suggests that we need to be careful when thinking about ancient letters in terms of modern *Gattungen*. It is not so that when someone wished to write a private or personal letter that he first had to consider which fixed form he would use, and was then bound to a fixed structure or rules of composition. The *Gattungen* of modern research are *descriptive* and were, in most cases anyway, never *prescriptive* in the ancient world.[263]

3 Recent Justification for Rhetoric

Biblical scholars interested in applying ancient rhetorical theory to the letters of the New Testament have paid surprisingly little attention to the relation between epistolography and rhetoric. Apart from H. D. Betz, whose work on Paul's letter to the

---

[262] E.g., G. A. Kennedy (1984, *New Testament*, 19f, 36 and passim), and B. L. Mack (1990, *Rhetoric*, 49ff). The same point is made by the classicist C. J. Classen (1993, "Epistles," 289). He suggests that ancient rhetorical theory will really only render service (and then within limits) in the areas of *inventio* and *elocutio*.

[263] Of course men such as Pliny the younger, who sought to revise his letters for publication in literary form, paid great attention to certain literary and epistolary rules, e.g., one subject per letter, relatively short length. But such rules apply to the form of a (literary) letter as letter, and not as a particular *form* or *Gattung* of letters. Such rules were in any event never binding. The requirement of short length, for example, was not infrequently violated among the literate. The purist approach of the theorists and some practitioners only proves that "violations" of such rules were common enough. Witness Demetrius' comments against those (he names Plato and Thucydides) who dress treatises ($\sigma\upsilon\gamma\gamma\rho\acute{\alpha}\mu\mu\alpha\tau\alpha$) in the form of letters (*Eloc.* 228). Such a practice, in fact, became much more common, cf. the letters of Dionysius of Halicarnassus, many of Plutarch's writings and the letters of Epicurus (preserved in Diogenes Laertius). Such theoretical epistolary rules were merely what was considered proper for a literary letter among the cultured elite of society. Such concerns could hardly have worried the ordinary man, unless concerned with pretentions to literary merit.

The similarity of many administrative papyrus letters have shown that there *were* probably set forms and formulae for certain administrative types of letters, but these are not mentioned by the epistolary theorists. Common formulae for the opening and closing of private letters do not receive much attention either (cf. the research of H. Koskenniemi, 1956, *Studien*), though Apollonius Dyscolus, *Synt.* 1.65-68; 2.42; 3.63-66, 77, 79 is an exception. This fact does not radically affect the point in question.

Galatians was built upon the premise that this letter was written in "the apologetic letter tradition,"[264] many scholars appear to have gone to work with little consideration of this relationship. This is the more surprising given that ancient rhetorical theorists paid virtually *no* attention to letter writing before the fourth century AD (when a short appendix on this subject was sometimes added).[265] The only work on rhetoric to take account of letters before then (and this is more a treatise on style) is Demetr. *Eloc.*, which includes a digression on letter writing (223-35).[266] Ancient opinion judged the letter to be a different thing than a rhetorical speech, cf. Cic. *Fam.* 9.21.1, *quid enim simile habet epistula aut iudicio aut contioni?* (For what does a letter have in common with a speech in court or in an assembly?)[267] Such a situation makes the following simple and unsupported remark of G. A. Kennedy, for example, *prima facie* suspect:

---

[264] See below, pp.106-108.

[265] See Iul.Vict. *Rhet.* 27, and the *de Epistulis* from Anon. *Excerpt..* By the fourth century the writing of letters had blossomed into a very popular and stylised literary form. The passage from Julius Victor is most probably a quotation or abbreviation from a (lost) work of Julius Titianus who lived late second century AD (see R. Giomini/ M. S. Celentano, 1980, "Praefatio," xxii-xxiii, and L. Radermacher, "Iulius," 877-78).

[266] In addition to the fact that Demetrius' treatise only deals with style (one aspect of a rhetorical treatise), there is also the consideration that, given his Peripatetic inclination, he would seem to have been led to digress on epistolary style by the fact that he had in his possession a collection of the letters of Aristotle with an introduction by Artemon covering this subject (cf. *Eloc.* 223).

[267] W. von Christ *et al.* (1920, *Geschichte*, 301n) have suggested that letter writing was early on a standard part of rhetorical schooling, coming under the *progymnasmata*. Theon *Prog.* ii p.115,22 Sp. is cited, but all that may be meant here is that προσωποποιίαι are generally used in panegyric speeches, protreptic essays, and letters.

It is also appropriate here to note that H. Probst's translation of Philostr. *Dial.* 1 is rather misleading (1991, *Paulus*, 99). He translates: "Der Brief soll gegliedert sein nach Art der öffentlichen Rede, aber durch Eleganz gefallen." This renders the Greek (re: epistolary style): συνκεῖσθαι μὲν πολιτικῶς, τοῦ δὲ ἁβροῦ μὴ ἀπᾳδεῖν. It is rather far fetched to construe συγκεῖσθαι πολιτικῶς here as "laid out in the manner of public speaking." A cursory reading of Philostratus' own letters should have put paid to that. A better translation would be: "(Letters) should be composed in an official style, but not without gracefulness." Probst continues by arguing that ancient letters in general were based upon the *divisio* of an ancient (deliberative) speech: *exordium, narratio, argumentatio,* and *peroratio.* His analysis, however, empties these terms of their *rhetorical* meaning. He maintains that this division, although derived from ancient rhetoric, has become distinct in ancient epistolary tradition (i.e., it does not follow "ancient school rhetoric"). Given this analysis, I have not deemed it fair to comment critically upon Probst's division of 1 *Ep.Cor.* 8 - 10 in chapter six. His treatment of Paul's first letter to the Corinthians is therefore not dealt with in this book.

The only work on epistolary theory which appears to interpret letter writing in terms of oratory is the appendix *de epistolis* in Iul.Vict. *Rhet.* 27. Here it is said that letters should be written using *omnia oratoria praecepta*, although this is mollified by the following words: *una modo exceptione, ut aliquid de summis copiis detrahamus et orationem proprius sermo explicet.* Precisely what is meant by *omnia oratoria praecepta* is not made clear, but it is extremely doubtful that the use of rhetorical genres or the divisions of a speech are intended. The appendix is probably a quotation from Julius Titianus (late second century AD, see above) who was an orator well-known for deliberately imitating the style of Cicero (a fact which shows through elsewhere in the appendix itself). In any event, the comment on the use of oratorical precepts in letters is unique.

"The structure of a Greco-Roman letter resembles a speech, framed by a salutation and complimentary closure."[268] The Greeks and Romans themselves appear to have thought otherwise! Certainly most ancient letters do not structurally resemble formal speeches. Yet as we shall see below there were exceptions.

The first to properly address this relationship, as far as I am aware, was H. Hübner.[269] Hübner takes account of the separation between rhetoric and epistolography in ancient theorists but appropriately remarks that, in addition to theory, we must also take account of practice. Unfortunately, Hübner himself doesn't do much with this. He continues by noting the definition of an ancient letter (as derived from the sources by H. Koskenniemi, 1956, *Studien*), that is, to bridge physical absence and turn it into presence. To put it otherwise, that a letter is one half of a conversation. For Hübner, "so ist dadurch die Diastase von Brief und Rede im Grundsatz durchbrochen."[270] But if by "Rede," rhetoric is meant in the ancient technical sense (the art of public speaking), then this does not necessarily follow. A personal conversation is quite different from a public speech, and this was precisely one of the points of the ancients in differentiating letters from speeches.[271] With respect to Paul, Hübner makes an interesting suggestion that bears some consideration. He remarks that Paul was in essence a preacher, and "sofern er schreibt, 'redend schreibt.'" In other words Paul's letters were substitutes not for a conversation, but for a sermon/ speech.[272] There is some point to this. After all, Paul wrote most of his letters to Christian churches, i.e., *groups* of people, and not individual friends. Of course Hübner assumes, but does not prove, that early Christian sermons could be classified in terms of Greco-Roman rhetoric.[273]

But more recently, due to the interest in rhetorical exegesis in recent years, biblical scholars concerned primarily with epistolography have also addressed this relation. So it is that S. K. Stowers devotes some attention to the matter. Stowers argues that ancient letters must be approached with a knowledge of both ancient epistolary *and*

---

[268]   1984, *New Testament*, 141.
[269]   1984, "Galaterbrief."
[270]   1984, "Galaterbrief," 245, cf. G. A. Kennedy above.
[271]   Cf. Cic. *Fam.* 9.21.1 cited above.
[272]   Cf. J. White (1983, "Paul," 439) who also references H. Thyen, *Der Stil der jüdisch-hellenistischen Homilie* (FRLANT 47; Göttingen: Vandenhoeck & Ruprecht, 1955) who argues that the body of Paul's letters is influenced by synagogue homily (59-63).
[273]   This question would seem to me difficult to prove. *If* by other means, some of Paul's letters could be shown to have the structural form of a Greco-Roman speech, then it could be perhaps concluded that he preached using such a structure. The only other way to determine the structure of early Christian preaching would perhaps be to analyse some of the early Christian letters which *appear* to be essentially sermons in form. Note, for example, Van Unnik's analysis of the first letter of Clement mentioned below (§ 4).

rhetorical theory. He views the letters of Paul as examples of paraenetic rhetoric, that is, hortatory argumentation as was developed in Greco-Roman rhetoric.[274] He proceeds (27f) to associate most types of ancient letters with epideictic rhetoric, which was often defined by the ancients in terms of praise or blame. Stowers makes the connection here by arguing that social relationships and structures were very important in the Greco-Roman world, and most letters had to do with these relationships. Further, "the giving of praise and blame was essential to the working of these institutions in antiquity" (27). Here is thus the connection he makes. One must ask whether such a general observation proves that the *methods* of rhetorical theory for epideictic *speeches* are relevant to letters. On pp.51f Stowers discusses this relationship in more detail. There he notes that there are letter types that would fit in each one of the traditional three types of rhetoric (forensic, deliberative, epideictic) and there are some that do not seem to fit any. He correctly adds that rhetorical theory tended to neglect discussion of the epideictic type which itself could become a catch-all category for whatever did not fit into the former two categories.

But in all this a crucial step has been missed. Is it correct procedure to apply *rhetorical* genres (i.e., genres formulated to apply to public speeches, e.g., forensic, deliberative, epideictic) to letters? Stowers (52) proceeds to acknowledge the independence of letter writing and rhetoric in antiquity and adds that because of this, "classification of letter types according to the three species of rhetoric only partially works." Another reason is the relation of many letters (including those of Paul in Stowers' opinion, 42f) to ancient paraenetic tradition, which is "only tangentally related to rhetorical theory." Elsewhere (93, cf. 107) he adds: "Exhortation transcends the rhetorical categories." Nowhere does Stowers discuss the all-important question as to whether ancient letters, even if they may loosely be categorised as epideictic or deliberative, use the *methods* prescribed for these genres by rhetorical theory. If the categorisation of ancient letters according to rhetorical genres is to have any real meaning, then these rhetorical genres must not be divorced from the methods associated with them in rhetorical theory.

On a different level, Stowers (56) also argues that the fact that letter writers generally had a rhetorical education means that they would have been well provided "with

---

[274] 1986, *Letter*, 23. Stowers relies here upon the work of Abraham Malherbe. In fact, Stowers is inclined to classify most Christian letters of the first and second centuries as hortatory (43). Christian letters of the fourth and fifth centuries became more stylised and can more frequently be classified in terms of rhetorical genres. Stowers rightly adds that Paul's style would have been deemed unacceptable in the fourth century (46). Letters such as those from Basil the Great are full of (at least stylistic) rhetorical flourish, and greatly influenced by Atticism.

techniques for the endless elaboration and development of the basic ideal captured in the handbook descriptions." By "handbook descriptions" he is referring to the sample letters provided with the epistolary types in [Demetr.] *Typ.* and [Lib.] *Ep.Char.*. Stowers thus means to say that even apart from the question of rhetorical genres, letter writers in antiquity may have been more generally influenced by rhetorical methods of elaboration and development.

4 Ancient Letter-Speeches

Despite the fact that ancient letters cannot automatically be classified into one of the three rhetorical-speech genres, there *were* letters in antiquity that were essentially rhetorical writings given an epistolary frame. This fact was already recognised by Dionysius of Halicarnassus in the first century AD. Dionysius, in a discussion of Plato's scanty rhetorical speeches, says: δημηγορία δὲ οὐδεμία, πλὴν εἴ τις ἄρα τὰς ἐπιστολὰς βούλεται δημηγορίας καλεῖν (But there is not one deliberative speech, unless perhaps someone wishes to call his letters deliberative speeches, *Dem.* 23, p.180,4-6 U.-R.). Dionysius definitely relates Plato's letters to deliberative rhetoric in some kind of way.[275] Further in *Th.* 42 he lists a number of δημηγορικοὶ λόγοι in Thucydides which he particularly admires. Among these is a letter sent by the general Nikias to the Athenians (Th. 7.11-15).

Sykutris has argued that the casting of a formal speech in letter form enabled the author to avoid strict conformance to the formal rules applying to the speech-genre.[276] Sykutris in fact refers to the *open letter* as a kind of letter-speech. "Der Inhalt eines publizistischen Briefes ist fast derselbe wie der einer Rede" (201). It was a type of literature using the letter form as a cloak. He gives as examples Demosthenes' letters from exile and the letters of Isocrates. He notes further that open letters became quite popular among the Romans, especially in the first century BC, but that under the monarchy the practice declined (but cf. Apollonius of Tyana, *Ep.* 103, 109, and Aristides, *Or.* 19 for Greek examples from the imperial period).

An interesting point is hinted at by Sykutris here, namely, that we may distinguish between letters which are nothing but a speech with a letter-opening and closing, and letters which, whilst clearly rhetorical, are not exactly constructed according to the form of a speech.

---

[275] See the discussion of Plato's letters below.
[276] 1931, "Epistolographie," 200.

Letters of the latter kind are dealt with in the work of J. Klek (1919, *Symbuleutici*). In defining the deliberative genre, Klek places it within the context of literary genres in general (29-41) and does not limit his definition to the boundaries of rhetorical theory. This is because he sees the origin of symbouleutic (deliberative) in the ancient poets (e.g., Hesiod's *Opera et Dies*). Thus by the time rhetorical theorists began using the term it was already an established genre. Klek's analysis of deliberative rhetoric is not at all bound to the *divisio* of a (deliberative) speech. Nevertheless, what he defines as deliberative rhetoric is broadly what rhetorical theory also meant.[277] His definition of the symbouleutic (deliberative) genre in general is: that genre in which "*certae personae, cuius voluntas regatur, et certae condicionis exstant vestigia atque artis rhetoricae leges cernuntur*" (41). By "laws of the art of rhetoric," he clearly means the kinds of arguments and advice prescribed by the rhetorical theorists, cf. 79. Of the *letters* belonging to this genre (and therefore conforming to rhetorical laws), he analyses Plato, *Ep.* 7 and 8; Q. Cicero, *Pet.* (a letter to his brother M. T. Cicero); Cicero, *Q.fr.* 1.1; Pliny, *Ep.* 8.24; 9.5; Isocrates, *Ep.* 1, 3, 6, 9; *Socraticorum Epistula* 30; and Sallust, *Rep.*. All these letters are defended as real and rhetorical, although he admits some were also written with a view to publication (e.g., Pl. *Ep.* 8, p.72).

There are, however, certain letters from antiquity which may profitably be analysed in terms of a rhetorical *speech*. J. A. Goldstein has shown, for example, that the first four letters of Demosthenes, written in exile to the assembly in Athens, are effectively deliberative speeches.[278] Demosthenes states that were he present he would address the Athenians himself, but because of his situation he must write his thoughts in a letter, *Ep.* 3.35 ταῦτα δ', εἰ μὲν παρῆν, λέγων ἂν ὑμᾶς ἐδίδασκον· ἐπειδὴ δ' ἐν τοιούτοις εἰμί, ... γράψας ἐπέσταλκα. What is important is the fact that the letters he wrote are structured using rhetorical methodology. Demosthenes *might* just as easily have made the same points in a more informal and epistolographical way. He didn't.

---

[277] Klek discusses the particular use of the deliberative genre by rhetorical theoreticians and schools on pp.157-62. Here he argues that rhetoricians treated deliberative speeches as a kind of exercise to build up to the more difficult (and for a rhetor much more important) judicial speeches. Because of this fact the nature of deliberative rhetoric amongst the rhetoricians underwent some modifications.

[278] 1968, *Letters*; see also the appraisal by D. M. Macdowell, 1970, "Review." Goldstein prefers the term "*demegoria*" which properly denotes political speeches, but in terms of rhetorical theory is equivalent to the term "deliberative speech." Goldstein's book has made a convincing case for the authenticity of the first four letters of Demosthenes. An important part of his case is the rhetorical analysis of these letters in terms of *demegoriae* conforming to the rhetorical rules and practice of fourth century BC Athens (133-81). For our purposes the question of authenticity is less important than the fact that such rhetorical letters were accepted as authentic in antiquity.

Early Christian tradition has also been clearly shown to utilise this way of letter-writing. W. C. van Unnik, for instance, has carefully analysed the form of the first letter of Clement.[279] Van Unnik shows beyond reasonable doubt that this letter consciously conforms to the deliberative genre.[280]

H. D. Betz was the first New Testament scholar who sought to place a letter of Paul in terms of an ancient Greek tradition of letter-speech.[281] In his commentary on Paul's letter to the Galatians he introduces the "genre of the apologetic letter."[282] He does this with reference to comments made by A. Momigliano, 1971, *Development*. Betz explains that this genre arose in the fourth century (Momigliano, p.62 is referenced) and that Momigliano "makes the Socratics responsible for creating the genre of the apologetic letter."[283] Thus via this authority in classics, Betz attempts to establish a backdrop for his analysis of the letter to the Galatians.

Yet there is a problem with Betz' literary analysis. Momigliano *not once* speaks of a "genre" of the apologetic letter! In his discussion of the development of Greek biography he mentions various examples of autobiographical literature in the fourth century BC. Among these examples is Plato's 7th letter. Now on page 60 Momigliano happens to call Plato's 7th letter "apologetic." But this is a far cry from saying that it is the first of a new genre for which the Socratics were responsible! Unfortunately, Betz only makes the misconstrual worse when he adds that the subsequent history of this genre is difficult to trace "since most of the pertinent literature did not survive." He immediately cites Momigliano (62):

> "We cannot, *therefore* [italics mine, R.D.A.], see the exact place of Plato's letter in the history of ancient autobiographical production. But one vaguely feels the Platonic precedent in Epicurus, Seneca, and perhaps St. Paul."

---

[279] 1970, *Studies*.

[280] This letter even calls itself τὴν συμβουλὴν ἡμῶν (58), and at 63: ... τὴν ἔντευξιν [i.e., "speech"] ἣν ἐποιησάμεθα περὶ εἰρήνης καὶ ὁμονοίας ἐν τῇδε τῇ ἐπιστολῇ. Van Unnik shows that deliberative speeches concerning peace and concord were a commonplace in antiquity. The clarity of (rhetorical) form in such a letter as this is *prima facie* nowhere to be seen in the letters of Paul. On rhetoric in the first letter of Clement see also B. E. Bowe, *A Church in Crisis: Ecclesiology and Paraenesis in Clement of Rome* (Harvard Dissertations in Religion 23; Memphis: Fortress Press, 1988).

[281] He is also one of the few New Testament scholars who have paid attention to the relation of rhetoric to epistolography in a rhetorical analysis of Paul's letter. His student M. M. Mitchell has produced an interesting dissertation on Paul's first letter to the Corinthians with careful attention to (among other matters) epistolary rhetoric. See the discussion below, chapter six, § 1.2.

[282] 1979, *Galatians*, 14-15; cf. 1975, "Composition," 353-79.

[283] Momigliano, pp.60-62.

It seems as if Momigliano is speaking in reference to the apologetic letter genre, however in context Momigliano is, in fact, referring to "autobiographical letters." Betz goes on to say that his analysis of the letter to the Galatians now shows that Momigliano's cautious "perhaps" is no longer necessary. Betz appears to mean that the letter to the Galatians is also apologetic, but Momigliano was referring to the element of autobiography![284]

D. E. Aune in his appraisal of Betz' work also noticed this discrepancy in argumentation and asked further how one can maintain that a particular composition belongs to a genre in which most of the examples from antiquity are no longer extant.[285] He has a point here, though for Betz this is overcome by the idea that the apologetic letter in its body conformed to the genre of the judicial speech. Aune goes on to ask how one can properly determine the genre (of apologetic letter) when those examples that have survived (and here he appears only to be thinking of the 7th letter of Plato) "have not been subjected to an intensive generic analysis?" His point is well taken, namely, that Betz does not analyse any examples of such letters to determine if the letter to the Galatians falls into the same category. He assumes that reliance on rhetorical theory is sufficient and proceeds to analyse Paul's letter as a formal defence speech complete with the *partes orationis*. In fact, had Betz attempted to analyse Plato's letter, he would have soon found that this letter defies *any* analysis in terms of rhetorical *partes orationis*![286] But Aune is further apparently unaware of the genre analysis of Plato's 7th letter by J. Klek.

Klek, writing in 1919, realised that many scholars tended to typify Plato's 7th letter as apologetic, yet he argued forcefully that whilst the letter certainly had an apologetic strain, the genre of the letter itself was clearly deliberative.[287]

---

[284] Betz' use of sources does not always appear to be the most careful. For a similar case detected by J. F. M. Smit, see 1989b, "Letter," 2n.

[285] 1981, "Review," 324.

[286] It should, perhaps, be noted that Betz did not see fit to alter this section in the German translation of 1988. The critique at this point is also not mentioned in his new preface, although a list of critical essays on the American edition is given in an appendix on p.574.

[287] One of the difficult features, structurally, of Plato's 7th letter is the fact that it contains mostly narrative. The broad structure includes an introduction, narrative of Plato's first sojourn in Sicily, narrative of his second sojourn, advice concerning the correct constitution of a state, and narrative of his third sojourn in Sicily. Plato opens the letter by stating that Dio's friends (the addressees) had written to him for advice (on the state). Plato agrees to give this if they are of the same mind as the late Dio. Plato proceeds to offer this advice by relating the (same) advice which he gave to Dio and Dionysius in Sicily. In the middle section where this advice is given, an important part is put in the mouth of Dio himself. According to Klek, the first narrative functions as the necessary background to support this. It shows how Plato and Dio came to the advice that he now offers. The second and third narratives are additions to which there is a distinct measure of self-defence, yet they are clearly not the main point of the letter, which is to give advice, cf. 330c ὑμῖν πρῶτον μὲν συμβουλεύσας ἃ χρὴ ποιεῖν ἐκ τῶν νῦν γεγονότων, ὕστερον τὰ περὶ ταῦτα [i.e., that what he did on his second sojourn was εἰκότα τε καὶ δίκαια] διέξειμι, τῶν ἐπανερωτώντων ἕνεκα τί δὴ βουλόμενος ἦλθον τὸ δεύτερον, ἵνα μὴ τὰ πάρεργα ὡς ἔργα μοι συμ-

It is unfortunate that Betz is apparently unaware of the study of Goldstein on the letters of Demosthenes (cited above). Goldstein has shown that *Ep.* 2 of Demosthenes is apologetic. Yet Goldstein also shows that this letter is not forensic, but deliberative. It is not addressed to a court, but to the assembly of the people who are at the same time his opponents. Therefore the proposition is not related to a point of law (namely, that Demosthenes be allowed to return from exile). Goldstein calls it an example of an apologetic δημηγορία. In a detailed rhetorical analysis he shows how the letter conforms to the rhetorical rules and expectations of deliberative rhetoric, as opposed to forensic rhetoric (157-66).[288]

Goldstein makes a good case for the existence of apologetic δημηγορίαι, i.e., apologetic defence speeches intended not for the court but for the assembly. He analyses Andocides' *de Reditu* in this vein (166-69) and concludes:

> "The appeals of Demosthenes and Andocides are apology throughout and bear considerable resemblance to forensic speeches. Nevertheless, their structure differs significantly from that of a defence before a court. ... there is no detailed discussion of the events which lay behind the accusations. The exact nature of the accusations is nowhere stated, and the opposition is nowhere named. Neither work contains personal invective. [Goldstein has argued that this was conventionally avoided in δημηγορίαι] ... Both orators begin with argument under the heads of the *telika kephalaia* [i.e., deliberative method of argumentation]." (169)

Demosthenes' 2nd letter would *prima facie* appear to be a much closer example to Paul's letter to the Galatians than Plato's 7th letter. It is both apologetic, and addressed to an assembly of people who are at the same time, in a manner of speaking, the writer's opponents. Betz' desire to place his vision of the letter to the Galatians within a classical letter-tradition that was both apologetic and related to the rules of rhetoric (including the *divisio* of a speech), would have been well served by Demosthenes *Ep.* 2.[289]

βαίνη λεγόμενα.
Interestingly, a recent analysis by H. Probst (1991, *Paulus*, 63-70) also argues against an apologetic interpretation. Probst does not seem to have been aware of Klek's work.

[288] For example, the charges against Demosthenes as such are nowhere mentioned as would be expected in a forensic defence (159). As arguments the τελικὰ κεφάλαια, typical of δημηγορίαι, are used first and only later does he take up a defence of his innocence in the Harpalus affair (cf. 164).

[289] For a critique of Betz' vision of the letter to the Galatians as a letter-speech, see the section on this letter below (chapter four, § 1).

5 Summary

We have seen above (§ 1) that to categorise Paul's letters onesidedly as fresh and real, thereby implying that they must be devoid of rhetoric, cannot be justified. If anything, there are various arguments which point to Paul's letters as being more closely related to the so-called literary letters of antiquity than those discovered among the papyri.

Yet we have also seen (§§ 2-3) that ancient letters cannot simply be forced into the threefold structural categorisation of ancient rhetoric. Letters could be classified in a variety of ways as they were in antiquity and still are in modern epistolary scholarship. This merely reflects the variety of forms letters could take. But this does not mean that letters can never be classified in terms of structural rhetorical categories (§ 4). Nevertheless, the first thoroughgoing attempt to do this in New Testament scholarship has rightly met with substantial criticism.

But this does not mean that Paul's letters may not have been influenced by rhetorical methods of style and argumentation more generally. We have indicated above several factors that suggest this to be likely. In fact, New Testament scholarship has of late devoted considerable attention to this aspect of Pauline studies. In the following section we shall attempt to review some of the work done in this area on Paul's letters to the Galatians, Romans, and the first letter to the Corinthians. These letters, particularly that addressed to the Galatians, have been the main focus of attention in recent years. Their generally accepted structural integrity and authorship make them quite suitable for a study on ancient rhetorical theory and Paul. In addition to the review of recent scholarship, we will also provide our own rhetorical analysis of the argumentative portions of the letters to the Galatians and Romans. The first letter to the Corinthians, as we shall show, is not suited to such an analysis.

IV The Letter to the Galatians 1 - 5.12

1 Recent Scholarship

With respect to Paul's letter to the Galatians, we have already made reference to the work of H. D. Betz.[290] Betz (unsuccessfully) attempted to place this letter in a so-called "apologetic" letter tradition. This aside, his analysis of the letter to the Galatians in terms of a forensic defence speech has merited further consideration. In fact his commentary has been the springboard for considerable debate as to the rhetorical genre of the letter. As far as rhetorical analysis is concerned, however, apart from a rhetorically based forensic outline, Betz does not make much use of ancient rhetoric in the actual text of his commentary. Although some have accepted his general analysis, most scholars have seen inescapable weaknesses in his use of the forensic model.[291] One obvious weakness is the difficulty of incorporating the paraenesis of *Ep. Gal.* 5-6 into a forensic scheme. Betz himself admitted that his *exhortatio* was not discussed by rhetorical theoreticians.[292]

---

[290] 1979, *Galatians*. See pp.106-108.

[291] It has been accepted (with minor modification) by J. D. Hester, 1984, "Structure"; cf. 1986, "Use"; and also apparently (I have not seen this book myself) by B. H. Brinsmead, *Galatians - Dialogical Response to Opponents* (SBLDS 65; Chico, Calif.: Scholars Press, 1982).

For criticism of the forensic structure see, e.g., P. W. Meyer (1981, "Review"); D. E. Aune (1981, "Review"); G. A. Kennedy (1984, *New Testament*, 144-52); G. W. Hansen (1989, *Abraham*); J. F. M. Smit (1989b, "Letter"); J. Schoon-Janssen (1991, "*Apologien*," 70-82); C. J. Classen (1993, "Epistles," 286-88).

R. N. Longenecker (1990, *Galatians*) criticises aspects of Betz' proposal on pp.cix - cxiii, especially the notion that Paul might be genealogically dependent upon rhetorical theory. He prefers to speak of an "analogical" approach. Rhetoric was "in the air." He also attempts to pay more attention to epistolographic formulae. Despite this, in the text of his commentary Betz' basic rhetorical scheme is *maintained*, although slightly modified. Longenecker includes a *narratio* (*Ep.Gal.* 1.11 - 2.14), *propositio* (*Ep.Gal.* 2.15-21) and *probatio* (*Ep.Gal.* 3.1 - 4.11). Even though he notes that *exhortatio* has no place in rhetorical theory, yet he classifies *Ep.Gal.* 4.12ff as *exhortatio* and states that Paul shifts here from judicial to deliberative rhetoric.

[292] Betz attempts to answer his critics on this point in the German translation of his commentary (1988, *Galaterbrief*). There he suggests that one should not expect paraenesis to be discussed in rhetorical handbooks: "Die Paränese findet sich ja in erster Linie bei den Philosophen und deren Rhetorik, angefangen mit Plato und Aristoteles. Die philosophischen Apologien, wie etwa Platos Apologie oder Brief VII, enthalten auch Paränese und sind insgesamt paränetisch ausgerichtet. ... Trotz der hier noch zu leistenden Arbeit kann jedoch schon jetzt gesagt werden, daß die Paränese des Galaterbriefes nicht in grundsätzlichem Widerspruch zur apologetischen Rhetorik steht" (2-3).

Betz, however, confuses two separate things, namely, philosophical discussions and treatises, and rhetorical theory and practice. Of course Aristotle was concerned with ethics and paraenesis. Yet even in Aristotle's *Rhetoric* there is no place given to paraenesis. That Betz finds paraenesis in Plato's 7th letter

In an attempt to overcome the problem, D. E. Aune suggested that the letter to the Galatians should be viewed as a mixture of forensic and deliberative rhetoric.[293] He was followed in this suggestion by G. W. Hansen.[294] However, such a classification seems, rather, to suggest that the standard rhetorical genres don't exactly fit this letter. And this is precisely the point made by the classicist C. J. Classen.[295]

Others have argued that the letter to the Galatians fits quite simply into the deliberative genre. So, for example, G. A. Kennedy, and his former student R. G. Hall.[296] Hall (277) insists that any rhetorical analysis of a document must first

---

may be true (not, however, the kind of general paraenesis found in *Ep.Gal.* 5), but then Plato's 7th letter is not organised according to the *divisio* of a forensic speech - even *if* one would allow that it may be considered an apologetic letter (see above, chapter three, § 4). With respect to the *Apologia* of Socrates, I presume he is referring to the advice Socrates offers his friends upon pronouncement of the penalty of death. At this point, however, Socrates' rhetorical speech has ended and his advice is added as a personal comment to his friends. It has nothing to do with rhetorical theory or practice.

One may also comment on Betz' insistence that *Ep.Gal.* 1.12 - 2.14 is the *narratio* of the defence speech. Were it a *narratio*, we should at least expect something like a description of how the Judaisers came into being, something of their history of trouble making, and how they came to Galatia and what damage they did there. For further comments on the rhetorical genre of the letter to the Galatians see p.166.

[293] 1981, "Review."

[294] 1989, *Abraham*, 58-59. Hansen, however, uses a modern rhetorical approach in his analysis. He attempts to combine an epistolary analysis with a rhetorical analysis. His epistolary analysis is interesting, highlighting many epistolary conventions in the letter to the Galatians. He views the basic structure as that of a rebuke-request letter and uses this to explain the different use of Abraham in *Ep.Gal.* 3 and 4 (each has a different function). Behind both he understands a background known to the Galatian Christians, hence their vagueness to us today.

The attempt of W. Harnisch (1987, "Einübung") to argue that the paraenetic section takes the form of the deliberative genre (i.e., προτρεπτικός/ ἀποτρεπτικός, citing Arist. *Rh.*, see pp.286-87) fails to understand the nature of a rhetorical deliberative speech.

[295] 1993, "Epistles," 286-88.

[296] Kennedy, 1984, *Testament*, 144-52; Hall, 1987, "Outline." Apparently N. Dahl had already suggested in 1973 that the letter to the Galatians "showed signs of fitting the symbouleutic or deliberative genre of speech" (in a paper submitted to the Paul Seminar of the Society of Biblical Literature, *vid.* W. Wuellner, 1991, "Rhetoric," 130). In addition, see M. Bachmann, 1992, *Sünder*, 156-60, and C. D. Stanley, 1990, "Curse," 491. Stanley's article makes little use of ancient rhetorical theory as such. His interpretation hinges on an incorrect interpretation of *Ep.Gal.* 3.10 which he paraphrases as follows: "Anyone who chooses to abide by the Jewish Torah in order to secure participation in Abraham's 'blessing' is placed in a situation where he or she is threatened instead with a 'curse,' since the law itself pronounces a curse on anyone who fails to live up to every single one of its requirements." This interpretation is defended on the basis of the so-called conditionality of ὅσοι. Stanley has failed to notice that the "conditionality" (if one wishes to use that term) of ὅσοι refers to those who may or may not live "by the works of the law." The connection between those who live "by the works of the law" and those "under a curse" is fixed (by the verb εἰσίν), and not conditional. Paul's point is that *if* you live by the works of the law, then you are (certainly) under a curse. Stanley's interpretation would require something like: ὅσοι γὰρ ἐξ ἔργων νόμου εἰσὶν, ὑπὸ κατάραν εἶναι κινδυνεύουσι. It is, perhaps, worth noting that Stanley has also misconstrued Calvin's paraphrase of the same verse. The translation "liable to the curse" in context quite clearly means "guilty" and is not intended to be conditional (Calvin's latin is *maledictioni obnoxios*).

determine the rhetorical species (i.e., judicial, deliberative, or epideictic). As far as the letter to the Galatians is concerned, he argues that if the so-called *exhortatio* is to be explained, the letter *must* be considered deliberative (281), and he goes on to provide his own outline for the letter on this supposition. This is, however, no solution. Rhetorical theorists never discuss general *exhortatio* at all, whether the genre is deliberative or not.

In an article published in 1991 Hall focuses on an interesting aspect of rhetorical theory, namely, the historical value of a διήγησις (*narratio*) in a speech.[297] He quite correctly shows that rhetorical theory allowed the orator to carefully invent matter for inclusion in the narration of a speech in order to make it more persuasive (310-14). In other words, rhetorical theory permitted the creation of a fictionalised account, providing it was crafted in such a way so as not to arouse suspicion. What Hall does not say, but ought to be added, is that the context of such advice in rhetorical theory is that of a *narratio* in a defence speech. This was the usual place for a *narratio*, since a defence lawyer would normally be expected to review the events of the alleged crime, interpreting them in his favour, or, as opportunity presented itself, inventing a version of the story that supported his client. It is important to note that such activity was not really considered morally wrong. The *defence* of a man, even if considered guilty, could be considered virtuous conduct (cf. Cic. *Off.* 2.51; *Vat.* 5; Quint. *Inst.* 12.1.33-45). In terms of application to the letter to the Galatians, Hall evidently does not wish to argue that Paul invented material, but he does wish to issue a caution as to the historical nature of what is said. By comparing *Ep. Gal.* 1.11-12 and 1 *Ep. Cor.* 15.1-3, he quite rightly demonstrates that Paul presents and interprets his material in accordance with the point he is making (314). He also argues that the journey to Jerusalem mentioned in *Ep. Gal.* 2.1 ("after fourteen years") does not have to mean that Paul was not more frequently in Jerusalem. But his argument here does not really depend on his analysis of rhetorical theory (i.e., that the truth may be stretched to make an argumentative point) for he argues that this whole passage is *not* apologetical, and that Paul's argumentative point is *not* that he did not ever visit Jerusalem between the stay mentioned in *Ep. Gal.* 1.18 and that in 2.1. In any case, it should be remembered that Hall wishes to view this letter as a *deliberative* speech/ letter. The character of a deliberative *narratio* should not simply be equated with that of a judicial defence speech.

W. B. Russell has also provided a general rhetorical analysis of the argumentation in this letter.[298] Russell follows Kennedy's methodology and consequently makes no

---

[297] 1991, "Inference."
[298] 1993, "Analysis."

real distinction between ancient or modern rhetoric.[299] He also chooses for the deliberative genre (351), arguing that the paraenetic section of the letter should be viewed as a
separate argument, namely, that only Paul's Gospel gives true deliverance from sin's
power through the Holy Spirit. This suggestion, however, belies the point that Paul
does not present his paraenesis as *deliberative argument*. Russell's analysis of the
argumentation of the letter to the Galatians (416-39) is mostly concerned with the
arrangement of the arguments (part of $\tau \acute{\alpha} \xi \iota \varsigma$), although he does not present much in the
way of specific application of rhetorical theory.

Another scholar who considers the letter to the Galatians to be deliberative
rhetoric is J. F. M. Smit.[300] Yet Smit's analysis and outline of the letter is considerably
different to that of Hall. Furthermore, Smit is of the opinion that the *exhortatio* cannot
be fitted into any traditional rhetorical genre. He argues that it is in fact a later inter-
polation(!).

The studies of Smit are interesting in several respects. He is one of the few
scholars who has seen the need to discern which are the most appropriate sources of
ancient rhetorical theory to utilise with respect to the letters of Paul. He stresses the
need to use sources more directly related to Hellenistic rhetoric and suggests that the
Rhetorica ad Herennium and Cicero's *de Inventione* meet this need.[301]

Smit's own interpretation of the letter to the Galatians is also rather interesting,
especially that of 4.12 - 6.18 as more fully worked out in 1986, "Redactie." He provides a persuasive case for the fact that a hortatory section such as 5.13 - 6.10 does not
fit in a rhetorical analysis of the letter - not even as deliberative rhetoric. He attempts
to make a case for viewing this passage (5.13 - 6.10) as a later redactional addition by

---

[299] See above, chapter one, § 5.
[300] 1989b, "Letter." Smit's essay is based on four other publications in Dutch: 1984, "Benadering";
1985b, "Heidenen"; 1985a, "Paulus"; but especially 1986, "Redactie."
[301] 1989b, "Letter." He adds that Cicero's later work *de Oratore* is based on his later experience (and
thus not on Hellenistic Greek sources). However, because of the fact that these sources concentrate
heavily on judicial rhetoric, Smit adds that the *Rhetorica ad Alexandrum* of *c.* 300 BC (which does not
exhibit this lopsided concentration) can also be useful. In (1991) "Genre," 194-95 he inadvisedly adds
Cicero's *Partitiones Oratoriae* as an acceptable source (on the philosophical nature of this treatise see
above, chapter two, § 2.2.1).
    Smit also argues that the use of Quintilian ought to be avoided as a later *Roman* development of
Greek rhetoric (but see p.79 and p.82 above). Quintilian is said to be too encyclopedic to be used with
profit and therefore introduces the danger of eclecticism. What precisely this danger amounts to Smit
does not say, but the comment occurs in the context of the observation that Betz often uses incidental
remarks from Quintilian (frequently interpreted in a strange way) to justify his rhetorical interpretation
(1989b, "Letter," 6). It is interesting to note that in 1991 ("Genre," 194-95) Smit states of Quintilian:
"Because of the encyclopedic character of this work I shall use it mainly to control whether the views,
brought forward in the other handbooks, are indeed generally accepted."

arguing that various concepts in this section are used in a way contradictory to the rest of the letter. As far as his rhetorical analysis itself is concerned, he makes a good case *prima facie* for viewing 4.12 - 5.12 as the *peroratio*/ ἐπίλογος of the speech/ letter.[302] This *peroratio* is said to be made up of three sections typically found according to rhetorical theory, namely, *conquestio*/ ἔλεος (arousal of pity, 4.12-20), *recapitulatio*/ ἀνακεφαλαίωσις (summary, 4.21 - 5.6) and *indignatio*/ δείνωσις (arousal of hostile emotions against some person or matter, 5.7-12). Having excised 5.13 - 6.10 he goes on to argue that 6.11-18 forms a fourth part of the *peroratio*, namely, the *amplificatio*/ αὔξησις. Smit, whilst noticing that Cic. *Inv.* 1.100-105 on *indignatio* is equivalent to the section entitled *amplificatio* in *Rhet.Her.* 2.47-49,[303] nevertheless states that *amplificatio* is elsewhere presented as a fourth part of the *peroratio*, next to the three abovementioned. However, he offers no proof of this apart from an irrelevant citation from J. Martin's *Rhetorik* (1974).[304]

Smit's characterisation of the *conquestio* is further interesting in that he too, just as Betz, sees here a series of τόποι. Betz had characterised 4.12-20 as a series of (epistolary) friendship τόποι and argued that this solved the problem of the rather loose thread that seemed to run through these verses.[305] Smit, however, argues that we have *loci misericordiae* here, i.e., τόποι designed to evoke sympathy.[306] He provides a rhetorical connection by showing that such τόποι belonged to the *conquestio* section of a peroration. His citation of Cic. *Inv.* 1.107 seems appropriate (the *locus* whereby one compares former prosperity with present evils).

According to Smit, Paul enlivens his *recapitulatio* by utilising the device of προσωποποιΐα, meaning that he personifies the law and brings it on stage, as it were, to argue for him. Smit notes that the use of this device is warmly recommended by the

---

302 1986, "Redactie," 125-27.

303 Both treatises present a tripartite division of the ἐπίλογος, and although the second section goes under a separate name in the respective treatises and is to some extent treated differently, both are very clearly based upon the *same* source.

304 1986, "Redactie," 136 note 65. One might, however, think of Arist. *Rh.* 3.19 where the ἐπίλογος is divided into four parts, 1) influencing the audience to think well of oneself and negatively of the opponent, 2) αὔξησις, 3) exciting the emotions of the audience, 4) ἀνάμνησις.

305 Betz (1975, "Literary Composition," 372) also attempted to provide rhetorical precedence by referring to Quint. *Inst.* 5.11.41 where Quintilian discusses the use of universal sayings and gives as an example: *ubi amici, ibi opes.* Yet Quintilian's point (in context) is that such sayings can function as a kind of authoritative precedent to be used to bolster a particular argument. This has nothing to do with a passage where various friendship sayings are supposedly linked together to form an argument all on their own. Betz has appropriately omitted reference to Quintilian in his commentary on this passage.

306 1986, "Redactie," 117.

rhetorical theorists for the summary in the conclusion of a speech (121).[307] He also characterises the questions in 4.21-22 as the device of *communicatio* (120).[308] Interestingly, in 1989b, "Letter," although retaining his point with respect to προσωποποιΐα (but dropping this technical term), he omits any mention of *communicatio*.[309]

Smit's article of 1989 provides a rhetorical analysis of the section he defines as the *confirmatio* (i.e., the proof section, 3.1 - 4.11), based upon Cic. *Inv.* 1.47ff (Cicero's section on arguments from probability in a *confirmatio*).[310] Here he sees an introduction (3.1-5) using the reception of the Holy Spirit as a *signum*, followed by three rounds of arguments (3.6-14; 3.15-29; 4.1-7). Each argument is said to begin with a *comparabile*. The first is basically a *iudicatum* (based on authority), and the second and third are characterised as *credibile* which Smit defines as "a conviction which is shared by the audience and which does not need corroborating evidence." The argument of 3.6-14 is "the confession of the oneness of God," and that of 4.1-7 "the faith that God, by sending his Son, has achieved the eschatological revolution." These arguments are followed by an emotional conclusion (4.8-11) evoking πάθος because of the use of *correctio* and *dubitatio*.

Smit has certainly seen that Paul's argumentation is well structured, and his analysis highlights this fact. Certainly 3.15; 4.1 and 4.8 are transition points of sorts. Yet the analysis seems to me to over-compartmentalise what is essentially one long connected argument of the apostle (see my analysis below, § 2.4). Further, his references to rhetorical devices are sometimes questionable. A *credibile* as defined by Cicero (*Inv.* 1.48) is one of several arguments based on probability.[311] It is the use of an opinion thought to be generally shared by the audience. An argument by appeal to an agreed

---

[307] He cites Cic. *Inv.* 1.100; Quint. *Inst.* 1.52.99 and adds that προσωποποιΐα is the first of nine τόποι for a conclusion mentioned by Apsines. Smit's identification of προσωποποιΐα here is, however, somewhat far-fetched.
[308] Whilst the notation of the figure is appropriate (in Greek, ἀνακοίνωσις, see the select glossary *s.v.*), Smit rather inappropriately cites Quint. *Inst.* 6.1.5 on p.126. Quintilian is here dealing not with rhetorical questions, but with actual questions the opponent will be expected to answer.
[309] Did he, perhaps, review his previous argumentation in the light of his criticism of Betz with respect to the eclectic use of Quintilian? It is noticeable that he also swapped the term *peroratio* (cf. Quint. *Inst.* 6.1.1) used in 1986, "Redactie," for the synonym *conclusio* (cf. Cic. *Inv.* 1.98; *Rhet.Her.* 2.47).
[310] 1989b, "Letter," 13-16.
[311] Smit also cites [Arist.] *Rh.Al.* 7, but Anaximenes' εἰκός is defined somewhat differently to Cicero's *credibile*. Anaximenes states: Εἰκὸς μὲν οὖν ἐστιν οὗ λεγομένου παραδείγματα ἐν ταῖς διανοίαις ἔχουσιν οἱ ἀκούοντες. By means of examples he explains that he means arguments that refer to the kinds of experiences (sorrow, pain, desire etc.) which everyone knows and can sympathise with. Clearly, common or shared (dogmatic) convictions (as, e.g., oneness of God, eschatological revolution in the sending of Christ) do not fall into this category.

dogma based on religious conviction would not be considered as merely probable (granting for the sake of argument that this is what Paul is doing)![312]

In 1986 J. D. Hester published an article entitled "The Use and Influence of Rhetoric in Galatians 2:1-14."[313] Hester, strongly influenced by Ch. Perelman/ L. Olbrechts-Tyteca, seeks to identify the use of τόποι and figures in this passage *and* relate them directly to their function in terms of argument (the emphasis of Perelman). Hester's analysis of τόποι follows Perelman's *New Rhetoric* (1969) and is thus of little interest for us here. He does, however, identify a number of figures with the help of ancient rhetoric, although his identifications are sometimes dubious.[314] His analysis of 2.11-14 as a χρεία and 2.15-21 as its development is an interesting suggestion. The passage, however, is not properly a *chria* since Paul is simply describing an incident related to his argument that happened to him personally. The point of a *chria* is to introduce an action or saying of a famous person.[315]

At the conclusion of his article (408) Hester makes the interesting suggestion that Paul may have left the composition of this letter to "one carefully versed in rhetoric." This brings up the difficult question of the place of a secretary in the letters of Paul, a point we shall briefly return to in the conclusions (chapter seven).

---

[312] For my own analysis of the relevant passsages see below, § 2.4.

[313] This substitutes an earlier suggestion made by Hester in 1984, "Structure."

[314] Take, for example, his identification of παράλειψις in 2.3-5 (398). Παράλειψις is the deliberate mention of something whilst stating that you will not mention it but pass it by. Cf. Demetr. *Eloc.* 263 who explains with respect to an example of παράλειψις: ἐν γὰρ τούτοις καὶ εἴρηκεν πάντα, ὅσα ἐβούλετο, καὶ παραλιπεῖν αὐτά φησιν, ὡς δεινότερα εἰπεῖν ἔχων ἕτερα. Hester suggests that the introduction of the controversy over the circumcision of Titus doesn't really flow smoothly in the argument and this motivates his admittedly cautious (cf. note 43) identification of παράλειψις. Yet his definition of it ("to introduce a matter that one proposed to pass over but managed to slip in anyway") omits to mention that this device always includes a statement to the effect that what the orator is speaking about, he will pass by or refuse to speak about. Incidentally, two good New Testament examples of this device are to be found in *Ep. Philem.* 19 and *Ep. Hebr.* 11.32ff.

Another example is the identification of ἀποσιώπησις at *Ep. Gal.* 2.3. According to Hester the thought breaks off at the end of the verse. What should follow is not implied by the context and therefore it is not an example of ellipsis but ἀποσιώπησις. But ἀποσιώπησις as a rhetorical (and not grammatical) figure also involves the orator letting his audience know that he is deliberately breaking off his thought. Even the passage cited by Hester (*Rhet. Her.* 4.41) makes this clear (cf. Quint. *Inst.* 9.4.54-57; Demetr. *Eloc.* 103, 253).

Hester validly points to considerable use of (the τρόπος) μετωνυμία (metonymy) and also περίφρασις (periphrasis), although with respect to the latter he tends to exaggerate. It should be borne in mind that περίφρασις was generally considered to be verbal decoration by rhetorical theorists and thus inessential to the argument (see select glossary cf. *s.v.*). One ought to be able to substitute a simple word (cf. *Rhet. Her.* 4.43).

[315] Hester as much as admits this in note 70 (404-405). Nevertheless, perhaps Paul's use of this incident and his development of what he at that time said (v.14) in verses 15-21 could be *likened* to a *chria* and its development. Yet I doubt this interpretation. That v.15 begins a development of the statement of v.14b seems most unlikely (see my analysis below, § 2.3)

The identification of a "chreia" was included by Hester in a broader article dealing with the epideictic character of *Ep. Gal.* 1 and 2.[316] He begins by having us understand *Ep. Gal.* 1.11-12 as the "*stasis* statement" of Paul's letter.[317] He notes earlier criticism of his speaking of a "*stasis* statement," but defends himself by saying that he means that it was in this statement that the Galatians discovered the *stasis* upon which Paul was to build the elements of his argument. This, however, still shows that Hester has not quite understood the nature and purpose of στάσις doctrine. Rhetorical theorists taught their students about στάσις doctrine to enable them to focus sharply on the point at issue. Treatises generally listed *loci* or ready-made arguments that could be used for each different στάσις. It was never the intention to include a "*stasis* statement*" in one's speech so that the audience would recognise which στάσις the orator had used (e.g., whether it was στοχασμός, μετάληψις, δικαιολογικός, etc.). This would have been a well-nigh impossible task anyway since there was no unanimity on the classification of στάσεις among the rhetorical theorists (see Quintilian's overview of his predecessors on this point, *Inst.* 3.6.29-62). Of course, a statement clarifying the issue at stake was often made in conjunction with the proposition, and an orator's own thinking regarding the στάσις of his speech would surely lie behind such a statement. But the point of such a statement was to clarify the issue to be addressed, and not to tell the audience anything about the orator's own στάσις theory.

Having categorised the στάσις of the letter to the Galatians as one of *qualitas*, Hester notes that it is this *stasis* "that is associated with the epideictic genre." Although he does not say so in so many words, Hester distinctly implies that the *stasis* of *qualitas* belongs with epideictic rhetoric and not forensic rhetoric. His analysis of the "*stasis* statement*" functions as the motivating factor for analysing *Ep. Gal.* 1 - 2 as epideictic rhetoric (281, 297). Unfortunately his only reference to prove this connection is from modern rhetorical theory. In ancient rhetorical theory, despite the occasional insinuation to the contrary, στάσις doctrine was effectively only applied to judicial rhetoric.[318] Moreover, *qualitas* was a *standard* στάσις *for judicial rhetoric*. Discussion under this στάσις generally concerned various means of justifying one's actions. Hester's confusing mix of ancient and modern rhetorical theory here is typical of his whole article.

---

[316] 1991, "Blame."

[317] Hester is building upon his analysis in 1984, "Structure," 226-28. On στάσις, see the entry in the select glossary appended to this book.

[318] See Quint. *Inst.* 3.6.1. Hermagoras seems to have applied his analysis of στάσις doctrine to all the kinds of speeches covered by the three common genres (forensic, deliberative, epideictic), although he does not appear to have used this genre classification, see *Fr.* 3 Matthes, and A. D. Leeman/ A. C. Braet, 1987, *retorica*, 78-79. However, even Hermagoras appears to have worked his στάσις doctrine out with a clear emphasis on judicial rhetoric.

He goes on to classify the letter to the Galatians as an epideictic blame letter. It should, however, be noted that blame in epideictic rhetoric was not usually (was it ever?) the blaming of the audience! Moreover, did an orator ever present an ἐγκώμιον of *himself* as Hester suggests for *Ep. Gal.* 1.11 - 2.21? He goes on to give a rather poor description of epideictic rhetoric in general, unfortunately confusing the picture by reference to the modern theory of Ch. Perelman/ L. Olbrechts-Tyteca.[319] My most significant criticism would be his insistence that "the basic arrangement of an epideictic speech followed that of the other genres." He proceeds to list a fourfold scheme: introduction, narrative, proofs, conclusion. Apart from the fact that deliberative rhetoric hardly ever used a narrative, there is little evidence that standard epideictic rhetoric ever used such a scheme. Of course it could have an introduction and a conclusion, but the methodology described by the ancient theorists for the arrangement of an epideictic speech is quite different. Quint. *Inst.* 3.7.15, for example, offers two methods, i) trace the life and deeds of the person to be praised in chronological order, ii) organise one's praise under the various virtues exhibited. Hester himself shows knowledge of such schemes (gleaned from T. C. Burgess, 1902, "Literature") on pp.295-97, but he emphasises the fact that such an ἐγκώμιον could form a *part* of a speech. Nevertheless, the kind of fully developed arrangement he gives on p.296 was hardly intended to be used for an encomiastic passage within a speech. His application of such a scheme to *Ep. Gal.* 1.11 - 2.21 is not convincing.

In general, Hester is yet another example both of those who tend to confuse ancient and modern rhetorical theory, and of those who show no real grasp of ancient rhetorical theory itself.

L. Wierenga's study of Paul's use of rhetoric in the letter to the Galatians is unfortunately rather thin on specific reference to ancient rhetorical theory.[320] There is in general a rather too heavy reliance upon Aristotle (no other rhetorical author is cited in his bibliography), especially in ordering his discussion of argumentation under "ethische," "logische" and "pathetische" means of persuasion (ethos, logos, pathos). In discussing ethos, for example, it is one thing to argue that the use of *sententiae* can have a good effect upon the image of a speaker's character, but quite another to conclude that because Paul supposedly uses many *sententiae* (he cites *sententiae* in 3.7, 9, 10, 11, 12, 13, but these are hardly statements of *communis opinio*!), these are auto-

---

[319] See pp.291-95. Epideictic rhetoric is, for example, defined as educational and concerned with the future behaviour of an audience. This hardly does justice to the varied nature of ancient epideictic, but *does* reflect the theory of Perelman/ Olbrechts-Tyteca.

[320] 1988, "Paulus."

matically evidence of the "ethical" character of his argumentation. In each case it needs to be shown that the use of the so-called *sententia* positively contributes to the speaker's image. Further, his classification of rhetorical questions under "ethical" persuasion is also not really demonstrable from ancient rhetorical theory.

Wierenga (30-32) goes on to give an analysis of *Ep. Gal.* 3.1-10 in terms of a gradual shift from *quaestio finita* to *quaestio infinita*. Unfortunately, his discussion does not properly take account of how rhetorical theory dealt with this matter. To make but two points: firstly, discussion of a *quaestio* in terms of its finite and infinite form goes back to Cicero's attempt to synthesize philosophy and rhetoric in the *de Oratore*. This kind of analysis was probably not common to contemporary school rhetoric. Secondly, Wierenga's analysis proposes a shift in the opposite direction to that recommended by Cicero (and following him, Quintilian), and further, they never speak of a *gradual* shift.[321] There is, however, something to be said for the suggestion that the διαίρεσις which Paul sets up between justification by works of the law or faith in Christ[322] is presented in general terms and thus could be likened to a θέσις (*quaestio infinita*). Paul's specific concern (cf. ὑπόθεσις = *quaestio finita*) is that the Galatians turn from the Judaising doctrine back to Paul's Gospel, but what Paul sets out to prove is that *no one* can be saved by works of the law and that *everyone* needs to be saved by faith in Christ (cf. θέσις = *quaestio infinita*). That Paul takes this line of reasoning, however, probably has more to do with the all-encompassing nature of his Gospel than that he was thinking in terms of θέσις/ ὑπόθεσις.

The ensuing analysis of *Ep. Gal.* 4.21-31 (34-38) does not really follow rhetorical theory as such, except to say that Paul is using an *exemplum*.[323]

In 1992 J. S. Vos published an interesting article on hermeneutical antinomy in Paul.[324] Vos presents an interesting attempt to apply certain κοινοὶ τόποι from στάσις doctrine to two passages in Paul's writings. He is here primarily concerned with *Ep. Gal.* 3 and *Ep. Rom.* 10 where Paul confronts his readers with at least two citations from the Torah which *prima facie* appear to be in opposition to each other. It is Vos' contention "daß Paulus in Gal 3 in starkem Maße, in Röm 10 in geringerem so argumentiert, wie es in den rhetorischen Handbüchern im Falle der leges contrariae empfohlen wird." He also backs this up with reference to a similar procedure amongst

---

[321] See further my critique of Hellholm, p.171f, and also chapter two, § 2.2.1.
[322] See p.135 below.
[323] Wierenga's analysis of the allegorical method is based on a *later* Christian method of dealing with allegory and has little in common with allegorical method in the first century AD.
[324] 1992, "Antinomie."

the Rabbis (concerning contradictory halakoth resting upon different texts from the Torah) and Philo.

Vos shows that in ancient rhetorical theory separate attention was given to the *status legum contrariarum* (e.g., Cic. *Inv.* 2.144-47; *Rhet.Her.* 2.15; Quint. *Inst.* 7.7). Among common arguments (κοινοὶ τόποι) suggested to overcome a possible contradiction between two laws he highlights the arguments *utra lex antiquior* and *utra lex potentior*. He also notes the common attempt to get at the *voluntas* or intent of a law, if there seems to be a contradiction at the level of its letter. Finally, there is also the point that the advocate ought to try to put such a construction on the law used by his opponent that it conforms to his point, and, if possible, show that the two laws in question do not really contradict each other.

Vos goes on to apply this to *Ep.Gal.* 3, basing his division of Paul's argument upon the schema suggested by late rhetorical theoreticians such as Sulpicius Victor. He suggests that Paul first discusses the Scripture supporting his position (3.6-9), and next that of his opponents, giving his own interpretation (3.10-11). He then proceeds to discuss the *voluntas* of the promise to Abraham (the point concerning σπέρμα, 3.15-16), the *comparatio - utra lex antiquior* (3.17-18), the *voluntas* of the Mosaic law (why was the law given?, 3.19-20), and finally the *comparatio - utra lex potentior* (the law did not give life, 3.21-22). Paul then adds several images to help explain his point.

Vos' analysis seems at first sight attractive. Yet, as the analysis of Paul's argumentation below shows, Vos' presentation does not really capture the essence of the argument. Nevertheless, it is true that in *Ep.Gal.* 3.19-22 Paul is concerned with the intent (*voluntas*) of the Mosaic law and interprets it in such a way that it does *not* contradict God's promises to Abraham. This concern that two laws or contracts should not contradict each other is reflected in rhetorical theory, as well as the consideration that one should examine the *intent* of the law as well as its letter. Yet these similarities are not sufficient to suggest dependence upon στάσις doctrine. The concern that Scripture not contradict itself was widespread among the Jews (cf. the evidence cited from rabbinical sources and from Philo by Vos himself, and also *Ev.Jo.* 10.35).[325]

Vos' case with respect to *Ep.Rom.* 10 is less strong, which he himself also admits.[326]

---

[325] Already above, I have suggested that the detailed τόποι of στάσις doctrine are not really relevant to the letters of Paul, see pp.58 and 88-89.

[326] See pp.267-68. *Ep.Rom.* 10 is much less clearly dealing with a *prima facie* contradiction between two laws or Scripture passages. Paul's argumentation here is intimately connected with his reasoning begun at 9.1 and continuing through to 11.36. It is difficult to envisage the beginning of chapter ten as a digression designed to resolve an apparent discrepancy within the law of Moses.

C. H. Cosgrove has also attempted a rhetorical explanation of *Ep. Gal.* 3:15-18.[327] Cosgrove argues that Paul, taking the premises of his opponents (which Paul himself does not accept), argues that God, who gave the covenant to Abraham as a promise, later tried to amend that covenant by bringing in the Mosaic law as a condition and thereby profoundly altering the terms of the original agreement. Yet God's attempt to do this fails because no one can add stipulations to a ratified covenant. Cosgrove argues on the basis of the phrase "*κατὰ ἄνθρωπον*" that Paul does not accept the premises of his own argument (which involves a characterisation of his opponents' position), but *concedes* the premises *hypothetically*. He further argues that this was a standard rhetorical technique, referring to Quint. *Inst.* 9.2.51. Two considerations show the weaknesses in Cosgrove's position. Firstly, his interpretation demands understanding v.17 to be indicating that there is a fundamental conflict between the introduction of the law and the Abrahamic covenant. This is supported by interpreting the words *οὐκ ἀκυροῖ* ("does not invalidate") as "is not able to invalidate." A straightforward reading of these words, however, renders perfectly good sense. Paul's point is then not about the *introduction* of the law *per se*, but its *function*. It is this function which is addressed in v.19. Furthermore, Cosgrove has misread the import of the word "*videmur*" in Quintilian. When Quintilian states: *concessio, cum aliquid etiam iniquum videmur causae fiducia pati*, he means to say that the concession made only seems to be injurious to one's case, not that the concession may only be hypothetical. This is all the more clear from the examples Quintilian provides. It should, however, be noted that Cosgrove's book (1988b, *Cross*), written subsequent to his article, drops any reference to Quintilian or ancient rhetoric in his interpretation of this passage (61-65). Here he explicitly rejects a rhetorical division of the letter (23-26, cf. 30).

Finally, it is necessary to refer to an essay by the classicist J. Fairweather.[328] Fairweather provides an interesting analysis of Chrysostom's use of rhetorical theory in commenting on Paul's letter to the Galatians.[329] She also provides a good overview of Paul's relation to Hellenism. Her own analysis of the letter to the Galatians (214-29) is rather general, but in the main ruled by a notable sobriety. Many of her suggestions are similar to those defended by me below.

Fairweather (214) appropriately takes cognizance of the difficulty presented by Paul's strong rebuke of the Galatians at the opening of the letter. Such a rebuke is hardly in accord with rhetorical theory. Yet, citing Arist. *Rh.* 3.14.12, she suggests

[327] 1988a, "Human."
[328] 1994, "Epistle."
[329] See my comments in note 331 below.

that Paul might be considered to be amplifying the importance of his subject here. This is certainly true, but does not remove the fact that the pronouncement of a curse can hardly be considered to be *deliberative*. Her playing down of the rebuking nature of Paul's letter allows her to classify the letter as belonging to the deliberative genre (219).[330] But she is quite frank when she admits to being able to find no "clear evidence" for "the general layout of Paul's argumentation," whether in "Greek rhetorical theory about deliberative oratory and θέσις-composition, or in actual philosophical letters and short treatises belonging to the period up to Paul's lifetime" (220). She further notes how Paul's argumentation is quite a contrast to the τελικὰ κεφάλαια of deliberative rhetoric (221), and goes on to make some quite interesting comments with respect to Paul's common sequence of doctrinal exposition followed by moral exhortation, a sequence which does not appear to have been common in antiquity (226-27). Her discussion of Paul's style will be referred to in my general conclusions (chapter seven, § 1).

2 Rhetorical Analysis
2.1 Introduction

The following analysis of the letter to the Galatians is restricted to the verses 1.1 - 5.12. The paraenetical section and epistolary closing are excluded, not because they are not necessarily integrally connected with the letter as such, but because they do not offer scope for an analysis with respect to ancient rhetorical theory. Paul's habit of closing his letters with general and specific paraenetic advice is closely related to popular philosophy (cf. esp. Sen. *Ep.* 94).

Although this book is not specifically concerned with rhetorical interpretation of Paul in the church fathers, this area is very much of related concern. I have, therefore, chosen to pay some attention to the commentary of Marius Victorinus on this letter as

---

[330] Fairweather's statement on the genre of the letter is fairly clear, although she does allow for "apologetic overtones" and "eulogistic touches." Earlier, in connection with "types of epistolary discourse," she suggests that the letter is of the "mixed" type (20). In private correspondence (dated 23 Nov. 1995) she also uses the term "mixed" of the letter's rhetorical genre.

In the context of her genre classification (219) Fairweather also reckons, among others, allegory as one of the "effective modes of persuasion" recognised by the rhetorical theorists. As noted below (§ 2.5, part two), Paul's use of the allegorical method in *Ep.Gal.* 4 is not the same as the rhetorical figure known as ἀλληγορία.

both a test-case and control on my own rhetorical analysis.[331] Victorinus (born in Africa) was a well-known professor of rhetoric teaching in Rome in the mid fourth century AD, where a statue was erected in his honour. His literary output was prolific, demonstrating a wide reading knowledge in both Greek and Latin. Among the extant works is a commentary on Cicero's *de Inventione*. Very late in life he converted to Christianity and began writing commentaries on the Pauline letters and also various theological tracts. The commentary on Paul's letter to the Galatians is the first Latin commentary on this letter extant.[332] Victorinus' commentary is, however, not a rhetorical commentary. He pays very little attention to matters of rhetorical theory or style. Yet occasionally he provides comment relevant to this study.[333]

In accord with both my comments on the usefulness of rhetorical genres in general,[334] and the comments above on this approach with respect to the letter to the Galatians, no *rhetorical* outline has been attempted in terms of any of the rhetorical genres. The letter does not fall naturally into the confines of a rhetorical genre, nor can it reasonably be divided into the various *partes* of a speech.[335] The following general comments on genre may be made. As noted above, Paul's letters *qua* length and language are closer to those letters extant in the literary tradition than those found among

---

[331]   I have used the edition of A. Locher (Leipzig: B. G. Teubner, 1972).

   J. Fairweather (1994, "Epistle," 2-22) has investigated Chrysostom's commentary on Paul's letter to the Galatians and deduces on the basis of it a rhetorical outline of Paul's letter. Structurally, she argues that Chrysostom interprets the letter as containing a mixture of rhetorical genres. Fairweather brings this back to the theory of ἐσχηματισμένος λόγος, in particular, to a method described by Ps.-Dionysius of Halicarnassus, *Ars Rhetorica* 8.8-12 (a treatise probably dating to the beginning of the third century AD). As noted in the select glossary, ἐσχηματισμένος λόγος was a method used when one wished to disguise what one had to say (usually criticism of one's audience) and thus enable the speech to come across in a more agreeable way. Various methods for accomplishing this are described by the rhetorical theorists, but so far as I am aware [D.H.] *Rh.* 8 is the only treatise to suggest what is called ὁ ἄγων ὁ συμπεπλεγμένος, namely, the idea that various genres may be disguised under another genre. Unfortunately, Fairweather does not really make the *purpose* of ἐσχηματισμένος λόγος clear, nor does she attempt to show, if Chrysostom really interpreted Paul in this way, what purpose Paul may have had in using this method and what he was trying to disguise. Needless to say I am sceptical as to the suggestion that Chrysostom analysed Paul in terms of this method. Chrysostom nowhere makes this explicit. That he uses various terms common to rhetorical genre terminology to describe what Paul does in this letter is true, but Chrysostom uses such terminology throughout his homilies. A more in-depth investigation of the treatises of Chrysostom would be needed in order to determine whether he means to say anything meaningful about genre through his scattered use of such terms.

[332]   For an extended overview of his life and works see Wessner, 1930, "Marius."

[333]   It is, perhaps, worth noting that Victorinus (*Gal.* 1146d) sums up the purpose of the letter as to correct the Galatians and call them back from Judaism that they may keep faith in Christ alone. Victorinus sees no direct apologetic purpose to the letter. It is a refutation (*refutare*) of what the Galatians have added to the Gospel and a confirmation (*confirmare*) of Paul's own Gospel.

[334]   See pp.82-90.

[335]   See p.166.

the papyri in Egypt.[336] In terms of epistolary theory, going by the analysis presented below, the letter to the Galatians may be broadly typified as belonging to the ἐπιτιμητικὸς τύπος ([Demetr.] *Typ.* 6, cf. [Lib.] *Ep. Char.* 34, 81). The letter is essentially a strong rebuke of the Galatian Christians who have apparently been under the influence of certain Judaising teachers. The letter suggests that at least one of the central points of these teachers was the necessity for the Galatians to be circumcised. Paul considers this Judaising Gospel incompatible with the Gospel which he first preached to them and thus calls them back to the true Gospel as originally preached by him.

The analysis concentrates on, i) understanding the argumentative flow in the letter, as a necessary precursor to, ii) comment on the use or lack of ἐπιχειρήματα (rhetorical syllogisms) and other forms of argumentation, as well as the use and, where appropriate, function of various tropes and figures. iii) Thirdly, following upon the analysis, certain comments will also be made upon the style in relation to both rhetorical and epistolary theory. This analysis is an attempt to approach the letter to the Galatians from the perspective of ancient rhetorical theory. The application of rhetorical terminology to what Paul does in this letter should not necessarily be taken to mean that Paul himself thought in these terms. Many methods of argumentation and figures were (and are) commonly used without any theoretical consideration. The approach is therefore maximalist, and more akin to how Paul's letter may have been interpreted by a contemporary professor of rhetoric (with some goodwill!). Following upon the analysis of several letters some remarks will be made concerning the likelihood of direct or indirect influence of Graeco-Roman rhetorical theory upon Paul.[337]

That portion of the letter considered here may be broadly divided into four sections as follows:

1.1-10 *Epistolary opening and rebuke*: The rebuke (1.6-10) replaces the regular thanksgiving section.
1.11 - 2.21 *Narrative Apology*: Independence and divine origin of Paul's Gospel.
3.1 - 4.11 *Argument*: The nature of the Galatians' initial reception of the Gospel followed by Scripture proof (3.1-14), and a didactic explanation of his position (3.15 - 4.11).
4.12 - 5.12 *Emotional appeal*.

---

[336] See pp.96f.
[337] Of course, the following analysis also presents various exegetical choices which have been made. It is, however, beyond the scope of this study to interact with exegetical material outside of a rhetorical purview.

2.2 Epistolary Opening and Rebuke (1.1-10)

The Argumentative Thread

A regular letter opening is extended by two additional thoughts: i) The expansion on Paul's apostleship (v.1). This could be considered the establishment of ethos (self-recommendation), but it is not effected along traditional rhetorical lines (by using the stock turns of phrase). Given the problem in the Galatian church, Paul has seen the need to emphasise the nature of his apostleship, and does this at the beginning. Rhetoricians also saw the need to establish credibility at the beginning of a speech, but this is a concept too common to attribute to the influence of rhetorical theory as such.[338] ii) The expansion on what Jesus Christ has done for his own and the conclud ing doxology (verses 4-5). Both the doxology and the specific form of the greeting (grace and peace) have Jewish backgrounds. The rather verbose extended form of this letter opening, particularly the second expansion, may be considered the kind of μακρολογία which Demetr. *Eloc.* 7 (cf. 242) states is appropriate to prayer, or in this case praise.[339]

The θαυμάζω ὅτι section (1.6-9) replaces a thanksgiving section (regular both in Paul and in Hellenistic letters generally). Although such use of θαυμάζω is common in the orators, it is also not unusual in Hellenistic letters.

The πάθος attained in verses 8-9 is certainly high, and due to: i) the very harsh judgment combined with the use of a foreign (Jewish) concept, ἀνάθεμα ἔστω.[340] It is as if Paul is so worked up that he reverts to an expression from his mother tongue. ii) The use of ὑπερβολή (hyperbole, "or an angel from heaven"); iii) emphatic repetition with a heightening the second time (εἰ for ἐάν). Such repetition, Arist. *Rh.* 3.12.3 says, should be varied the second time. It is highly dramatic and for that reason inappropriate to written work, i.e., if read it comes across as ὁ τὴν δοκὸν φέρων (a proverb explained by Photius as one of many ἐπὶ τῶν ταὐτὰ ποιούντων καὶ μηδὲν περαινόντων, cited in Leutsch/ Schneidewin *Corpus Paroemiographorum Graecorum*,

---

[338] Vict. *Gal.* 1147c suggests that Paul adds the brothers with him as addressees to shame the Galatians by showing that their error is contrary to them all. He also notes that Paul may have had Matthias (who replaced Judas) in mind when he says that he was not sent by men (1147d).

[339] It should be noted that [Lib.] *Ep.Char.* 51 recommends a simple letter opening: ὁ δεῖνα τῷ δεῖνι χαίρειν. Additional adjectives ought to be avoided. Apollonius Dyscolus, however, in a discussion on articles in epistolary syntax (*Synt.* 1.65-68), suggests several cases in which adjectives may be necessary. Neither author appears to envisage the kind of extensive expansions present in Paul.

[340] It is interesting that Paul assumes that the Galatians will understand this term (a Septuagintalism, see below, note 413). If the Galatians were not Jewish, they had been under Jewish influence, or had done a lot of Old Testament study.

1.168n). This πάθος is maintained in v.10 by the two/ three short rhetorical questions in a row (cf. select glossary, s.v. ἐπερώτησις).[341] The point is that Paul no longer *persuades* men (let alone God - another ὑπερβολή).[342] The thought is repeated in other words, thus equating the action of πείθειν with ἀρέσκειν. Πείθειν thus has a negative sense here, as more frequently in popular criticism of rhetoric (i.e., pleasing men with rhetorical flourish rather than stating the matter plainly).[343]

Paul thus approaches an emotional climax as he introduces a narrative excursus in v.11.

Rhetorical Notes

1.7 The phrase ὃ οὐκ ἔστιν ἄλλο is an example of μεταβολή (self-correction, see select glossary s.v.). Here it has the opposite effect to that described in *Rhet.Her.* 4.36. The initial overstatement heightens the seriousness of the offense.

2.3 Narrative Apology (1.11 - 2.21)

The Argumentative Thread

Having pronounced a strong rebuke against the Galatians, Paul next takes up a lengthy defence of the divine origin and authority of his Gospel. His proposition is formally introduced using the common disclosure formula (γνωρίζω). Paul begins this defence by recounting the fact that he received his Gospel directly from God via a revelation and thus not via the mediation of men (i.e., of the other apostles). This revelation was probably well known to the Galatians.

The establishment of the divine origin of Paul's gospel lends divine authority to its message. Paul next argues that after this revelation he had minimal contact with the

---

[341] Γάρ in abrupt or short interrogative questions generally has no conjunctive force, LSJ s.v. I.4, contra J. B. Lightfoot (1865, *Epistle, ad loc.*) and J. van Bruggen (1973, *Veertien*, 136) et al.. Compare also Denniston on progressive γάρ (i.e., no causal force, *Part.*, 81-85, esp. 82-83). Denniston suggests that this usage is confined to drama (84), but it ought to be noted that the *terminus ad quem* for his research is 320 BC. K.-G., *Gram.*, 2.2 pp.335-37 (§ 545, 7) note that adverbial γάρ (i.e., of emphasis) in questions is common.

[342] The expected answer to the question is thus, "neither." J. van Bruggen's objections to this interpretation, that the word order clearly suggests an alternative proposition, are not conclusive (*op. cit.*, 138n). The fact that πείθω comes after ἀνθρώπους (instead of ἄρτι γὰρ ἀνθρώπους ἢ τὸν θεὸν πείθω;) may merely serve to emphasise ἀνθρώπους, the words ἢ τὸν θεόν coming as a hyperbolic afterthought.

[343] Paul can also use the verb πείθω in a positive sense, cf. 2 *Ep.Cor.* 5.11. An alternative interpretation is to view πείθω and ἀρέσκω as in opposition to each other (taking πείθω in a positive sense). The first question is then an alternative, does Paul persuade men or does he persuade God? Obviously he persuades men, for he submits to God (being a slave of Christ). That is why he cannot be a men-pleaser. For this interpretation see J. van Bruggen, *op. cit.*, 135-40.

apostles. He was, therefore, never their student. Yet Paul does not explicitly draw this conclusion. As more often in Paul, the conclusion is left out as self-evident. Whilst this certainly may be appropriate according to rhetorical theory, one needs to be careful that ambiguity does not arise and that the conclusions are in fact crystal clear from the context. This is not always the case in Paul and is a weakness in his argumentation, as we shall see below.[344]

The following narrative concerning himself, therefore, has the nature of an *argument*. As scholars have frequently noted, there is a strong element of personal defence here. It seems as though certain rumours had been spread around which denigrated his authority and his Gospel.[345] Paul, therefore, finds it necessary to defend the divine origin of his Gospel. As noted above, this section cannot rightly be compared to the διήγησις of a speech.[346] Already Victorinus (*Gal.* 1152b) had realised this. He notes that this section does indeed have the character of a *narratio de se*, but that its function is to *prove* (*probare*).[347]

Now the main purpose of the letter is to rebuke the Galatians for following the Judaisers and to call them back to the pure Gospel. This is what is initially presented in the letter (1.6-9) and also argued for and explained in the argument of 3.1 - 4.11. The narrative of 1.11 - 2.21 appears, therefore, to have a purpose somewhat different to the other sections of the letter. It forms a kind of excursus. Of course, the narrative does lay an important foundation for the argument and teaching to follow. This foundation is provided both by showing the divine nature of Paul's Gospel and his authority as its messenger, and by using the narrative itself to introduce the main point of Paul's argument to come, i.e., the διαίρεσις between faith in Christ and the works of the law.[348]

Such an extended apologetic excursus was not a regular feature of either rhetorical theory or practice, *but* it is certainly not without precedent (see below).

One of the most important functions of the προοίμιον in the rhetorical theory of this age was the effective presentation of the character (ἦθος) of the speaker. The orator had to make sure that his audience were prepared to listen to him. If the audience had particular prejudices, these had to be first removed before he could proceed to his argument (cf. Cic. *Inv.* 1.22). Both *Rhet.Her.* 1.9 and Cic. *Inv.* 1.23 advise the use of a

---

[344] See pp.139-41.

[345] For Chrysostom's reconstruction of charges made against Paul, see J. Fairweather, 1994, "Epistle," 3-4.

[346] See note 292.

[347] Victorinus further divides this section into four parts (*divisiones*) and shows how they help to prove that Paul's Gospel was independently received by divine revelation.

[348] See p.135 below.

cautious insinuating προοίμιον when the audience is hostile for one reason or another. Paul does not opt for this approach, nor was it universally supported by rhetorical theorists (cf. the critical comments in Quint. *Inst.* 4.1.37-39, 42ff). Instead, Paul tackles the problem head on by the presentation of a lengthy apologetic narrative.

In this respect we have two fairly close parallels in the 5th speech of Demosthenes and the 40th speech of Dio Chrysostom.

Demosthenes' speech, delivered in 346 BC, was a short attempt to convince the Athenians that it was politically necessary to accept the peace which had been made with Philip. After a regular προοίμιον (§§ 1-3), Demosthenes inserts an apologetic narrative concerning his lone, yet (in his view) correct, counsel to the Athenians on earlier occasions (§§ 4-12). The *propositio* is then provided at §§ 13-14a. The function of this personal defence is quite clearly to build his ἦθος before he goes on to give what (for him) must have seemed rather unlikely counsel. Given that the whole speech only takes up 25 roughly equal sections, the apologetic narrative forms a significant portion of the whole.[349]

Dio delivered his 40th speech to the citizens of Prusa in AD 101, having been invited to speak to the debate on the motion "that concord ought to be concluded with Apameia." The speech is itself essentially deliberative, however, Dio realised that his audience were potentially quite hostile to him. For this reason he begins with a lengthy *apologetic* προοίμιον. In fact, he goes so far as to insert a separate apologetic speech into the προοίμιον. This takes the form of a narrative concerning his past actions which defends the proposition that he did not prove false to his native land nor cheat them from the promise he made. Thus the προοίμιον of his speech has the following structure:

προοίμιον (§§ 1-2): (concerned with the speaker's ἦθος)
    Insert (§§ 3-15): (apologetic narrative)
προοίμιον continued (§§ 16-19):

Given that the whole speech is divided into only 41 roughly equal sections, this extended προοίμιον also takes up an abnormally large proportion of the speech (19 sections).

---

[349] F. Vouga (1988, "Gattung") briefly compares this speech with Paul's letter to the Galatians as evidence that the letter should be categorised as deliberative. Whilst the speech makes a good comparison in respect of the apologetic narration, Vouga goes too far when he characterises sections 24-25 as an *exhortatio* (comparing *Ep.Gal.* 5.2 - 6.10). These sections form a regular ἐπίλογος to Demosthenes' speech wherein he reiterates his main point and anticipates possible objections. It is in no way comparable to Paul's paraenesis.

These extended apologetic narratives may be effectively compared with the space taken up by Paul's apologetic narrative. Paul's letter, of course, does not have a formal rhetorical προοίμιον, but a modified letter opening (see above). Nevertheless, just as Demosthenes and Dio, Paul found it necessary to include a rather lengthy narrative (in his case to defend the divine origin and independence of his Gospel) before he began to deal with arguments more directly related to the issue at stake. Unlike the two examples above, Paul neatly joins his narrative to the more formal argument by introducing a speech/ rebuke he made to Peter.

It is to be noticed that from 2.1 the narrative is extended from the original plan (presented in 1.11) in order to show how, in fact, the other apostles *supported* his Gospel, and that it was the pseudo-apostles who crept in and tried to change things. Paul follows this up by recounting how, when in Antioch Peter changed his behaviour (on account of the arrival of the Jacobites), he effectively rebuked Peter. He includes a *précis* of his rebuke at that time within this letter, on account of its direct relevance to his argument. Within the précis of this rebuke, Paul develops the διαίρεσις which pinpoints from his perspective the nub of the issue, namely, justification by works of the law or through faith in Christ. The issue is simply and starkly presented. In Paul's view, the doctrine that circumcision is still necessary for Gentile Christians (implying the necessity of keeping the whole Mosaic law), in this context, is tantamount to trying to earn justification by works.

Rhetorical Notes

1.11 γνωρίζω δέ (a better reading than γάρ) announces a proposition (in this case accompanied by a short reason, cf. Quint. *Inst.* 4.4.8) which will be proved in the following paragraphs. The ὑπερβατόν (hyperbaton) of ὅτι (which should be construed with γνωρίζω and belongs immediately before τὸ εὐαγγέλιον) emphasises the οὐκ and the immediately following phrase which is the crunch of Paul's argument.

1.12 οὔτε ἐδιδάχθην is an example of πλεονασμός (pleonasm). It is considered by Quint. *Inst.* 8.3.53-55 a style fault unless deliberately used *adfirmationis gratia.*

1.16 σαρκὶ καὶ αἵματι is a common περίφρασις (periphrasis) both in Paul and other Judeo-Christian texts (cf. 1 *Ep.Cor.* 15.50; *Ep.Eph.* 6.12; *Ep.Hebr.* 2.14; *Ev.Matt.* 16.17; LXX *Si.* 14.18; 17.31).

1.20 Midway through the narrative, Paul finds it expedient to use an oath. Here we see a tacit acknowledgement of the fact that Paul *cannot prove* his own account of his past (cf. [Arist.] *Rh.Al.* 17.1), at least not with hard evidence. The oath, therefore, functions to magnify the trustworthiness of his testimony. It is effectual because of its setting here. Paul, as a God-fearing apostle, is not likely to perjure himself in this way. The standard courtroom refutation of oaths (that criminal types who don't fear the gods in their deeds are unlikely to worry about divine revenge for a false oath) is not applicable.

1.23 ὁ διώκων seems to be used as a timeless substantive. J. B. Lightfoot compares ὁ καταλύων at *Ev.Matt.* 27.40.[350] The sudden switch to a clause in the first person whilst engaged in narrative is discussed by [Longin.] 27, who notes that if it is done just at the right moment it supplies a certain outburst of passion (ἐκβολή τις πάθους). Nevertheless, his examples (from Homer and Hecataeus) are more abrupt and have more πάθος than Paul here. Paul's citation is prepared for by ἀκούω and introduced by ὅτι. Yet his citation is more effective dramatically than had he said: ἀκούοντες ἦσαν τὸν διώξαντα αὐτούς ποτε νῦν εὐαγγελίζεσθαι τὴν πίστιν.

2.2 ἀνέβην δέ (repeating the same verb from the previous verse) is a clear case of διλογία as described by Demetr. *Eloc.* 103 which makes the style μεῖζον. It would have been less forceful to say ἀνέβην κατ' ἀποκάλυψιν εἰς Ἱεροσόλυμα κτλ.. It also emphasises the revelation (cf. *Eloc.* 197).

It seems more likely that the verbs in the phrase μή ... τρέχω ἢ ἔδραμον are both indicative than that the first is subjunctive.[351] If so, then τρέχω and probably κηρύσσω should be considered historic presents. Ps.-Longinus (§ 25) argues that the use of the historic present transforms narrative into an ἐναγώνιον πρᾶγμα (energetic/ vivid event). Ps.-Aristides (*Rh.* 2.134) states that it produces ἀφέλεια (simplicity). Paul's clause may be interpreted in two ways. 1) He is admitting that he was just possibly (πως) on the wrong track and thus communicated his Gospel to the reputable men to make sure. If this is the case the clause is an example of *concessio* as defined in Quint. *Inst.* 9.2.51. 2) Perhaps more probably Paul is reflecting on the possible danger that his Gospel preaching would be thwarted by a more Judaistic Gospel accepted by the men of repute.

Τρέχω is here metaphorical of running in a race, a μεταφορά common in Paul and elsewhere (cf. 5.7 and LSJ *s.v.* II.2).

2.4-5 Regarding these verses J. B. Lightfoot appropriately speaks of a "shipwreck of grammar."[352] This is a flagrant example of solecism and these verses form an ade-

---

[350] 1865, *Epistle*, 86.
[351] The use of the indicative with μή (= ἵνα μή) is more common in later Greek, but strictly speaking incorrect. Mayser, *Gram.Pap.* 2.2.549 notes μή + indic. in subordinate clauses used of doubtful questions.
[352] 1865, *Epistle*, 104.

quate indication that Paul did not revise the language of the letter.[353] The verb
ἠναγκάσθη is probably to be understood with verse 4a.

Paul's language here comes close to what was called ἐσχηματισμένος λόγος due
to his use of ἔμφασις (see select glossary s.v.). The point is that by running down those
who wanted Titus to be circumcised as "infiltrating pseudo-brothers," he *hints* that he
would consider anyone who supported circumcision in like terms. The undrawn conclusion is that the Galatians have taken the side of infiltrators and traitors. The ἔμφασις
here is, however, quite open, and as we have seen, Paul is not afraid to accuse the
Galatians directly. His letter cannot, therefore, be interpreted as ἐσχηματισμένος
λόγος in general.

Paul's disparaging use of the term ψευδάδελφος is an interesting coinage. It
appears to conform quite well to Demetrius' description of the forceful use of compound words which have been coined (*Eloc.* 275).

2.6-10 The following verses are quite complex and full of various figures which
heighten the emotion of the passage. In 2.6 and 8 we have two examples of παρένθεσις
(parenthesis). Both are short, related to the matter in hand, and not syntactically complex, in accordance with the advice of rhetorical theorists. Both are, however, syntactically separate from the main sentence, and the first parenthesis is not followed by a
syntactical completion of the sentence originally started. 2.6a is thus an anacoluthon.
The first parenthesis also contains an example of ὑπερβατόν (hyperbaton): πρόσωπον
[ὁ] θεὸς ἀνθρώπου. Yet this is not such a highly emotional example as those discussed
in [Longin.] 22. The dogmatic statement: πρόσωπον ... λαμβάνει is an example of a
κεκριμένον, i.e., the use of a commonly accepted opinion to prove a point (in this case
an opinion accepted among Jews and Christians and ultimately based upon Old Testament revelation). The underlying argument (which in this case is not difficult to follow)
is that if God is not a respecter of persons then neither should Paul himself be, which is
why it does not matter to him what kind of people the men of repute used to be.

This statement may be interpreted in two ways. If Paul's use of οἱ δοκοῦντες car-
ries a negative connotation, then he would seem to be saying that the fact that the other
apostles were once those chosen to be the special disciples of the Lord Jesus on earth is
of no consequence in terms of making a judgement upon the nature of the Gospel. But
why would Paul want to interject this comment? After all, he goes on to narrate how

---

[353] One might think of a very early occuring haplography of the words ἠναγκάσθη περιτμηθῆναι, were
it not made rather improbable by the well attested δέ following διά.

the apostles were in complete agreement with his Gospel! Would not the added reputation of the apostles be an advantage to his argument, rather than a disadvantage?[354]

A second possibility (taking οἱ δοκοῦντες positively) is that Paul is referring to the low station of the other apostles, namely, the fact that they were for the most part fishermen from the region of Galilee, whilst Paul himself was a rabbi, trained under no less an authority than Gamaliel. The thought is then a form of εἰρωνεία, since in telling the Galatians that the fact that his superior training and social standing makes no difference to his judgment of them (nor to that of God), he at the same time reminds them of that very difference! Considerations of character presentation (ethos) are thus mixed together with the first round of proof.

The thought resumed after the first parenthesis is (as noted above) begun over with a different grammatical construction. The structure of the sentence (2.6a versus 2.7-9) is an ἀντίθεσις (of thought), but it is not proportional (which would be out of place here).

2.7 The μετωνυμία (metonymy) of ἀκροβυστία and περιτομή in 2.7, according to *Ep.Eph.* 2.11, was common Jewish terminology (cf. *Ep.Gal.* 2.12; *Ep.Rom.* 2.26-27; 3.30; 15.8; *Ep.Col.* 3.11; 4.11; *Act.Ap.* 10.45; 11.2). They therefore cannot have had much creative effect.

2.9 στῦλοι in verse 9 is a μεταφορά which also occurs elsewhere (cf. 1 *Ep.Ti.* 3.15; *Apoc.* 3.12; E. *IT* 57; cf. Ph. *Migr.Abr.* 124). The same metaphor occurs with the word κίων (cf. Archil. 16 D.; Pi. *O.* 2.90; *Vit.Aesop.* G § 106 [p.68,9-10 Perry, ὁ κίων τῆς βασιλείας, of Aesop]).

2.9 also contains another example of ὑπερβατόν: δεξιάς ... κοινωνίας. This example seems more artful (the ὑπερβατόν actually encompasses the rest of the clause) and emphasises Paul's point. The artfulness of this clause seems somewhat incongruent with the grammatical disorder of the foregoing.

2.10 The ὑπερβατόν of τῶν πτωχῶν (to be construed with μνημονεύω) in 2.10 serves to emphasise the fact that the exception only concerned the *poor.*[355]

2.14 ὀρθοποδέω appears first here. It reappears in Christian writers from the time of Origen, and in secular literature in an unpublished third century AD papyrus cited in BAGD *s.v.*. It would thus *seem* that Paul has coined the word here, though we must be careful with the argument from silence as concerns Greek lexicography. It is a common

---

[354] This interpretation is often coupled with the hypothesis that the Galatians, for the reason suggested, considered the other apostles as more authoritative than Paul.
[355] Elliptical ἵνα in commands is more common, cf. LSJ *s.v.* II.3.b.

enough μεταφορά (cf. εὐθυπορέω) though if Paul has introduced a πεποιημένον (word-coinage) here (based on ὀρθόπους), the metaphor may be accentuated.

2.14b-21 The structure of 2.14b-21 has always given trouble to commentators. Where does Paul's citation of his speech to Peter stop? *Prima facie* it appears that the citation continues until v.21.[356] Before then there is no formal indication of any transition. That the citation is continued at v.15 is indicated by the words ἡμεῖς φύσει Ἰουδαῖοι which cannot easily refer to himself and his audience. The Galatians were hardly a group of Jews! Yet the way the argument flows, especially in terms of how Paul ends up giving a personal testimony of his relation to Christ, and the lack of any particular application to Peter or to the matter of circumcision has led scholars to think that these last verses cannot have been a part of his rebuke to Peter. J. B. Lightfoot, for example, suggests that Paul's thoughts and language drift away from Peter at Antioch to the Judaisers in Galatia.[357] Without wishing to deny the possibility of such a solution (a break after v.16 might be considered, as, for example, Vict. *Gal.* 1164b), rhetorical theory may point us in another direction. If the verses 14b-21 are to be viewed as Paul's own *précis* of what he said in public to Peter at Antioch,[358] then it may be that Paul employed a well-known and certainly not uncommon rhetorical method, ἐσχηματισμένος λόγος.

Rhetorical theorists explain how such figured speech may be used in a variety of circumstances, for a variety of motives, and in a variety of ways. One important motive was εὐπρέπεια (propriety) when the necessity of rebuking someone of standing presented itself. This is precisely the situation Paul found himself in at Antioch. The point of ἐσχηματισμένος λόγος is to present one's rebuke in such a way that it comes across, but without unnecessarily offending the person to be rebuked. Now it must be admitted that Paul begins in 2.14b by directly accusing Peter of compelling the Gentiles to Judaise (πῶς ... ἀναγκάζεις). This seems to have been the position of the party of the circumcision, but it was probably *not* Peter's intent. As Paul himself has stated, Peter acted in concert with the Jacobites out of fear. Yet Paul hereby equates his action with agreement to the Jacobite party policy. It is a mild form of ὑπερβολή, but justified. It shows Paul's anger (cf. Arist. *Rh.* 3.11.15), an anger appropriate to the situation. But in what follows, Paul mollifies his direct rebuke by the use of ἐσχηματισμένος λόγος.

---

[356] This solution is also accepted by J. Fairweather (1994, "Epistle," 14), following Chrysostom.
[357] 1865, *Epistle*, 114.
[358] It is probable that Paul's actual rebuke was considerably longer, and also impromptu. This recollection is no doubt polished somewhat, but we should expect that it recounts the essential points Paul made at that time.

He does this in two ways. Firstly, he includes himself in what is said (ἡμεῖς φύσει Ἰουδαῖοι), immediately creating a bond between himself and his addressee. He then proceeds to show how his arguments apply to himself personally without making the direct application to Peter, nor mentioning the precise point at issue at the time. Instead, the issue is broadened to the question of righteousness by works or by faith. Whilst on the one hand this makes Peter's conduct the more serious, on the other hand, the fact that no direct application to either Peter or the matter of circumcision is made softens the blow. Certainly, this application is *clearly* implied, but respect for Peter allows him to make the application for himself, and that is precisely the point of ἐσχηματισμένος λόγος.

Paul thus repeats a speech he made at that time within his letter. Of course this incident (and the speech) is repeated because of its direct connection with the problem in the Galatian church.

2.16 The point that justification is by faith in Christ and not by works of the law is repeated several times in this verse. Such tautology shows how Paul desires to emphasise this point, but stylistically does not come across very well. It should be considered a fault here (cf. Quint. *Inst.* 8.3.51). Ταυτολογία is more fitting to prayers or laments (cf. Demetr. *Eloc.* 7).

καὶ ἡμεῖς. This is διλογία used for the sake of clarity, Demetr. *Eloc.* 197, cf. 196.

πᾶσα σάρξ is a Hebraism common in the LXX (although not actually in the text which is probably here alluded to, *Ps.* 143 [144].2). The allusion is not cited as an authoritative witness, but introduced much like a γνώμη (maxim). Its position at the end of an argumentative consideration would also seem appropriate and in line with rhetorical theory (cf. Demetr. *Eloc.* 110-11). The fact that it is an *Old Testament* allusion immediately secures the sympathy of his audience.

In 2.16 Paul's argument is an example of the common form of argument known among rhetorical theorists as διαίρεσις (cf. select glossary *s.v.*). Two or more possibilities are listed of which only one can be valid. The argument allows no room for any third possibility, which can be a risk, but not in this case.

2.17 uses a rhetorical question answered by Paul himself. The use of such a figure certainly heightens the emotional tension as the ancient theorists point out, and thus is also used *after* Paul has made his main point. The rhetorical question therefore serves as αὔξησις, ramming home the point of his argument to Peter, not really adding anything new.

ἁμαρτωλοί is here ἀντονομασία (antonomasia) for ἔθνη. Paul hereby stresses the Jewish view of other peoples as sinners because they do not hold to Jewish customs.

His point is that in seeking to be justified in Christ, Jews have become Gentiles, sinners in the sense that Mosaic rituals are abandoned. I do not necessarily see any irony here (*contra* J. B. Lightfoot, 1865, *Epistle*, 115). Paul lays a verbal trap by showing how Peter's position would make Christ a servant of sin.

In the phrase ἁμαρτίας διάκονος, ἁμαρτία is personified. Arist. *Rh.* 3.11.3-4 (cf. Demetr. *Eloc.* 81; Quint. *Inst.* 8.6.11-12) appropriately notes that portraying inanimate things/ concepts as animate makes the matter quite vivid (ἐνέργεια). Those all *too* familiar with the text of the New Testament are inclined to miss the striking vividness of Paul's personification of abstract concepts.

2.17-19 The suggestion that Christ is a minister of sin is of course to be answered in the negative by all parties. But what is Paul's point? It would appear that he is intimating that ἁμαρτία here is of a different kind than that implied by the comment that Gentiles are ἁμαρτωλοί. In other words, sin is not to be defined by the ritual commandments of the Mosaic Law. Whilst this may very well underlie Paul's thought, he does not proceed to explain himself in this way. Instead, he states metaphorically that one proves oneself a transgressor if he attempts to rebuild what he has once destroyed, i.e., that he proves that the act of destruction was wrong. This statement is an example of ἀλληγορία (in the rhetorical sense, see select glossary, *s.v.* and comments at 4.1-2 and 5.9). It seems to rest upon the accepted fact that Peter *et al* had earlier all agreed (and presumably still agreed in principle) that the rituals of the Mosaic Law were no longer binding. Therefore, their concessions to the Judaisers are tantamount to an admission that their earlier decisions on this matter (confirmed with pledges, v.9) were *wrong*.

2.19 A second argument follows. The γάρ refers back to v.17 and is co-ordinate with the γάρ of v.18. Verse 19 seems rather enigmatic, but was probably not intended as such. Ambiguity is a trait the rhetorical theorists generally considered a result of poor workmanship. Nevertheless, going by what is more broadly presented in the letter to the Romans, the meaning is probably that Paul, through trying to obey the law, died to the law (personified and characterised in terms of its sanctions). The following ἵνα is somewhat clumsy, as if Paul had deliberately killed himself in the presence of the condemning law. This is surely not intended. The thought is rather that this death to the law happened in order that *in Christ* he might live to God (in the newness of the Spirit-led Christian life). That is to say, Paul did not just die before the judgment-seat of the law, but he was crucified together with Christ, implying also union with the new life which Christ received at his resurrection (v.20). For *this* reason Christ cannot be considered a minister of sin. Although the rituals of the Mosaic law are abandoned, nevertheless, followers of Christ still live for God. The ambiguity, poor stylistically, is of no great consequence as this main point is amply clear and further developed in the following verses. He has been crucified with Christ, i.e., cut off from the law (crucifixion being the ultimate curse of the law). The verb σταυρόομαι thus *hints* at cutting off from the law (ἔμφασις). Paul follows this up by means of his personal testimony, showing how he now identifies with the (living) Christ. This, of course, is meant as paradigmatic for any who would follow Christ.

2.20 The two clauses: ζῶ δὲ οὐκέτι ἐγώ, ζῆ δὲ ἐν ἐμοὶ Χριστός are a clever jingle. We have here the kind of artfully constructed ἀντίθεσις (using παρίσωσις and παρομοίωσις) generally condemned by rhetorical theorists, at least in serious contexts (cf. Thphr. *Fr.* 692 FHS&G; D.H. *Isoc.* 12 (p.72,12-14 U.-R.) and also §§ 13-15; *Dem.* 4 (p.135,19-22 U.-R.), 20, 25-26; Demetr. *Eloc.* 27-28, 247; Quint. *Inst.* 9.3.102; and the endnote to the select glossary). A short chiasm follows (ζῶ ἐν σαρκί, ἐν πίστει ζῶ, cf. [Hermog.] *Inv.* 4.8 re: κύκλος).

2.21 The *précis* of the rebuke to Peter finishes with a climactic sentence serving to sum up the issue as Paul sees it. If righteousness is by law, then Christ died in vain! Rhetorical theorists in general recommended that speeches close with great πάθος. Paul's climax also, however, contains once again unstated implications (ἔμφασις). The phrase "righteousness by law" is clearly meant to be a reference to compulsory circumcision and implies that its effect is to make one's salvation dependent upon justification by works. The implication is then that if circumcision is demanded, Christ died in vain.

2.4 Argument (3.1 - 4.11)

Part One: The Argument Itself (3.1-14)
The Argumentative Thread

At 3.1 Paul turns on the Galatians and asks, "who bewitched *you*?" (emphasis in Greek text via word order). The implication is that just as Peter was misled, so also are they. Paul has now quietly passed from his original point on the origin of his Gospel (1.11) to what he sees as the error of the Galatians, namely, that by reintroducing circumcision *et al* they have in effect abandoned salvation by faith in Christ for a Gospel of works. In doing so they have made the death of Christ to be vain.

Paul's next argument (3.2-14) is rather complex and involves tying three different strands together, namely, i) justification from God, ii) the experience of the Galatians in receiving the special gifts of the Holy Spirit, and iii) the significance of Christ's death (alluded to in the foregoing, 2.19 - 3.1).

The central point of the argument appears to surface only after the opening series of rhetorical questions concerning how the Galatians received the gifts of the Spirit. It comes with the scriptural example of Abraham. The *proposition* itself is introduced by the verb γινώσκω (3.7, cf. 1.11), namely, that those living by faith are sons of Abraham. This is later coupled with the opposite consideration, those living by the works of the law are under a curse (3.10).

The argument thus begins with the question of the reception of the Holy Spirit (3.2-5). Paul continues with the διαίρεσις which he set up in his speech to Peter, namely, that of salvation/ justification by works of the Law or by the hearing of faith.

Paul then cites the example (παράδειγμα) of Abraham. Abraham *believed/ had faith* in God, and it was this that was reckoned to him as righteousness (LXX *Ge.* 15.6). Paul clearly assumes that the Galatians have knowledge of the story of Abraham and recognise that the promise which Abraham is said to have believed was that his descendants would be a vast multitude (LXX *Ge.* 15.5).

He goes on to explain why the example of Abraham is relevant to the Galatians and introduces thereby his main point here, those who live *by faith* are the descendants of Abraham.

In doing this he makes the citation of Abraham function as a *proof*. Normally παραδείγματα would function to reinforce a position already argued for. Because of Abraham's position as *the* forefather of the Jewish faith, and because of the promise made to him with respect to Gentile nations, the citation of Abraham is much more than an historical comparison. The authority of Scripture recording God's promise that the nations would be blessed in Abraham has the stature of a prophecy, and thus a *necessary* proof. If the nations are to be blessed *in Abraham*, then that blessing must come about *by faith*, just as Abraham received God's favour *by believing God/ having faith in him*.

Paul's next step is to show that the other possibility of his διαίρεσις, i.e., obtaining righteousness by works, cannot work. It only produces a curse. Although Paul does not spell it out, his clear presupposition is that no one is able to fully obey the law as demanded, and that everyone attempting to gain favour from God via this route is therefore cursed (a point made more explicit in his letter to the Romans). He also attempts to show that Scripture clearly distinguishes the way of works from the principle of faith.

He then moves on to reintroduce the strand of Christ's death. He states that Christ has redeemed *us* from the curse of the law by dying on the cross. Paul clearly intends the Galatians to be included by the word "us," although here again there is a missing link in his argumentation which can be supplied from the letter to the Romans. Paul clearly viewed all men, Jews and Greeks, as condemned by the curse of the law. This is why Christ's death as freedom from the law's curse has significance to both Jews and Greeks. Here in this letter Paul merely adds that the effect of Christ's death releasing us from the law's curse is that we might partake of the blessing of Abraham in Christ. The two ἵνα clauses in 3.14 are probably meant to be co-ordinate, and so Paul ties the matter of the blessing of Abraham to the Galatians' reception of the gifts of the Spirit. Although the two are related, they should not, however, be identified. The Spirit was promised by Christ to his apostles whilst on earth, though Paul is perhaps thinking of the promise recorded by Joel and cited by Peter on the day of Pentecost. In any case, as Luke's record in *Act.Ap.* clearly shows, the reception of the special gifts of the Spirit among the Gentiles was received as a demonstration that Gentiles too had received repentance unto life (cf. *Act.Ap.* 10.44-48; 11.15-18). The reception of the promised Spirit was thus a seal of their reception of the blessing of Abraham, namely, justification (this is the connection made in *Ep.Gal.* 3.8) by faith.

What is the nature of the argumentation involved in the three different strands? i) Justification by faith is argued by the authoritative example of Abraham (see above). ii) The Galatians' reception of the Holy Spirit is argued from their own experience. The special manifestations of the Spirit among them have thus the nature of a necessary sign (τεκμήριον). The Galatians know full well that they received these gifts of the Spirit by believing (probably via the laying on of Paul's hands, cf. *Act.Ap.* 8).[359] iii) The significance of Christ's death as taking away the curse of the law for Jews and Gentiles is only partially argued for (and actually only partially explained! Cf. the significance of "us"). The connection between Christ's death and the curse is argued for by reference to LXX *De.* 21.23.

A structural outline of Paul's argument from 3.6-14 helps to show not only its structure, but also how many gaps there are in the logic which need to be filled in by the audience (marked off by square brackets).

- "Abraham believed God and it was reckoned to him for righteousness"
- [the promise he believed was that he would have a multitude of descendants]
- therefore those of faith are sons of Abraham

---

[359]   The fact that Gentiles received the special gifts of the Spirit directly in *Act.Ap.* 10 is one of the reasons for the great surprise of Peter *et al.* After Pentecost the reception of such gifts for subsequent believers came via the laying on of hands by the apostles. *Act.Ap.* 10 is a sort of second Pentecost.

- God is justifying the Gentiles by faith
- proved by Scripture's promise to Abraham: "in you all nations will be blessed"
- [the nations here refer to the promised multitude of descendants]
- therefore those of faith are blessed together with the believer Abraham

- those of the works of the law are under a curse
- it is written: "all who do not obey the law are cursed"
- [no one is able to completely obey the law]
- [therefore everyone is cursed]

- no one is justified with God by the law
- proved by Scripture: "the just-by-faith shall live"
- the law is not by faith
- proved by Scripture: "the doer of the laws shall live by them"

- [we are all cursed under the law, Jews and Gentiles (who have the principles of the law in their heart)]
- Christ has redeemed us from this curse by becoming the curse for us
- proved by Scripture: "everyone hanging on a tree is cursed"
- [Christ was crucified, and therefore cursed by God]
- therefore the blessing of Abraham came to the Gentiles
- therefore we receive the promise of the Spirit by faith

Clear ἐπιχειρήματα (rhetorical syllogisms) these arguments are not, despite the fact that our rhetorical sources allow for the omission of premises, explanations, or even the conclusion *if they are self-evident*. Too much is left unstated (noted in square brackets). It is interesting to note how the structure is varied. Paul begins by deducing a conclusion (underlined) which is stated after the premise. The second conclusion or proposition is stated first, and then argued for (cf. Cic. *Part.* 47; *Inv.* 1.76). Each proposition once argued, is again supported by another similar consideration.

The fact that so much must be understood between the lines, as it were, would suggest that Paul may be repeating points made to the Galatians in his earlier preaching to them. Such a consideration may be supported by the fact that we are able to fill in the gaps from his letter to the Romans, a letter probably reflecting much of his general presentation of the Gospel to established churches.[360]

---

[360] The two letters are probably to be dated quite close to each other. The letter to the Romans was written from Corinth, late AD 55 to early 56 or late 56 to early 57 (see C. E. B. Cranfield, 1975/79, *Commentary*, 1.12-16), whilst the letter to the Galatians (on the North Galatian theory) dates anywhere between AD 53-56. The argument in the letter to the Galatians is more compressed and difficult to follow than that in the letter to the Romans. Several factors contribute to this: i) The fact that in the letter to the Galatians Paul is writing to a congregation where he has personally preached and taught, and so may presume knowledge of his teaching. ii) The fact that we have no knowledge of the precise nature of the Judaistic heresy, nor of their use of Old Testament Scripture. It is probable that Paul's argumentation to some degree reacts to this. The letter to the Romans on the other hand is written to a congregation which Paul has never seen nor ministered to, which explains his fuller presentation of the Gospel. The letter to the Romans does not necessarily polemicise against specific problems within the Roman congregation. It

That Paul's argument is no logical demonstration is clear. Many questions remain, e.g., how is the sacrificial system which provided the possibility of atonement for the sins of the Israelites to be viewed in connection with Paul's interpretation of LXX *De.* 27.26 and *Le.* 18.5?

Furthermore, many aspects of the argument are not proved, but merely stated. Paul is here also *teaching* and instructing the Galatians. At the same time, he attempts to prove (mostly from Scripture) certain key points of his teaching, but even this is sometimes left open to question. Why is a certain text to be interpreted in that way? We may answer that as a divinely appointed apostle, he *interprets* the Scriptures for the Galatians. But Paul would probably expect his interpretation to be accepted as reasonable, although it also comes with his divinely based authority.

Rhetorical Notes

3.1 To rebuke one's audience as strongly as Paul does here was never recommended by rhetorical theorists, who are always concerned with ensuring that one's words are persuasive and not inciting opposition (cf. Quint. *Inst.* 3.8.69). Even when strong words were required, the rhetoricians suggested various ways in which the rebuke might be softened or made palatable, see select glossary *s.v.* παρρησία. With this rebuke, as with Paul's concentration on his divine authority, Paul departs from rhetorical theory. Such rebukes are more the province of popular philosophical literature.

βασκαίνω: a μεταφορά referring to the use of the evil eye.[361]

Paul indicates that his preaching of Jesus Christ as crucified was vivid, placing this fact before their eyes. The importance of vivid description is very frequently described by the rhetorical theorists (and others in antiquity) as setting the matter "before the eyes" (Arist. *Rh.* 3.10.7 - 11.5; Cic. *de Orat.* 3.202; *Orat.* 139; [Longin.] 15.1; Quint. *Inst.* 9.2.40-44; Plb. 2.56). His implication is that if they had kept this fact before their eyes, they would not have succumbed to the evil eye.

3.1-5 The πάθος of his letter reaches fever pitch, not only by the strength of his rebuke, but also by the string of accusatory rhetorical questions addressed to the

---

is therefore quite warranted to use it, with caution, in order to aid understanding of the letter to the Galatians. Of course, an eye must be kept to certain differences. In the letter to the Galatians, for example, Paul is thinking of the law primarily as a set of outward rules, do not touch, do not taste, etc.. In the letter to the Romans, the law is envisaged more as the concretisation of a general moral code.

[361] The references in H. D. Betz (1988, *Galaterbrief,* 241n) to the use of this word among the orators are not really germane since the term is there used in quite another way, namely, of maligning. The semantic context does not permit that meaning here (cf. LSJ *s.v.*).

Galatians. These questions are opened in v.2 in a way which initially disguises the fact
that they are rhetorical, and seems to imply that Paul really wanted to learn their answer (τοῦτο μόνον θέλω μαθεῖν ἀφ᾽ ὑμῶν). The irony of the rhetorical questions which
follow in 3.2 and 5 is hereby heightened. At 3.2 he expects the Galatians to answer "by
the hearing of faith." They know that they received the Spirit (and its concomitant
gifts, the δυνάμεις v.5) by faith. This answer (ἐξ ἀκοῆς πίστεως) is again assumed at
3.6 where Paul continues ... καθὼς ᾿Αβραάμ.

Demetr. Eloc. 279 notes that such a string of rhetorical questions leads the
audience to perplexity, seeming as if they are under cross examination with nothing to
answer. Quint. Inst. 9.2.7-8 also notes how such rhetorical questions can be used to
threaten (instandi gratia). Rhetorical theorists may, perhaps, have questioned the use of
such great πάθος at this point in the argumentation. Πάθος is something to be especially reserved for an effective peroration so that a speech may end with a resounding
climax. However, the nature of this letter as primarily a rebuke explains the high
degree of πάθος throughout.

3.4 contains an example of μεταβολή (correction, see select glossary s.v.).
Demetrius lists it as one of the τόποι which may function to help make the audience
favourable (Eloc. 148). Paul here provides the Galatians with an option to repent. Their
previous experiences/ sufferings (the sense is unclear) do not have to have been in vain.

3.8 presents us with a kind of micro-προσωποποιΐα. The Scripture is here personified and made to preach the Gospel to Abraham. Such personification is not elsewhere found in the New Testament, apart from the standard phrases such as λέγει
("Scripture says").[362] Because of the emotional character of προσωποποιΐα, rhetorical
theorists recommended its use at the end of a speech.

3:10 contains ἐπιφορά (successive clauses ending in the same word, here εἰσίν).

Part Two: Didactic Explanation (3.15 - 4.11)
The Argumentative Thread

Having established the mutual opposition of salvation by faith and by works, i.e.,
of blessing/ promise and law, Paul turns to the question of the relationship of the two
in the Old Testament. He appears to deal with a possible objection to his argumentation
here, namely, that the Mosaic law coming later superceded or changed the nature of the

---

[362] Ph. Leg.All. 3.118ff is an excellent parallel. Here Philo personifies ὁ ἱερὸς λόγος and, just as Paul,
has "him" speak via a citation (i.e., προσωποποιΐα). Whether Philo and Paul represent a typical Jewish
way of speaking is an open question. The rabbinical phrase referred to by Str.-B. 3.538 is not really a
true parallel.

Abrahamic διαθήκη. It is interesting that he does not deal with the possibility of another interpretation of the Abrahamic διαθήκη. This may suggest that either his opponents agreed with his interpretation, or that an interpretation of it was not germane to their own argumentation.

Paul's (human) comparison at 3.15-18 calls for some comment. In the first place, what Paul does here is introduce an argument from the lesser to the greater, not a σύγκρισις as such.[363] If a ratified human διαθήκη is not set aside or changed, then this applies all the more to a divine διαθήκη (3.17).

Now Paul states, with respect to a διαθήκη among humans, that no one sets it aside or adds to it. *Prima facie* it would seem that Paul's consideration is contradicted by a κοινὸς τόπος (in the sense of a set argument) with respect to laws and contracts which was common in rhetorical theory, namely, that a later contract, law or any written document invalidated an earlier one (cf. Arist. *Rh.* 1.15.25; Cic. *Inv.* 2.145; Quint. *Inst.* 7.7.8 and also Just. *dial.* 11).[364] The question arises as to what Paul intends by the term διαθήκη.

In the Septuagint (in secular literature but rarely) διαθήκη refers to a contract or covenant. Nevertheless, the normal Greek usage of the term was that of a last will and testament.[365] Although Paul does not seem to think of a διαθήκη in terms of the necessary death of anyone, he does relate the term to κληρονομία (inheritance). Paul probably interpreted the Septuagint to be referring to a kind of testament in the sense of a promise of some kind of inheritance.

Paul's comment that no one sets aside or alters a human διαθήκη is thus made with reference not to a contract, but to a will. This distinction does not really help solve the descrepancy with the rhetorical κοινὸς τόπος, however. Rhetorical theory generally included all kinds of written documents, including wills, under what it said

---

[363] A σύγκρισις is a comparison between the subject in hand and something else in order to show how the one is better, worse, or equal to the other.

[364] J. S. Vos (1992, "Antinomie," 261 and note) attempts to relativise this κοινὸς τόπος by stating that whilst Cicero says the youngest law is always valid, others leave the question open. It is, however, clear from the sources that, special cases excepted (e.g., that a more recent contract was based on deceit), the most recent law was *always* to be considered binding. Where this is not specifically stated (e.g., in Quint. *Inst.* 7.7.8) it is clearly assumed as common knowledge.

Was this κοινὸς τόπος used to promote the Mosaic law over against the promise made to Abraham by the Judaisers?

[365] Paul's language is not specific enough to be referring to the Jewish מתנת בריא, described by H. D. Betz (1979, *Galatians*, 155) as a "transaction of property from donor to donee, which takes place at once and is not conditional upon the donor's death, although he may retain his right to usufruct during his lifetime." It is even doubtful whether the מתנת בריא is a realistic option. See further, Betz (1988, *Galaterbrief*, 280-81) and the literature cited there. Betz supports this interpretation.

concerning laws (cf. Cic. *Top.* 96; Quint. *Inst.* 7.5.6). In any case, in antiquity a testator always had the right to make modifications to his will, or to substitute a new will in place of an older one.[366]

But what does Paul mean to indicate by speaking of a κεκυρωμένη διαθήκη? *Prima facie* he would seem to indicate a will which is legitimately drawn up. A phrase such as ἡ διαθήκη κυρία (or similar) was a common formula in all kinds of legal documents throughout the Greek world, evidenced from classical times through to the fourth century AD. It was designed to secure the legal status of the document.[367]

Nevertheless, it seems rather unlikely that Paul would not have realised that wills could be modified or replaced. For this reason, it is just possible that Paul means to speak of a will which has come into force, i.e., in a human situation, by the death of the testator (cf. *Ep.Hebr.* 9.16-17). Of *such* a will, it could properly be said that no one adds to it or sets it aside. The comparison is, however, not exact. The διαθήκη of God granting an inheritance to Abraham and to his seed is not brought into force by the death of the testator (God)! Perhaps Paul would have argued that it was brought into force by the death of the sacrificial animals and birds in the covenant rite. In any case, Paul appears to want to compare a last will and testament that has come into force, with the covenant/ will which God made with Abraham and *brought into force* at that time (cf. *Ep.Gal.* 3.17).

Given this explanation, the κοινὸς τόπος from rhetorical theory referred to above is irrelevant.

Paul next turns to the intent of the *adding* of the Mosaic law (3.19-22).[368] His point is that unlike illegal additions to a will which has come into force and which may

---

[366]   Cf. E. Bund, 1979, "Testamentum," esp. § I.4b; I.7a-b; II.1-2. Certain examples of wills among the papyri from Egypt evidence a clause effectively prohibiting additions, e.g., the will of Taharpaesis which states at the closing (§ 18), Ἄλλῳ [γ]ὰρ οὐδενὶ οὐδὲν τῶν ἐμῶ[ν κα]ταλείπω. D. Kamp, who published this papyrus, notes other examples (1968, "Testament," 128). Nevertheless, such a will could still be replaced by the testator at another time with a completely new document.

   Antipas is known to have contested the validity of the later will of his father Herod (cf. J. *BJ* 2.20; *AJ* 17.224). The grounds, however, were the soundness of Herod's judgement at the time of writing the later alteration (cf. J. *BJ* 2.31, 35-36; *AJ* 17.244).

[367]   Of wills, see D. Kamp, 1968, "Testament," 94 (§ 18) with commentary; *PEleph.* 2.15 (284 BC); *POxy.* 494.26 and 29-30 (AD 156-65). Of other contracts (a few examples from the first centuries BC and AD): *PTeb.* 104.39 (92 BC); 110.13-14 (92 or 59 BC); *BGU* 998.13 (101 BC); 1103.26 (13 BC); *POxy.* 261.17-18 (AD 55); 269.12-13 (AD 57); 270.50 (AD 94); 275.33-34 (AD 66).

[368]   H. D. Betz (1988, *Galaterbrief*, 163) describes 3.19-25 as a *digressio*, i.e., not a new argument but a digression preventing a wrong conclusion. In his view v.26 begins a new proof section based on ecclesiastical tradition (Betz interprets 3.26-28 as the citation of a baptism liturgy). Yet as our analysis shall show, 3.1 - 4.11 is one long, essentially unified, argument. Although in v.19 Paul does begin to explain the intent of the adding of the law, he does this in such a way that his explanation is highly relevant to the main point of his letter, namely, that the Galatians turn from the Judaistic version of the Gospel they have adopted. In this respect the pericope cannot be considered a digression, nor does Paul include anything like the popular ἄφοδος (cf. Quint. *Inst.* 9.3.87) to call himself back to his main sub-

thereby *alter* the conditions for inheritance, the addition of the law does not contradict the promise. It had an entirely different purpose. The law was not given in order to grant life, but was added on account of transgressions.

Whilst Paul's main point is clear, the argument of verses 19-20 is not so transparent. The point would appear to be connected with the initial answer to the question, why the law? He states, "it was added for the sake of transgressions ... having been ordained through angels by the hand of a mediator." The introduction of the concept of a mediator/ arbitrator (in this case Moses, cf. OT *Ex.* 20.18-19) implies the existence of *two* estranged parties which need to be brought together. Verse 20 stresses the point that the presence of a mediator implies two parties, and adds that God is but one of those parties. God alone is, therefore, not responsible for the introduction of the law. In fact the estrangement was Israel's fault, for it was on account of their sin that the law was added. Paul seems to be arguing here that the introduction of the law was a measure designed to bring God and Israel back together. Had man not sinned, the introduction of the Mosaic law (again, here considered as material regulations) would not have been necessary. The metaphors of verses 22-25 illustrate how the law functioned to bring God and his people together, primarily, by leading Israel to the coming Christ, the object of the faith by which man is justified by God (and so reconciled to him).

In v.22 Paul states that the Scripture (once again personified) has, by bringing in the law, "confined" (a metaphor of imprisonment) all things under sin. This is a reference to the argumentation presupposed at 3.10, namely, that the presence of the law, which is impossible to completely obey, only demonstrates that all men fall under its curse, i.e., are sinners before God. The adding of the law (here in this letter, in particular, a law of material regulations) only serves to highlight man's plight (cf. *Ep.Rom.* 5.20) and cannot possibly provide righteousness (the suggestion refuted in v.21).

The intent of the giving of the law is now further illustrated by two metaphors (3.23-25). Paul first modifies the metaphor of imprisonment introduced in v.22. He describes "us" as having been held in custody by the law (personified) awaiting the faith to come (i.e., $\mu\varepsilon\tau\omega\nu\nu\mu\dot{\iota}\alpha$ for the content of that faith, Jesus Christ).[369] The use of

---

ject. In fact, we see instead that v.26 is integrally connected to v.25. The $\gamma\dot{\alpha}\rho$ indicates that Paul will now explain why it is that a $\pi\alpha\iota\delta\alpha\gamma\omega\gamma\dot{o}\varsigma$ is no longer needed when "faith" came.

[369] That $\dot{\upsilon}\pi\dot{o}$ refers to the agent in v.23 (and does not mean "under" in the sense of the previous verse) is indicated both by the verb and by the personification in the following verse. The use of $\sigma\upsilon\gamma\kappa\lambda\varepsilon\dot{\iota}\varepsilon\iota\nu$ $\tau\iota\nu\dot{\alpha}$ $\varepsilon\dot{\iota}\varsigma$ $\tau\iota$ was a common metaphorical construction in Hellenistic Greek (cf. $\sigma\nu\gamma\kappa\lambda\varepsilon\dot{\iota}\omega$ in LSJ I.2 and BAGD 2.), though $\varepsilon\dot{\iota}\varsigma$ invariably refers to *place*. The Septuagint, however, also uses $\varepsilon\dot{\iota}\varsigma$ to refer to the purpose for which someone is imprisoned (cf. LXX *Ps.* 77 (78).50 $\tau\dot{\alpha}$ $\kappa\tau\dot{\eta}\nu\eta$ $\alpha\dot{\upsilon}\tau\dot{\omega}\nu$ $\varepsilon\dot{\iota}\varsigma$ $\theta\dot{\alpha}\nu\alpha\tau\sigma\nu$ $\sigma\nu\nu\dot{\varepsilon}\kappa\lambda\varepsilon\iota\sigma\varepsilon$, v.62 $\sigma\nu\nu\dot{\varepsilon}\kappa\lambda\varepsilon\iota\sigma\varepsilon\nu$ $\varepsilon\dot{\iota}\varsigma$ $\dot{\rho}\sigma\mu\varphi\alpha\dot{\iota}\alpha\nu$ $\tau\dot{o}\nu$ $\lambda\alpha\dot{o}\nu$ $\alpha\dot{\upsilon}\tau\sigma\dot{\upsilon}$, and *Ep.Rom.* 11.32).

the first person plural is rather vague. Does it refer to Paul and the Galatians, or to Paul and others as Jews? The most obvious application is to the Jews, but Paul's transformation of the metaphor at 4.4-5 and its application at 4.8-11 makes it clear that he does not wish to exclude application to the Galatians themselves. He then changes the metaphor by calling the law a παιδαγωγός, i.e., the man (usually a slave) responsible for conducting a child to and from school. Such παιδαγωγοί were also responsible for the discipline of their charges, and frequently carried a rod with them.[370] Just as the παιδαγωγός led his boy to school, so the law led the Jews to Christ. The comparison of law to a παιδαγωγός is also found in Plut. *Mor.* 645b.[371] The function of these metaphors is clearly to illustrate what Paul has argued for in verses 19-22.

Paul continues in v.26 with an explanation of the conclusion drawn from his last metaphor, namely, that when "faith" came there was no longer need for a παιδαγωγός. This leads Paul into a new theological turn which seems rather confusing to the reader until explained at 4.1-7. Given the argument so far, one would expect Paul to say that after Christ came (i.e., "faith"), those who believe in him become sons of Abraham, inheriting the promise through faith in Christ (who was the promised seed of Abraham). Instead, however, we are surprised to hear that the παιδαγωγός is no longer necessary because the Galatians are sons of *God*! The surprising turn (cf. παράδοξον, Quint. *Inst.* 9.2.22-24) is perhaps deliberately emphasised by the change from first person plural to second person plural.

Paul's method at this point could be assessed in two ways. It could be argued (with some justification) that this new turn is quite confusing and likely to confuse the listeners (remember that the letter would have been read aloud to the congregation). However, it could also be argued that Paul is at any rate attempting to grab his audience's attention and hold it in expectation (cf. Quint. *Inst.* 9.2.22-24). By throwing out this new twist without explanation, he causes his audience to prick their ears up and listen for the connection. Paul doesn't answer the connection right away, or straightforwardly, but chooses first to amplify the connection of the believer with Christ, and then via a similar illustration to explain what he means.

---

[370] Cf. Pl. *Prt.* 325c-d; Theon *Prog.* ii, p.98,32f Sp.; Quint. *Inst.* 1.9.5 and for a stereotyped picture of the παιδαγωγός in general, Lib. *Chr.* 3, p.85,13 - p.86,1 F.. On the Greek παιδαγωγός, cf. S. F. Bonner, 1977, *Education*, 38-39.

[371] J. B. Lightfoot (1865, *Epistle*, 149) cites a passage gleaned from Wetstein which he references as Liban.iv.437 ed. Reiske. Wetstein references the passage as Lib. D.XXV p.576 C. This passage is not to be found in the equivalent section of Förster's edition, nor is it to be located using the *Concordantiae in Libanium* (ed. G. Fatouros *et al* [Hildesheim: G. Olms, 1987-8]). Comparisons of the law to leaders, guides or teachers were common (cf. Chrysipp. *Stoic.* 3.77; Ph. *Ebr.* 198; D.Chr. 75.1-2, 9).

At 3.27-29 Paul begins his explanation of the surprising twist. The connection of
the believers with Christ is illustrated (via a metaphor) by referring to baptism as an act
of putting Christ on as one would clothing, a common metaphor in the LXX, of
σωτηρία 2 Ch. 6.41; of αἰσχύνη Jb 8.22; of δικαιοσύνη Jb 29.14; of φόβος Jb 39.19,
etc.. The effects of this unity with Christ are also described, and the expected conclusion is drawn that if there is unity with Christ, then they may also be called seed of
Abraham and heirs of the promise. But this was what was initially expected. Paul needs
now to explain how they are sons of *God*.

The metaphor of 3.24 is now altered and presented as an ἀλληγορία (in the
rhetorical sense, cf. select glossary *s.v.*), namely, an illustration stating one thing in
straightforward language, but signifying something else.[372] The period under law is
likened to that of a son under age.[373] But instead of the term νόμος as in 3.24, the
phrase τὰ στοιχεῖα τοῦ κόσμου is now substituted as a περίφρασις (periphrasis). It is
not really germane to this study to examine the hundreds of interpretations of this
phrase. It will suffice to briefly give my own understanding as it affects the description
of Paul's argumentation.

Paul's reason for this περίφρασις is neither ornamental nor to deck some
indecent expression (the two reasons given in the rhetorical sources, cf. for example,
Quint. *Inst.* 8.6.59-61), but to indicate what aspect of the Mosaic law he is here
highlighting. That the phrase is co-ordinate to νόμος is clear from the context and the
use of the phrase ὑπὸ νόμον in the two following verses. We should, therefore, not
expect "the elemental things of the world" to refer to the four elements here, nor to the
heavenly bodies (whether considered as divinities or not). The terminology is quite
vague and we should be careful not to impute too specific a meaning to the phrase.
Paul is most probably referring to the Mosaic law as a law code containing elemental
laws of the world, namely, ritual regulations requiring various outward observances but
having no direct spiritual or ethical significance.

This interpretation also fits Paul's use of the same term at v.9 where it refers to
pagan religion. The στοιχεῖα, mentioned in v.9, are clearly in some way connected

---

[372] In this sense, any example or illustration presented without a *preceding* explanation functions as an
ἀλληγορία, cf. Quint. *Inst.* 8.6.52.
[373] The precise nature of Paul's comparison remains unclear. H. D. Betz suggests the *tutela
testamentaria* of Roman law, i.e., the right of a father to stipulate guardians in his will in case those
named in the inheritance are under age at the time of his death. The specification of a time by the father
does not function in Roman law, however, as the guardianship (*tutela*) ends when the child comes of age,
although see Betz' comments on *testamentaria* found in the provinces (1988, *Galaterbrief*, 357). The
death of the father is also an aspect of the comparison which does not function in Paul's application. It
may be that Paul is not thinking in terms of the death of the father, but of a father's arrangements for the
management and upbringing of his children.

with the observance of days, months, seasons and years. The term occurs again in *Ep. Col.* 2.8 and 20 where the context is not dissimilar. Paul is rebuking the Colossians for returning to regulations such as μὴ ἅψῃ μηδὲ γεύσῃ μηδὲ θίγῃς (*Ep. Col.* 2.21) involving food and drink or in respect of a feast, new moon or sabbath. The Colossians had clearly been influenced by some kind of Judaic syncretism,[374] and it is not impossible that the form of Judaising troubling the Galatians was also somewhat syncretistic, although the days, months, seasons and years can also be interpreted solely in terms of Jewish law.

By paraphrasing the Mosaic law in v.3 in terms of the elemental things of the world Paul effectively constructs a link between this aspect of Mosaic law and heathen ritual law which the Galatians came out of. Christ was born ὑπὸ νόμον and the lack of the definite article is probably significant here. Christ has redeemed those enslaved by (ritual) law (v.5, τοὺς ὑπὸ νόμον [*sc.* δεδουλωμένους]), whether Mosaic or heathen.[375] This link between Jewish and pagan law is made more explicit in verses 8-11.

At verses 4-5 the statement that they are sons of God is finally explained by showing that their connection with Christ is a connection with Christ as the son of God. The comparison becomes mixed at this point. Had Paul elected to continue with his original comparison he would have had to say that the Galatians at a certain point in time came of age and *therefore* were entitled to the inheritance. This thought, implying entitlement because of something in and of themselves, is theologically unacceptable to Paul. The comparison is thus altered and those who were first considered sons under age and therefore *likened* to slaves, are now considered to *be* slaves who need redemption. Thus, Paul states that Christ *redeemed* those under the law (i.e., those in slavery) that they might be adopted as sons of God and therefore have an entitlement to the inheritance. At this point Paul also ties in the reception of the Spirit, which is where this lengthy argument began. The Spirit is the Spirit of God's son, Jesus Christ, and thus is a σημεῖον of their union with Christ and their sonship in respect of God.

At 4.8-11 Paul concludes the long section of argument from Scripture beginning at 3.1. Paul now explicitly identifies the Galatians' current observance of Mosaic ritual as a *return* to the weak and impoverished elemental things of their own previous pagan religion (cf. the emphasis in the words πάλιν ἄνωθεν).[376] This is strong language, the

---

[374]   In how far one may argue syncretism on the basis of stipulations involving drink is, however, questionable, cf. Aristeas 142.

[375]   At this point we may notice that Paul's comparison of Mosaic and heathen law differs from that in *Ep. Rom.* 2 where the moral aspect of the law is in view.

[376]   The words πάλιν ἄνωθεν seems to be a variation of the more common πάλιν αὖ(θις), cf. LXX *Wi.* 19.6.

more so as it is couched in a rhetorical question. The identification should probably be considered as ὑπερβολή, considering Paul's general respect for the law elsewhere (e.g., *Ep.Rom.* 7.12). Aristotelian tradition (as distinct from Hellenistic rhetorical theory, cf. Arist. *Rh.* 3.11.15; Demetr. *Eloc.* 124-27, 161-62, 182-86 and contrast, for example, Str. 3.2.9) considered the use of ὑπερβολή too emotional for rhetoric. It was often merely an expression of anger. Paul's use of ἐπερώτησις and ὑπερβολή contributes to the πάθος here which is appropriately increased at this concluding point of this line of argumentation. Their ritual observances are at once summed up, and the list is made to feel very long by the use of πολυσύνδετον (multiple use of conjunctions or connecting particles, cf. Demetr. *Eloc.* 54, 63). These lines probably had some shock effect on the Galatians who would not have expected their observance of Jewish law to be compared with the pagan religion they had abandoned. Paul concludes with an emotional suggestion similar to that which he made at the beginning of the argument (3.4). Has his work been in vain?

Rhetorical Notes

3.16b Within the argument of verses 15-18, verse 16b seems somewhat out of place. It contributes nothing to the argument in hand (lesser to greater), yet the point that the promise was made to Christ (seed singular) is taken up later on. Paul appears to add a proleptic explanation of the promise to Abraham here. It is not related to his specific point at this place, but will be important later on. Such an argument, that a collective noun should nevertheless be treated as referring here to a singular subject, would not be acceptable as an explanation of a human document, but becomes possible due to the prophetic nature of Scripture in the eyes of Paul (and presumably his audience).[377]

3.19 The use of αἰτιολογία (a short inquiring question, which is answered by the speaker, cf. v.21) implies a conversational style such as is appropriate for letters. It also helps to hold the audience's interest (cf. *Rhet.Her.* 4.23-24).

3.28 Vivid repetition. This resembles what Quint. *Inst.* 9.3.49 says was called διαλλαγή, the ramming home of a point by using different or similar terms to describe it.

4.1 The statement that the child differs in *nothing* from a slave is ὑπερβολή, emphasising the point.

---

[377] It seems unlikely to me that Paul intended to say that σπέρμα did not also refer to the Jewish race descended from Abraham, cf. *Ep.Rom.* 4.18; 9.7.

4.4-5 ἀναφορά (anaphora) using first γενόμενον and then ἵνα. Compare Hebrew parallelism.

4.9 We have here a good example of μεταβολή (see select glossary *s.v.*) used to emphasise the point made by the correction. Note that this figure does not necessarily imply that the original statement was completely incorrect.

2.5 Emotional Appeal (4.12 - 5.12)

Part One: Personal Plea (4.12-20)

The following paragraph (4.12-20) contains a personal plea from Paul that they be like him. Paul reminds them how he first came to them in physical need, and of their caring response. Has he become their enemy by telling the truth? A criticism of his opponents follows together with a rather bold metaphor referring to his efforts to correct the Galatians. Paul closes the section with a sigh of perplexity with respect to them.

This whole appeal is both quite emotional and replete with rhetorical devices. Some of these devices give direct aid to the πάθος of the pericope whilst others are artful, figures commonly considered more suited to epideictic.

The πάθος of the section is supported by the direct rhetorical questions and the appeal itself which continues the rather direct contact with the audience (cf. ἀνακοίνωσις). The very dramatic metaphor of v.19 underlines this. Such a bold metaphor was not generally considered suitable for prose among the rhetorical theorists. It probably underscores the emotional nature of Paul's appeal. The desire to be present with the Galatians (v.20) was an epistolary commonplace of the time, but this should not be made to detract from the sincerity of Paul's wish.

The more "studied" devices are, for example, the words οὐκ ἐξουθενήσατε οὐδὲ ἐξεπτύσατε in 4.14. J. B. Lightfoot remarks (probably correctly): "As ἀποπτύειν is more usual than ἐκπτύειν in this metaphorical sense, the latter seems to be preferred here for the sake of the alliteration."[378] The phrase is an example of ἀντενναντίωσις (the casting of a positive statement in a negative form, cf. Alex. *Fig.* 2.23; Tryph. *Trop.* 2.15 where it is classified as a kind of ἀντίφρασις), and is emphasised by the repetition of the thought by an added synonym (cf. *Rhet.Her.* 4.38, *interpretatio*). Such an ἀντενναντίωσις frequently has the effect of an understatement (cf. *Rhet.Her.* 4.50). In this case the understatement is immediately followed by an overstatement (ὑπερβολή)

---

378   1865, *Epistle*, 175.

in the form of two similes (εἰκόνες), namely, that he was received as an angel of God or even as Christ Jesus himself. The use of ὑπερβολή was common in the ancient world (cf. Quint. *Inst.* 8.6.75), and also generally recommended by rhetorical theorists.[379] The thought conveyed by this verse (4.14) is significantly emphasised by the use of these figures.

In v.17 we have a word-play (ζηλοῦσιν ὑμᾶς ... αὐτοὺς ζηλοῦτε) not dissimilar to ἀντιμεταβολή (cf. *Rhet.Her.* 4.39; Quint. *Inst.* 9.3.85; Rut.Lup. 1.6). It also demonstrates the figure κύκλος (chiasm, cf. [Hermog.] *Inv.* 4.8). The critique of Dionysius of Halicarnassus (*Th.* 48, reflected generally in other rhetorical theorists) that παρονομασία does not produce πάθος but ἐπιτήδευσις probably reflects a practice popular among many with which many theorists did not approve. Verses 17-18 contain a double πολύπτωτόν (cf. *Rhet.Her.* 4.31; Quint. *Inst.* 9.3.37), ζηλοῦσιν, ζηλοῦτε, ζηλοῦσθαι and καλῶς, καλόν, καλῷ.[380]

Part Two: An Allegory (4.21 - 5.1)

A rather abrupt change of mood occurs between 4.20 and 21. Paul has just noted how he could wish to be with the Galatians and is perplexed over them. He then lashes out with another rhetorical question in an evident emotional outburst of anger (Vict. *Gal.* 1185a rightly speaks of *indignatio*). The anger is heightened by the use of αὐτονομασία which theorists note could be used for praise or censure (e.g., *Rhet.Her.* 4.42). Here the censure is evident when Paul calls the Galatians οἱ ὑπὸ νόμον θέλοντες εἶναι. Paul also speaks with a hint of irony (εἰρωνεία) when he asks if they listen to the law, for his interpretation of the story of the birth of Isaac and Ishmael will turn the straightforward interpretation on its head! Instead of the Jews being the sons of Isaac (i.e., sons of the promise), Paul uses an allegorical interpretation to draw the *opposite* conclusion. The Jews are the sons of the slave woman, whilst those living by faith are the sons of the promise. He adds a further prickling thrust by daring to apply LXX *Ge.* 21.10 to the situation. The obvious implication is that the Galatians should cast the Judaising teachers out from their midst. It is thus striking that by the end of the paragraph Paul's anger (and for the readers, his implicit rebuke in 4.21) is no longer directed at the Galatians themselves, but at the Judaisers who must be cast out. The emotion is thus directed to instigate among the Galatians an appropriate feeling of animosity towards the Judaisers.

---

[379] The Peripatetic tradition is a minor exception in that it discouraged the use of ὑπερβολή. See my forthcoming *Glossary*, *s.v.*.

[380] Strictly speaking this kind of πολύπτωτόν refers to the case endings of nouns or adjectives, but the same principle is here at work with a verb.

But what does Paul mean precisely when he says that the story of Abraham's two sons ἐστιν ἀλληγορούμενα?

With respect to the term ἀλληγορία it is important to distinguish between two quite distinct activities, namely, that of the use of ἀλληγορία in *speaking* (or writing), and its use in *interpretation*. These two distinct uses of the term have unfortunately often been confused. The use of ἀλληγορία when speaking is discussed by the rhetorical theorists (see select glossary *s.v.*), but they never address the quite distinct question of allegorical interpretation. A good example of rhetorical ἀλληγορία is provided by Paul in *Ep. Gal.* 5.9. Here a proverb is quoted as an ἀλληγορία. Symbolic or metaphorical language is used to make a point. What is literally said may be true or false, but it is not the point. The point being made is the inner or figurative meaning lying behind the expression.

Rhetorical theory when discussing the use of ἀλληγορία usually confines itself to examples consisting of short comments couched in metaphorical language. The discussions of the theoreticians do not often extend to the use of a mythical story deliberately told as an allegory. Such deliberate allegorical stories (apart from the question of the interpretation of the poets) were not common in Greek literature. Nevertheless, it has been suggested that, given the penchant of many rhetors for using short citations of Homer allegorically, treatises dedicated to an allegorical explanation of Homer may have been used as source books.[381]

When we come to the question of an allegorical interpretation of stories in the Old Testament, the allegorical interpretation of Homer forms an obvious analogy. This interpretative method had become popular amongst (particularly Stoic) philosophers.

> Although such allegorical interpretation of Homer has a long history, especially among Stoic philosophers, there are really only five major sources of this approach extant. Of these, the three earliest fall within the first or second centuries AD, namely, Cornutus, *de Natura Deorum* (first century AD); Heraclitus, *Allegoriae* (= *Quaestiones Homericae*, probably first century AD) and Ps.-Plutarch, *de Vita et Poesi Homeri* (second century AD).[382]
> It is clear that the allegorical interpretation of the ancient poets (primarily Homer) rested upon the same basic definition of ἀλληγορία as was common in rhetorical theory.[383] In fact, Heraclit. *All.* 5-6 even goes so far as to defend his interpretation of Homer by showing first how (rhetorical) allegory was common in the poets. As in rhetorical theory so also in the allegorising of Homer it is the inner meaning that is being communicated. The truth or falsity of the myths concerned does not matter. In fact, for the Homeric interpreters this was an important point, for they wished to exonerate Homer from writing blasphemous myths about the gods.
> In this respect, it is significant that these sources argue that Homer himself *spoke* in ἀλληγορίαι, that is to say, that Homer *intended* to communicate philosophy by means of the

---

[381]   See F. Wehrli, 1928, *Geschichte*, 96.

[382]   The other two sources are Porphyry, *Quaestiones Homericae*, and the scholia to the *Iliad*.

[383]   In respect of the relation between rhetoric and allegory, see J. Leopold, 1983, "Rhetoric."

mythical stories which he wrote.[384] Of course, such an opinion needed defence. Apart from the question why Homer may have wished to speak in this way, there was also the consideration that for ἀλληγορία to be effective, the audience had to recognise that the language was figurative. Heraclit. *All.* 1-3 offers a defence of this opinion, worked out in the rest of his treatise. He even goes so far as to argue that Homer, by writing in this way, is *not* ambiguous, but made his own method quite clear (§ 5, p.8,9-20 Oel.),[385] although he elsewhere likens the allegorical myths to τελεταί which a hierophant must expound (§ 64). Maximus Tyrius (10, cf. 26, second century AD) also defends the view that the poets deliberately spoke of philosophy via myths. Although Maximus speaks in terms of αἰνίγματα and not ἀλληγορίαι, he frequently uses the term αἰνίγματα in a broad sense equivalent to ἀλληγορίαι, even if at § 6 he notes that the μύθους λόγου μὲν ἀφανεστέρους, αἰνίγματος δὲ σαφεστέρους.[386] Ps.-Plu. *Vit.Hom.* 92-160, in his enthusiasm for Homer as the originator of every scholarly pursuit, with respect to philosophy also argues that Homer was *speaking* in αἰνίγματα (cf. 92.3; 100) and ἀλληγορίαι and so *deliberately* expounding all manner of philosophical doctrine via his mythical stories. The verb ἀλληγορέω is here clearly used in the sense of *speaking* in allegory (as opposed to *interpreting* in allegory), even though allegorical interpretations of Homer are presented (cf. § 96.1; 102.2).

The *raison d'être* for this approach to Homer was the criticism by others of the scandalous way Homer spoke of the gods, cf. Cic. *N.D.* 2.64-71; [Longin.] 9.7 (Heraclitus specifically polemicises against Plato and Epicurus). If Homer was to remain an ethically responsible pedagogical text, then he *had* to be interpreted allegorically. It was, however, not enough to just *interpret* Homer allegorically, one had also to maintain (and attempt to prove) that Homer *intended* to speak allegorically of philosophy. In this way, the allegorical approach to Homer may be seen as an extension of rhetorical theory on ἀλληγορία (although rhetorical theory never discusses the question whether the poets spoke their myths allegorically).

Naturally this approach to Homer *et al* did not satisfy everyone, and there is a history of critique down through the centuries (cf. Pl. *R.* 378d). In the first century AD we hear from Seneca (*Ep.* 88.5) the complaint that by the use of allegory Homer had been made the originator of mutually exclusive philosophies. Plutarch (*Mor.* 19e) speaks of those who use ἀλληγορία as an interpretative method to force and twist the stories of Homer (especially those commonly slandered) so as to make them refer to more acceptable dogmas. He also explains that this usage of the word ἀλληγορία was modern in his day and that the older term was ὑπόνοια.[387] This does not mean, however, that Plutarch himself never used an allegorical method of interpretation. In fact, the allegorical method is very important in his tract on Isis and Osiris. Plutarch, however, uses the verb ἀλληγορέω in the sense of "*interpret* allegorically" (*Mor.* 363d) and nowhere explicitly suggests that the authors/ narrators of the myths deliberately *spoke* allegorically.[388] This probably has

---

[384] It ought to be noted that Corn. *ND* takes another approach. Cornutus argues that it was the "ancients," whose genealogies the poets describe, that were inclined πρὸς τὸ διὰ συμβόλων καὶ αἰνιγμάτων φιλοσοφῆσαι (§ 35, p.76,4-5 L.). Cornutus actually blames the poets (e.g., Hesiod) for adding in a mythical way to what the ancients handed down and so corrupting the ancient θεολογία (§ 17).

[385] Here we see an important difference with the ἀλληγορία in rhetoric which was a *figure*, effectively used especially because of its inherent ambiguity (cf. Demetr. *Eloc.* 99-102). Homer does not use ἀλληγορία as a figure, but his whole epic consists of ἀλληγορίαι designed to *teach* philosophy.

[386] Corn. *ND* also uses the term αἰνίττομαι instead of ἀλληγορέω. Note that Strabo (64/3 BC - c. AD 21) also believed that Homer spoke allegorically when relating myths, cf. 1.2.7.

[387] The terms ἀλληγορία and αλληγορέω are common enough in the first century BC, though their first appearance appears to be in the works of Cicero (see the select glossary *s.v.* for references). This suggests that the term has a Hellenistic origin.

[388] At *Mor.* 361e he reasons that ὑπόνοιαι were deliberately infused into the secret rites, but such a consideration is expected of the mysteries. A similar comment is not made with respect to the myth itself. In this respect Leopold's comments on how Plutarch dealt with the question of how the allegorical message got into the text of the myth are not convincing (1983, "Rhetoric," 158-59).

to do with the fact that Plutarch accepted most of the myth as actually having occurred.[389] The actual myth as such is just as important as the allegorical interpretation of it. In this respect we are a step removed from the function of ἀλληγορία in rhetorical theory. It seems that Plutarch's criticism of others who twist the Homeric myths may have been directed against the use of this method to explain away difficult myths by suggesting that Homer intended to speak allegorically. With respect to Isis and Osiris, Plutarch merely dismisses the myths he considers too fantastic to be true (cf. *Mor.* 374e, 358ef). Around the same time, Dio Chrysostom found it difficult to decide whether it really was the custom among the poets of Homer's age to write φυσικοὶ λόγοι in the form of myths, or not (D.Chr. 53.3).

Allegorical interpretation also became popular among Jewish interpreters from an early date.[390] The letter of Aristeas (dated somewhere between the third and first centuries BC) contains an interesting passage where ritual regulations of the law are allegorically interpreted in terms of ethics. Aristeas does not use any of the regular technical terms to describe his approach. Instead we encounter the first use of the verb τροπολογέω (§ 150).[391] Aristeas' view is that the lawgiver himself intended to communicate this allegorical meaning to those with understanding (§ 148, ὁ νομοθέτης [*sc.* ταῦτα] σημειοῦσθαι τοῖς συνετοῖς).

Philo describes how he came across this interpretative method among the sect of the Therapeutae (*Vit. Cont.* 78, using both terms, ὑπονοία and ἀλληγορία), a Jewish ascetic group just outside Alexandria. Here the law was likened to a living being of which the body has the literal commandments whilst the soul contains the invisible meaning stored up in the words. The context implies a certain Platonic dichotomy between body and soul. Philo also attributes this method to the Essenes who philosophised διὰ συμβόλων (*Omn. Prob. Lib.* 82).[392] In addition, in some 67 other passages Philo rather generally refers to other allegorists, a tradition of interpretation which seems to have been of long standing (cf. *Spec. Leg.* 1.8).[393] At least some such allegorists appear to have used their interpretation to justify neglect of the literal commandments, *Migr. Abr.* 89-93.[394]

Allegorical interpretation is also especially popular in the exegesis of Philo himself.[395] Philo's own approach seems to vary. At *Som.* 2.31 he clearly uses the verb ἀλληγορέω of an allegorical *interpretation* of his own. Speaking of the sheaves in LXX *Ge.* 37.7 he says: δράγματα δ' ἀλληγοροῦντές φαμεν εἶναι πράγματα. Yet it is clear that Philo believed Moses to have deliberately spoken allegorically, and goes so far as to call him a ἱεροφάντης, communicat-

---

[389] See J. G. Griffiths, 1970, *De Iside*, 100-101.

[390] See I. Heinemann, 1952, "Allegoristik." Heinemann, however, works with a definition of allegory which demands that the literal sense be negated. Although allegorical interpreters of Homer often worked in this way (embarrassed by the literal text), use of the allegorical method by no means demands that the literal interpretation is *per se* negated.

Aristobulus of Alexandria is not infrequently cited in connection with allegorical interpretation, but the relevant extant fragments of his works show that he was concerned with explaining anthropomorphisms in the books of Moses (see Eus. *p.e.* 8.10.1-17; Eus. *p.e.* 13.12.1-2 [= Clem. *Str.* 1.150.1-3 = Eus. *p.e.* 9.6.6]; Eus. *p.e.* 13.12.3-8; Eus. *p.e.* 13.12.9-16 [= in part, Eus. *p.e.* 7.14.1; Clem. *Str.* 6.137-42]). His interpretations are not allegorical in the strict sense, nor does he employ the technical vocabulary of allegorical interpretation (cf. Heinemann, *op. cit.*, 133-35). I cannot, therefore, agree with the statement of P. Borgen that Aristobulus "largely uses the allegorical method" (1984, "Philo," 274. The fragments of Aristobulus are discussed on pages 274-79).

[391] The verb τροπολογέω next occurs (frequently) in the works of Origen (third century AD) and from then on becomes popular in patristic authors. The cognate τροπολογία (in the sense of allegorical interpretation) is first found in Just. *dial.* 57.2 (second century AD).

[392] Another technical term for ἀλληγορία, cf. Demetr. *Eloc.* 243; Corn. *ND* 35.

[393] These references are noted and discussed by D. M. Hay, 1979/80 "References."

[394] See Hay, 1979/80, "References" 47-51 for discussion of this passage.

[395] For a short introduction see, Y. Amir, 1973, "Philo."

ing the secret mysteries to his special disciples (*Cher.* 49; *Gig.* 54). As such, the allegorical meaning was for Philo clearly more important than the literal meaning. Yet Philo did not accept the view that Moses spoke myths (cf. *Op.Mund.* 1-3; *Gig.* 7, 58). Furthermore, it is clear from *Migr.Abr.* 92-93 that Philo did not wish the use of allegorical interpretation to undermine the literal commandments.[396] There is, however, some evidence that Philo knew and adapted allegorical interpretations from Greek philosophers.[397]

Josephus also appears to have been influenced by the popularity of this method. In an interesting passage at *AJ* 1.24 he explains that Moses (the lawgiver) presents the law in three ways, using αἴνιγμα, ἀλληγορία, and straightforward speech: πάντα γὰρ τῇ τῶν ὅλων φύσει σύμφωνον ἔχει τὴν διάθεσιν, τὰ μὲν αἰνιττομένου τοῦ νομοθέτου δεξιῶς, τὰ δ᾽ ἀλληγοροῦντος μετὰ σεμνότητος, ὅσα δ᾽ ἐξ εὐθείας λέγεσθαι συνέφερε ταῦτα ῥητῶς ἐμφανίζοντος.[398] A hint of what Josephus is getting at is provided in *BJ* 5.212-23 where he suggests that the colours of the temple veil signify darkly (αἰνίττεσθαι) the four elements of the universe (cf. *AJ* 3.179-87).

Yet at *Ap.* 2.255-56 Josephus shows antagonism to the use of τὰς ψυχρὰς προφάσεις τῶν ἀλληγοριῶν (the frigid pretexts of the allegories) in order to interpret the poets philosophically. Philo also mentions others who opposed the application of the allegorical method to the Scriptures (cf. *Mut.Nom.* 60).

Given that Paul is here dealing with the allegorical interpretation of a story (whether intended to be spoken allegorically by the author or not), citations from rhetorical sources on the use of ἀλληγορία are irrelevant to an analysis of Paul's own rhetorical or argumentative method in this pericope.[399]

We are faced with two important questions. First, what does Paul mean by the words: ἅτινά ἐστιν ἀλληγορούμενα? Second, what argumentative force did Paul see in his use of allegorical interpretation?

With respect to the first question, we should note that Paul does *not* say that this story "is *able to be* interpreted allegorically." The clause is not hypothetical, and ἐστιν is not used impersonally in the sense of "it is possible," but is part of a periphrastic verbal construction.[400] The words ἐστιν ἀλληγορούμενα are virtually equivalent to

---

[396] Here, as described above with reference to the Therapeutae, he likens the literal commandments (e.g., circumcision) to the body and the allegorical interpretations to the soul.

[397] See Y. Amir, 1984, "Transference."

[398] The reference here is to *speaking* in allegory, not interpreting as allegory. The passage is thus incorrectly cited in BAGD *s.v.* ἀλληγορέω.

[399] Orators sometimes *spoke* figuratively, and this is what is discussed by the theorists. Paul is engaged in the *interpretation* of an ancient narrative which he argues was spoken allegorically (see below). He is not speaking allegorically himself at this point. H. D. Betz' introduction to this passage (1988, *Galaterbrief*, 412-14) is for this reason beside the point. Betz, although recognising the distinction between speaking and interpreting allegorically on pp.418-19, appears not to have considered the difference between the rhetorical use of metaphorical language to make a point in a speech (rhetorical ἀλληγορία), and the allegorical interpretation of a story from ancient tradition (whether it is argued that the author spoke allegorically or not).

Vict. *Gal.* 1185c cites the rhetorical definition of ἀλληγορία when discussing this passage and then appropriately notes that Paul means something different.

[400] It should not really be necessary to state this, but several commentaries on this epistle (notably embarrassed by the allegory) seem to treat this verse as if this is what was said.

ἀλληγορεῖται.[401] The relative ἅτινα is probably just equivalent to ἅ, as commonly in the New Testament. Does Paul mean to say that this story "is interpreted allegorically" or "is spoken allegorically?" The context must be decisive in favour of the latter. There is no signal in the text directing the reader/ hearer to understand Paul to be saying that the story "is interpreted allegorically." We would then, for example, need some indication as to who might interpret it so. Nor could he mean that it is *frequently* so interpreted, for apart from the fact that this is not explicitly stated, there is also the consideration that there is little evidence which would support such a claim. It seems clear that Paul means to say that this Bible story is *spoken* allegorically.

This is what Paul says. But what does he mean? There are a number of disconcerting considerations. i) It is rather unlikely that Paul was led to think that the passage was spoken allegorically because he was embarrassed by its literal interpretation. Nor does the more complex theory that Paul understood two levels of interpretation, the one literal, and the other allegorical (or as some would argue, typological) satisfy.[402] The two interpretations (literal and allegorical) in this case plainly contradict each other. This fact is remarkable and is not the kind of allegorical interpretation reflected in the tradition (whether of Homeric or Scriptural allegorical interpretation). ii) Nowhere else in Paul's writings do we find such explicit allegorical interpretation.[403] iii) In terms of the argumentative structure of the letter to the Galatians we would not expect a new argument from Scripture at this point. Paul has presented his Scripture proof and explanation in 3.1 - 4.11. This argument from Scripture (4.21 - 5.1) follows closely on the heels of an emotional personal appeal (4.12-20) and is itself followed by a recapitulation of the main thrust of Paul's rebuke.

Now, to argue that this passage is an interpolation is rather far-fetched and without hard evidence. Such a drastic measure is also not really necessary. Taking into

---

[401]   The preponderance of such periphrastic constructions in the New Testament has been attributed to the influence of Aramaic. For discussion see M.-T., *Gram.* 3.87-88.

[402]   For example, Chrysostom on this passage, who suggests that Paul, contrary to custom, uses the term allegory instead of τύπος. See J. Fairweather, 1994, "Epistle," 17.

[403]   Nowhere else does Paul use any of the normal technical terminology with respect to allegorical interpretation, although this does not necessarily mean that other examples of allegorical interpretation of the Old Testament are not present in his writings. A possible contender *might* be 2 *Ep.Cor.* 3.16-17 where OT *Ex.* 34.34 is cited and interpreted, but it seems doubtful to me that Paul would have considered his interpretation here to be allegorical in nature. 1 *Ep.Cor.* 5.6-8 is not a good example in that it is not clear that Paul means to say that the Old Testament spoke allegorically with respect to the passover. A better example might be 1 *Ep.Cor.* 9.9-10, referring to the law: οὐ κημώσεις βοῦν ἀλοῶντα. Paul asks: μὴ τῶν βοῶν μέλει τῷ θεῷ; But even here, Paul's ensuing interpretation really only shows that the principle embodied in the law is what is important, and that this principle can also be applied to ministers of the Gospel, just as it is applied to oxen in the law.

account the fact that this passage is preceded by an emotional personal appeal, and the fact that this paragraph itself begins with a highly charged rhetorical question, the solution would seem to lie in the direction of a continuation of Paul's *emotional* appeal to the Galatians. Swept up in emotional indignation, Paul engages in a *sarcastic* exposition of this Bible story (cf. σαρκασμός, Quint. *Inst.* 8.6.57; Alex. *Fig.* 1.18; Ps.-Plu. *Vit.Hom.* 69; Tryph. *Trop.* 2.20).[404] This is the only solution that properly takes account of the fact that the allegorical interpretation leads to a conclusion exactly *opposite* to that of the literal interpretation. The tables are turned. The Jews are *not* descended from Sarah, but from Hagar! Why? Is it not obvious that Mt. Sinai (where the giving of the Law took place) is to be found in Arabia (4.25)? Paul's point seems to be that Sinai in his own day was part of the territory of the Nabateans, popularly said to be descended from Ishmael, Hagar's son (J. *AJ* 1.214; cf. LXX *Ba.* 3.23). The fact that this was certainly not Nabatean territory in Moses' day is not relevant. The argument is sarcastic.[405] Those who accept Paul's Gospel (inheritance via the promise) are the people descended from Sarah, the free woman. The net effect of the passage is to reiterate Paul's anger and perplexity at the Galatians (cf. 4.20 ἀποροῦμαι ἐν ὑμῖν).

We can further note that the argumentative effect of such an inventive allegorical interpretation may be appropriately compared to that of a μῦθος (fable). Rhetorical theory does not discuss the use of allegorical interpretations of stories, but Paul's use of such an obviously *invented* interpretation comes close to the definition of a *fable*. Theon (*Prog.* ii, p.72,28 Sp.) defined the μῦθος as a λόγος ψευδὴς εἰκονίζων ἀλήθειαν (an untrue story which images truth) and recommended that it be used *after* the setting out of one's argument. In the working out of a fable, Theon recommends that it be weaved together with a narrative. He gives as an example the fable of the camel which craved after horns, but ended up being deprived of its ears. Theon suggests that one could continue as follows: παραπλήσιόν μοι δοκεῖ τι παθεῖν τῇ καμήλῳ ταύτῃ καὶ Κροῖσος ὁ Λυδός, etc. (It seems to me that Croesus the Lydian experienced something similar to that camel ..., *Prog.* ii, p.75,14-15 Sp.). The application of a fable to a sub-

---

[404] It is possible that the *raison d'être* may have been the use of this Old Testament passage by the Judaisers, but this is no more than speculation.
[405] It is not my intention to discuss here the text critical problems attending *Ep.Gal.* 4.25, nor the various interpretations of this verse. The interpretation summarised above seems to me to be the most probable. There is the question as to whether the Galatians could have been expected to realise that Nabatean territory extended as far as Mt. Sinai, and that they were popularly believed to be descended from Ishmael. If there were Jews in the congregation it is probable that this could have been explained. In any case, we have already seen that Paul's letter generally presupposes a high level of Old Testament knowledge. We have no way of knowing whether Paul appropriately gauged the level of his audience's knowledge or not.

ject reflects Paul's application of an *invented* interpretation of a story from the Law to the Galatians. It was generally recognised that the fable lent credence via its emotive power to portray the point being argued (cf. Cic. *Part.* 40; Theon *Prog.* ii, p.76,6-7 Sp.).

Rhetorical Notes

4.25a should probably be considered a παρένθεσις. The subject of συστοιχεῖ is then μία [διαθήκη].[406]

4.24ff Paul again shows his penchant for personification by personifying the two διαθῆκαι. This is classified from the time of Aristotle on as the most vivid way of speaking.

Part Three: Summary (5.2-12)

Paul now concludes the formal section of his rebuke (i.e., before engaging in paraenesis) with a short, but still emotionally charged, summary of the nub of the issue. This is backed up by a strong appeal to his authority as an apostle, upon which his following statements are based ('Ἴδε ἐγὼ Παῦλος λέγω ὑμῖν, 5.2). He closes with a backlash at the Judaisers themselves.

The emotion here is climaxed by the rather clear cut proclamations given by Paul in 5.2-6. The twofold διαίρεσις (works of the law versus faith in Christ) is now expressed in terms of what must have been for Paul a key issue, namely, the compulsion to circumcision. Circumcision functions in this context as the sign and seal of salvation by the works of the (Mosaic) law. Christ and compulsory circumcision cannot be combined. This is the nub of the διαίρεσις. The ἔμφασις (see select glossary *s.v.*), clearly also present (cf. 3.10-12), is that if they have been made debtors to the whole law, then they are under a curse, being unable to keep it perfectly.

At 5.7 Paul returns to rhetorical questions, yet his tone becomes milder to the Galatians. In fact he goes so far as to express his confidence in their agreement with him (v.10, a sentiment which in contemporary rhetorical theory might be expected in the προοίμιον, cf. *Rhet.Her.* 1.8 [& 3.7]; Quint. *Inst.* 4.1.14).[407] Paul's anger is now directed at the Judaisers themselves. He reiterates the fact that he does not support this view and then even goes so far as to express a wish that the Judaisers would *sever* their

---

[406] So J. B. Lightfoot, 1865, *Epistle*, 181.
[407] Note, however, that Arist. *Rh.* 3.14.7 suggests that the prosecuting speech should attack the opponent in the ἐπίλογος.

own genitals (i.e., make themselves eunuchs).[408] With this parting shot Paul closes his argued rebuke of the Galatians and embarks on a section of παραίνεσις before closing his letter. The attack on the Judaisers, combined with the stated confidence in the Galatians themselves, functions to mollify the Galatians after his rather stern rebuke. Paul thus attempts to bring his audience back into a frame of mind congenial to him and prepared to accept the παραίνεσις he brings next.

It should, however, be noticed that the whole final section (i.e., the emotional appeal from 4.12 - 5.12) functions effectively as a kind of ἐπίλογος to his argument. The πάθος in this whole section is high, as is Paul's evident desire to win the Galatians over. It is also interesting to note the high degree of correspondence between the three parts of this appeal and the three parts of an ἐπίλογος prescribed by Cic. *Inv.* 1.98-109. The agreement is not complete, nor are the three parts in the same order, but considering the fact that Cicero is writing with respect to a forensic speech, the degree of agreement is striking. Cicero states that a peroration has three parts.[409] Firstly, an *enumeratio*, i.e., a recapitulation of the main points. This corresponds neatly to *Ep.Gal.* 5.2-6 or more broadly considered 5.2-12. The second part is the *indignatio*, a section wherein the orator tries to evoke indignation or hatred against his opponents. Fifteen *loci* are listed here to give the orator ideas on how this may be done.[410] Whilst these *loci* are more directly related to a forensic speech, as we have seen, the net effect of Paul's allegorical interpretation (*Ep.Gal.* 4.21 - 5.1) is to arouse negative feelings against the Judaisers. The third part of the peroration according to Cicero is the *conquestio*, a section wherein the orator tries to arouse the pity (ἔλεος) of the audience. Here there is less direct agreement. Paul in *Ep.Gal.* 4.12-20 is not trying to arouse pity, but he is strongly appealing to the Galatians' former acceptance of both himself and his Gospel.

This kind of tripartite division described in Cic. *Inv.* (with a variation in *Rhet.Her.* 2.47-50) was not the only way rhetorical theorists around this era dealt with the ἐπίλογος. Quint. *Inst.* 6.1-2 describes two alternative methods of dealing with it. One may either recapitulate the main points, or one may engage generally in exciting the emotions. Quintilian spends a lot of space dealing with the appeal to the emotions,

---

[408] There may well be an additional hint of εἰρωνεία here in that the Mosaic law forbade eunuchs to enter the assembly of the Lord (OT *De.* 23.1).

[409] Cicero's tripartite division: *enumeratio*, *indignatio* and *conquestio* are clearly based upon the same source as the tripartite division in *Rhet.Her.* 2.47-50 (*enumeratio*, *amplificatio* and *misericordia*), although there are differences.

[410] See R. D. Anderson, (forthcoming) *Glossary, s.v.* αὔξησις for the relation of these *loci* to αὔξησις and to the equivalent section of *Rhet.Her.*.

and at *Inst.* 6.2.1-7 waxes eloquent on its important persuasive force. It is clear that the final section of Paul's rebuke to the Galatians may be generally so characterised. It is significant that he reserves his strong emotional appeal until after he has presented his more formal argumentation.

Of course, in Paul's case there still follows a paraenetic section, but as noted above, this has more connection with παραίνεσις in popular philosophy generally. Detailed comment on Paul's παραίνεσις is material for a separate study.

Rhetorical Notes

5.2-3 For the emphatic repetition of the thought in these two verses, see above, p.126, on *Ep.Gal.* 1.6-9.

5.3 μαρτύρομαι should probably not be taken in the sense of an asseveration (i.e., "protest," "call to witness" [without an explicit direct object]), but in the sense of "bear witness." This must surely be the sense in LXX 1 *Ma.* 2.56 and *Act.Ap.* 26.22, which would lead one to suspect that other constructions of this verb with the dative should be taken similarly, cf. *Act.Ap.* 20.26 and H. Strathmann, 1942, "μάρτυς," 4.511n.[411] It should thus not be interpreted as an oath formula, *contra* H. D. Betz (1988, *Galaterbrief*, 443).

5.4 This verse is chiastic: κατηργήθητε ἀπὸ Χριστοῦ ... τῆς χάριτος ἐξεπέσατε. The verb ἐκπίπτω may just mean "deprived of," or (as often) may be used here as the passive of ἐκβάλλω and include a reference back to 4.30 (ἔκβαλε τὴν παιδίσκην).

5.5 ἐλπίς here (the object hoped for) is a not an uncommon example of μετωνυμία (cf. πίστις in 3.25).

5.7 For τρέχω as metaphor, see at 2.2.

In the phrase ἀληθείᾳ μὴ πείθεσθαι, Paul has substituted the word "truth" for "my Gospel." Arguably this is an example of ἔμφασις, implying (without stating in so many words) the stupidity of the Galatians in allowing themselves to be seduced away from the *truth*.

5.8 πεισμονή appears first here in Greek literature. The περίφρασις for God at the end of the verse is common.

5.9 Paul uses a proverb (παροιμία, cf. 1 *Ep.Cor.* 5.6) as an ἀλληγορία (in the rhetorical sense), Quint. *Inst.* 5.11.21, cf. 8.6.57.[412] The meaning is not entirely clear.

---

[411] Although LSJ do not suggest this possibility, BAGD *s.v.* 1. include it, although the references to Pl. *Phlb* 47d; J. *BJ* 3.354; POxy. 1120.11; PAmh. 141.17 and PStrassb. 5.14 do not belong. This is thus a late usage.

[412] Aside from the two references in Paul, however, this proverb has not elsewhere been identified.

The intention may be that if circumcision is admitted into their religion, ultimately the whole Mosaic law must be admitted. It may, however, be more general in the sense that the admittance of anything extraneous to the Gospel will ultimately affect it completely. Or again, the admittance of a few troublemakers causes trouble for the whole church. The use of proverbs is recommended in epistolary style (cf. Demetr. *Eloc.* 232).

2.6 Style

Without going into too much detail, it is pertinent to make a few remarks on the style of the letter to the Galatians. Firstly, as is well known, the language itself is basically Hellenistic with considerable Semitic influence (traceable to the Septuagint).[413] Paul, therefore, cannot be classified as participating in the Atticist trends popular in his time, also among some of the extant rhetorical theorists concerned with matters of style.

As far as sentence structure is concerned, the style is generally paratactic, showing no use of extended periods.[414] There is no attempt to avoid hiatus, not even in cases

---

[413] A select list of Hellenisms follows: The use of ὅστις for ὅς (*passim*); popularity of the periphrastic construction, cf. 1.7, 22, 23; 4.24; instrumental ἐν (common in later Greek, esp. biblical under the influence of Hebrew בּ *instrumentalis*), 1.6. Χάρις signifies here a generous favour done, in this case Christ's self sacrifice on the cross (v.4). Ἄρτι used in the sense of νῦν, 1.9; εὐαγγελίζομαι with the accusative (instead of dative), 1.9; προσανατίθεμαι in the sense "take counsel with τινι," 1.16 (note that Vict. *Gal.* 1154d appears to have read προσανεπαύσθην!); ἵνα with fut. indic., 2.4; πιστεύω with prepositions, e.g., 2.16; συνιστάνω is Hellenistic, occurring as early as Polybius, 2.18; μία μέν for ἑτέρα μέν, 4.24; ἀναστατόω is Hellenistic. The earliest citation appears to be LXX *Da.* 7.23 although it also appears in a first century BC papyrus (*BGU* 1858.12, cited in BAGD *s.v.*), 5.12.
    Examples of Septuagintalisms: ἀνάθεμα in the sense of "accursed" is only found in Jewish/ Christian texts (from חֵרֶם), 1.8-9; the idiom πρόσωπον λαμβάνειν is a Hebraism derived from the LXX, 2.6; ἐὰν μή for ἄλλα is classified as a Septuagintalism by M.-T., *Gram.* 4.91-2, *Ep.Gal.* 2.16; δωρεάν meaning "in vain," "for no reason" is a Septuagintalism which arose from the etymologically based translation of חִנָּם (from חָנַן), 2.21. Σκάνδαλον is a late word for σκανδάληθρον, used in the LXX and then the New Testament; LSJ also cite *PCair.Zen.* 608.7 from the third century BC which would suggest that the word originated in Egypt, 5.11. Ὄφελον as a wish would normally take the infinitive. The construction with a second or third person verb appears to be under the influence of LXX usage, 5.12.
    In addition the use of καταργέομαι (5.4) in the sense "be parted" is peculiarly Pauline (cf. *Ep.Rom.* 7.2, 6), although, as J. B. Lightfoot (1865, *Epistle*, 204) hints, it may have more to do with a pregnant use of the preposition ἀπό (separated from), cf. *Ep.Rom.* 9.3; 2 *Ep.Cor.* 11.3; *Ep.Col.* 2.20.
[414] I use the word "period" here in a restricted sense, namely, of a sentence containing at least two subordinate clauses wherein the main clause, interrupted by the subordinate clauses, is left in suspense and only completed by the last few words of the whole sentence. A good example is the opening sentence of Luke's Gospel (*Ev.Luc.* 1.1-4). Paratactic sentences, in contrast, are strings of clauses joined by copulatives such as καί, τέ, δέ, etc.. Sentences containing subordinate clauses in general may be described as hypotactic. Whilst Paul's style is frequently hypotactic, he generally prefers to introduce subordinate clauses with particles such as ὅτε, ὅτι, ὡς, εἰ etc., and tends to avoid the use of subordinate participial constructions (which are otherwise common in Greek literature).

where this was standard practice. Consequently collocations of vowels difficult to pronounce (and thus stylistically poor) are not uncommon, e.g., κατὰ ἄνθρωπον in 1.11 and 3.15; ἀλλὰ ἀπῆλθον in 1.17; κατὰ ἀποκάλυψιν in 2.2; cf. 1.10 εἰ ἔτι; 1.18 τρία ἀνῆλθον, etc..[415]

Paul is well known for favouring a varied use of prepositions, and to some extent constructions, without any variation of semantic nuance. Examples of this variation also appear in the letter to the Galatians, e.g., εὐαγγελίζομαι with the dative in 1.8 and the accusative in 1.9; μαρτυρέω in 4.16 and μαρτύρομαι in 5.3 used synonymously; μετά with the accusative in 1.18 and διά with the genitive in 2.1 both meaning "after."

Paul's style seems in certain respects anomalous. On the one hand he is very fond of ἀντίθεσις, examples of which are too many to detail.[416] Yet Paul makes only scant use of the typically Greek μέν ... δέ construction.[417] Paul's Greek can be at times very careless (see the comments above on 2.4-6). Yet as we have seen he can also make use of rather artificial rhetorical figures (see, for example, the comments on 4.12-20).

His use of such figures, particularly in strongly emotional contexts, flies in the face of the advice of rhetorical theorists (see the endnote to the select glossary, and my note on 2.20). The rhetorical theorists advise their readers to steer generally clear of the use of such artificial figures. A small sprinkling of them is sometimes permitted, but even this is discouraged in contexts where a serious or emotional point is being made. Yet as shown in the endnote to the select glossary, the rhetorical theorists were at this point polemicising against a popular trend, a trend not only clearly in evidence among the schools of declamation, but even present in the lawcourts. It would appear, in this respect, that Paul's style breathes the language popular among the more or less

---

[415] Of course we can only speak of stylistically poor *writing* here. Appropriate ellisions would probably have been made in *reading* the letter aloud.

[416] In the main, Paul's ἀντιθέσεις are not balanced by παρίσωσις or the like (the few examples of which have been noted), but are simple ἀντιθέσεις of thought. This is characteristic of his style and their preponderance is no doubt also to be accounted for by the ease with which his subject matter lends itself to such ἀντιθέσεις.

For a separate investigation into Paul's use of ἀντίθεσις see N. Schneider, 1970, *Eigenart*. Schneider's analysis is not, however, based upon ancient rhetorical theory, although the study purports to use definitions taken from ancient rhetoric. Unfortunately no rhetorical sources seem even to have been consulted! Schneider's information on rhetorical theory is all taken from H. Lausberg's (1973) *Handbuch*. The sole use of this work has the result that Schneider presents a rather complex systematic overview of the ἀντίθεσις as *the uniform doctrine* of rhetorical theory. This is historical nonsense. Schneider unfortunately also misinterprets the concept of *correctio* (cf. the much too wide definition of *correctio*, pp.47-52), a concept which holds an important place in his dissertation. Nothing is said about the value judgements of ancient rhetorical theorists on the use of ἀντίθεσις.

[417] There are several places in the letter to the Galatians where we might reasonably have expected this construction: cf. 1.22 ἤμην δέ, where we should have expected μέν in better Greek. In 2.9 we would expect ἵνα ἡμεῖς μέν, and in 3.20 we would expect ὁ μὲν μεσίτης.

educated masses of his day. His language does not, in any respect, measure up to the ideals of the theorists. It is, however, interesting to note that the worst examples of careless Greek appear in the beginning of Paul's letter (cf. 2.4-6), and the best examples of artificial polish towards the end (cf. 4.12-20). Rhetorical theorists suggested that the προοίμιον should contain little splendour or finish of style (cf. *Rhet.Her.* 1.11; Cic. *Inv.* 1.25; Quint. *Inst.* 4.1.55-60), but that the ἐπίλογος was the place for magnificence of style (cf. Quint. *Inst.* 6.1.51-52[418]).

One might conceivably argue that Paul's avoidance of periodic style and great use of conversational figures (e.g., rhetorical questions) demonstrate a style which conforms to the canons of epistolary theory (cf. Demetr. *Eloc.* 223-25, 229; Philostr. *Dial.* 1; Cic. *Fam.* 9.21.1; Sen. *Ep.* 75.1; Quint. *Inst.* 9.4.19).[419]

Given that Paul's letter has the nature of a strong rebuke and thus comes across quite forcefully, it is, perhaps, interesting to briefly compare Paul's style in this letter with Demetrius' recommendations on the forceful (δεινή) style (*Eloc.* 240-304).[420]

As customary, Demetrius discusses this style under the threefold analytical scheme of πράγματα, σύνθεσις and λέξις. To this is added a short discussion of smoothness in σύνθεσις and a very short description of the erroneous counter-style to forcefulness.

---

[418] This passage should, however, be tempered by *Inst.* 9.3.100-102. Quintilian seems to come close to contradicting himself. At the least, we may say that *Inst.* 6.1.51-52 needs qualification.

[419] Note that Demetrius advises such a plain style for the kind of letters *he* regards as true examples of the epistolary genre, namely, letters which in terms of content restrict themselves to φιλοφρονήσεις (§§ 231-32). To write a letter as one προτρεπόμενος is not to write a letter as such, but a contrivance (μηχανή). Demetrius himself, therefore, would not have intended his comments on appropriate epistolary style to be applied to a letter such as that to the Galatians. Demetrius' views on which matters most suit a letter are essentially based on his ruminations upon the letters of Aristotle. A more typical epistolary theorist such as [Demetr.] *Typ.* (c. first century BC) was broader in his views, and it is largely on the basis of his work that the letter to the Galatians can be typified as a rebuke-letter (see above). But [Demetr.] *Typ.*, unfortunately, says virtually nothing with respect to style, except that letters should be written ὡς τεχνικώτατα (*proem.*). Nevertheless, the general stylistic remarks with respect to letters made by Demetrius are also common to epistolary theory in later centuries, and can therefore probably be appropriately related to Paul's letters.

That the warning against letters being turned into συγγράμματα (Demetr. *Eloc.* 228) ought, however, to be taken into account when reflecting upon style is clear from Quint. *Inst.* 9.4.19. Quintilian repeats the commonplace among epistolary theorists that letters ought to be written in a loose style (i.e., non-periodic), but excepts from this canon those letters which treat material *supra naturam suam*, giving as examples philosophy and politics. In this context, serious reflection upon religion must be considered equivalent to philosophy. This fact will need to be borne in mind when reflecting upon the style of Paul's letter to the Romans.

[420] In our rhetorical analysis we have noted how Paul's language can be quite forceful. It is all the more surprising that Augustine characterised the style of the letter as a whole as belonging to the *submissum genus* (*Doct.* 4.20.44 - Augustine is applying the threefold stylistic theory of Cicero's *Orator*).

Demetr. *Eloc.* 240 does not really give us a good idea as to what kind of πράγματα are suitable to the forceful style. He assumes that this will be known to the reader. The only point made is that the use of δεινὰ πράγματα will make the speaker seem to be speaking in a forceful style (although this would be a wrong conclusion, cf. § 75).

In terms of σύνθεσις (§§ 241-71) Demetrius emphasises brevity. Κόμματα should be preferred to κῶλα, and περίοδοι should be no longer than two κῶλα. The use of ἀντίθετα and παρόμοια should be avoided in periods (περίοδοι), since these only make them bombastic. Such short periods may be used in quick succession and thus produce the effect of a forceful metre. But forceful brevity is particularly marked by the use of ἔμφασις and ἀλληγορία. Periods can be very effective if they are bound tightly at the end (§ 244). Demetrius, I think, means to say that the final words of a period, which tie the meaning of a sentence together, should be particularly separated from their precursor, thus heightening the tension and energy in the sentence. At § 249 he adds that those words of a sentence which contain a forceful or unexpected expression should be left until the end.

Other effects which may contribute to forcefulness include ill-sounding word order (κακοφωνία), or the injection of forceful humour.

In terms of figures, Demetrius naturally recommends those figures which tend towards brevity and/ or ἔμφασις. Recommended are thus ἀποσιώπησις, παράλειψις and even προσωποποιία. Figures used in forceful κόμματα are also mentioned, e.g., ἀναδίπλωσις, ἀσύνδετον, (ἐπ)αναφορά. The figure κλῖμαξ may also be forcefully used.[421]

Demetrius' comments on λέξις (§§ 272-98) are also governed by what is short, and contains hints of ἀλληγορία and ἔμφασις. Use of μεταφοραί and εἰκασίαι are thus recommended, but παραβολαί are considered too long-winded. Further, a forceful use of compound words, rhetorical questions, ἐπιμονή and ἐσχηματισμένος λόγος, among others, are discussed. Smoothness of σύνθεσις (§§ 299-301), which Dionysius of Halicarnassus would call "harmony," is said not to be fitting to forcefulness.

If we review what has been said in our analysis of the letter to the Galatians concerning various matters of style, then Paul in many respects uses figures and effects which Demetrius would consider appropriate to the forceful style. We have noted a few cases of rhetorical ἀλληγορία, and several of ἔμφασις. There is even a minor case of

---

421   On the various figures see my forthcoming *Glossary*, *s.v.*.

(micro) προσωποποιΐα. Paul is particularly fond of the forceful use of rhetorical questions. He also shows the ability to coin a particularly forceful compound (ψευδάδελφος). His clauses are often short and sharp, although ἀναφορά is not much used (cf. 4.4-5), nor can we point to the forceful use of ἐπιμονή, ἀναδίπλωσις, ἀσύνδετον, κλῖμαξ, παράλειψις or ἀποσιώπησις. We have noted above that Paul's "harmony" cannot be characterised as smooth, although I very much doubt that this is deliberate on his part, given that this lack of smoothness is apparent in *all* his letters. The greatest difference to Demetrius' characterisation lies in the fact that Demetrius quite clearly assumes that even the forceful style will make plenteous use of appropriate periods. Periods are wholly absent in Paul's writing. We have also noted above Paul's seemingly inappropriate use of artificial figures.[422] One final difference (taking "style" in a rather broad sense) is Paul's forthright critique of the Galatians, shown particularly in the curse at the opening, and in his memorable ἀποστροφή, "Ὦ ἀνόητοι Γαλάται" (3.1). Demetrius may well have suggested to Paul that judicious use of ἐσχηματισμένος λόγος would have been more forceful than λοιδορία.

2.7 Conclusions

What does Paul accomplish in this letter? He begins by showing how his Gospel has independent authority, and goes on to cast the problem in terms of a choice between faith and the works of the law (1.11 - 2.21). He then sets out to prove that his Gospel of justification by faith is the true Gospel. He argues on the basis of the way the Galatians received the Spirit (3.2-5), and follows with proof from Scripture (the example of Abraham), noting how Scripture also shows the fallacy in the dogma of his opponents (3.7-14). The significance of Christ's death is also woven into the argument. Meeting a possible objection which may arise from his Scripture proof, he explains how his Gospel is related to the law of Moses (3.15 - 4.11). He then begins an impassioned appeal to the emotions. He first appeals to the Galatians' past acceptance of him (4.12-20). Next, his anger and perplexity at them climax in the sarcastic allegory of Abraham's two sons (4.21 - 5.1). This anger is eventually focused more specifically against the Judaisers themselves. Paul then crowns his argument with several clear and

---

[422] One might also suspect that Demetrius would have considered the didactic sections of Paul's letter inappropriate to the forceful style, but this consideration cannot weigh too heavily. After all, considerations of style cannot be permitted to outweigh the importance of including certain important items of content.

simple statements which sum up his rebuke of the Galatians on the basis of his own authority.[423]

Wherein does the letter to the Galatians differ from a judicial speech? Apart from the basic structural problem of the concluding παραίνεσις, we have already noted above (in chapter two, § 5) that Paul nowhere appeals to the typical *loci* of forensic speeches. Rhetorical theory in his time provided lists of such *loci* (organised under the στάσεις) to be used in the preparation of a judicial speech. Paul's letter is simply not related to this aspect of rhetorical theory.

Is Paul's letter then deliberative rhetoric? Deliberative rhetoric was advisory, i.e., advising the audience that one particular path of action was better than another. In this sense, Paul is not advising but *insisting* that adherence to his Gospel is the *only* way of salvation. Furthermore, Paul uses none of the so-called τελικὰ κεφάλαια (arguments related to such concepts as justice, legality, advantage, etc.), which were the central arguments for deliberative rhetoric.[424]

Against both forms of rhetorical genre it must be reiterated that Paul is not simply trying to persuade his audience, he is giving them a solemn rebuke! He makes a strong appeal to his authority as an apostle, derived from the fact that he received his Gospel direct from God through a revelation of Jesus Christ. Not only does his initial apologetic narrative defend this authority and independence of his Gospel, but Paul also appeals to his position when he sums up his rebuke in 5.2. It is within this framework that he continues with argumentation intended to lend weight and persuasion to his initial rebuke (1.6-9). This should not be interpreted to mean that Paul now needs to *justify* his initial pronouncement of anathema. No, his authority as an apostle of Jesus Christ is sufficient. Nevertheless, he seeks to underline the weight of what he has said by supplementary argumentation intended to bolster conviction of his main point. Even here, the persuasive argument is really limited to 3.1-14. What follows is of a more didactic than persuasive nature, although it may be interpreted in terms of the clearing up of a possible objection. But all things considered, in this letter Paul is better likened to a philosopher whose pupils have departed from his doctrines than to a defendant on trial, a prosecutor in court, or a politician in an assembly. Indication of this may be seen in the fact that attacking the convictions of the audience (as Paul surely does!) was in rhetorical theory regarded as a faulty method of argumentation (cf. *Rhet.Her.* 2.43; Cic. *Inv.* 1.92; *de Orat.* 2.304-305).

---

[423]   Although the παραίνεσις and letter closing is here left out of the picture, this should not be taken to suggest that there is no integral connection between these sections and the foregoing. My point is only that these sections preclude rhetorical analysis.

[424]   Cf. J. Fairweather, 1994, "Epistle," 221.

Nevertheless, despite the fact that Paul's letter cannot really be classified into any one of the three most popular rhetorical genres, we have seen that it is possible to make some comments on the arrangement of the letter as a whole. The main portion of Paul's letter (that part dealt with here) does have a beginning (1.1 - 2.21) - προοίμιον if you will, a middle (the "proof"), and an end (the emotional appeal). It has, therefore, been possible to make some remarks on certain parallels in rhetorical theory as regards, for example, what is appropriate to a προοίμιον or to an ἐπίλογος.

V. THE LETTER TO THE ROMANS 1 - 11

1 Recent Scholarship

The letter to the Romans has also been subjected to rhetorical genre analysis in recent scholarship. Already in 1976 W. Wuellner published an article arguing that this letter is essentially epideictic.[425] Wuellner's approach is a mixture of modern and ancient rhetoric. He isolates *Ep.Rom.* 1.1-15 as an *exordium* (I would be inclined to say an epistolary substitute for an *exordium*) and uses this to argue that the rhetorical genre must be epideictic. He then goes on to note that δικαιοσύνη was a traditional special topic for ceremonial discourse (135 note 41).[426] As with the letter to the Galatians, the paraenetic section is a problem for rhetorical genre analysis. Wuellner looks to modern rhetorical theory for an answer and comes up with the solution that the paraenesis "spells out the practical commitment of those who took part in the argumentation" (143). He adds that the paraenesis functions as an *exemplum* and is a *digressio* (144), but the terms are hardly used in their ancient sense.[427] His "solution" cannot satisfy, at least not in terms of ancient rhetorical theory.

Nevertheless, Wuellner's analysis has been accepted by some.[428] In particular, R. Jewett has attempted to build upon it and pin down just what kind of epideictic genre the letter to the Romans is.[429] Jewett's thesis is as follows:

---

[425] 1976, "Rhetoric."

[426] Without reference he adds that H. Lausberg (1973, *Handbuch*) assigns a leitmotif to each rhetorical genre, that of epideictic being love. He is referring to §§ 241 and 437 where Lausberg speaks of "Leitaffekte" referring to pairs of opposite emotions deemed most important to each of the three genres. Apart from the misleading way in which Wuellner speaks of what Lausberg is saying, Lausberg's own classification is deceptive. The two *Leitaffekte* for deliberative rhetoric (*spes et metus*) are taken from a seventh century AD Latin treatise (Isid. *Orig.* 2.4.4), however the rhetorical theory of the period examined in this book surely understood the two so-called *Leitaffekte* of judicial rhetoric (*indignatio et conquestio*) to be applicable to deliberative rhetoric. Lausberg does not provide a reference for his idea that love and hate are the *Leitaffekte* of epideictic rhetoric. The dangers inherent in the use of Lausberg's *Handbuch* apart from consultation of the sources themselves are evident.

[427] If one does not mean to use the terms in their ancient rhetorical sense, then why use an ancient language?

[428] Cf. D. Fraikin (1986) and R. Jewett discussed below. G. A. Kennedy, though not mentioning Wuellner, also considers the letter to the Romans to be "more epideictic in intent" (1984, *New Testament*, 152). He adds that since the pastoral headings are concerned with "belief and attitude, not with action, they do not, as elsewhere, convert the letter into deliberative rhetoric" (154).

[429] 1982, "Romans."

"Romans is a unique fusion of the "ambassadorial letter" with several of the other sub-types in the genre: the parenetic letter, the hortatory letter, and the philosophical diatribe. Its purpose is to advocate in behalf of the "power of God" a cooperative mission to evangelize Spain so that the theological argumentation reiterates the gospel to be therein proclaimed and the ethical admonitions show how that gospel is to be lived out in a manner that would ensure the success of this mission."

Jewett classifies an ambassadorial speech as epideictic based upon Burgess' study on epideictic literature.[430]

Thus the letter to the Romans is an ambassadorial epideictic letter. The proof that it is ambassadorial consists mainly in i) references to typical ambassadorial formulae (not demonstrated, but reference is made to other sources), and ii) the demonstration of how the letter to the Romans can be so interpreted, especially given that Paul elsewhere describes himself as an ambassador of Christ. Jewett conveniently ignores the fact that an ambassadorial speech, as outlined by Burgess, is a speech presented to a ruler, and therefore an important part of this genre is the praise of that ruler. The letter to the Romans is hardly close to this category - even if Paul considers himself an ambassador of God to a church.

In 1991 Jewett returned to this letter and provided a rhetorical outline, particularly of the proofs, which is rather loosely based upon the terminology of ancient rhetoric. But his analysis is not really very helpful since the ancient terminology loses much of its original meaning through a rather innovative application.[431] This short arti-

---

[430] T. C. Burgess, 1902, "Epideictic." This aspect of Jewett's article is problematic. Burgess' discussion is based upon the analysis of "epideictic" literature in two late sources, namely, Ps.-Dionysius of Halicarnassus and Menander (late third century AD). These sources use the term "epideictic" in a broad sense. Further, Jewett notes that Burgess had shown that epideictic also commonly contained the element of persuasion or advice (8) and he gives as an example Lysias' *Olympiacus*. But Lysias deliberately distances himself from typical epideictic show in this speech and says that he will engage in συμβουλεύειν! It was not uncommon in the fourth century BC for an orator to deliver an essentially deliberative speech at a ceremonial occasion - especially if the orator was self-conscious about criticism against oratory merely for the sake of show. At this point we cross the problem of defining epideictic according to occasion or content. For example, Lysias' *Olympiacus* seems to have been a deliberative speech presented at an epideictic occasion (only the preface, and a summary by Dionysius of Halicarnassus is preserved).

If we define epideictic narrowly as an oratorical showpiece, would not ambassadorial speeches - which usually have a specific request - be better classified as deliberative rhetoric? Compare the example from Philo (*Leg. Gaj.* 276-329) mentioned by Jewett (9). His whole discussion ignores the problem of the definition of epideictic in terms of style.

[431] Jewett seems to realise what he is doing since he admits on p.271 that "these categories are ordinarily applied to shorter blocks of material." But this is to vastly understate the transformation of terminology that has taken place. Two small examples of his procedure follow: i) He defines 1.18 - 15.13 as the *probatio*, a typical ancient term for the main section of a speech containing the proof. He then isolates four rounds of proof and names the first *confirmatio* (= βεβαίωσις), a term in ancient texts frequently used as a synonym for *probatio*. By *confirmatio* Jewett means a section in which the basic proof is provided and upon which the other three rounds are developments (271). This definition, however, cannot be found in ancient rhetorical theory. ii) The fourth proof is broadly categorised as *exhortatio* which he maintains must be considered a rhetorical category because Hermogenes uses it to define the

cle cannot in any way be deemed to demonstrate "the dynamics of ancient rhetoric" (277) in Paul. It is unfortunately a rather extreme example of disturbing trends in recent rhetorical studies, namely, the confusion of ancient and modern rhetorical theory, and the misuse or misunderstanding of ancient terminology and texts.[432]

A similar problem is found in the article of D. Hellholm (1993) who attempts an analysis of the macro-structure of the letter to the Romans by a combination of linguistics and ancient rhetoric. His grip of ancient rhetoric is, however, not very good.[433]

Hellholm identifies *Ep.Rom.* 1.16-17 as the "thematic proposition" of the letter and summarises it as "the gospel of the universality of justification by faith" (137). He sees the *probatio* or proof contained in 1.18 - 11.36. This *probatio* is further divided into θέσις (1.18 - 8.39) and ὑπόθεσις (9.1 - 11.6). The θέσις is then itself divided into *refutatio* (1.18 - 3.20) and *confirmatio* (3.21 - 8.39). Whilst this sub-division is said to be "obvious" (135), I have my questions. There is no comment given to the common analysis of *Ep.Rom.* 6.1ff and 9.1ff in terms of the objections raised in 3.3 and 3.5. If anything looks like *refutatio* (which Hellholm himself speaks of in terms of the refutation of arguments from opponents) then surely consideration should be given to this common analysis.[434]

There are other problems with his use of the θέσις/ ὑπόθεσις distinction. In ancient rhetoric the *quaestio* (question at issue) of an actual speech was a concrete case, a *quaestio finita* or ὑπόθεσις. Cicero in the *de Oratore* suggests that in order to prove one's case, one ought to first prove the general *quaestio* which underlies the specific *quaestio* under consideration (*de Orat.* 3.120). Quintilian, who follows Cicero in this respect, offers a good example: One must prove first that marriage is desirable before

last part of an argumentation based upon a *chria*. The working out of a *chria*, however, is quite a different thing to the construction of a speech!

[432] I bypass, as not properly related to rhetorical theory, Jewett's article "The Rhetorical Function of Numerical Sequences in Romans" in *Persuasive Artistry*, 1991, 227-45.

[433] This may be seen in his confusion of the distinction between θέσις and ὑπόθεσις (in reference to a *quaestio*) with the doctrine of *status*. The two are, however, quite separate. Compare only the exposition of Quintilian who discusses θέσις and ὑπόθεσις in *Inst.* 3.5 and *status* in *Inst.* 3.6. In fact, Quintilian even notes (*Inst.* 3.5.16) that the *status* of a definite *quaestio* (i.e., ὑπόθεσις) is the same as its abstracted indefinite *quaestio* (i.e., θέσις). In other words the distinction between definite and indefinite *quaestiones* (ὑποθέσεις and θέσεις) does not affect the doctrine of *status*. Hellholm is incorrect in suggesting a parallel between the doctrine of *status* and *parole*, *partes orationis* and *langue*, and *parole* and θέσις/ ὑπόθεσις.

[434] The point with respect to 6.1ff and 9.1ff is still valid even if Hellholm accepts S. K. Stower's analysis of 3.1-9 as a diatribic dialogue (1984, "Paul's Dialogue"), which from the analysis on p.139 appears to be the case.

one can prove whether Cato should marry (*Inst.* 3.5). On the basis of this doctrine it is theoretically possible to divide the *probatio* of a speech into proofs concerning the underlying θέσις and those concerning the ὑπόθεσις itself. A good example of this approach occurs in the 38th speech of Dio Chrysostom (an orator turned philosopher).

Nevertheless, it ought to be noted that Cicero's preoccupation with θέσεις in the *de Oratore* has to do with his attempt to synthesize philosophy and rhetoric in this treatise. Θέσεις were the province of philosophy, and Cicero's incorporation of them into his rhetorical theory represents his own personal approach, not that of school rhetoric in general.[435] That Quintilian also advocates this approach has to do with his admiration for Cicero, and cannot count as evidence that such a doctrine was further popular in the school rhetoric of the time (whether Greek or Latin).

Apart from the fact that this doctrine is not representative of school rhetoric, there is also a problem in the way Hellholm applies it. He considers the *quaestio finita* (ὑπόθεσις) of Paul's letter to be "God's δικαιοσύνη and Israel's disobedience and unbelief." According to the theory, this should then be *the* theme of the letter to the Romans. But this, in Hellholm's view, is not the main proposition of the letter itself (see his description of the *propositio* of 1.16-17, p.137, cf. 142-43). Rather, he views the *quaestio finita* as "the special treatment of the theme." This is all very well, but his θέσις/ ὑπόθεσις division as such no longer conforms to Cicero's theory.

One final point worth noting is that Hellholm also comes up against the problem of exhortation in this letter. His "solution" (without comment) is simply to label 12.1 - 15.13 as *exhortatio*. The criticism noted above with respect to Betz' similar proposal in the letter to the Galatians is also applicable here.[436]

Another example of the disturbing trends in recent rhetorical scholarship is the work of A. H. Snyman. In 1984 he published an article entitled "Style and meaning in Romans 8:31-9." Although some use of ancient rhetoric is made, the article is essentially a modern rhetorical and stylistic analysis based on the principles of E. Nida *et al;' Style and Discourse*. Rhetorical figures are again misappropriated.[437]

Similar problems are apparent in his article of 1986 "Stilistiese tegnieke in Romeine 7:7-13" which is basically an exercise in discourse analysis.[438] He does,

---

[435] On θέσεις in rhetorical theory, see chapter two, § 2.2.1.

[436] See p.111.

[437] Προσωποποιία is incorrectly identified in *Ep.Rom.* 8.35, 38-39. Despite reference to appropriate Graeco-Roman sources (100-102), namely, Demetr. *Eloc.* 265-66 and *Rhet.Her.* 4.66, he neglects to notice that προσωποποιία is always defined as introducing a specific character (person or thing) and letting it speak. Snyman has confused the modern term "personification" with the much more specific Greek figure προσωποποιία, cf. also Cic. *Orat.* 85; Quint. *Inst.* 9.2.29-37. See also the discussion below on the work of S. K. Stowers.

[438] Personification (this time of ἁμαρτία) is again incorrectly confused with προσωποποιία.

however, note an interesting case of ἀντίθεσις in 7.10, which is at the same time supported by a clash in the syntax. He argues that we have here deliberate rhetorical effect in the grammar which illustrates the application of the principle that style must be πρέπον (fitting).

In 1988 Snyman published a modified form of his article from 1984. This article was now reworked using the "methods" of G. A. Kennedy and Ch. Perelman/ L. Olbrechts-Tyteca.[439] Snyman now even went so far as to categorise this *pericope* (*Ep.Rom.* 8.31-39) into one of the three species of rhetoric (epideictic)! For this he has been rightly criticised by N. Elliott (95n) who traces this problem back to Kennedy.[440] Elliott alleges that Kennedy "gives the misleading impression that a 'rhetorical situation' can be identified for segments of a text."

Another case of ill-considered rhetorical analysis is provided by M. R. Cosby, "Paul's Persuasive Language in Romans 5" (1991).[441] Cosby is unfortunately careless both in his critique of others (cf. the note on J. T. Kirby below) and in his description of rhetorical figures. One example will suffice.

In commenting on v.17 Cosby complains that οἱ τὴν περισσείαν τῆς χάριτος καὶ τῆς δωρεᾶς τῆς δικαιοσύνης λαμβάνοντες is an unusual construction in that the article is so far from its participle. He claims that this, and the fact that the comparison made in this verse is not exactly parallel, show lack of "rhetorical sophistication."

Yet οἱ ... λαμβάνοντες is hardly unusual Greek. The object of λαμβάνω is quite properly placed between the article and the noun. It would be unusual if a non-related word were placed there.[442] It is true that the comparison is not parallel, but this is surely more a result of Paul's deliberate variation at this point.[443] Despite variation of terms, the conceptual comparison is still valid. When heard in a continuous reading, the hearer does not have the time to think everything logically through - but he does hear

---

[439] See above, chapter one, §§ 3-5.
[440] N. Elliott, 1990, *Rhetoric* (cf. G. A. Kennedy, 1984, *New Testament*, 34-35).
[441] Consider also the rather bombastic article by M. Schoeni (1993) concerned with sublime hyperbole (i.e., hyperbolic metaphor and simile) as described by Ps.-Longinus 38. Schoeni unfortunately misinterprets Longinus at this point by stating that at 38.5-6 he means to say that after a particularly high emotional instance of hyperbole, one needs to bring the audience "down" via the use of humour (177). Longinus, however, says nothing of the kind. All he means to say with respect to humour is that humorous hyperbolic expressions *work* (i.e., sound convincing) precisely because they are funny. There is no theory of humour used as a "come down" from emotional hyperbole. Given that the rest of Schoeni's article is based upon this incorrect interpretation, his contribution says little concerning the use of ancient rhetorical theory.
[442] That would then be the rhetorical effect of ὑπερβατόν of which Basil the Great, among others, was so fond.
[443] See below p.201.

the parallel constructions and, we may assume, does recognise a conceptual comparison.

Cosby does not do very much with the results of his rhetorical analysis of *Ep.Rom.* 5, except to say that with the rhetorical techniques "the Roman Christians would find Paul's presentation more persuasive than they would if he had merely provided substantiating data without rhetorical techniques." One wonders if such a conclusion is really sufficient.[444]

At this point we have progressed from rhetorical genre analysis to rhetorical textual analysis.[445] It would seem that a number of scholars becoming discontented with the results of genre analysis have instead directed their study of ancient rhetoric and Paul towards textual rhetoric.

A. B. Du Toit, for example, appropriately critiques what he terms as the "overriding influence of Greek rhetoric."[446] On p.195 he provides an example of this in his critique of Wuellner for superimposing an *exordium* and its characteristics on the epistolary opening of the letter.[447] Du Toit concludes his opening remarks as follows: (195-6) "... to force Romans into a rhetorical scheme or to speculate whether this letter belongs to the epideictic or any other rhetorical genre would be methodically unacceptable." For Du Toit, the letters of Paul remain letters whilst they may have rhetorical characteristics.

In his article, Du Toit seeks to understand the rhetoric of argumentation in *Ep.Rom.* 1.1-17. Aspects of ancient rhetorical theory are utilised in doing this, for example, viewing verses 11-12 as *correctio* (207). He characterises Paul as striving to be cautious and avoid the impression of self-commendation. The point is to give readers a positive impression of his apostolic capabilities. "By means of the *correctio* Paul actually scores his point, while at the same time he avoids any suggestion of over-inflated self-esteem." Du Toit adds that by 15.17ff such caution is no longer necessary, i.e., Paul's credentials are sufficiently established.

---

[444] A second example of Cosby's poor rhetorical analysis may be seen in Paul's alleged use of *transitio* (a statement wherein the speaker is expected to announce what he will next speak upon and distinguish it from what has gone before) in 5.1-2 (and 3.23 and 8.1), pp.213, 225. Whilst Paul does occasionally summarise what he has said (cf. 3.9), it seems to me that he rarely in any structural way introduces what he will next treat of (except in the epistolary περί clauses of 1 *Ep.Cor.*).

[445] For the term, see above pp.21-22.

[446] 1989, *Persuasion*, 194.

[447] In all fairness to Wuellner, I don't think he means *exordium* in the sense of ancient rhetorical theory, but in the sense of modern rhetoric (i.e., functional).

Another example of the application of rhetoric to exegesis is shown by an article by J. T. Kirby.[448] Kirby argues that καὶ οὕτως in *Ep.Rom.* 5.12 should be interpreted as answering to ὥσπερ, therefore obviating the need to consider the verse an anacoluthon. Apart from the grammatical considerations,[449] he argues that the rhetorical care of the rest of the following pericope would contrast strongly with a "violent anacoluthon and the need to posit a lengthy and cumbersome ellipsis." With respect to rhetorical care, he points to the isocolon in v.15 as an example.

Whilst it is true that rhetorical care is evidenced in this whole chapter (see the analysis below), it must also be said that there are a number of examples of significant ellipsis here (compare, e.g., 5.11, 16, 18). More to the point, the presence of anacolutha (and even worse grammatical slips) are not uncommon in Paul, cf. *Ep.Rom.* 2.20.[450] In addition, Kirby's main grammatical consideration hardly seems very strong. He does not show that an inversion of the normal word order οὕτως καί really does serve to emphasise the fact that an ellipsis is present.[451]

In recent years there have also been at least two full scale monographs on the letter to the Romans which give significant attention to textual rhetoric.

---

[448] 1987, "Syntax." See, further, the study of D. A. Black (1989, "Love Command"). Black basically takes up J. Muilenburg's challenge to analyse the textual rhetoric of a passage and attempts to utilise this in terms of an exegesis of the argumentation. He analyses the stylistic (rhetorical) arrangement of *Ep.Rom.* 12.9-13 and insists that the exegetical interpretation of the cola should reflect the rhetorical grouping. Black's textual rhetorical analysis is sound as far as it goes. The application to exegesis is interesting, but not related to ancient rhetorical theory.

[449] E.g., inversion of the word order of the regular οὕτως καί to emphasise the fact that δι᾽ ἑνὸς ἀνθρώπου should be understood.

[450] The presence of an anacoluthon does not have to be considered "violent," nor a grammatical, error. It may rather suggest a conversational style entirely appropriate to a letter.

[451] No other examples of *such* inverted word order are cited, and I have not been able to turn any up myself. An example of οὕτως καί *with* ellipsis was not hard to find (cf. Pl. *Grg.* 476b) and that is not surprising. The word order ὥσπερ ... οὕτω καί is rather fixed (cf. K.-G., *Gram.* II/2 256) and I would submit that if one wanted to suggest an answering clause to ὥσπερ, with or without an ellipsis, the best way to do so would be to use the regular word order οὕτως καί. By inverting the word order, the reader is quite naturally inclined to take the καί as conjunctive, as does Origen (*comm. in Rom.* M. 14.1005). Origen judges the verse to be an anacoluthon and is clearly embarrassed by the fact that it might show a deficiency of style. He goes on to argue, however, that there is really no stylistic deficiency present. Nevertheless, he does not seem to have noticed the possibility of treating καὶ οὕτως as the answering clause.

Kirby's interpretation has been accepted by N. Elliott (1990, *Rhetoric*, 230). M. R. Cosby (1991, "Language") also accepts the basic point but has criticisms. Unfortunately, Cosby inexplicably states that Kirby thinks v.12 is the isocolon (220). Kirby is referring to v.15.

In 1990 N. Elliott published *The Rhetoric of Romans: Argumentative Constraint and Strategy and Paul's Dialogue with Judaism.* He writes:

> "Our premise in this work is that the ancient and modern discussions of the dynamics of argumentation may help us to evaluate the cogency of some of the inferences that have been made from Romans in 'classical' historical treatments." (18-19)

His interest is clearly with textual rhetoric, and on p.64 he even notes the problems of identifying Romans with one of the traditional three rhetorical species. Yet despite this, Elliott does provide a rhetorical "*divisio*" of the letter. For example, he treats the letter opening and closing (1.1-15; 15.14-33) as functioning as, or corresponding to, the *exordium* and *peroratio* of an oration (69). His careful choice of words (in terms of functional correspondence) suggests that this is really the application of modern rhetorical theory.

We are once again confronted with a study that intends to provide a mix of ancient and modern rhetoric. The emphasis, however, is clearly upon modern rhetoric.[452] He adds on p.66:

> "the constraining power of audience and exigence in relation to Paul's persuasive purposes, as this may be analyzed through Paul's choice and development of topics, is the proper object of the rhetorical criticism of Romans."

In general, he wishes to see the whole of the letter to the Romans as serving the paraenetic goal of 15.14-16, namely, that the Gentile Christians will become participants in the cosmic offering of the Gentiles by sacrificing themselves to God in spiritual worship.

Elliott does, however, make a number of exegetical suggestions related to ancient rhetorical theory. For example he suggests that *Ep.Rom.* 5.1ff is the *propositio* of the letter, and that chapters one to four are an introduction by way of *insinuatio* (ἔφοδος) (233). This implies an audience not predisposed to accept Paul's statements in chapter five. The point seems somewhat far-fetched however. If the proposition begins in chapter five, then the introduction is out of all proportion to the rest of the letter (cf. Quint. *Inst.* 4.1.62). Elliott also attempts to overcome the fact that he had already defined 1.1-

---

[452] Evidence of this may be seen in the lack of a proper grasp of ancient rhetoric. For example on p.63 he confuses the philosophical λόγος προτρεπτικός (a separate literary genre) with προτρέπειν as a subcategory of deliberative rhetoric. (For a definition of λόγος προτρεπτικός see Philo of Larissa *Fr.* 2 Mette [= Stob. 2.7.2]).

15 as the functional *exordium* by saying that chapters one to four are "an extended *exordium* leading to the explicit *propositio* in Rom. 5" (234n).

On p.236 he proposes that "the sustained deliberative tone and syllogistic progression evident" in 6.1 - 8.13 are characteristic of *ratiocinatio*. He admits that this term was variously explained by ancient authors (referring to Cic. *Inv.* 1.57 and *Rhet.Her.* 4.23-24), but does not explain why he seems to think both usages which he cites seem to apply here, or how they apply.

A better suggestion is made on pp.288-90 where he argues that Paul applies various strategies from forensic rhetoric in emphasising "the immoral actions of the accused (1.18-32), denying any plea of ignorance (1.19-20, 32; 2.2) and accusing his 'defendant' of willfully presuming on the mercy of the divine 'court' (2.3-5)." There would appear to be something in this.

The second full scale monograph on the letter to the Romans attempting to grapple with ancient rhetoric was published by D. A. Campbell in 1992 (*The Rhetoric of Righteousness in Romans 3.21-26*).[453] Campbell devotes a separate chapter to a (textual) rhetorical analysis of his chosen passage, relying upon Quintilian as, in his view, the best source for Pauline investigation. He begins with a stylistic analysis designed to show that *Ep.Rom.* 3.21-26 is set off from the surrounding context by a distinct style (79-83). The context around this pericope is described as diatribic style (taken from S. K. Stowers, 1981, *Diatribe*), but within the pericope itself he describes the style as follows:

> "The sentences are more complex and use balanced cola and commata with a distinct rhythmical lilt. The diction is more elevated, and theological motifs (like νόμος) figure centrally in sweeping enthymemes." (81)

This sounds good and Campbell attempts to relate this to ancient rhetorical theory on style, but the point is not argued for in any detailed way.

Nevertheless, Campbell's rhetorical analysis of these verses (pp.70-101) is interesting and challenging, especially as it impinges upon the difficult question of the

---

[453] Campbell's article "Determining the Gospel through Rhetorical Analysis in Paul's Letter to the Roman Christians" (in 1994, *Gospel in Paul*, 315-36) concerns the application of modern rhetorical theory only.

syntactical structure of vs 22b-24a.[454] He sees various rhetorical devices at work here, especially ἀντίθεσις and ἐπαναφορά (anaphora). Using these notions he argues that οὐ γάρ ἐστιν ... χάριτι is an antithetical parenthesis, and that the prepositional phrases with διά c. gen. in verses 22, 24, and 25 are co-ordinate (he calls them an example of ἐπαναφορά). A careful reading of the passage with this in mind will demonstrate the exegetical consequences.

Whilst certainly challenging and worth thinking about, I am not in the end convinced by Campbell's analysis. It seems to me that he has been too concerned to put some logical and rhetorical balance and structure into Paul's sentence(s) which really just isn't there. It is difficult for me to see how someone reading the Greek would, for example, naturally distinguish διὰ τῆς ἀπολυτρώσεως κτλ. from τῇ αὐτοῦ χάριτι in v.24. A co-ordinate relationship with διὰ πίστεως κτλ. in v.22 just isn't clear enough. One would need some kind of extra marker (i.e., co-ordinating particles) to indicate this.

A significant problem in this part of Campbell's study is the lack of discussion of syllable length in connection with rhythm. He mentions the concept of rhythm a number of times, and it also comes up in the sources he cites, but nowhere does he note or pay attention to the question of syllable length so important to rhythm in ancient Greek and Latin. Whether Paul paid attention to this or not needs at least to be discussed if one wishes to discuss Pauline rhythm.

Nevertheless, I believe that Campbell's rhetorical analysis proceeds along a better path methodologically than many recent studies. He is concerned to apply ancient rhetorical theory at a textual level as an aid to exegesis. He quite appropriately sees the need to discuss not only figures of speech, but also more general considerations of style. Campbell himself characterises his approach as a concentration upon *elocutio*, one of the five traditional divisions of ancient rhetoric. The rhetorical insights thus gained function for him as "the interpretative pivot" upon which his whole investigation turns (77).

Finally, notice should be made of the challenging monograph of S. K. Stowers (1994, *A Rereading of Romans*). Stowers attempts to set Romans within its own

---

[454] In other respects the stylistic analysis is pushed a bit too far, for example, when νόμος, used twice in v.21, is not only seen as ἀντίθεσις (which is possible, if then rather inelegant as Campbell admits) but also as παρονομασία (word-play). He sees a pun in the fact that the two uses of νόμος are used to indicate different functions of the law. Frankly, this seems a pretty weak pun, and I can hardly think that it was intended as such.

cultural context and provide a fresh interpretation from this perspective.[455] The book is certainly challenging, though in the end I believe its general interpretation is unconvincing. However, we must restrict ourselves here to what Stowers says of ancient rhetorical theory. Although use of the word "rhetoric" is frequently made in this book, its sense is invariably very broad and not related to ancient rhetorical theory as such. Stowers' use of ancient rhetorical theory is effectively limited to his discussion of προσωποποιΐα (see especially pp.16-21). Given the popularity of this figure among New Testament exegetes and its frequent misinterpretation, it is worthwhile to consider his discussion in some detail.

Stowers identifies five passages in the letter to the Romans which he labels as προσωποποιΐα: 2.1-5; 2.17-29; 3.1-9; 3.27 - 4.2; and 7.7 - 8.2. We shall turn to these passages in a moment. It is first of all necessary to note how his discussion and definition of προσωποποιΐα (which he translates as 'speech-in-character') concentrates upon identification of this figure. He argues that προσωποποιΐα normally had to be identified in literature by means of stylistic and grammatical considerations, that is to say, that examples of προσωποποιΐα were *not* normally formally introduced. This is, naturally, important to Stowers, given that Paul has no formal introductions indicating προσωποποιΐα in his letter to the Romans. But it is at this point that his argument is quite weak. Essentially four arguments are presented for his case, and I shall briefly comment on each.

Firstly, he cites Quint. *Inst.* 1.8.3 where Quintilian is speaking of the appropriate use of the voice when reading out loud. At *Inst.* 1.8.3 he notes that προσωποποιΐαι ought not to be declaimed/ pronounced (*pronuntiari*) in the way of comic actors. The unfortunate use of the word "indicate" used to translate *pronuntiare* in the *Loeb* translation of H. E. Butler has led Stowers to surmise that *identification* of προσωποποιΐαι is also implied by the passage. The question of identification is simply not addressed by Quintilian here.

The second argument comes from Aristarchus of Byzantium's interpretative principle of τὸ πρόσωπον τὸ λέγον ("the person speaking") with respect to analysis of the poetry of Homer. Stowers refers the reader to A. Roemer's monograph on Aristarchus (1924, *Homerexegese*). Roemer's discussion (253-56) of the principle of τὸ πρόσωπον τὸ λέγον, however, shows that it concerns the solution of *prima facie* contradictions in Homer by appealing to the fact that one must distinguish what Homer himself says as poet from the words he puts into the mouths of other characters in his poem. There is

---

[455] He builds upon interpretations already argued for in (1981) *Diatribe* and (1984) "Dialogue."

nothing in the context which suggests anything connected with *problems of identification* as to who might be speaking in any given passage as such.[456]

His third reference (Quint. *Inst.* 9.2.37) is the only relevant evidence for his point. Here Quintilian, at the close of his discussion of προσωποποιΐα, notes that a speech may be inserted without indication of the person. However, his only example is from epic poetry and Quintilian goes on to note that omission of notification of the person speaking should itself be considered the use of the figure *detractio*.

The fourth argument is an unfortunate misreading of the fifth or sixth century AD treatise of Emporius, *de Ethopoeia*. On p.20, after discussing Quint. *Inst.* 9.2.37, Stowers goes on to say that Emporius distinguishes three ways of beginning a "characterisation." He then cites three examples taken from Emporius and categorises the beginnings as i) "the character starting to speak about herself or himself in the first person," ii) "an apostrophe, with the author addressing the fictional character," and iii) "by introducing the circumstances" of the occasion. Stowers states that these ways of beginning a προσωποποιΐα *exclude* specific introduction and identification of the speaker. This presentation of Emporius' treatise, however, badly misrepresents what is said. The reference is to Empor. *Eth.* p.563,1-12 H., where Emporius is indeed discussing various ways of beginning an example of what he calls ἠθοποιΐα (i.e., προσωποποιΐα of a person as opposed to a thing). Emporius' discussion concerns the subjects or topics with which one may begin the speech of the person concerned. However, he distinguishes not three subjects with which to begin, but four, namely, the person, the matter, time, or place. Beginnings taken from the person are further divided into the person of the speaker of the speech, the person to whom the speech is addressed, or a person described in the speech itself. Examples of each of these categories are provided from Vergil's *Aeneid*. It ought to be stressed that Emporius' concern is the kind of subjects/ topics with which one may *begin* one's προσωποποιΐα or introduced speech. Emporius does *not* mean to imply that such speeches ought not to be formally introduced and their speaker explicitly identified. In fact, *in every single example* he quotes (and he quotes no less than 11 examples), *the speaker is explicitly introduced and identified!*[457]

---

[456] It is interesting to note that the problem of τὸ πρόσωπον τὸ λέγον was also discussed by Origen in his commentary on the Song of Songs (fragment preserved in *philoc.* 7.1). Here the *identification* and *change* of speakers is Origen's paramount concern. He admits that the Scriptures (particularly the Prophets) are often unclear in their swift skipping from person to person.

[457] The quotations are from Verg. *A.* 1.37; 12.931; 1.65; 11.124; 5.781; 7.359; 8.185; 11.14; 8.374; 6.687; and 6.673.

If we return to Quint. *Inst.* 9.2.37 for a moment, we may note that Quintilian's discussion clearly views the omission of notification of the speaker as an exception. Furthermore, in his example, taken from Verg. *A.* 2.29, there is little room for misunderstanding that προσωποποιΐα is being used. In fact, if we look to the actual use of προσωποποιΐα in both rhetorical and philosophical texts then we find that a formal introduction and identification of the speaker is inevitably present. A lengthy list of examples is provided in the select glossary *s.v.* προσωποποιΐα. In each case, without exception, the speaker is identified.

Of Stowers' five examples in the letter to the Romans, the first two may be readily dismissed. As he himself indicates, both 2.1-5 and 2.17-29 are examples of ἀποστροφή. No speech is put into the mouth of another party, and thus no προσωποποιΐα can be spoken of.[458] The third and fourth examples (3.1-9 and 3.27 - 4.2) are interpreted as dialogues and for this reason termed προσωποποιΐα. As I have shown in the select glossary, certain ancient authors did include dialogue as a kind of προσωποποιΐα. Nevertheless, Stowers' case that these passages represent actual dialogue is not convincing.[459]

The final passage is the first person account of 7.7 - 8.2. This is more interesting in that Stowers also discusses Origen's attempt to see a kind of προσωποποιΐα in this passage. It is, perhaps, best to briefly review Origen's own interpretation first.[460] Origen had little trouble with *Ep.Rom.* 7.7-13, interpreting the difficult statement in v.9 of Paul and "every man's" early childhood. Yet Origen encountered problems at 7.14 and following. Quite rightly, he noted that Paul seems to be contradicting himself here. How can Paul speak of himself as σάρκινος and πεπραμένος ὑπὸ τὴν ἁμαρτίαν? Origen cites several other Pauline texts to highlight the contradiction. In light of this *problem*, he *tentatively* suggests that Paul may be using various examples of

---

[458]   It is possible that Stowers used the term προσωποποιΐα of these passages because he understands Paul to be putting on a certain character here. As to the first, he understands Paul to be speaking as a Jewish missionary preacher, and as to the second, he characterises it as the "philosopher-talk" of a teacher correcting a fellow Jewish teacher. *If* Stowers means that this is the introduction of the speech of these characters, and not of Paul himself, then his use of the term προσωποποιΐα is a little more understandable. Nevertheless, the lack of any identification of these speakers must weigh heavily against this interpretation which cannot have been obvious to the audience.

[459]   See footnote 483 below.

[460]   Unfortunately we no longer possess the text of Origen's massive commentary on Paul's letter to the Romans and must discern his views from a variety of sources. For *Ep.Rom.* 7 we rely upon Greek extracts in the *catena* and in the *Philocalia*, Rufinus' abbreviated Latin translation/ paraphrase, and Jerome's use of Origen in *Epistle* 121. A good discussion of Origen's commentary on *Ep.Rom.* 7 is to be found in C. P. Hammond Bammel, 1981, "Philocalia."

προσωποποιία (he suggests one kind of weak person for v.14 and another for v.15).[461] Yet evidence from Jerome (supported by Rufinus) shows that this was not the only interpretation Origen proffered for this passage.[462] Nevertheless, as Stowers notes (*Rereading*, 268-69), the use of the figure of προσωποποιία to solve the difficulties in *Ep.Rom.* 7 became more common (apart from Rufinus and Jerome who merely "translate" Origen, other interpretations using προσωποποιία are to be found in works of Didymus the Blind and Nilus of Ancyra).[463]

Origen's caution in suggesting the application of προσωποποιία here, combined with the fact that he is led to this suggestion *because* of the difficulties encountered in the text, do not inspire confidence in the correctness of this interpretation.[464] In fact, the complete lack of any introduction or identification of the speaker of any supposed προσωποποιία, combined with the absence of any other markers in the context suggesting that Paul means anyone other than himself by his use of the first person, must weigh heavily against this interpretation. The same consideration must also be applied

---

[461] ζήτημα ἀνακύπτει ... εἰ μή που εἴπωμεν ὅτι προσωποποιίας ἔχει διαφόρους ὁ λόγος ... (Catena 41). The caution is clear from the use of the subjunctive after εἰ μή and the insertion of που ("except, perhaps, we should say"). Stowers (*Rereading*, 362 n39) correctly notes that Hammond Bammel's argument for Origen's "guardedness" from the verb ἀμόζω is weak. Nevertheless, Stowers does not recognise the careful caution of the εἰ μή clause.

[462] See Hammond Bammel, *op. cit.*, 70-71, 74. She cites Jerome's words (70) that Paul "*non de se loquitur, sed de eo, qui post peccata uult agere paenitentiam, et sub persona sua fragilitatem describit condicionis humanae, quae duorum hominum, interioris et exterioris, pugnantium inter se bella perpetitur.*" By showing connections between Jerome's exposition and Rufinus' "translation" Hammond Bammel is able to make a good case for the fact that these words of Jerome are taken from Origen. Stowers, having denied the tentativeness of Origen's suggestion of προσωποποιία, prefers to regard Rufinus' exposition as correction of Origen, and Jerome's interpretation as influenced by his Western theology (*Rereading*, 362 notes 40 and 43). Although not impossible, Stowers' interpretation seems much less likely.

[463] Didymus (*Rom.* p.1-6 Staab), although a follower of Origen in many respects, has a different interpretation of *Ep.Rom.* 7. He understands *Ep.Rom.* 7.7-24 to be προσωποποιία of Adam. Like Origen's, his interpretation is motivated by perceived contradictions in these verses with other statements of Paul. The brief exegetical fragments in Nil. *epp.* 1.152 and 1.153 suggest that he thought of multiple use of προσωποποιία (he uses the term ἠθοποιία, a word used in late rhetorical theory of προσωποποιία in respect of a person as opposed to an abstract concept). *Ep.Rom.* 7.9 is interpreted of a non-Jew, and 7.23 is interpreted of one (certainly not Paul) who is swept away by his carnal passions. It is interesting to note that Nilus speaks of ἠθοποιία as an exegetical tool, not as a figure employed by Paul himself (*epp.* 1.153).

[464] One wonders if Origen's rather broad application of προσωποποιία is related to his theory of the inspired προσωποποιία of the Holy Spirit. In a fragment of his fourth homily on the Acts of the Apostles (preserved in *philoc.* 7.2) Origen argues that the Holy Spirit "makes persons" (προσωποποιεῖ) in the prophets. He means to say that when the prophets speak in the name of someone else (e.g., of God, or of Christ), then it is really the Holy Spirit, through the prophet, who is speaking in the character of the person concerned (whether, for example, in the person of God or Christ). Origen is led to this digression by the mention of a Psalm of David whose words Origen interprets to be the words of Christ (OT *Ps.* 108 cited in *Act.Ap.* 1.16).

to Stowers' contention that 7.7 - 8.2 is an example of προσωποποιΐα of a Gentile attempting to live by the works of the law.

We must conclude that despite other merits this book may have, it is ultimately not very helpful when it comes to the application of ancient rhetorical theory to Paul's letter.

2 Rhetorical Analysis
2.1 Introduction

As in the case of Paul's letter to the Galatians, the paraenesis in the letter to the Romans (beginning at chapter twelve) has been excluded from this analysis. Once again, this is not to say that the paraenesis plays no important role in the letter, nor that it is not in some way connected with the foregoing argument. The only point is that it is less feasible to analyse this section of the letter in terms of ancient rhetorical theory. Our analysis will, therefore, be restricted to the first eleven chapters.

Prima facie the letter to the Romans would appear to offer more scope for a rhetorical analysis than the letter to the Galatians. It is less obviously epistolary in content and length, and offers a more connected extended argument. The letter does not suffer from the apparent disconnectedness of thought present in the letter to the Galatians, nor is it so obviously tied to a particular situation regarding which we are left guessing. In writing to the Christians in Rome, Paul is writing to churches he has never personally visited.[465] This at least means that we are presented with a more clear presentation of what Paul wishes to say. The kind of argumentative lacunae found in the letter to the Galatians do not appear here.

We may also, I believe, sidestep the rather vexed and much debated question as to the purpose of the main body of the letter.[466] It is safe to say that Paul nowhere explicitly reveals why he chose to include the material of *Ep.Rom.* 1.16 - 15.13. In particular, the argumentative section (chapters one to eleven) can be quite simply understood apart from the presupposition of any concrete situation in Rome. That is not to say that a particular situation in Rome may not have influenced what Paul wrote, or,

---

[465] That we may speak of *churches* (ἐκκλησίαι) in Rome is clear from *Ep.Rom.* 16.5a. That Paul had never visited Rome is not to say that he necessarily had no knowledge of the situation there. In this respect, J. van Bruggen's analysis of the implications of *Ep.Rom.* 16 is quite enlightening (1970, *Raadsel*). Van Bruggen cogently argues that the churches in Rome were founded by missionary teams sent out by Paul sometime after AD 50 (see also, 1967, *Oorsprong*).

[466] That is, aside from the obvious purposes mentioned in *Ep.Rom.* 1.1-15 (mutual prayer) and chapter fifteen (his forthcoming visit and intended trip to Spain).

perhaps, the way he wrote it, only that we have no hard evidence from which to reconstruct such a situation. In any event, chapters one to eleven may be understood as a summary of the Gospel which Paul generally preached to believers in the Roman empire.[467] This section, however, is certainly no dogmatic treatise since the nature of the argument and its emphases show clearly the kind of ideas Paul found it necessary to emphasise and to combat during his missionary travels. The great mystery of the Gospel, namely, salvation revealed in Christ not only for Jews but also for Gentiles, raised a number of problems and questions among the early churches, and some of these show clearly through in Paul's argumentation.

The rhetorical analysis offered below, as for the letter to the Galatians, is written from the point of view of a hypothetical professor of rhetoric. As such it is a maximalist approach and should in no way imply that Paul thought or even deliberately wrote in these rhetorical terms or categories. The question as to Paul's conscious use of rhetorical theory will be discussed in the conclusion to this book.

2.2 Ep.Rom. 1 - 5

The first 15 verses follow modified epistolary conventions. An expanded opening (1.1-7) is followed (as per convention) by a thanksgiving paragraph.[468] The desire to visit is also an epistolary commonplace, although this fact should not be interpreted to mean that the desire is not real. The epistolary introduction may be interpreted to show concern for *captatio benevolentiae* (cf. ethos) in a number of respects, but none of the traditional rhetorical τόποι are employed.[469]

---

[467] I would emphasise the words "to believers." Paul is writing to those already converted and whom we may presume (as Paul evidently does) already know the basics of the Gospel story of Christ's life on earth, his suffering, death and ascension to heaven. That Paul must have preached on these basics to new Christians is clear from passages such as 1 *Ep.Cor.* 11.23-26 and 15.1-8.

[468] A conventional thanksgiving sentence (or short paragraph) would have concerned a prayer regarding the health or prosperity of the addressee. Paul, instead, gives thanks to God (using his own favourite verb εὐχαριστέω instead of the regular χάριν ἔχω) that their faith is proclaimed throughout the whole world.

[469] Paul's expanded address provides a rather full identification of his office (an apostle of God's Gospel concerning Jesus Christ). As noted above in respect of the letter to the Galatians, Paul's expanded openings are quite unusual in terms of Graeco-Roman epistolary tradition. The suggestion that certain credal formulae have been introduced here is interesting, but can hardly be proved. It is noteworthy that whilst Paul identifies the subject of God's "good news" (Jesus), he does not at this point reveal what the actual *good* news is. The tone of this description of his office is considerably different to that of the opening of the letter to the Galatians. His own subservience to Jesus Christ (the anointed king) is especially emphasised by the phrase δοῦλος Χριστοῦ Ἰησοῦ, carrying distinctly Eastern connotations (a slave of the great king) which are supported by the Septuagintal background.

If J. van Bruggen's hypothesis is correct, that Paul is writing to churches which have been established through missionary teams sent out by him (1970, *Raadsel*), then the description of his calling to office as an apostle (esp. 1.1 and 5) would probably be sufficient to remind his audience of his excep-

Paul captures the goodwill of his audience in a number of ways: i) by emphasising their inclusion, together with himself, as subjects of Jesus Christ (1.6), ii) his
modification of the thanksgiving formula in noting that their faith is proclaimed
throughout the whole world (a hyperbolic emphasis). This fact is further emphasised by
the ensuing oath that he personally spreads the news of their faith around continually.[470] The use of an oath here has nothing in common with rhetorical theory on
oaths in a forensic setting, but the use of humble prayer in an *exordium* is recommended by Cic. *Inv.* 1.22 as one way of attaining goodwill. iii) The use of correction
($\mu\varepsilon\tau\alpha\beta o\lambda\dot{\eta}$) to emphasise his humility in not just wanting to strengthen their faith, but
in expecting mutual encouragement.

The theme for the rest of the argumentative section of the letter is introduced in
verses 16b-17, namely, that the "good news" is God's power for deliverance to everyone who believes, since God's justice is revealed in it by the connection of faith.[471]
Formally the proposition for the letter as a whole might be considered to be v.15. It is
this statement (that it is Paul's desire to preach the Gospel to the Roman Christians)
that forms the basis for Paul's following remarks (indicated by the ensuing series of
causal conjunctions [$\gamma\acute{\alpha}\rho$]), and also seems to be reflected upon again at the end of the
"sermon" (15.5ff). It would seem that the main body of this letter functions as a
temporary substitute for Paul's personal presence and preaching. If this is correct, it
confirms our comments above on the viability of understanding at least the first eleven
chapters as the summary of a message Paul more frequently felt a need to emphasise to
Christian congregations, given their faith in a Gospel which emerged out of a Jewish
context.

A global picture of Paul's argument in the first five chapters may be schematised
as follows:

> 1.16-17 *Theme:* God's (saving) justice is revealed in the Gospel by the connection of faith.
> 1.18 - 3.20 *Counterpoint:*
> > - God's anger revealed against man's profanity and injustice, who supresses the truth with
> >   his injustice.
> > - Because they see God's eternal power and divinity in creation.

---

tional apostolate (i.e., having been commissioned not by Jesus on earth, but through an exceptional
manifestation, cf. *Act.Ap.* 1.21-22; 9.1-19).
[470] A comma should be placed at the end of v.9 and not after $\mu o v$ in v.10. The near synonymous
adverbs $\dot{\alpha}\delta\iota\alpha\lambda\varepsilon\dot{\iota}\pi\tau\omega\varsigma$ and $\pi\acute{\alpha}\nu\tau o\tau\varepsilon$ indicate the beginning of separate clauses. Furthermore, this punctua-
tion makes the best sense of the $\gamma\acute{\alpha}\rho$ in v.9. Paul is able to say that their faith is proclaimed around the
world *because* he is continually engaged in doing this!
[471] That v.17 also belongs with the theme seems clear from the way in which these opening lines are
picked up on in 3.21-22. The Gospel as God's power is not emphasised again in the letter.

- Therefore they are without excuse.
- Because knowing God they dishonour him by image worship of creatures.
- Therefore God gave them over to their own lusts - which they have engaged in. They are full of sins, both in deed (e.g., murder etc.) and thought (e.g., greed etc.).

2.1-16 ἀποστροφή *to man in general:*
- Therefore *you* are without excuse, *everyone* who judges such sin, since you are not free from it yourself.
- No one escapes God's judgement.
- God judges impartially both Jew and Greek (on the basis of his law). When Gentiles *do* the law (although not in physical possession of it) they will be judged accordingly.

2.17 - 2.29 ἀποστροφή *to Jew:*
- Jewish hypocrisy attacked and set off against Gentile obedience of law. Conclusion is that it is the inward Jew that is important (i.e., he who obeys, not he who is physically circumcised), i.e., further proof that God judges impartially both Jew and Greek.

3.1-9 πρόληψις: (still directed to Jew, cf. 3.5-9 *1st* pers. pl.)
- What then is benefit of Jew? Entrusted with God's oracles.
- Brief refutation of two objections related to God's trustworthiness and justice, and the idea that Paul's Gospel implies a license to sin.

3.9-20 *Summation* of main point of argument thus far: the whole world is accountable to God because of sin (failure to obey his law).

3.21-23 But now God's righteousness is revealed through faith in Christ.
3.27 Therefore boasting is excluded
3.29 Argument from oneness of God
3.31 πρόληψις
4.1 Example of Abraham
5.1 Beneficial results of justification in Christ
5.12 σύγκρισις between Adam's transgression and God's act of justification in Christ.

Paul's announcement that God's δικαιοσύνη is revealed in the Gospel requires some comment, as does his usage of the verb δικαιόω. To Greek readers unfamiliar with the Septuagint, the use of δικαιόω in the sense of "to justify τινα" instead of "seek justice against τινα" (i.e., "to punish") must have caused a lexical-shock. Thus in *Ep.Rom.* 4.5 the phrase τὸν δικαιοῦντα τὸν ἀσεβῆ means "he who justifies the ungodly man" and not "he who *punishes* the ungodly man"! Frequent readers of the Septuagint and/ or New Testament become somewhat immunised against the lexical shock effect this must have had to a reader/ listener unfamiliar with these writings. Nevertheless, the context of the earliest occurrence of this verb in the letter to the Romans must have shown uninitiated readers/ listeners what Paul meant by the term, although it may initially have caused some confusion (the first usage is *Ep.Rom.* 2.13).[472] Despite what is

---

[472] It is interesting to postulate how an uninitiated listener may have heard the first few occurences of δικαιόω upon hearing the epistle read to him. A listener would not have too much time to think while the epistle was being read. If the first occurrence of δικαιόω at 2.13 raised questions and caused some confusion, then the second occurence at 3.4 in a difficult context (see below for the elliptical argumentation) would not help. It is unlikely that the uninitiated listener would misunderstand the gist of 3.20, although the peculiarity of the Septuagintal (Hebraic) ου ... πᾶσα σάρξ may have hindered the listener from quickly perceiving what the grammatical or lexical problem, which he must have perceived, amounted to precisely. By 3.24 the listener may well have perceived the trend since the context again makes the meaning clear. This is reinforced in the following verses. Paul's usage would, therefore, probably not have

said here, it should be remembered that Paul's audience were converted Christians and it may be expected that some (if not most) of them were familiar with the peculiar Greek of the Septuagint (which must have been used in regular worship).

With regard to the noun δικαιοσύνη, we should be careful before importing any kind of special meaning from background sources, and first let Paul's own usage speak for itself.[473] Paul begins by saying that God's δικαιοσύνη (righteousness) is revealed in the Gospel, and then sets this off against the fact that God's ὀργή (anger) is revealed against the ἀδικία of men. Whilst δικαιοσύνη and ὀργή are set off against each other, they are not strictly speaking opposites. God's δικαιοσύνη is contrasted with man's ἀδικία. The true opposite to God's ὀργή against man's ἀδικία, is his χάρις manifested to men through faith in Jesus Christ (cf. 1.5; 3.24; 4.4-5).

Having announced that God's δικαιοσύνη by faith is revealed in the Gospel, Paul immediately supports his contention with testimony from Scripture. The text refers to the ὁ δίκαιος ἐκ πίστεως, which may be considered to involve συζυγία (argument from a cognate word), although the argument is hardly based on συζυγία as such.

Having provided a short but strong support for his major contention, Paul immediately moves to the contrasting discussion of the revelation of God's anger against man's ungodliness and wickedness, and his impartiality in judgement. The function of the following section (1.18 - 3.20) is clearly to show that man's works can avail him nothing before God. Paul is therefore carefully constructing the same twofold διαίρεσις with which he was concerned in the letter to the Galatians: justification may be conceivably attained in only two ways, namely, by the works of the law or by faith. Since it cannot be obtained by the works of the law (which only produce God's anger, cf. 4.15), it must be by faith, a contention also attested by the Old Testament Scripture itself.

A skeletal outline of the flow of argumentation was given above. Of particular interest is the way Paul dwells upon the consideration that God has handed men over to their own lusts (because of their wickedness). In fact Paul repeats those words no less than three times (1.24, 26, 28), emphasising his point rather dramatically by this

---

caused gross misunderstanding, although it may have led (initially at least) to some measure of ambiguity and confusion.
[473] I must admit that I was formerly inclined to read δικαιοσύνη here in terms of its use in the Septuagint as more or less equivalent to deliverance or vindication, cf. LXX Ps. 97 (98).2, ἐγνώρισεν κύριος τὸ σωτήριον αὐτοῦ, ἐναντίον τῶν ἐθνῶν ἀπεκάλυψεν τὴν δικαιοσύνην αὐτοῦ. Paul's contrast of God's δικαιοσύνη with man's ἀδικία, however, belies this interpretation.

ἀναφορά.[474] Each time, however, the recipient of the verb παραδίδωμι is varied, although essentially indicating the same thing. This variation prevents the ἀναφορά from appearing too wooden (or in Greek terminology, ψυχρόν). In addition, the emotional tension is heightened by personifying these recipients.[475] They are as follows:

> 1.24 (ἐν ταῖς ἐπιθυμίαις τῶν καρδιῶν αὐτῶν) εἰς ἀκαθαρσίαν
> 1.26 εἰς πάθη ἀτιμίας
> 1.28 εἰς ἀδόκιμον νοῦν

The effect produced by this repeated attacking is heightened with each new variation. In the second sentence Paul becomes more explicit as to what he means by the dishonouring of their bodies mentioned the first time around. In the third sentence Paul pulls out all the stops, as it were, including various examples of παρονομασία (wordplay, ἐδοκίμασαν ... ἀδόκιμον 1.28; φθόνου, φόνου 1.29; ἀσυνέτους, ἀσυνθέτους 1.31) and increases the tempo of his language by the extended ἀσύνδετον (asundeton). In addition, a whole host of sins are now listed in no particular order and including both serious crimes (e.g., murder) and sinful desires (e.g., greed). The mixture is probably deliberate and serves to include more comprehensively all kinds of people within the same category of men who stand under God's wrath as sinners and are therefore deserving of death (1.32, cf. 5.6; 6.21).

Such use of ἀναφορά combined with other figures such as ἀσύνδετον to provide a highly emotional attacking effect is well described in [Longin.] 20.1-3. However, as in the letter to the Galatians, we may note that Paul considers the use of παρονομασία appropriate in highly emotional contexts, a practice condemned by our extant rhetorical theory. The whole passage (1.24-32) may be considered as a good example of ἐπιμονή, a rhetorical lingering on a particular thought by repeating it several times in varied ways. This figure was considered by the theoreticians to be particularly forceful. The main point made in the ἐπιμονή is that the disgusting sins present in the world (e.g.,

---

[474] The judgemental overtones are, perhaps, augmented by the fact that Paul's emphasised phrase is itself taken from a Psalm in the Scripture, LXX *Ps.* 105 (106), also used in the context of God's anger, although there it is God's anger directed against Israel. It is clear from the parallels in *Wi.* 13-14 that Paul has adapted traditional argumentation against the sins of the Jewish people to his own context of God's anger against the sins of mankind generally. The relevant portions from *Ps.* 105 (106).40-41, 46 read as follows: καὶ ὠργίσθη θυμῷ κύριος ἐπὶ τὸν λαὸν αὐτοῦ ... καὶ παρέδωκαν αὐτοὺς εἰς χεῖρας ἐθνῶν ... καὶ ἔδωκεν αὐτοὺς εἰς οἰκτιρμούς. Incidentally, the phrase καὶ ἐλογίσθη αὐτῷ εἰς δικαιοσύνην (cf. *Ep.Rom.* 4) is also used in this psalm (v.31) of a *deed* of Phineas, in contrast to the statement about Abraham (where it is his *faith* that is concerned).
[475] See above p.136.

homosexuality) are evidence of God's anger against man for his sinful turning away from the true God.

Paul uses the forceful tension which he has built up to suddenly turn upon the reader, whoever he may be, and accuse him of falling into this category of person (2.1), and therefore being without excuse before God.[476] The reader, up until now, may have been expected to be in full agreement with the condemnation of such blatant sins, but in a surprising turn (cf. παράδοξον, Quint. *Inst.* 9.2.22-24) he now finds himself roundly condemned! Paul achieves this by addressing anyone who would dare judge those that commit the kind of sins just enumerated (those who don't judge them have already been condemned in 1.32). He asserts that such judges cannot escape the charge of hypocrisy. At this point, Paul's inclusion of common sins of thought within his climactic list at 1.29-31 must be in the background. No one can realistically claim that they never also indulge in such sins.

Because of the intensity of the foregoing, the *apostrophic* accusation is all the more forceful (see select glossary *s.v.* ἀποστροφή). The πάθος is maintained by the use of rhetorical questions (ἐπερώτησις) at 2.3-4. The effect is one of threatening cross examination (cf. Quint. *Inst.* 9.2.7-8; [Longin.] 18).[477]

Paul goes on to argue that God's judgement will come on the basis of man's works and will be the same for both Jews and Gentiles. God is impartial in judgement. This point is clearly important to Paul as his discussion of it takes up the rest of the chapter (2.6-29).

It should be noted that by this point Paul has already effectively accused all mankind of unrighteousness and sin. This must be presupposed in the ensuing discussion and is further confirmed by Paul's remarks at 3.9-20. What Paul now sets out to

---

[476] It has been argued that this ἀποστροφή must be seen in connection with Paul's attack on the Jews in the second half of this chapter, but there is no indication of that here (so, correctly, S. K. Stowers, 1994, *Rereading*). Keeping in mind the necessity of reading an ancient text *linearly* (see G. A. Kennedy, *New Testament*, 5), one cannot expect the reader to have interpreted the διό of 2.1 as referring to anything else but the foregoing (cf. J. Weiss, 1897, "Beiträge," 216). C. E. B. Cranfield's argument (1975/79, *Commentary*, 1.138) that the notable points of contact with LXX *Wi.* 11 - 15 in this section suggest that Paul was thinking of Jewish assumptions is not at all cogent. It is true that Paul's argumentation here seems related to *Wi.* 11 - 15 which is directed against the Jews, but it should be remembered that 1.18-32 is *also* related to these chapters of *Wisdom* (particularly 13 - 14), yet no one would argue that Paul is singling out the Jews there! Paul has clearly adapted the argumentation of this book and made it suit his own purposes. It should be added that there is equally no indication in the text that Paul's argument from 1.18ff is restricted to Gentiles. Paul is referring to mankind in general, both Jew and Greek (*contra* Stowers, 1994, *Rereading*).

[477] Incidentally, Paul's thought at 2.4 is clearly based on the general message of LXX *Ps.* 105 (106), cf. esp. v.1 and 47. This psalm (as noted above) was very clearly in Paul's mind when writing the letter.

prove is that God's judgement of mankind is impartial. Both Jew and Greek are judged on the basis of God's law.

Paul must be speaking of the law of Moses in these chapters. It is this law that the Jews have in their hands, and the task of which, Paul argues, the Gentiles have written on their hearts. Paul, however, clearly makes a distinction between the law of Moses as a moral law (applying equally to the Gentiles, cf. OT *Le.* 20.22-23) and certain ceremonial aspects applicable only to the Jews, e.g., circumcision (cf. 2.27 where Paul speaks of a hypothetical Gentile who keeps the law and yet is uncircumcised). This distinction is taken for granted and not argued for. Paul clearly expected it to be known and accepted by his audience.

Yet the central point of the rest of this chapter, God's impartiality in judgement, clearly concerned Paul. It seems clear that he thought that this point could *not* be taken for granted. Thus he states quite emphatically that God will judge men on the basis of their *works* whether good or bad (2.6-11). Paul gives the hypothetical outcome of this judgement both for those who seek immortality by endurance in good work, and for those who disobey the truth. At this point, the question of how someone might be able to gain eternal life is out of the picture. Paul has argued that all men are under sin's dominion and will go on to argue that only by faith in Jesus Christ can one be justified before God and receive his Spirit which empowers the believer to accomplish good works. Yet these considerations are not pertinent here. The point is God's impartiality.

In the ensuing verses (2.12-29) Paul combats, in particular, the idea that Jews are right (δίκαιος) before God by virtue of their possession of his law. Paul distinguishes *hearing* the law from *doing* the law. Whatever one's position in this life (whether Jew or Greek), it is *doing* the law which is the determining factor in God's judgement. In this respect the Gentiles stand equal before God with the Jews.

God's basic impartiality and his judgement on the basis of man's deeds are stated rather than argued for, and Paul would no doubt have expected them to be generally acceptable (these points are clearly enunciated in the Old Testament). They are thus used as κεκριμένα (accepted opinions or judgements). Paul goes on to apply these κεκριμένα in a way that breaks down any perceived differences between Jew and Gentile. These commonly accepted dogmata are thus used to prove a less commonly accepted point. He argues that Gentiles too possess knowledge of God's law. Their outright condemnation, therefore, cannot just be assumed because they do not possess the physical rolls of the *Torah*. Paul highlights their equality in judgement by comparing a Gentile who may actually in some respects *do* the law of God, with a hypocritical Jew.

The ἀποστροφή to such a Jew (Paul addresses *one* hypothetical Jew in the singular)[478] functions as an example in order to make it clear to the audience that God must surely judge the law-abiding Gentile more positively than the flagrantly disobedient Jew.[479] The matter of circumcision (implying the covenant privileges of the Jew) does not make any difference in this respect. True circumcision is of the heart - a well-known Old Testament metaphor (cf. OT *Le.* 26.41; *De.* 10.16; 30.6; *Je.* 4.4; 9.25-26). When Paul adds that true circumsion is ἐν πνεύματι (presumably a reference to the Holy Spirit), we see a hint that he really only believes that someone could be genuinely acceptable to God through the power of the Holy Spirit, which as he later shows, is given to those who have faith in Jesus Christ.

The argumentative function of the ἀποστροφή to the Jew, therefore, is to set in high relief Paul's contention that a Gentile stands on precisely the same footing before God's judgement seat as the Jew. Surely God will recognise and take account of the law-abiding Gentile and condemn the hypocritical Jew. The ἀποστροφή thus functions as clarification rather than rational argumentation.[480]

Having broadly outlined the argumentative structure of chapter two, we can now return and make a few more detailed remarks more specifically related to rhetorical theory.

In 2.14-16 Paul appeals to the fact that Gentiles are known to perform duties of the law (τὰ τοῦ νόμου) in order to suggest that they have the task of the law (τὸ ἔργον τοῦ νόμου) written in their hearts. This is further demonstrated by the activity of the conscience and their inward thoughts which will give testimony on judgement day. Even though they do not have physical copies of God's law, God will still hold them

---

[478] S. K. Stowers, (1981, *Diatribe*, cf. 1994, *Rereading*) has correctly shown the similarity of this kind of ἀποστροφή with those in contemporary popular philosophical writings (even if I would quibble with his use of terminology), cf. Teles, Epictetus, Dio Chrysostomus. Individual opponents are clearly addressed.

[479] Paul is concerned here with the *relative* judgement of God at the last day. He nowhere directly suggests that certain Gentiles may actually merit eternal salvation by virtue of their obedience to God's law. In fact, he goes on to emphatically *deny* this. Nevertheless, Paul implies that God's judgement of man's deeds will be fair. Those non-believers who have nevertheless followed God's law in many respects will be judged differently from others who have been flagrant criminals.

[480] Seen in this light, one ought not to look in this passage for arguments that Jews as a whole are sinners. The "προῃτιασάμεθα Ἰουδαίους τε καὶ Ἕλληνας πάντας ὑφ' ἁμαρτίαν εἶναι" of 3.9 has been shown in 1.18 - 2.5. Not only does the *apostrophic* passage *not* prove this point (not all Jews were thieves, adulterers or temple robbers!), but its form as an individual ἀποστροφή should warn against a general application where that is not indicated in the text (contrast the *clear* corporate use of the singular in 11.17-24 where its use is influenced by the metaphor of the *single* wild olive tree with its branches reflecting the individual Gentiles).

accountable at judgement day on its basis (cf. 3.19-20) and take into account as much of his law as they have kept. As noted above, Paul speaks here of Gentile obedience over against Jewish disobedience in order to highlight the Gentiles' equality with Jews before God's judgement seat.[481]

In these verses (2.14-16) Paul comes quite close to the notion of common/ natural law which was widespread in antiquity.[482] Rhetorical treatises often discussed how to use the notion of common law if the written law did not seem to support one's case. Here, however, Paul holds up the idea of common law as evidence that all mankind has some knowledge of the task required by God's law. We may note that the phrase τὸ ἔργον τὸ τοῦ νόμου is used at Arist. *Rh.* 1.15.7 to mean "the task of the law" (as distinguished from the written law itself) within the context of a discussion on common law (ὁ κοινὸς νόμος which is said to be κατὰ φύσιν). Given the general acceptance of the principle of common or natural law in antiquity, this part of Paul's argument would have been readily accepted. Paul, of course, takes for granted the fact that the Jewish Scriptures are God's law revealed to man and that it is the task of *this* law that is written on the hearts of Gentiles. He is, after all, speaking to an audience already committed to the Christian faith.

---

[481] I have suggested what I believe to be the most acceptable interpretation of these verses, but it ought to be noted that there are certainly other interpretations. S. K. Stowers (1994, *Rereading*) has suggested that 1.18 - 2.5 concerns only Gentiles, and then only Gentiles in a broad corporate sense. He argues that Paul means that some Gentiles could earn salvation (contrast my note 479 above). Whilst there are many things quite attractive about Stowers' interpretation of these opening chapters (his arguments cannot be listed in full here), his interpretation flounders with his attempt to water down the strong all-inclusive language of 3.9-20. C. E. B. Cranfield takes a more traditional position when he argues that the positive statements in chapter two proleptically refer to Gentile *Christians*. Cranfield's position becomes difficult at 2.14. He interprets the verse to be referring to people who do not possess the law "by virtue of their birth" (1975/79, *Commentary*, 1.157), i.e., Gentile Christians. Cranfield's desire to interpret φύσει as referring back to τὰ μὴ νόμον ἔχοντα reflects his difficulty in that he is forced to maintain that Paul's point is that these Gentiles didn't grow up with the law. Being Christians, they naturally now have access to it. Paul's point, however, is that these Gentiles emphatically do not have physical copies of the law, and the fact that they are still capable of performing certain things that the law requires (τὰ τοῦ νόμου) shows that they may be considered to have the task of the law (τὸ ἔργον τοῦ νόμου) written on their hearts. The argument fails if it can be maintained that they now have access to the physical rolls of God's law anyway! Cranfield's interpretation (*Op. cit.*, 1.195-96) leads him to further problems at the exegesis of 3.19-20 where he is forced to maintain that those ἐν τῷ νόμῳ must be only the Jews. This position is rather weak given the conclusion deduced in 3.19b-20 that the whole world is thus held responsible to God. Paul's point is related to the fact that he has already shown in 2.14-16 that the Gentiles are also considered to be subject to God's judgement in the same way as the Jews, namely, on the basis of God's law.

[482] The concept was widely discussed in philosophical, rhetorical and legal treatises. A mere sampling of references follows: Zeno *Fr.* 162 (*Stoic.* 1.42-43, the Stoics identified natural law with the divinity); Arist. *Rh.* 1.10.3; 1.13; 1.15.4-8; *Rhet.Her.* 2.14, 19, cf. 3.4; Cic. *Inv.* 2.65-67, 161; *Off.* 3.69; *Leg.* 1.18ff; Quint. *Inst.* 7.1.46-47; Gaius *Inst.* 1.1, cf. D.H. *Th.* 40 (ὁ κοινὸς τῆς φύσεως νόμος) and Ph. *Abr.* 4-5.

At 2.17 Paul directs his ἀποστροφή to the Jew in particular. Again we are confronted with a series of threatening questions which may be likened to cross examination where the person questioned is simply left speechless. Such charges of hypocrisy were common in the ancient world (cf. Max.Tyr. 31.6), especially against Jews (cf. Arr. *Epict.* 2.9.20-21). In the run-up to these questions (2.17-20) Paul again carefully builds an increase in tempo into his language by beginning paratactically and then introducing ἀσύνδετον. The sentence is broken off in notable agitation as Paul launches into the accusatory questions.

The apparent downplaying of the value of circumcision at 2.25-29 leads Paul to briefly introduce a πρόληψις (prolepsis) of two objections (3.1-9). Rhetorical theory does not provide much concrete information on when and how to use such προλήψεις, but it is clear that this brief digression (παράβασις) is warranted (cf. [Arist.] *Rh.Al.* 18.11-15; Rut.Lup. 2.4; Quint. *Inst.* 9.2.16-17. The somewhat more concrete advice in Hermog. *Meth.* 23 is not really applicable here.).

The nature of Paul's ἀποστροφή to the Jew also changes somewhat at this point, for Paul begins to ask questions to which he supplies his own short answers. Instead of accusatory rhetorical questions we have an example of αἰτιολογία (a short inquiring question which is answered by the speaker, cf. *Rhet.Her.* 4.23-24; Alex. *Fig.* 1.8). *Rhet.Her.* notes that this figure is very well adapted to conversational style (*sermo*), and that it holds the audience's attention both by its *venustas* (charm) and by expectation of the reason to follow. Such conversational style changes the tone of Paul's language as he attempts to show how these possible objections to what he has been saying are unfounded.[483]

The first objection (whether the unbelief of certain Jews renders God's trustworthiness of no effect, i.e., makes God *un*trustworthy, since he entrusted them

---

483 The idea that Paul launches into a fictitious dialogue at this point is improbable. Although S. K. Stowers (1994, *Rereading*) has shown that such dialogues do occur in popular philosophical literature, they are always of such a nature that the remarks of the two speakers concerned are immediately identifiable without the aid of separate markers in the text (cf. the examples Stowers himself mentions, Teles *Fr.* 1; Arr. *Epict.* 3.26.36-37). This is precisely the problem in this pericope. In order to make sense of a dialogue here, the division between the two speakers becomes rather complex. Stowers' division (*Op. cit.*, 165-66) as he isolates it with appropriate markers does make sense, but it is not obvious from the text. A reader/ hearer of the letter could not be expected to immediately discern which statements belong to which person. The passage is, therefore, much better characterised as dialogue-*like* due to its use of αἰτιολογία, an established procedure discussed by ancient theorists. With respect to dialogue, it should be noted that unless it is absolutely obvious from the text which words belong to which person, the ancients indicated this in the text (e.g., "he then said/ says"), cf. Cic. *Clu.* 70-72 (reported dialogue); *Planc.* 12-13 (dialogue in conjunction with προσωποποιΐα); *Ep.Rom.* 11.19.

with his oracles [containing his promises of salvation to them]) is answered by means of a κεκριμένον, namely, the common judgement (expressed also in the Scriptures) that God cannot be false.[484] Further refutation is left until chapters nine to eleven.

The motivation behind the second objection (whether God is unjust if he vents his wrath, since man's wickedness establishes the fact that God is in the right) cannot be understood without knowing the words of LXX *Ps.* 50 (51) immediately preceding the line quoted.[485] The whole sentence in LXX *Ps.* 50 (51).6 is as follows:

σοὶ μόνῳ ἥμαρτον
καὶ τὸ πονηρὸν ἐνώπιόν σου ἐποίησα,
ὅπως ἂν δικαιωθῇς ἐν τοῖς λόγοις σου
καὶ νικήσῃς ἐν τῷ κρίνεσθαί σε.

Paul evidently understands this verse in its *prima facie* sense, namely, that the psalmist (here, according to the superscript, David confessing his sin in regard to Bathsheba) confesses to have committed this sin before God's eyes *in order that* God might be justified in his words. It would seem probable that Paul understood the content of "ἐν τοῖς λόγοις σου" to be explained by the following verse:

ἰδοὺ γὰρ ἐν ἀνομίαις συνελήμφθην,
καὶ ἐν ἁμαρτίαις ἐκίσσησέν με ἡ μήτηρ μου.

The γάρ (not represented in the Hebrew text) makes this interpretation quite reasonable. The point is thus that David's sin in God's sight has justified God's words that man is conceived in sin, i.e., has a sinful nature.

The objection is once again answered with a κεκριμένον, this time the fact that God will judge the world. Paul's argument is that since this proposition may be taken

---

[484]   The παρονομασία in 3.2-3 on the root πιστ- does not make it easy to grasp quickly and accurately Paul's point here. Nevertheless, it is the answer to the objection (that God cannot be false) which shows that ἡ πίστις τοῦ θεοῦ must be taken in the sense of God's trustworthiness, and that the whole phrase must refer to making God untrustworthy. That the unbelief of certain Jews could be considered to make God untrustworthy has to do with the *promises* which God gave to them, and it must be these promises which are foremost in Paul's mind when he speaks of the oracles (τὰ λόγια) entrusted to the Jews. Paul's tendency towards elliptical argumentation is not totally absent in this letter.

[485]   Others (e.g., C. E. B. Cranfield, 1975/79, *Commentary*, 1.183-84) have attempted to explain the objection on the basis of 3.3-4 equating ἀδικία ἡμῶν with the unbelief of certain Jews and θεοῦ δικαιοσύνη with God's trustworthiness. Apart from forcing the meaning of δικαιοσύνη, this explanation still cannot account for how, on the basis of 3.3-4, one could conclude that God's trustworthiness or δικαιοσύνη is *established* or *shown up* by the injustice of certain Jews in not believing. This is nowhere implied by Paul's words in verses 3-4.

for granted, then the idea that God is unjust in venting his wrath must be incorrect.[486] This point is reiterated in v.7 in more personal terms. Paul then continues with a *reductio ad absurdum* in v.8, a proposition of which others had apparently accused him.[487]

The question must also be asked whether the second objection raised by Paul would have been fully understood by his audience. This is, of course, impossible to answer. One may have doubts, although the answer would, at least partly, also depend in how far these verses of LXX *Ps.* 50 (51) were discussed within first century Judaism. If this Psalm was as popular then as it is in certain ecclesiastical quarters today, then it may be fair to assume that these difficult verses were fairly well known. Later Rabbinical explanations do in fact argue, on the basis of this Psalm, that David deliberately committed the sin with Bathsheba in order to benefit God, or confirm his word with respect to man's sinfulness (see Str.-B. 3.135-36).

Paul next (3.9) leads his argument quite smoothly back to where he had brought it at the end of chapter two.[488] He briefly recapitulates his main point thus far, namely, that both Jews and Greeks are all under sin. This is then supported by the strongest argument yet, in rhetorical terms a necessary ἄτεχνος proof. In Christian terms, he provides direct Scripture proof of his contention. His conclusion is then once again summarised at 3.19-20 and put into the terms familiar from the letter to the Galatians. Nobody can be saved ἐξ ἔργων νόμου. We are thus faced with the same twofold διαίρεσις as in that letter. Salvation is either by the works of the law or by faith. Since it cannot be by works, it must be by faith. Here, in the letter to the Romans, Paul has given extended argument to prove that salvation cannot be by works (1.18 - 3.20) and provided what for him is an exceptionally clear summation of his point in 3.9-20. No doubt about his central point may be entertained.

In the following paragraph (3.21-26) Paul returns to his main proposition (enunciated in 1.16-17), namely, that the Gospel is God's power for salvation *to everyone who believes*, both Jew and Greek, since God's δικαιοσύνη is revealed in it.

---

[486] The words κατὰ ἄνθρωπον λέγω may be taken as an apologetic παρένθεσις for putting this obvious proposition in the form of a rhetorical question.

[487] This *may* suggest that Paul had earlier used LXX *Ps.* 50 (51).6-7 in his teaching programme, but that the comments he made with respect to the Psalm were misunderstood (and even deliberately twisted).

[488] The interpretation of the first words of this verse are, however, difficult. Assuming that the Nestle/Aland[26] text is correct (the variants are not widely supported), then it seems clear that we have two questions followed by οὐ πάντως. That οὐ πάντως should be taken in its regular sense "not quite" (as opposed to πάντως οὐ) is clear from Paul's correct usage at 1 *Ep.Cor.* 5.10 and 16.12. Given that this is the answer, the preceding question should perhaps be interpreted to mean "are we better/ do we excel?" (taking the verb προεχόμεθα as medial with active meaning, even though this is not elsewhere attested). The other two possibilities unfortunately do not make very good sense (i.e., as a passive "are we surpassed?," or as a medial without the expected object "are we making excuses?").

It is interesting to note that Paul states here that this δικαιοσύνη is witnessed to by the law and the prophets. This fact is merely mentioned and not argued for. Paul is probably referring to the story of God's sending of Jesus Christ to earth and of his suffering, death, resurrection, and ascension to heaven - i.e., the "Gospel story." He clearly presupposes that his audience (Christian converts) are familiar with this story and the Old Testament testimonies to Christ's activity (of which all four Gospels provide examples). This letter is not written as an "evangelical sermon" in the modern sense of that term. Paul's concern is that these believers recognise that God's justifying activity implies that *all* men need to be justified by faith in Jesus Christ, and that there is no place for the works of the law in respect of this justification.

An interpretative problem for many a commentator on this passage is the fact that whilst on the one hand verses 24-26 are so important and foundational *theologically*, yet *grammatically* these thoughts are all part of a series of dependent clauses, beginning with δικαιούμενοι. Grammatically, the main clause here is contained in v.23, namely, that all have sinned and fall short of the glory of God. The grand redemptional content of the following verses seems merely to be some added thought. Commentators not infrequently busy themselves with considerations which might show that verses 24-26 are, nevertheless, the main thought of the apostle.

Whilst not at all wishing to denigrate the important theological content of these verses, I believe that there is good reason to follow the *prima facie* grammatical structure in our interpretation of this passage. Paul's main argument thus far has been to show that all men are guilty before God when held before his divine law. The Jew is no exception to this. Paul concludes that, therefore, nobody can earn his salvation by keeping the law. This enables Paul in 3.21-23 to argue that God's righteousness (δικαιοσύνη) in Jesus Christ is available for *all who believe*. There is no distinction, both Jew and Greek need to be saved by faith in Jesus Christ. Now it is precisely this point that Paul emphasised in his opening proposition in 1.16-17. This is where the *argument* has been leading. At the risk of repeating myself, Paul's central proposition is that both Jew and Greek must be saved by faith in Jesus Christ and not by the works of the law. It is also this point that is reinforced by the considerations of 3.27-31. Paul again explicitly states in v.28: "For we are arguing that one is justified by faith apart from works of the law." It is again this proposition which is supported by the example of Abraham in chapter four. What, therefore, Paul says of the *nature* of God's justifying work in Jesus Christ, whilst important theologically, is here merely provided by way of explanation. It is important to note that whilst Paul has been busy providing *arguments* for his case thus far, *no arguments* are provided for the statements in verses 24-26. They are an explanation.[489]

---

[489] Given that these statements are not argued for, it would seem probable that Paul presupposed some basic knowledge on the part of his audience as to the significance of Christ's death in terms of their justification. The wonder and importance of the subject may have led him to this discursive explanation.

Paul resumes his argument at 3.27 by drawing a consequence from the διαίρεσις he has thus far argued. If justification is by faith and not by works, then it is *God's* work and we have nothing to boast about. Up to this point the substance of Paul's argument has been to show conclusively that justification by works cannot be possible and therefore justification must be by faith. He now adds another argument in support of his contention, namely, that the oneness of God (an important Jewish confession, reiterated in the *Shema*) implies his position as God of all mankind and that he will have but *one* way of justifying people. That one way must of course (on the basis of the foregoing) be by faith.

Before launching into the extended παράδειγμα (example) of Abraham, Paul briefly engages in another πρόληψις, assuring his audience that he does not hereby nullify the law, but rather establishes it. There is no real explanation or argument showing how this is so. At this point, Paul finds it sufficient to give his audience this assurance and so to settle any uneasiness they may be feeling on this matter.

In chapter four Paul introduces an extended discussion of his παράδειγμα, Abraham. Rhetorically Paul's use of Abraham has much more persuasive power than a standard παράδειγμα, since the record of Abraham is taken from the Scripture (considered as authoritative divine text). The παράδειγμα thus functions at the same time as a necessary proof.

Paul's use of a παράδειγμα at this point conforms in several respects to the comments of Arist. *Rh.* 2.20. Aristotle advises that the normal place for a παράδειγμα is after the presentation of one's arguments. The only exception is when multiple παραδείγματα are used as an argument by induction, but this procedure is not recommended. When arguments have been presented only one good παράδειγμα is necessary.

Paul introduces the παράδειγμα in connection with the question of boasting just referred to. His point, however, is clearly to use the example of Abraham to bolster the main point of justification by faith and not by works. He therefore cites OT *Ge.* 15.6 wherein Abraham is said to have believed God, and this is reckoned to him for righteousness. Paul first explains the words ἐλογίσθη αὐτῷ εἰς δικαιοσύνην in verses 4-8. The necessity for this explanation may have been a popular Jewish interpretation of the passage extolling Abraham's faith as a meritorious act.[490] Paul begins with an argu-

---

490 See C. E. B. Cranfield, 1975/79, *Commentary*, 1.229-30. Note that, although Paul's explanation does *define* this phrase, it shows little relation to rhetorical theory on ὁρισμός (definition).

ment in the form of the abstract τόπος ἐκ τῶν ἐναντίων (4.4-5, cf. Arist. *Rh.* 2.23.1; Cic. *Top.* 17, 47-49; *de Orat.* 2.169; Quint. *Inst.* 5.10.73), a fairly common form of argument. His further reasoning is, however, somewhat elliptical. Essentially, his point is that since it is faith that is reckoned, then works must be excluded (the whole concept of his διαίρεσις is presumed to have force here). Further, if works are excluded and faith is mentioned, we must presume that the person concerned is a sinner who is justified *by grace.* These considerations are backed up by reference to the testimony of David's words who refers to the blessed man whose sin is not reckoned by God. The state of blessedness is considered to be equivalent to being reckoned righteous.

Paul's argument continues in a way that might rhetorically be characterised as the τόπος τοῦ χρόνου, although again this is a common form of argument. Paul is concerned with the question *when* Abraham was circumcised. By showing that his circumcision came after the imputation of righteousness, Paul is enabled to conclude that Abraham is also the father of uncircumcised people who believe. Paul, of course, assumes that the relation here described between God and Abraham (as the forefather *par excellence*) is paradigmatic for later generations.[491]

This last conclusion is now buttressed by several supporting arguments. Firstly, Paul argues that Abraham may also be considered the father of uncircumcised believers because the promise that he would inherit the world (understood here as becoming the world's *father*) was made not by the law (which is associated with circumcision), but through the righteousness attained by faith. Furthermore, it could not have been fulfilled by the law since the law has been shown to produce God's anger. Therefore it must be by faith, so that the promise is assured. Paul's essential argument, based upon his twofold διαίρεσις, is thus made explicit.

Paul continues with a number of subordinate clauses which are further developed to 4.22. Herein Paul returns to the παράδειγμα of Abraham and provides some more context which helps him to develop the parallel between the faith exercised by Abraham and that exercised by Christians. Just as Abraham's faith was a firm trust in God's promise of life to one as good as dead, so also the faith of the Christian is a firm trust in God who resurrected Jesus from the dead and whose death and resurrection

---

[491]　There is some grammatical confusion at 4.12. Paul would appear to be describing the Gentiles in v.11 and the Jews who not only are circumcised but also follow in the footsteps of Abraham's faith in v.12. The problem is the article τοῖς before στοιχοῦσιν which would suggest that two groups are meant. This suggestion is, however, countered by the position of οὐ *after* and not *before* the first τοῖς in the verse. Although some commentators are inclined to bracket the second τοῖς, Paul's grammatical lapses elsewhere may suggest that it belongs in the text, especially given the unanimous textual support for this reading.

resulted in his (i.e., the Christian's) justification. Note that Paul presumes that his audience recognise that the words οὕτως ἔσται τὸ σπέρμα σου cited in 4.18 were the content of God's promise made to Abraham immediately before the Scripture records the statement about the imputation of Abraham's faith.

The argumentation Paul attaches to the presentation of his παράδειγμα is much more than is envisaged by rhetorical theory, which suggests that the presentation of the παράδειγμα itself should be sufficient, perhaps concluded with a γνώμη (maxim) or an ἐνθύμημα (in the sense of a short argument from contraries, see select glossary, s.v. ἐνθύμημα). Paul's argumentation is, however, relevant and necessary due to the nature of the παράδειγμα he has chosen. His argumentation does not so much concern *what* Abraham did, as *how* this event is described by the Scripture. It is this emphasis, requiring the explanation, which makes the παράδειγμα rather atypical in terms of rhetorical theory.

At 5.1 Paul turns to the beneficial results of justification in Christ. One might suggest, in rhetorical terms, that this chapter expands on the συμφέρον (benefit) of justification by faith. At any rate, it is clear that Paul uses various common literary/ rhetorical devices to expand on the benefits of justification. Most of these devices are related by one or other rhetorical theorist to αὔξησις, i.e., rhetorical expansion and embellishment upon matters which either do not need proof (e.g., as in epideictic rhetoric) or have already been proven (as here, and as commonly in other forms of rhetoric).[492] In rhetorical theory αὔξησις was frequently discussed in connection with the ἐπίλογος since its use assumes that the matters in hand have already been proven (cf. Arist. *Rh.* 3.19.1-2; *Rhet.Her.* 2.47-49; 3.15 [compare Cic. *Inv.* 1.100-105]; Cic. *Part.* 52-58). Paul's use of it here suggests that he believes that he has adequately proven his contention of justification by faith (i.e., in terms of 1.17, that God's δικαιοσύνη is revealed in the Gospel by the connection of faith).

Paul introduces the main benefit of justification as peace with God. In v.2 Paul goes on to describe the Christian response by introducing an effective παράδοξον (a surprising twist, cf. Quint. *Inst.* 9.2.22-24). He states that Christians *boast* in hope of the glory of God (which non Christians lack, cf. 3.23).[493] At 3.27ff Paul had carefully

---

[492] Lists of methods for αὔξησις may be found in [Arist.] *Rh.Al.* 3; Arist. *Rh.* 1.9.38-40; Thphr. *Fr.* 679 FHS&G; *Rhet.Her.* 2.47-49 (cf. Cic. *Inv.* 1.100-105); Theon *Prog.* 7; [Longin.] 11.2; Cic. *Part.* 55-58; *de Orat.* 3.104-108; Quint. *Inst.* 8.4.

[493] It is important to note that whilst I speak here of Christians in the third person, Paul has been speaking in the first person plural including himself and his audience in the benefits of the Christian faith which he is describing.

argued that since justification is by faith, Christians have nothing to boast about. It is because of this that the παράδοξον takes its effect. Paul immediately adds another παράδοξον by stating that Christians also boast in their tribulations (θλίψεις), a rather unexpected thing to boast about. This is explained in the ensuing κλῖμαξ (lit. "ladder") where Paul climbs from θλῖψις through to ἐλπίς, showing that ultimately boasting in hope amounts to boasting in tribulation, since tribulation produces hope. Of course, what I have just said in one short sentence, Paul states in a very rhetorical way which serves to emphasise and drive home his point.

The use of κλῖμαξ, as at v.3, is aptly described by Demetr. *Eloc.* 270 who notes that it seems as if one is climbing to greater and greater things. [Arist.] *Rh.Al.* 3.11 and [Longin.] 11.2 both classify this figure as a method of αὔξησις.[494] The steps of the "ladder" are emphasised both by ἀσύνδετον and ἐπεζευγμένον (several phrases relying on the same verb).

At v.5 the top of the κλῖμαξ is reached with the statement that hope does not disappoint. This statement is then supported by the consideration that the love of God has been poured out. Paul then briefly dwells on this thought in a way rhetorical theorists term ἐπιμονή (see select glossary *s.v.*), a device clearly linked to αὔξησις (cf. [Longin.] 12.2; Alex. *Fig.* 1.10) wherein one repeats one's thought in varied ways, often adding reasons etc.. Paul expands on this thought by the consideration that God's love is shown in Christ's death on behalf of ungodly people. He goes on to highlight how significant this fact is.[495] Verse 7 emphasises the fact that it is rare even for someone to die for a just or good man![496] This is a good example of παρομολογία (partial admission, cf. Rut.Lup. 1.19) where Paul makes a concession, but one that rather reinforces his point than detracts from it. The concession made is appropriate since it was not an uncommon sentiment for one to be willing to die for one's good friends or family (cf. the popular story of Achilles being willing to die to save Patroclus, Arist. *Rh.* 1.3.6; Pl. *Smp.* 179e; *Ap.* 28cd; Aeschin. 1.145-50 etc.; and in general, Arr. *Epict.* 2.7.3; Philostr. *VA* 7.12; *Herc.* 1044.22,3-11[497]). The essence of Paul's thought is then repeated in v.8.

---

[494]   The text of Ps.-Longinus at this point is based on a probable emendation.

[495]   I would translate 5.6 as follows (interpreting the second ἔτι as emphatic repetition, cf. select glossary *s.v.* ἀναδίπλωσις, which is correctly said to produce δεινότης): "for *still*, even though we were weak, *still* at the right time Christ died for the ungodly."

[496]   It is clear from the context that both δικαίου and ἀγαθοῦ should be taken as masculine nouns. I do not think that we should force a distinction between the two terms. Paul repeats the same thought in varied words for emphasis (cf. Arist. *Rh.* 3.12.2-3).

[497]   Edited by W. Crönert, 1900, *Epikureer.*

In v.9 Paul uses the thought of Christ's death to bring himself back to the main thought of this paragraph, namely, that having been justified Christians have peace with God. This thought is repeated by means of another κλῖμαξ (verses 9-10), although this time the terms are varied and Paul lays emphasis on the fact that if the preceding is true then the following step must be much more true. The basic structure is: justification by Christ's death leads to salvation from God's anger (i.e., reconciliation = peace with God), and this reconciliation through Christ's death leads to salvation in Christ's (new) life.

The following verse is a kind of afterthought wherein Paul reminds his audience that they are not only reconciled (the participle καταλλαγέντες should be understood after οὐ μόνον δέ)[498], but they now also *boast* in God.

At v.12 Paul embarks on a σύγκρισις (a developed comparison) between Adam's transgression and God's act of justification in Christ.[499] However, Paul breaks off his initial comparison in order to insert a parenthetical explanation concerning the effect of sin between Adam and Moses (5.13-14). Paul's initial sentence is not resumed and instead he first outlines two differences between the matters being compared (5.15-17),[500] before dealing with their similarity (5.18-19). The differences concern the fact that the two matters are opposites and have diametrically opposite effects. The similarity consists in the relation of one to many. In the verses dealing with the differences, Paul deliberately seems to vary his terms of reference so that the antithetical propositions, whilst parallel in concept, are not exactly parallel in form. When presenting the similarity, Paul maintains verbal parallels. This is obviously a matter of style, although any motivation beyond a desire for variation remains elusive.[501]

The use of σύγκρισις is listed by Theon *Prog.* ii, p.108,3-15 Sp. as a method of αὔξησις. Further details or τόποι from rhetorical theory (e.g., Theon *Prog.* 9) are not relevant to this passage however.

As noted above, the verses 13-14 form a short parenthetical explanation. The argumentation is, however, somewhat elliptical. Paul begins in v.13 with two state-

---

[498] The ensuing participle καυχώμενοι demands that a participle be understood after οὐ μόνον δέ. Furthermore, the verb καταλλάσσω also makes sense of Paul's reference to καταλλαγή at the end of the verse. The suggestion that σωθησόμεθα be understood fails to account for either consideration.

[499] It should be noted that, although the precise terms of the σύγκρισις vary, the comparison is *not* between the persons Adam and Christ as such.

[500] The words πολλῷ μᾶλλον in verses 15 and 17 refer to the stronger logical consequence of the proposition stated (as compared to the previous clause), just as at 5.9-10.

[501] One might, perhaps, suggest that the differences are varied by using *different* terms, whilst the similarities use *similar* terms.

ments which seem to lead to a particular conclusion. These statements may be charac-
terised as the major and minor premises of a rhetorical syllogism (cf. $\grave{\epsilon}\pi\iota\chi\epsilon\acute{\iota}\rho\eta\mu\alpha$).[502]
The major premise is the fact that up until the time of the (Mosaic) law sin was in the
world. This needs no supporting argumentation since Adam's sin and its spread to all
mankind are assumed to be well known (cf. v.12). The minor premise is also a necessary statement requiring no proof, namely, that sin is not imputed where there is no law
(cf. 4.15b; 7.8b). Now the expected conclusion from such premises is that sin was not
imputed during the period from Adam until Moses. However, this is not what Paul
states, and he indicates that his conclusion is contrary to expectation (another
$\pi\alpha\rho\acute{\alpha}\delta\phi\xi o\nu$) by introducing it with the adversative $\grave{\alpha}\lambda\lambda\acute{\alpha}$.[503] In fact, says Paul, death
(personified) reigned during this period, even over those who did not transgress like
Adam.[504] The statement in and of itself is an obvious truth, but Paul's point is that
God's law *was* effectual during this period, despite the fact that the Mosaic law was not
yet in existence. This must be so since the fact that death reigned shows that sin was
imputed. Paul has here stated the logical consequence of his conclusion instead of
saying that sin was nevertheless imputed. Cicero (*Inv.* 1.74) recommends this procedure when the conclusion is quite obvious, but Paul's reason for doing so here is
probably the fact that it is the logical result of his conclusion (i.e., the fact that death
reigned) which *proves* that his unexpected conclusion ($\pi\alpha\rho\acute{\alpha}\delta\phi\xi o\nu$) is correct. Paul does
not argue the point further, but it is clear that his earlier contention (ch. 2) that we *may*
speak of God's law being present even if the physical rolls of the Mosaic law are
unknown (e.g., in the case of Gentiles) supports his reasoning.[505] Paul essentially continues his explanation at 5.20-21 where he uses the later addition of the law to highlight
the superabundant outpouring of God's grace (a further reflection of the contrast
brought out in 5.15-17).

---

[502] A good and straightforward discussion of the rhetorical $\grave{\epsilon}\pi\iota\chi\epsilon\acute{\iota}\rho\eta\mu\alpha$ is given in Cic. *Inv.* 1.57-77.
The discussion in *Rhet.Her.* 2.28-30 seems to be based on a misunderstanding of the ultimate (Greek)
source common to both treatises, see W. Kroll, 1936, *Epicheirema*, 5-8.
[503] C. E. B. Cranfield (1975/79, *Commentary*, 1.282-83) attempts to explain the words $o\grave{\upsilon}\kappa$ $\grave{\epsilon}\lambda\lambda o\gamma\epsilon\hat{\iota}\tau\alpha\iota$
in a relative sense, i.e., that sins were blameful before Moses, but were not reckoned to the extent that
they were when the law came in. His explanation naturally runs into trouble when he has to explain the
adversative $\grave{\alpha}\lambda\lambda\acute{\alpha}$ at v.14. The adversative clearly indicates that Paul will turn the expected conclusion on
its head.
[504] Paul's point is that Adam's death was the result of his breaking a positive law of God (eating from
the forbidden tree). Paul does not state whether he thought there may have been more positive laws of
God between Adam and Moses (cf. OT *Ge.* 26.5), and the question is not really to the point here.
[505] This is precisely the point made by Origen who also explains the text in this way (though without
reference to rhetorical theory), cf. Catena 36.43-47 (A. Ramsbotham in *Journal of Theological Studies*
14 [1913] 12). We may add that this interpretation is consonant with 5.20 where it is stated that the
reason the (Mosaic) law was added was to *increase* transgression, i.e., not to initiate it.

Rhetorical Notes

1.3-4 We may note here both the ἀναφορά (τοῦ ... τοῦ) and the typical stylistic variation of prepositions common in Paul's writings. This variation is very pronounced in the ensuing verses.

1.11 This verse contains an interesting example of ὑπερβατόν (τι ... χάρισμα ... πνευματικόν). Its use here seems merely for the purpose of elegance (cf. *Rhet.Her.* 4.18).

1.20 Paul's penchant for παρονομασία may also be seen in the oxymoron here: τὰ ἀόρατα ... καθορᾶται. The term ὀξύμωρον does not appear to be attested before the fourth century AD.

1.26 The phrase ἡ φυσικὴ χρῆσις is a good example of περίφρασις in order to avoid an indecent expression (cf. Quint. *Inst.* 8.6.59).

1.27 The metaphor ἐξεκαύθησαν is fairly common and also appropriate (cf. 1 *Ep.Cor.* 7.9).

2.5 θησαυρίζεις σεαυτῷ ὀργήν is a picturesque metaphor not without parallel in antiquity, and especially popular in the Septuagint (cf. *Pr.* 1.18; 2.7; 16.27; *Am.* 3.10; *PsSal.* 9.5; *Ev.Matt.* 6.19-20).

2.8 An example of personification: ἀλήθεια and ἀδικία (cf. p.136).

2.9-10 Here we have an example of πολύπτωτον caused by the varied construction (again merely for the sake of adornment it seems). In the first verse we have ἐπί + accusative, in the second we have the simple dative. The general chiasm of verses 7-10 should also be noted.

2.19 The metaphors here are typical of the Old Testament.

2.20 The ὑπερβολή in the words: παιδευτὴν ἀφρόνων, διδάσκαλον νηπίων adds to the great contrast made between the high position the Jews regard themselves in (a position not contradicted by Paul), and their hypocrisy.

2.21 The use of chiasm here is in line with Paul's general use of studied figures in emotional contexts.

2.27 For the μετωνυμία of ἀκροβυστία here and elsewhere in the letter see above, p.133.

3.2 Paul's ἀπαρίθμησις (listing of items, cf. Hermog. *Id.* 1.11 [p.288 R.]; [Aristid.] *Rh.* 1.70) is not continued here. The list is, however, given at 9.4-5.

3.3 The τινες is arguably an example of understatement (cf. 10.16; 11.17). It appears to be used for the sake of softening a very harsh reality.

3.25-26 We should note the emphatic repetition of ἔνδειξιν τῆς δικαιοσύνης αὐτοῦ which is a good example of διλογία (repetition) which provides μέγεθος (grandeur) and contributes to ἐνάργεια (vividness), cf. Demetr. *Eloc.* 103 and 211.

4.1 Abraham is introduced as τὸν πατέρα ἡμῶν κατὰ σάρκα.[506] The words κατὰ σάρκα already hint that Paul will argue that Gentiles may also refer to Abraham as their father (in faith). Such a hint may be rhetorically construed as an example of ἔμφασις (see select glossary *s.v.*).

4.14 It is interesting to note that Gregory of Nyssa (*hom. in 1 Cor. 15:28* M. 44.1324) considered Paul's use of κεκένωται πίστις here to be an example of κατάχρησις (catachresis, *in malam partem*). It would seem that Gregory thought the metaphor out of place.

5.2 Another clear example of παρονομασία: ἐσχήκαμεν ... ἐστήκαμεν.

5.4 The term δοκιμή is so rare, it may well be Paul's own coinage.[507] Another coinage in this letter is to be noted at 8.26 (ὑπερεντυγχάνω found elsewhere only in a few patristic texts). There seems to be no obvious stylistic motive behind either example of word coinage. Both are quite clear in terms of their meaning.

5.5 The metaphorical use of ἐκχέω is more common. Here it is probably influenced by its common metaphorical use in the Septuagint, especially of pouring out God's wrath or mercy.

5.9 τὸ αἷμα is used colourfully as μετωνυμία for ὁ θάνατος.

5.12-21 Throughout the σύγκρισις presented in these verses, Paul maintains a vivid style by his personification of ἁμαρτία, θάνατος and χάρις (cf. p.136).

5.14 τοῦ μέλλοντος is here used as ἀντονομασία for τοῦ Χριστοῦ. No specific reason for its use is apparent. Rhetorical theory (cf. *Rhet.Her.* 4.42; Quint. *Inst.* 8.6.29-30) suggests hinting at some praiseworthy or censorious feature, but that does not seem to be the case here.

2.3 *Ep.Rom.* 6 - 8

We have seen that the formal argumentation for Paul's proposition closes at the end of chapter four. In chapter five Paul expands upon the benefits of justification. In the next chapters (six to eight) he deals *pastorally* with a possible misunderstanding of

---

[506] The reading πατέρα is more probable, in my opinion, than προπάτορα.
[507] The word occurs in a few mss of Dioscorides 4.184, but is probably an interpolation. The few patristic examples are probably due to Paul's influence. Besides our text, Paul uses it again at 2 *Ep.Cor.* 2.9; 8.2; 9.13; 13.3 and *Ep.Phil.* 2.22.

what he has said concerning the relationship of the believer to sin. This misunderstanding had already briefly been mentioned and dealt with in 3.5-8. As others have sometimes remarked, it seems as if in chapters six to eleven Paul intentionally returns in detail to the two objections briefly raised in 3.1-8. The second objection is dealt with first (6 - 8) and then the first objection is treated (9 - 11). Whilst this aspect of the structure of the letter to the Romans ought not to be neglected, it ought also to be noticed that Paul does not formally indicate that this is what he is doing. Rather, his discussion of these objections, or possible misunderstandings, flows on quite smoothly from the immediate context. Thus the opening questions in 6.1 refer back to a possible wrong application of what was said in 5.20-21.[508]

The character of what Paul has to say in these ensuing chapters is, however, quite different from what has gone before. Paul is no longer attempting to construct a persuasive argument, but engages himself in *teaching* and *exhortation*. He appeals to the doctrine which he presupposes the Roman Christians to have been taught and accepted (ὁ τύπος διδαχῆς which they have been handed down).[509]

Although I shall briefly outline the structure of Paul's discourse below, it ought to be apparent that the lack of sustained *argumentation* severely limits the applicability of rhetorical theory to these chapters.

Paul begins by appealing to what the Roman Christians must have been taught concerning their baptism, namely, that it symbolises a union with Christ's death.[510]

---

[508] In both 3.5-8 and 6.1 the error to be refuted concerns a continuing license to sin, however the motivation for this license differs in the two passages. In 3.5-8 the erroneous reasoning is that since sin establishes the fact that what God has said about man's sinful nature remains true, then the more we sin the more truthful God appears. In 6.1 the erroneous reasoning is that since God's grace must be greater than sin, the more we sin the more God is gracious.

[509] The clause ὑπηκούσατε δὲ ἐκ καρδίας εἰς ὃν παρεδόθητε τύπον διδαχῆς (6.17) is difficult. However, the proposal (cf. C. E. B. Cranfield, 1975/79, *Commentary*, 1.324) to explain εἰς ὃν παρεδόθητε τύπον διδαχῆς as an abbreviation of τῷ τύπῳ τῆς διδαχῆς εἰς ὃν παρεδόθητε (in the sense: "you became obedient to the pattern of teaching to which you were handed over") cannot really be sustained. This is not an abbreviation so much as an attempt to rewrite what is present in the text in a more acceptable form. Paul's construction is grammatically difficult because a construction with εἰς does not normally follow the verb ὑπακούω. We may say, I think, that Paul has used a construction typically found with the (in this context) near synonym πιστεύω. The fact that Paul might expect the Roman Christians to have been taught such a "pattern of teaching" lends support to J. van Bruggen's exegesis of *Ep.Rom.* 16 (that Paul is greeting groups of missionaries acting in Rome on his behalf, 1970, *Raadsel*). This obviates the less likely interpretation of F. W. Beare (1958/59, "Interpretation") that τύπος διδαχῆς is personified and Paul is speaking about the transfer of slaves from one master to another.

[510] This appeal to an accepted doctrine (i.e., here, doctrine they have previously been taught and accepted), along with the appeals in 7.1, 14 and 8.22, 29 may be likened to the appeal in rhetorical theory to an accepted judgement of some sort (τὸ κεκριμένον).

Paul adds that the implication of this is that believers walk (in the sense of moral conduct) in newness of life (parallel to Christ's resurrection). The theological implication of union with Christ's death is justification from sin (6.7). This symbolic death implies death to sin (6.2, 10). On this basis the Roman Christians are *exhorted* not to let sin rule them, but to present the members of their bodies to God as weapons of righteousness.

Paul continues his exhortation by *explaining* that, in a sense (6.19a), the Roman Christians must still consider themselves slaves, only bound to a new master. Whereas they were previously slaves of sin, they are now slaves of obedience/ righteousness (i.e., ultimately slaves of God).

Paul consistently personifies ἁμαρτία throughout these chapters. Opposite to sin stands God in 6.13, and this is the essential contrast throughout the rest of the chapter. Paul's substitution of the terms ὑπακοή and δικαιοσύνη only serve to emphasise that being the slave of a new master (God) *still* implies obedience (which forbids continuance in sin).

At 7.1 Paul continues the same theme by introducing another explanatory consideration which he assumes the Roman Christians will be familiar with. The logical structure of 7.1-6, however, appears at first glance to be rather confused. At this point Cranfield provides a rather insightful analysis of the passage. He rightly notes that Paul's main point is the proposition of v.1, that the law is only one's master as long as he is alive. It is this legal principle that Paul expects the Roman Christians to be familiar with. Verses 2 and 3 supply an illustration of this principle (in rhetorical terms a παράδειγμα) in order to clarify it. Paul's παράδειγμα, however, does not exactly illustrate the principle as enunciated, but "its corollary, namely, that the occurrence of a death effects a decisive change in respect of relationship to the law."[511] Verses 4-6 apply the legal principle *as stated in verse one* to the symbolic death of Christians. They are dead to the law in that they are considered to have been crucified with Christ. The law is therefore no longer their master, but they have a new master in Christ risen from the dead.

On this reading of the text, Paul's reasoning process makes sense. The confusion comes because of the fact that it *seems* as if the application of 7.4-6 must somehow be related to the illustration of 7.2-3. If this is attempted, only hopeless confusion of terms results. On a linear reading (or hearing) the passage is, therefore, not very clear and open to an incorrect interpretation of Paul's reasoning process. The result is not so

---

[511]   C. E. B. Cranfield, 1975/79, *Commentary*, 1.335.

much a serious misinterpretation of Paul's words, but plain confusion. A rhetorical theorist might rightly suggest that Paul lacked the important virtue of speech, σαφήνεια (clarity), at this point.[512]

Paul next proceeds to correct a wrong impression that may have arisen from what he has just been saying, namely, that the law is not to be identified with sin. The rest of the chapter is set in the first person singular as Paul describes what must be interpreted as his own experiences.[513] Of course it is clear that Paul intends his own experience to be paradigmatic for the Roman Christians.[514] The whole passage from 7.7-25 is thus a personal παράδειγμα.[515]

Having described his symbolic experience of death under the condemnation produced by sin (still personified) which took its occasion through the presence of the law, Paul goes on to ask if the law then (put in terms of τὸ ἀγαθόν) must still be blamed (7.13). The answer is negative, and Paul goes on to set up the hypothetical problem of the Christian, speaking in his own person.[516] This hypothetical problem of the Christian concerns he who desires to follow Christ/ God and yet recognises the power of sin in his life up until his conversion. Paul describes this experience using military metaphors of the struggle between one's mind or inner person (ὁ ἔσω ἄνθρωπος) which wants to obey God, and one's flesh which is a slave to its master Sin.[517]

The solution to the great wail of exasperation in 7.24 is provided in 8.1-11. Whilst Paul sketched the problem in the first person singular, using himself as a paradigm, the solution is presented in terms explicitly incorporating the Roman

---

[512] The lack of clarity may have been overcome if Paul had either omitted the illustration of 7.2-3, or had re-enunciated his main principle before embarking on the application at 7.4-6.

[513] There are no signals in the text that Paul has introduced another speaker into his discourse here (e.g., Adam), and therefore προσωποποιΐα must be ruled out. Neither is there any hint that these verses are to be interpreted as any kind of generalised voice. The reader/ hearer of these words *must* have interpreted them of Paul's experience.

[514] There are various exegetical difficulties in this passage which do not need to be mentioned in this discussion, e.g., the meaning of 7.9.

[515] Note also the use of a short παράδειγμα within this passage to illustrate the contention that Paul would not have known sin except by means of the law (7.7b-8a).

[516] That Paul is not referring to pre-conversion experience in 7.13-25 is clear from, i) the consistent use of the present tense, ii) the analogy of the inner struggle in *Ep.Gal.* 5.16-18, iii) the order of the thoughts in 7.24-25, iv) the tension then created with 3.11b-12. Nevertheless, the tension between the statements in 7.14ff (that he is sold [i.e., in slavery] under the power of Sin) and what was said in chapter six and what will be said in chapter eight is too great to argue that Paul is here referring to normal Christian experience. His statements here are in contradiction to the exhortation of 6.12ff. Furthermore, the internal struggle described here is a *human* struggle between the mind and the flesh. No mention is made in this context of the effective work of the Holy Spirit.

[517] Compare the military metaphor in 6.13 where God and Sin are described as opposing generals to whom men's bodies may be presented as weapons.

Christians.[518] This suggests a certain cautiousness in Paul's presentation, a sort of
ἐσχηματισμένος λόγος for the sake of propriety (εὐπρέπεια, see select glossary s.v.
for references).

After giving thanks to God, obviously for the salvation provided in Christ, Paul
resumes his line of thought. Having summed up the problem once again, he describes
how in Christ's death the condemnation of the law is removed and the Holy Spirit is
granted to believers. It is by means of the power of this gift of the Spirit that believers
are enabled to do what was thought impossible, namely, not only to want to obey God,
but to actually *do* it. The body that was dead because of sin (8.10) will now be
revitalised by the power of the Spirit.[519] This is precisely the point where Paul had
begun at the beginning of chapter six.[520]

In the preceding discourse Paul has thus clarified that the law is not sin, but (as
they already knew, 7.14) holy and good. What is more, its condemnation against them
is taken away in the Gospel, and they are enabled to obey it and thus please God.[521] In
this way, something of the implications of his earlier assurance (3.31) that his Gospel
does not nullify but establishes the law, has been shown.

The verses 8.12-30 serve to draw out some of the consequences of the Spirit's
dwelling within believers, especially in terms of their sonship. This passage closes with
heightened πάθος via the effective use of κλῖμαξ and ἀναφορά (8.29-30) expressing
the certainty of God's dealings with those who love him.

This πάθος is sustained in the closing paragraph of this section (8.31-39) where
Paul draws out the implications of God's love for (the Roman) Christians. After introducing his conclusion via αἰτιολογία (a short inquiring question, which is answered by
the speaker), he answers with an emotional battery of rhetorical questions, the last three
of which are given added punch by the ἀναφορά of τίς. We may also note the effective
use of correction (μεταβολή) in v.34. The phrase Χριστὸς ὁ ἀποθανών[522] answers to
θεὸς ὁ δικαιῶν of the previous verse, but Paul "corrects" this by adding, in a series of

---

[518] The second person pronoun in 8.2 is not textually certain, but cf. 8.4 (first person plural) and 8.9-
11 (second person plural).
[519] There is nothing in the context to suggest that ζωοποιήσει should be taken to refer to the future
resurrection of the body. Ethical revitalisation fits the context much better.
[520] It ought to be added that Paul clearly does not envisage that the presence of the Spirit will enable
Christians to fulfill God's law perfectly. Such a view would remove the seriousness of his exhortation to
the Roman Christians in 6.12ff, and also belie his general awareness (throughout his correspondence) of
the remaining sinfulness in Christians.
[521] For Paul, the new obedience of the Christian is clearly obedience to God's law, cf. 7.22, 25; 8.4,
7.
[522] The name Ἰησοῦς probably ought to be omitted on both textual and stylistic grounds.

clauses, the much more powerful events connected with Christ, namely, his resurrection, ascension and intercession for them. The final question asking who will separate them (Paul included) from the love of Christ is answered by a list of afflictions made to seem endlessly lengthy by the πολυσύνδετον (repeated ἤ, cf. Demetr. *Eloc.* 54, 63). It is crowned with an Old Testament citation intended to show that the sufferings of God's people are nothing new. Yet Paul insists that through Christ/ God who has loved them all, they more than conquer these afflictions. Again a list of items follows (verses 38-39, cf. Arr. *Epict.* 1.11.33) which, Paul assures them, cannot separate them from God's love. Once again πολυσύνδετον makes the list seem endless (repeated οὔτε), and its effect is heightened by the all-encompassing nature of the items (death, life, height, depth, time present and future, celestial beings). This imposing list of intangible entities is effectively reduced to size by Paul's closing words in which he implies that they are after all only κτίσεις, things created by God in the first place.

The πάθος created by the subject matter combined with the rhetorical figures is appropriate to the conclusion (ἐπίλογος) of a section of discourse.

The style of this section (chapters six to eight) as a whole may be characterised as conversational. This effect is achieved by the consistent use of αἰτιολογία (6.1-3, 15; 7.8, 14; 8.31; 9.14, cf. *Rhet.Her.* 4.23-24; Alex. *Fig.* 1.8), and is naturally appropriate to a letter. As may be expected from a section which is primarily concerned with *teaching*, we have seen that Paul's reasoning process is characterised by the use of παραδείγματα (not as inductive proof, but explanatory) and accepted truths (cf. κεκριμένα).

2.4 *Ep.Rom.* 9 - 11

From the high emotional state of rejoicing in the last few verses of chapter eight, the mood suddenly plummets to the depths of sadness and solemnity at the opening of chapter nine. The sudden change of mood and subject is quite unexpected and unprepared for. Paul begins this new section with an oath that serves to underline the solemnity of the mood, and proceeds with a wish/ prayer for his own (eternal) death in place of his countrymen (an allusion to Moses is highly probable).[523] In this way he (re)introduces the problem of the Jews' rejection of the Gospel and its Messiah. Chapters nine to eleven thus take up problems related to the first of the two objections briefly dealt with in 3.3-9.

---

[523] Once again, the use of an oath here is unrelated to comments on oaths in rhetorical theory.

Having established the solemnity of his new topic (i.e., his deep personal feeling for his countrymen), he highlights its pathos by listing the benefits of the Israelites (this list completes the enumeration begun at 3.2). Paul uses πολυσύνδετον to help create the effect of an endless list of benefits (cf. Demetr. *Eloc.* 54, 63). At 9.6 the actual hypothetical objection is introduced, namely, that it is emphatically not the case that the Word of God has failed.

Paul now embarks on a line of argumentation (primarily from the Scriptures) in order to *prove* his point. He begins by showing how God has from the beginning made a selection out of Israel. In Paul's words, not all who are of Israel are Israel. The examples of Isaac versus Ishmael and Jacob versus Esau are cited. Particularly with the latter example (where God's choice is made before the twins are born) Paul is able to argue that God's calling cannot be based on works. This theme of election by grace, not by works, is emphasised several times in the ensuing discussion (cf. 9.32ff; 11.6) and supports his main argument in chapters one to five (justification by faith, not by works).

At this point (9.14) Paul's main line of argument is broken off and not properly resumed until chapter eleven, although what is said in between (particularly 9.30 - 10.21) is important for the main argument.

Paul breaks off the argument to raise an important possible objection in the minds of his audience, namely, whether there is injustice with God (in view of what seems to be arbitrary choice). Paul answers by citing two examples of God's choice from Scripture. His process of argumentation may be likened to the use of παραδείγματα by induction, instead of as confirmation (cf. select glossary *s.v.* παράδειγμα). This procedure was not generally recommended due to its being argumentatively weaker than argumentation by reasoning, however, the nature of Paul's examples as (authoritative) Scripture negate this consideration.

The two examples *prima facie* appear to emphasise the sovereignty of God, and this is certainly a point Paul wishes to make, particularly in regard to the second example (of the hardening of Pharaoh's heart). Paul emphasises this point with a παραβολή[524] concerning a potter and his clay (standing for God the creator and his creatures). Yet it is striking that Paul contrasts God's hardening with his *mercy*. This emphasis on mercy is maintained throughout the pericope (9.15-16, 18, 23). It is not improbable that Paul understands God's choice to save an elect number against the

---

[524] Hypothetical example, cf. Cic. *Part.* 40 and 55; and *Rhet.Her.* 4.59 who also suggests that the *similitudo* can be used as a proof.

background of the general guilt and condemnation of *all* men argued in chapters one to three. Since all men deserve condemnation, God's choice to save some must be characterised as an act of *mercy*. Paul, however, does not make this point explicit, but seems to assume it. We may consider it another example of his not altogether crystal clear clarity.

At 9.24 Paul applies his παραβολή of the potter and clay to God's decision to show mercy upon people both from the Jews as well as from the Gentiles. This is an important point which not only relates to the main argumentation in chapters one to five (for Paul argued that justification by faith implies availability of salvation both to Jews and Gentiles), but which Paul will also go on to relate to the problem of Jewish rejection of the Gospel. He thus first establishes the point by Scripture proof, showing that God has chosen both Gentiles and a remnant of the Jews. Paul then proceeds to sum up the problem: Gentiles have received a righteousness/ salvation which they were not pursuing, whilst the Jews who *were* pursuing righteousness did not arrive at it.[525] The Jews' problem is that they pursue righteousness not by faith but "as if" by works.[526] Before *explaining* what this means, Paul again reassures his audience of his heartfelt desire for the salvation of his countrymen. Paul quite rightly considers this necessary, given that he is about to criticise his own people. Essentially Paul explains that the Jews have missed the point that Christ is the goal (τέλος) of the law.[527] Paul cites the Mosaic law first in reference to their own attitude (righteousness by works implying the necessity of complete obedience - an obedience Paul has already argued to be impossible), and then in reference to Christ. The second citation is, however, put in the mouth of ἡ ἐκ πίστεως δικαιοσύνη personified, and may be characterised as a form of προσωποποιΐα. The effect is a rather lively presentation. The content of this presentation (10.6-8) is used to reinforce important points made by Paul thus far, supported by further Old Testament citations (10.9-13). Paul reinforces the point that salvation is by faith and that this applies to *all* men, whether Jew or Greek. The argument from the oneness of God is also repeated (from 3.29) only this time it is Christ who is referred to as κύριος.

---

[525] The phrase νόμον δικαιοσύνης in 9.31 is not very clear and has thus caused various interpretations. I believe that Paul means to indicate the law of Moses, but it would have been clearer had he written τὴν δικαιοσύνην τοῦ νόμου.

[526] The insertion of ὡς (which in later Greek often equals ὡσεί) is interesting. It is as if Paul is admitting that his Jewish compatriots may not have phrased their pursuit of righteousness in precisely this way.

[527] That τέλος in 10.4 is used in the sense of "goal" is made probable by Paul's interpretative demonstration of how "righteousness by faith" (personified) speaks, i.e., interpreting words from the Mosaic law in reference to Christ.

Having dealt with the Jews' incorrect approach to the law, Paul goes on to establish their inexcusableness for rejecting the Gospel, particularly at stumbling over God's
mercy upon the Gentiles. Paul begins with an argumentative κλῖμαξ in the form of
rhetorical questions (10.14-15), connecting God's calling with the preaching of the
Gospel by those sent from God. Of course one could make the same argumentative
point without using the figure of κλῖμαξ. The point of using this figure (here in combination with ἐπερώτησις - rhetorical questioning) is to provide a rhetorical effect. The
effect is to enhance the value of the battery of rhetorical questions. Rhetorical theorists
rightly noted that such a battery of questions has the effect of making the (hypothetical)
opposition seem speechless (cf. Demetr. *Eloc.* 279). The points made come across in a
way that suggests they *must* be true. In this context the κλῖμαξ enhances what seems to
be a step by step logical procedure and helps to make the point more *forcefully* (cf.
Demetr. *Eloc.* 270).

Paul goes on to note that this Gospel has been preached all over the world by the
apostles (he uses words cited from LXX *Ps.* 18 [19] but not introduced as a quotation).
He then cites Old Testament prophecy to prove that the Jews should have known God's
plan to offer salvation to the Gentiles, and this in the context of the obstinate disobedience of the Jews to provoke them to jealousy.

This brings Paul back to the problem of Jewish disobedience to the Gospel. Paul
had first argued from Scripture that not all Israel is Israel. God selects a remnant. He
now uses this to argue that God has not thrust *his* people aside (the pronoun makes us
think of the list of the benefits of Israel with which Paul began). Paul is able to use
himself as an example of God's selection of a remnant who are saved. He then backs
this up with another citation from Scripture, this time of the 7,000 God kept for himself in the time of Elijah. At this point Paul demonstrates that what he has said is con-
gruent to his prior argumentation, namely, that salvation can only be by grace and not
by works. The hardening of most of Israel at this time is further demonstrated by citations from Scripture.

The rest of chapter eleven (11.11-36) contains Paul's account of the reason for
Israel's hardening at this time. There is less argumentation here than explanation,
although Paul's account is based on the prophecy of Scripture (cited in 10.19) that God
would provoke Israel to jealousy by means of the Gentiles. This is illustrated by the
extended metaphor of the ingrafting of a wild olive branch into a domestic olive tree
(11.17-24). The extended metaphor is a lively and clear illustration of what Paul wishes
to communicate. Its liveliness may be attributed to the metaphor itself, the consistent
use of the second person singular to address the Gentiles with it, and the use of

διάλογος (dialogue) to represent possible objections (cf. 11.19 which is very close to Quint. *Inst.* 9.2.36). Paul uses this illustration to *exhort* the Gentiles against boasting over the Jews. He then goes on to reveal the μυστήριον (which in Paul's language refers to a truth, previously obscure, which is now made plain to all). Paul appears to suggest that when the fulness of the Gentiles have entered in (i.e., the olive tree), that the Jews *en masse* will return to God,[528] this as a new demonstration of God's mercy. Paul closes the whole section with an ἀποστροφή (not directed at anyone in particular) praising the wisdom and ways of God. Rhetoricians, naturally, more often used ἀποστροφή to express grief or outrage and so heighten the emotion directed either towards them or against their opponents. Paul's ἀποστροφή directs the emotions towards the praise of God, a fitting close to this section since it radiates Paul's conviction that he has definitively shown that the possible objections against God and his word are false. One must rather praise God for his wise and merciful dealings with man.

As already indicated, these chapters are more argumentative than their counterpart in chapters six to eight. The argumentation, however, is predominately based upon citation from Scripture and so less immediately relevant to rhetorical theory. The style is conversational, arguably more so than even chapters six to eight. Paul makes much use of conversational figures: αἰτιολογία (9.14, 30, 32; 11.1, 7, 11), ἀποστροφή directed at his audience (10.1; 11.25), διάλογος with respect to hypothetical objections (9.19; 11.17-20, cf. Paul's frequent interjection of λέγω, 10.18-19; 11.1, 11, 13).

2.5 Style

The general features of Paul's style noted in respect of the letter to the Galatians recur here in the letter to the Romans. There is the same use of late Hellenistic Greek mixed with Semitic influence often traceable to the Septuagint.[529] There is also the

---

528   This passage is, however, another example of Paul's lack of clarity. Another interpretation would understand the "all Israel" of v.26 to refer to the new Israel of the Gospel, i.e., the remnant of believing Jews combined with believing Gentiles. The key verse is 11.26, and particularly the meaning of the phrase καὶ οὕτως.

529   A select list of examples follows: Late Greek: Χάρισμα (appears to be first extant in Philo) 1.11 etc.; εἰς τὸ εἶναι of result (instead of purpose), 1.20; οἵτινες for οἵ, 1.25; πληρόω + dat. of contents (see refs in BAGD *s.v.* 1b), 1.29; καυχᾶσαι, 2.17, 23; καταργέω in the causative sense is not attested before the Septuagint. The evidence of *POxy.* 38.17 (dated to AD 49/50), however, suggests that it should probably be classified as late Greek (and not strictly a septuagintalism). Paul's metaphorical usage appears to be unattested elsewhere outside of patristic authors, 3.3 (cf. 6.6; 7.2, 6); διακρίνομαι of doubting, 4.20; ἵνα of result (instead of purpose), 11.11; the use of ἄρα as first word in a sentence, 7.3 etc.; συγκοινωνός is first extant in the New Testament (first occurence outside the New Testament appears to be an AD 110 papyrus, *Bilabel* 19.2) 11.17; κατακαυχάομαι appears to be first extant in the

same general lack of concern for hiatus, even in cases where avoidance is quite normal, e.g., 2.2 κατὰ ἀλήθειαν; 3.8 τὰ ἀγαθά; 3.5 κατὰ ἄνθρωπον; 4.4 κατὰ ὀφείλημα; etc..[530] The sentence structure is generally paratactic. Subordinate participial constructions are not frequent, let alone periods,[531] and there is the same predilection for varying syntax and prepositions without any semantic implications. There is a similar extensive use of ἀντίθεσις and yet skant use of the μέν ... δέ construction.[532]

Paul also shows the same high regard for the use of stylised figures, particularly παρονομασία, and also a preponderant use of rhetorical questions.

There are some differences with the letter to the Galatians, although these are more quantitive than qualitative. Firstly, the kind of extensive grammatical jumbles encountered in Ep. Gal. are not to be found in Ep. Rom.. Nevertheless, discounting regular kinds of ellipses and attraction, there are still a number of solecisms.[533] The solecism at 2.8 is particularly telling of Paul's anomalous style; a grammatical slip right in the middle of an otherwise carefully constructed passage - an ἀντίθεσις (2.7-8), followed by another ἀντίθεσις (2.9-10) so constructed as to form a chiasm with the first.

Secondly, the general argumentative flow is much smoother than in Ep. Gal.. The kind of extensive and very difficult ellipses in argument evident in Ep. Gal. are not present in Ep. Rom.. This would tend to confirm the suggestion made above that the

---

LXX, though there does not appear to be a direct connection with the New Testament, 11.18; ἀποτομία is late but well-attested from the first century BC on, 11.22; πώρωσις, possibly apart from references in Hippocratic writings, first appears in the NT, 11.25.

Septuagintalisms: Δικαιόω meaning "to justify"/ "vindicate" instead of "to punish." Ἀλλάσσω τι ἐν τινι is taken directly from LXX Ps. 105 (106).20 (but cf. S. Ant. 945), 1.23; ψυχή in the sense of Hebrew נֶפֶשׁ as "person," 2.9; προσωπολημψία - one of a number of like nouns coined (and found only in the New Testament) on the basis of the LXX (Hebraic) expression λαμβάνειν πρόσωπον, cf. LXX Ps. 81 (82).2; 1 Es. 4.39; Si. 4.22, 27; 42.1; 4 Ki. 2.9; the Hebrew way of expessing total denial οὐ ... πᾶσα σάρξ = nobody (here echoing LXX Ps. 142 [143].2). Σάρξ (= בשׂר) here means "person," 3.20; εὑρηκέναι, cf. the common LXX phrase εὑρίσκειν χάριν/ ἔλεος, 4.1; ἀνάθεμα in the sense of "accursed" is only found in Jewish/ Christian texts (from חרם), 9.3; κοίτη in 9.10 seems to be related to the common LXX expression (based on a Hebrew phrase) κοίτη σπέρματος, cf. also Nu. 5.20; σάρξ in the sense of Hebrew בשׂר as "blood relations," 11.14; ἀνεξιχνίαστος first appears in the LXX and then in the New Testament (same kind of contexts). Secular examples are much later, 11.33.

[530] It would be interesting to know why Paul sometimes uses ἀλλ' before a vowel (e.g., 5.15) and other times not (e.g., 5.14).

[531] Even long involved sentences like 1.1-7 are not carefully constructed periods (using subordinate participles) but long series of parallel clauses.

[532] For example, one might have expected μέν instead of δέ at 4.4; and the use of the μέν ... δέ construction might also have been expected at 4.19-20.

[533] For example: 2.8 where ὀργὴ καὶ θυμός should be accusative; 4.12 where the second τοῖς is unwanted; 8.3; 9.10; cf. 9.22-24 where the ellipsis is probably to be taken from the previous question (οὐκ ἔχει ἐξουσίαν), and the οὕς at 9.24 is masculine ad sensum.

argumentative ellipses in *Ep.Gal.* may have to do with the fact that Paul is presuming prior knowledge of aspects of his argumentation on the part of the Galatian Christians. Nevertheless, although on a smaller scale, there are still some argumentative ellipses in *Ep.Rom.*, as noted above. These occur particularly where Paul is assuming knowledge of the context of his Scriptural citations.

This latter point brings us to the question of clarity in general. Paul's Greek is more than often annoyingly ambiguous (witness the myriad variances of interpretation in the commentary tradition). This ambiguity is more often than not caused by a rather vague use of genitives in connection with nouns, and by an imprecise and underuse of the article. One might add that his predilection for variation of constructions and prepositions doesn't help. Of course, this point shouldn't be blown out of proportion. I believe that the main line of Paul's argument is quite plain (as outlined above), but many secondary points are not evident upon first reading, and several minor points of interpretation remain obscure.

Clarity ($\sigma\alpha\phi\acute{\eta}\nu\varepsilon\iota\alpha$) was one of the traditional virtues of style among rhetorical theorists from the time of Theophrastus onwards. It was universally present, both in philosophical and school rhetoric, and often referred to. Its importance is, perhaps, underscored by the fact that Dionysius of Halicarnassus (who utilised a rather extended list of virtues) considered it one of the three *necessary* virtues (along with pure language and brevity).

With respect to virtues of style, our hypothetical rhetorical theorist examining these letters of Paul, would almost certainly complain of the lack of $\sigma\alpha\phi\acute{\eta}\nu\varepsilon\iota\alpha$, if not also the lack of purity of language. With respect to the virtue of propriety ($\tau\grave{o}$ $\pi\rho\acute{\varepsilon}\pi o\nu$) - another very important virtue in rhetorical tradition, one could argue that the general conversational tone of both *Ep.Gal.* and *Ep.Rom.* befits the epistolary genre. We have noted above the various conversational figures used in *Ep.Rom.*. For their appropriateness in epistolary style, see the discussion of style under the section on *Ep.Gal.*.[534]

2.6 Conclusions

Our description of the general argumentative section of Paul's letter to the Romans (chapters one to eleven) has shown that the main argumentative concern is dealt with in chapters one through five, where chapter five functions as a kind of

---

[534] Note there the caveat concerning the relation of epistolary style to what is considered appropriate *content* for a letter. See p.163.

ἐπίλογος, magnifying the benefits of the point argued in the preceding chapters (that in the Gospel God's δικαιοσύνη is revealed by faith). Although chapters six to eight flow on quite smoothly from the end of chapter five, they are of a different character, more in the nature of exhortation and teaching. The three chapters immediately following (nine to eleven) do not flow on so smoothly, but do have an intimate connection with the main argumentation of chapters one to five. When seen in this light, the suggestion that in chapters six to eight and then nine to eleven Paul is taking up the problems briefly addressed in 3.1-9 becomes attractive. Chapters six to eight take up the ethical objection as to whether Paul's Gospel implies that one may continue in sin. This is dealt with pastorally rather than argumentatively. Chapters nine to eleven take up the problem of the Jews' general rejection of the Gospel (and the concommitant implication that God's promises of old have thus failed). The nature of these chapters is more argumentative, but argument primarily by Scriptural citation. The authority of God's prophetic word is here paramount. Of course, it is also a key part of Paul's argumentation in chapters one to four, but there it functions more as a confirmation of points already reasoned out.

We now come to a consideration of Paul's main argumentative proposition (found at 1.16-17). In discussing Hellenistic school rhetoric, it was noted that one of the first distinctions made by treatises typical of our period was that between the θέσις and ὑπόθεσις. The θέσις is an argumentative treatment of a theme lacking the specifics of person and circumstances, whilst the ὑπόθεσις is an argumentative treatment of a specific case.[535] However, that does not mean that the theme of a θέσις may not contain certain more specific parameters (cf. Quint. *Inst.* 3.5.8; Theon *Prog.* ii. p.128,3-7 Sp.). Our excursus on the θέσις also showed that θέσεις were a common form among the Hellenistic philosophers. Theon quite appropriately notes that θέσεις were commonly found in the lecture hall (*Prog.* ii, p.120,22-23 Sp., ἀκρόασις = ἀκροατήριον here).

When set against this background, it becomes clear that the theme of the letter to the Romans (that the Gospel is God's power for salvation to everyone who believes since God's δικαιοσύνη is revealed in it by the connection of faith) is much more reminiscent of a θέσις than an ὑπόθεσις. At that, it is much more reminiscent of a *philosophical* θέσις, than a rhetorical θέσις (which tended to deal with matters of public policy).

---

[535] A good discussion of the difference is provided in Quint. *Inst.* 3.5.5-18. See also our discussion above, pp.49-50.

Having made this classification, we can see another reason for the limitations placed on the application of rhetorical theory to this letter. There is, however, in Theon's *Progymnasmata*, a short discussion of the writing of a philosophical θέσις (*Prog.* ii, p.125,21 - 128,3 Sp.). But Theon's advice is of little help to us. He suggests the use of the same τόποι listed for the rhetorical θέσεις, i.e., those common to the deliberative speech (the so-called τελικὰ κεφάλαια), as well as τόποι of similarity, greater/ lesser etc.. Paul's argumentation is not related to the method described and illustrated here.

Cicero's treatment of θέσεις does not really get us much further. The most we can say is that the proposition of the letter to the Romans could be classified as a *thesis ad cognoscendum* of the *modus definitionis* (cf. Cic. de Orat. 3.113-17). This might sound good, but it doesn't help our analysis of the letter any.

There is, however, another dimension to the classification of Romans as a philosophical θέσις, namely, the point of contact with the discussions concerning Paul and the so-called διατριβή.

Ever since R. Bultmann's dissertation (1910, *Der Stil*) it has been popular to associate Paul's letters with the so-called *diatribe* style.[536] Bultmann attempted to connect the preaching style he found in Paul's letters to the style of the wandering Cynic philosophers which he associated with the *diatribe* (Bultmann's analysis of Paul's use of similies, metaphors and examples is still valuable). It was a form of speaking for mass communication to the man on the street. At the beginning of this century it was common for scholars to refer to the *diatribe* as a literary genre, defined by modern stylistic criteria. This idea that the *diatribe* was a *literary* genre, however, soon came under attack.[537]

Two more recent studies have taken up and modified Bultmann's work, S. K. Stowers, *The Diatribe and Paul's Letter to the Romans* (1981) and T. Schmeller, *Paulus und die "Diatribe": Eine vergleichende Stilinterpretation* (1987). Both authors agree that the term διατριβή was *not* used to indicate a literary genre in antiquity. They, however, use the term to describe a style which they believe moderns are able to discern and describe in various philosophical writings of antiquity (e.g., Bion of Borysthenes, Teles, Musonius Rufus, Epictetus, etc.). Stowers views this style as set against the background of the philosophical school. In his view the term *diatribe* "is an appropriate and useful term for these works which either had their origin in the

---

[536] Bultmann's study, of course, has its precursors, cf. J. Weiss, 1897, "Beiträge," 167-68; C. F. G. Heinrici, 1900, *Brief*, 442, 454-55; 1908, *Charakter*, 66-68).
[537] See, for example, O. Halbauer, *De Diatribis Epicteti* (Dissertation; Leipzig, 1911).

philosophical school or which imitate the style of the school discourse" (77). Stowers views dialogue as one of the key elements of his *diatribe* style, along with various other dialogue-like figures, e.g., the raising and answering of objections (which in his view are always to be interpreted as the questions of students, not the objections of opponents). Schmeller (rightly I believe) criticises Stowers' restriction of these writings to a school situation, and prefers to view them as concerned with instruction in the widest sense. Bultmann's restriction of the style to the wandering Cynics also comes in for criticism. Schmeller rightly notes that the works used as evidence of *diatribe* style tend to vary in their relation to the spoken word. Some are more literary than others.

Whilst an in-depth investigation of modern research into the so-called *diatribe* style is out of place in this book, it is sufficient to note that although the same authors are often referred to, there is no real consensus in defining the precise contours of this so-called style itself. Schmeller (whose own analysis of rhetorical devices is very weak) was at least correct in noting that the style of individual authors concerned does indeed vary, and this is only to be expected. It is of course true that these popular philosophers have much in common, but the wisdom of using such a term as *diatribe* to describe what is common in their style is questionable.

Against this background we turn again to the question of the θέσις. Already E. Norden had noted a connection between what was then accepted as the literary genre of the διατριβή, and the θέσις.[538] It was this assumed connection which led H. Throm to investigate more fully the nature of the θέσις in his dissertation, *Die Thesis: Ein Beitrag zu ihrer Entstehung und Geschichte* (1932). Throm agreed with the criticism of the διατριβή as a literary genre, noting, in particular, the difficulty of defining a genre on the basis of stylistic criteria. In his words: "Der Stil an sich ist etwas viel zu Individuelles, als daß er eine literarische Gattung begründen könnte" (10). Throm's dissertation discusses the θέσις as a literary genre recognised and defined by the ancients, and used both in the realm of philosophy and of rhetoric. He quite rightly suggests that most of the writings that had been designated by scholars as διατριβαί (i.e., as the modern literary genre) could be better identified and termed θέσεις (77). The term θέσις was at least fairly well defined by the ancients, and used by them as a term for genre classification. The question of style, however, does not really enter into the definition.[539]

---

[538]   1898, *Kunstprosa*, 1.309.

[539]   The style of θέσεις handled by popular philosophers can vary considerably, from the careful, affected literary θέσεις of Maximus Tyrius, to the much more conversational style of Epictetus (whose style has long been likened to Paul in several particulars).

The brief discussion here suggests that further research into the relationship between the θέσεις of popular philosophers and Paul's letter to the Romans might well prove fruitful.[540]

---

[540]   See the interesting article of D. T. Runia who applies the literary form of the θέσις to a tract of Philo, comparing it structurally (among others) with Plutarch's περὶ τοῦ πότερον ὕδωρ ἢ πῦρ χρησιμώτερον ("Philo's de Aeternitate Mundi: The Problem of its Interpretation," *Vigiliae Christianae* 35 [1981] 105-151, esp. pp.112-21).

VI. THE FIRST LETTER TO THE CORINTHIANS

1 Recent Scholarship

Our discussion of recent scholarship on Paul's first letter to the Corinthians is divided into three sections. We discuss first various articles on details of rhetorical theory in the letter, together with articles undertaking a genre analysis of distinct sections of it. Next we discuss separately the important work of M. M. Mitchell who engages in a serious attempt to understand the first letter to the Corinthians as a whole in terms of a Graeco-Roman speech. On the basis of this work we are enabled to draw certain conclusions concerning the application of rhetorical theory to this letter. Finally, we deal with recent studies on the first four chapters of the letter with respect to the relation of rhetorical theory to Paul's self-characterisation of his preaching.

1.1 Rhetorical Textual Analysis

In 1985 B. Fiore published an interesting article entitled ""Covert Allusion" in 1 Corinthians 1-4." Fiore concentrates on what Paul says in the difficult text of 1 *Ep.Cor.* 4.6, in particular, his use of the verb μετασχηματίζειν. He argues that Paul is referring to a not uncommon way of using figures of speech (σχήματα in Greek) as described in various rhetorical treatises. In rhetorical theory the term "figure" (e.g., of speech) often has the same meaning as it has in English, but it can also refer to a more specific use of figures, frequently designated ἐσχηματισμένος λόγος. This more specific use of the term refers to the use of figures to hide or cover what one actually wants to say. It is a way of softening one's critique, especially if that critique was to be presented to those high in authority. Various reasons for using figures in this way are given in the treatises, the most popular being ἀσφάλεια and εὐπρέπεια ("caution" and "propriety"). Fiore suggests that Paul has deliberately employed this method in the first four chapters of 1 *Ep.Cor.*, and refers to this in 4.6 where he makes explicit what he has up until then covertly said. Fiore argues that μετασχηματίζειν thus refers to "covert allusion" and that the ταῦτα of 4.6 refers to all four chapters. His reasons for this are: i) that all four chapters use figures commonly associated with this practice (he lists hyperbole, irony, contrast, metaphors, similies and allegory, with text references);

ii) that τὸ μὴ ὑπὲρ ἃ γέγραπται must refer to more than just the labourers' analogy in chapter three; iii) that the final allusion to factionalism refers back to all four chapters; iv) and that the "we" in 1.18 - 3.4 could be Paul and Apollos.

Such a suggestion is indeed quite interesting, but it is not clear to me what, according to Fiore, Paul is precisely saying. He states that "Paul and Apollos become figures themselves, to which the community is to look for their own improvement" (94). They are "exemplary apostolic labourers in order to incite the wayward to emulation and to a desire of like praise (4:5)" (95). Whether this means that there were no real parties of Paul and Apollos (or Peter or Christ) is not addressed.

Fiore's article is not really very convincing in and of itself. Chapters one to four are certainly much more than a presentation of Paul and Apollos as exemplary teachers. Paul uses a rather extended argument about the nature of his Gospel (brought not with wise or persuasive speech but in demonstration of the Spirit) in 1.17 - 2.16 to apply to the problem of divisional strife (3.1 - 4.4). Furthermore, it is simply not enough to note that use is made of various figures in chapters one to four which *could* be used in a style of "covert allusion." It needs to be demonstrated that such figures are indeed used in this way. This is not addressed at all.

P. Lampe has also recently published an article arguing along the same lines (1990, "Wisdom"). Lampe interprets μετασχηματίζω in a similar way, defining it as "to hint at something in a disguised speech without saying it *expressis verbis*" (129, note 15). Lampe, however, explains a little more what he considers the covert allusion to be. It is not found in an abundance of figures of speech as Fiore,[541] but in the argumentation of 1.18 - 2.16 which, although it does not attack the problem of divisions by name, nevertheless is designed to criticise it. 1 *Ep.Cor.* 1.18 - 2.5, by criticising Jews and Greeks, also gives a silent criticism of wrong attitudes in Corinth, and 2.6-16, by arguing that the apostles have their wisdom from God's Spirit, underlines the fact that one cannot boast in apostles but only in God. This silent criticism Lampe seems to refer to as ἔμφασις - an appropriate figure (see select glossary *s.v.*).[542] He goes on to suggest that Paul used such covert speech in order not to hurt the feelings of the influential personages, Apollos and Peter (130). Unlike Fiore, Lampe does not

---

[541] It should be noted that Lampe gives no sign of being aware of Fiore's study. The two studies appear to be independent of each other.
[542] Lampe brings his exegesis into rhetorical focus on pp.128-31. His terminology is, however, vague. Despite what one feels as hesitation with respect to explicit application of rhetorical theory (Lampe does not give the impression of having done much study in this area), his suggested application is as a whole more persuasive than the more technical study of Fiore.

address the apparent inconsistency that Paul would at 4.6 reveal his own use of covert speech thus seeming to undo the caution expressed up until then.

These articles raise a particularly interesting problem, namely, how Paul typifies his argumentation in 1 *Ep.Cor.* 4.6. To what is he referring and what does μετασχηματίζειν here mean? The matter becomes even more interesting when it is realised that Chrysostom (*hom. 3 et 12 in 1 Cor.*) understood Paul to be using a form of covert allusion in the specific sense outlined above. Chrysostom argues that Paul is here saying that he has transferred to Apollos and himself what was said in Corinth of others. There were no Paul or Apollos parties, but Paul has spoken of the matter in this way in order to make his admonition palatable to the Corinthians. If he had hit the issue head on, his rebuke would probably not have been so readily received. By introducing it under the guise of Paul and Apollos parties he is able to avoid a knee-jerk reaction of anger. Once the basic admonition has been made, Paul can "unveil the real stage scene" to which his comments applied (as he does in 4.6).[543] Chrysostom's description of Paul's tactic must be seen against the background of rhetorical theory on this point which describes just this kind of ploy (cf. Demetr. *Eloc.* 292; Quint. *Inst.* 9.2.65). Chrysostom's application goes further however. The point of "figured speech" was to hint at something without explicitly saying it, but not to contradict one's point or to say anything that was not true.[544] It is not, however, clear to me that Chrysostom necessarily sees a reference to this rhetorical tactic in the verb μετασχηματίζω.

---

[543]   Chrysostom: Ἕως μὲν αὐτῷ τῶν φορτικῶν ἔδει ῥημάτων, οὐκ ἀπεκάλυψε τὴν σκηνήν, ἀλλ' ὡς αὐτὸς ὢν ὁ ταῦτα ἀκοῦων, οὕτω διελέγετο, ἵνα τὸ ἀξίωμα τῶν ἐγκαλουμένων προσώπων τοῖς ἐγκαλοῦσιν ἀντιπίπτον, ἀπὸ τῶν ἐγκλημάτων εἰς ὀργὴν ἐξενεχθῆναι μὴ συγχωρήσῃ· ἐπειδὴ δὲ ἀνεῖναι λοιπὸν ἔδει, τότε ἀπαμφιάσας αὐτὸ, καὶ τὸ προσωπεῖον ἀπάρας, ἔδειξε τὰ κρυπτόμενα πρόσωπα ἐν τῇ τοῦ Παύλου καὶ Ἀπολλὼ προσηγορίᾳ. Διὸ καὶ ἔλεγε· Ταῦτα δὲ, ἀδελφοί, μετεσχημάτισα εἰς ἐμαυτὸν καὶ Ἀπολλώ.

"So long as he needed to use coarse words, he did not reveal the stage-scene, but reasoned as if he himself was the one who heard these things, in order that the dignity of those accused, being resistant to the accusers, would not permit them to become angry because of the accusations; but when it became necessary to proceed further, at that point having stripped it off and taken away the mask, he showed the persons that were hidden by the names of Paul and Apollos. For that reason he was also saying: 'But these things, brothers, I have applied to myself and Apollos.'" (For comments on the translation of μετασχηματίζω see below.)

[544]   Quintilian remarks that we make a hint *non utique contrarium, ut in εἰρωνείᾳ, sed aliud latens et auditori quasi inveniendum* (9.2.65). Demetrius gives the example of subtly critiquing a tyrant by telling him about the cruelty of another tyrant (292). This is not quite the same as Paul *inventing* the parties of himself and Apollos to disguise his critique. Furthermore, these sources do not cater for the idea that figured speech is only used to *introduce* the discussion of a subject which is later stated with full force (Chrysostom's point). Of interest, however, is the apparent allusion to just such a use of figured speech by certain theorists in [D.H.] *Rh.* 8.1 - a tract probably to be dated to the third century AD (cf. L. Radermacher, 1929, "Praefatio," xxiii - xxiv). Could Chrysostom be under the influence of such (late) rhetorical theory? To be fair to Chrysostom, he nowhere explicitly states that his analysis is an example of "figured speech."

Such a meaning for this verb is simply assumed in F. H. Colson's oft cited article (1916, "Μετεσχημάτισα") which does not even address the possibility that μετασχηματίζω in Paul or Chrysostom could refer to something other than a rhetorical use of σχῆμα. His argumentation against Chrysostom's exegesis is based on this assumption.

But one would not at face value expect μετασχηματίζω to mean something like "transform *something* by way of a (covert) figure." The rhetoricians quite rightly use the simplex σχηματίζω to refer to making something into a (covert) figure of speech, for when σχῆμα means "figure of speech" it refers not a change of the "form" or "shape" of words, but bringing them into a particular "form" (cf. Quint. *Inst.* 9.1.10-14). The prefix μετα-, however, implies a *change* from one form to another. Μετασχηματίζω is to change an existing σχῆμα (whatever sense σχῆμα might have) into another σχῆμα. As such, one would not expect σχῆμα here to mean "figure of speech."[545] This consideration may be overly pedantic, but in the absence of other evidence for such a technical usage we should be careful.

What then does μετασχηματίζειν τι εἰς τινα mean? Here we should also be careful. It is too simple to say that it means "to transform something into something else." A better equivalent would be "to change the form of something to another form." It is in this way that Paul uses the pass./mid. with εἰς (2 *Ep.Cor.* 11.13-14). A possible analogue is also provided by the usage of σχηματίζω (cf. LSJ *s.v.* II.1). This verb is often used in the sense of giving a certain form to something, e.g., σχηματίζειν τὸ ἁρμόσσον σχῆμα [*sc.* τὸ ὀθόνιον] Hippocrates, *Art.* 37 (cf. μετασχηματίζεσθαι in *Ep.Phil.* 3.21). There is also the following interesting passage from Achilles Tatius (a romantic author of the second century AD): σχηματίζειν τὸ πρόσωπον εἰς ἡδονήν, Ach.Tat. 6.11. This would appear to be equivalent to "giving the face a ἡδονικὸν σχῆμα," compare LXX 4 *Ma.* 9.22: ἀλλ' [ὁ νεανίας] ὥσπερ ἐν πυρὶ μετασχηματιζόμενος εἰς ἀφθαρσίαν, i.e., the form (σχῆμα) of the young man becomes immortal. If so understood, then μετασχηματίζειν ταῦτα εἰς Παῦλον would mean "to change the form of these things to a Pauline form (Παυλιανὸν σχῆμα)," which then (in context) may effectively mean "apply these things to Paul." This may be further confirmed by the following citation from Cyril of Alexandria (*Ps. 10:1*) πῶς ἡμᾶς χρὴ διακεῖσθαι, μετασχηματίσας ἐφ' ἑαυτῷ τὸν λόγον, πειρᾶται διδάσκειν, καί φησιν·

---

[545] In fact, the only technical use of μετασχηματίζω I have found in rhetorical treatises is the device (mentioned in several late works) called μετασχηματισμός which involves *changing* the form of a word for metrical or artistic reasons, cf. Joseph of Rakendutus, σύνοψις ῥητορικῆς (ed. Walz, 3.569); Polybius of Sardis, περὶ σχηματισμοῦ (ed. Walz, 8.611-12); Cocondrius, περὶ τρόπων (ed. Walz, 8.784).

"*ἐπὶ τῷ κυρίῳ πέποιθα*" ("Having applied the matter to himself, he tries to teach us how we ought to act, and says; 'I trust in the Lord'").

Chrysostom's interpretation, though perhaps initially attractive, fails to convince in the end.[546] Paul's opening remarks on party strife would be more bewildering than veiling. The remarks of Photius on 1 *Ep.Cor.* 4.6 seem to have captured Paul's point better. He states that the purpose of Paul's *μετασχηματισμός* was to apply the rebuke (*ὁ ἔλεγχος*) to himself and Apollos so as to avoid undue offence by singling out certain people. The rebuke he refers to would seem to be that of 3.5, namely, that neither Paul nor Apollos have anything to boast about for they function merely as servants of God who performs his own work through their ministry. This is then more generally applied in 4.6ff.[547]

Studies on other aspects of textual rhetoric in the first letter to the Corinthians include D. F. Watson's analysis of the rhetorical questions in 1 *Ep.Cor.* 10.29-30 (1989, "1 Corinthians"). Watson rejects one of the so-called traditional interpretations of verses 29-30, namely, that Paul is raising objections that he anticipates the strong will raise, stating that the following verses do not seem to form a response to these objections (308-309). Yet his own interpretation ends up being almost identical, namely, that these questions are an anticipation of objections from opponents which are

---

546 If correct, it would solve a particularly difficult problem in the letter itself, namely, how any supposed party divisions are supposed to be related to the content of the rest of the letter. It has long been noted by interpreters that the issues presented in the rest of the letter do not lend themselves to delineating supposed theological differences between various parties. In recent scholarship this has led to the idea that the supposed parties in Corinth must have existed along sociological and not theological lines (cf. S. M. Pogoloff below, § 2). Moreover, Paul addresses the entire congregation of Corinth as a whole, and does not appear to pay attention to individual parties. Such divisions resurface again only in 11.17ff and are perhaps presupposed in the use of the metaphor of the body in chapter twelve. But Paul is surprisingly hesitant with respect to divisions in 11.18. Chrysostom's interpretation would effectively solve this problem by treating the mention of Paul or Apollos parties as a rhetorical tactic, and not as a real situation.

547 Photius was of course very well versed in ancient literature, including the great Greek orators, as his famous *Bibliotheca* shows. His remarks on 1 *Ep.Cor.* 4.6 can be found in Cramer's *Catenae*, 5.81: Διατί "δι' ὑμᾶς μετεσχημάτισα εἰς ἐμαυτὸν καὶ Ἀπολλώ;" "δι' ὑμᾶς," φησίν, ἵνα μὴ ἀνίασω ὑμᾶς, ὀνόματι καθαπτόμενος· διορθοῦσθαι μὲν γὰρ ἔσπευδεν· ἀνιᾶν δὲ ἐφυλάττετο· διὰ δὲ τοῦ μετασχηματισμοῦ, φησίν, ἀμφότερα ὑμῖν βουλομένοις ἔσται· καὶ τὸ διορθωθῆναι, καὶ τὸ ἀλυπώτερον ἀκοῦσαι τῶν ἐπὶ τῇ διορθώσει ἐλέγχων· ἐποίει δὲ τοῦτο καὶ ἵνα μὴ ὡρισμένα πρόσωπα τῷ ἐλέγχῳ καθυποβάλλων, δόξῃ ἀνθρωπίνῃ τινὶ προσπαθείᾳ ἢ ἀντιπαθείᾳ τοὺς μὲν ἐᾶν, τῶν δὲ κατατρέχειν· ἄλλως τε δὲ καὶ ἵνα μὴ ἐν τῇ τοιαύτῃ διακρίσει, ὧν μὲν καθήψατο, τούτους εἰς ἀπόγνωσιν ἐμβάλλῃ, ἢ εἰς ὀργὴν καὶ φιλονεικίαν μείζονα ἀνάψῃ· ὧν δ' οὐκ ἐπὶ τοῖς ἐλέγχοις οὐκ ἐμνήσθη, τούτους δὲ ἄρα διὰ τοῦτο τύφου μᾶλλον καὶ ἀπονοίας ἐμπλήσῃ. διὸ εἰκότως ἐξ ὀνόματος οὐ καθήψατο· ἀλλ' εἰς ἑαυτὸν καὶ Ἀπολλὼ τὸν ἔλεγχον μετασχηματίσας, καθαρὰν καὶ εὐπρόσοδον τὴν νουθέτησιν κοινὴν ἅπασιν ἐποιήσατο. Compare Ambrosiaster *ad loc.*, a passage pointed out to me by J. Fairweather.

then, for comparison, placed side by side Paul's own position in v.31ff (he references [Arist.] *Rh.Al.* 34, 1440a.25). Watson has unfortunately adopted a very wooden interpretation of his sources. The point of Anaximenes (= [Arist.] *Rh.Al.*) is that one should raise likely objections from opponents and then refute them by comparing them with one's own position, making the views of the opponents smaller and your own greater. Were this the case, one might expect that Paul would introduce the questions as the possible objections of his opponents, and one would certainly expect that the objections would be answered and appropriately compared with his own position. But Watson has already admitted that the objections do not appear to be answered in what follows. This indicates that he would appear to think that the mere setting of two different thoughts side by side without comment fulfills the conditions of what Anaximenes is describing. The reading of the sources is shallow and shows little appreciation of the application of rhetorical theory in practice.[548]

We may close our discussion of rhetorical textual analysis by briefly noticing M. M. Mitchell's article on rhetorical shorthand in Paul's Corinthian correspondence (1994, "Shorthand").[549] Mitchell provides a commentated checklist of Paul's use of various terms for the Gospel which she classifies under βραχυλογία (use of a noun instead of a description), συνεκδοχή (part for whole) and μεταφορά (metaphor).

We turn now to several studies which insist on providing a rhetorical genre analysis (complete with the *partes orationis*) of various *portions* of Paul's letter.

In a dissertation published in 1983 (*Briefformular*), M. Bünker attempts to use both epistolary theory and rhetorical criticism to help him discern the sociological position(s) of the implicit audience (as opposed to the explicit audience) of the first letter to the Corinthians. By showing that this letter uses various expressions related to

---

[548] Another example of such reasoning may be adduced from p.304 where he argues that v.24 is a κρίσις or common opinion used to buttress an argument *that seems unlikely*. The whole point of a κρίσις is that it is introduced as common opinion, and not just the opinion of the speaker (thereby giving it more weight). This is also quite clear even from the sources Watson cites (Quint. *Inst.* 5.11.36-44; cf. Cic. *Inv.* 1.48). But Paul does not introduce his thought here as common opinion (even if it was a common thought - which is not demonstrated). It comes across as his very own advice. Therefore it can hardly be termed a κρίσις. If anything, one might argue that v.26 is a κρίσις, though of a special kind. If the citation was well enough known to be recognised as Scripture then it needed no introduction as such, although the authority of Scripture is of course of a different kind than that of *communis opinio*. Pages 314-15 show yet another example of forced reasoning (with respect to Quint. *Inst.* 5.11.5).

[549] It is difficult to say anything substantial about W. Wuellner's short article on digressions in 1 *Ep.Cor.* (1979, "Rhetoric"). The notion of digressions in Greek rhetoric is inadequately defined by Wuellner and per consequence the reader must simply accept his (improbable) isolation of three major digressions and his argumentative analysis. There is little substantiated proof.

epistolary theory (with respect to friendship), and that the argumentation may be compared to Seneca's letters to Lucilius, he concludes that the implicit audience belongs to the "sozial Höhergestellten" in the congregation (75).[550]

This conclusion is further supported by his rhetorical analysis of two passages, 1 *Ep. Cor.* 1.10 - 4.21 and chapter fifteen. He understands the passages to be based on forensic rhetoric as the most influential form of school rhetoric at that time. His analysis is, however, forced; its greatest flaw being the attempt to trace a complete rhetorical disposition within a fragment of a letter.[551] Yet Bünker's analysis of disposition does not even conform to rhetorical theory, e.g., *argumentatio, peroratio, argumentatio* II, *peroratio* II.[552] In giving his analysis Bünker appears to rely almost solely on H. Lausberg's *Handbuch* (1973). This seems to be a more general trend, yet it often has a somewhat distorting effect on the way rhetorical theory is applied. There is no substitute for a personal reading of the rhetorical theorists (in their own language), and the reading and application of this theory to typical speeches of the time. I believe this would have a salutary effect on rhetorical scholarship in general.

Another article providing a genre analysis of a portion of the letter is D. F. Watson's "Paul's Rhetorical Strategy in 1 Corinthians 15" (1993a). Watson provides a rhetorical analysis of 1 *Ep. Cor.* 15 as if it were a mini-speech.[553] However, he explicitly acknowledges the fact that chapter fifteen stands within the proof of the body of the whole letter. Yet he still feels justified in providing a complete "rhetorical analysis" of this chapter (232). At two points he indicates reasons for this procedure. On p.235 Watson cites Arist. *Rh.* 3.14 (1415b) and Quint. *Inst.* 4.1.72-75 to argue that the "functions of an *exordium* were commonly given to any portion of a work as needed." However, the point of the theorists here is only that one can often add a remark such as "now pay attention to what I have to say" anywhere in one's speech. Such a remark

---

[550] On p.34 Bünker draws the strange conclusion that use of "philophronetischer Phrasen und Wendungen" in 1 *Ep. Cor.* shows that Paul stands in the tradition of "(Schul-)Gebildeten, für die der Brief wesentliches Mittel der Pflege der Beziehung zwischen räumlich Getrennten darstellt." Had Bünker studied a selection of the papyrus letters found in Egypt, he would have realised that such phraseology was extremely common, even among the barely literate!
[551] The fact that Bünker holds to a partition theory of this letter does not alter this criticism. Even on his own theory (cf. 52f) these two passages do not represent complete letters.
[552] Bünker's analysis appears to have been adopted by R. Pesch, 1986, *Paulus.* On p.79 Pesch notes (without citation) that recent scholars have detected three separate apologetic speeches within the first letter to the Corinthians, namely, 1 *Ep. Cor.* 1.10 - 4.21; 9.1-27; and 15.1-58. It is contended that each apology deals with Paul's apostleship. Pesch's analysis shows that he is thinking (among others) of the work of Bünker mentioned above. Pesch uses this work as additional evidence that 1 *Ep. Cor.* is in fact a composite of four different letters (cf. 72-73, 81), cf. W. Schenk, 1990, "Korintherbriefe." Schenk also supplies a rhetorical *divisio* for 1 *Ep. Cor.* 1.10 - 4.21 (629-30, different from Bünker).
[553] Compare also B. L. Mack, 1990, *Rhetoric*, 56-59.

was a commonplace at the end of an *exordium*. These citations simply do not justify the classification of *exordia* throughout various stages of argumentation in a letter or speech. A similarly irrelevant citation is given for the justification of finding a *narratio* in 1 *Ep.Cor.* 15 (Arist. *Rh.* 3.16, 1417b on p.236). Although speaking in the context of a discussion about *narrationes* (διηγήσεις), Aristotle is at this point only referring to the narration of a piece of history that will function as an example in the proof.

A number of lesser studies on various passages from 1 *Ep.Cor.* exhibit some of the same problems. Examples are H. van de Sandt's study on 1 *Ep.Cor.* 11.2-16[554] and J. F. M. Smit's studies on 1 *Ep.Cor.* 12 through 14.[555] Along the same lines as Smit's analysis of 1 *Ep.Cor.* 13 as epideictic rhetoric is J. G. Sigountos' analysis of the same passage as an *encomium* (1994, "Genre").[556] Sigountos' analysis is, however, some- what more careful than that of Smit. He argues that 1 *Ep.Cor.* 13, like two passages that have often been compared with it (LXX 1 *Es.* 4.34-40 and Plato, *Symposium* 194e - 197e), are all to be classified as *encomia*.[557] What makes his suggestion more per- suasive is the fact that he compares the preliminary exercises for *encomia* prescribed in the rhetorical προγυμνάσματα. These exercises were frequently much shorter than a normal speech, as can be seen from the examples in Aphthonius or those preserved under the name of Libanius.[558] In fact such exercises were often viewed as material that could later be incorporated into a larger work.[559] Sigountos also has some *prima facie*

---

[554]   1988, "1 Kor. 11,2-16." He argues that this passage is "een op zichzelf staande redevoering" (411). Problems only begin when he argues that v.3 is the *propositio* and yet maintains that the passage itself is concerned to convince women to veil their heads.

[555]   Whilst Smit clearly regards 1 *Ep.Cor.* 12 - 14 as a unit, yet he insists on analysing the separate chapters as if they were practically separate speeches. Thus in (1989a) "Rangorde," he analyses 12.1-30 as a deliberative speech and even goes so far as to treat verses 4-6 as a *partitio* (i.e., the topics to be dealt with). In (1991) "Genre," he analyses 12.30 - 13 as an epideictic speech, providing two further points of detail (a case of irony, and of parenthesis) in (1993) "Puzzles." The conclusions of these studies are repeated, and an analysis of 1 *Ep.Cor.* 14 provided, in (1993) "Argument." Here he treats chapter four- teen as another deliberative speech with its own *partitio*. Unity to the whole is brought by considering 14.37-40 as a *peroratio* to all three chapters and by considering chapter thirteen as a *digressio*. Given the fact that i) these chapters are hardly long enough to be considered independent speeches; ii) that they are parts of a larger argumentative whole, at least 12 - 14, but apart from that a *portion* of a letter; and iii) the outline of *dispositio* provided for these three chapters is nowhere mirrored in ancient rhetorical theory nor contemporary speeches; such an approach can hardly be considered persuasive. Apart from this we should also note that Smit's discussion of rhythm in connection with 1 *Ep.Cor.* 13 (pp.204-205) does not discuss the problem of syllable length (a serious omission noted above in connection with Campbell's dissertation on *Ep.Rom.* 3.21-26, chapter five, § 1).

[556]   See also B. Witherington, 1995, *Conflict*, 264-65.

[557]   The passages in 1 Esdras and Plato are quite clearly *reports* of encomia that were supposedly held.

[558]   The reports of *encomia* in 1 Esdras and Plato are also short, however these examples may only be intended as summaries. Compare the length of the speeches in the *Acta Apostolorum*.

[559]   For a fuller discussion of the προγυμνάσματα see above under the section on Theon (chapter two, § 3.3).

evidence in the structure of 1 *Ep.Cor.* 13. A standard and important part of an encomium was the description of the deeds of whatever it was that was being praised (and abstract qualities were often used as subjects of *encomia*). Verses 4-7 seem to fit this very well. After a description of the deeds there was usually a comparison, which seems to fit verses 8-12. Having said all this however, a couple of points should be noted. Firstly, even though *encomium* exercises tended to be relatively short, none are as short as 1 *Ep.Cor.* 13. Secondly, and more importantly, it seems to me that 1 *Ep.Cor.* 13 is better viewed as a comparison in and of itself. The chapter begins by comparing love with other gifts, showing that love is always essential if the other gifts are to be meaningful. This is merely continued in verses 8-12. It ought to be noted that the σύγκρισις or *comparison* was also a separate kind of exercise in the προ-γυμνάσματα.[560]

1.2 Genre Analysis of 1 *Ep.Cor.* as a Whole

We turn now to what must be considered by far the most important rhetorical analysis of the first letter to the Corinthians, at least as far as rhetorical genre analysis is concerned. M. M. Mitchell's *Paul and the Rhetoric of Reconciliation* (1991) is a work which seeks to understand 1 *Ep.Cor.* as a whole to be a letter cast in the form of a deliberative speech on concord. The strength of this work clearly lies in its careful methodology. Right at the start five important mandates for rhetorical criticism are outlined (6).

> 1) Rhetorical criticism as employed here is an historical undertaking.
> 2) Actual speeches and letters from antiquity must be consulted along with the rhetorical handbooks throughout the investigation.
> 3) The designation of the rhetorical species of a text ... cannot be begged in the analysis.
> 4) The appropriateness of rhetorical form or genre to content must be demonstrated.
> 5) The rhetorical unit to be examined should be a compositional unit, which can be further substantiated by successful rhetorical analysis.

Points one and two are especially important. Mitchell does not wish to deny that modern rhetorical criticism may have its own value, but she wishes to separate it from

---

560 Several of the τόποι listed in Theon *Prog.* 9 would seem to be relevant. It should be emphasised that chapter thirteen should not be considered a set piece in and of itself. It forms an important link in the chain of argumentation from chapters twelve to fourteen. This fact does not, however, mean that Paul could not have applied a particular kind of method, commonly practised in school exercises, to a portion of his argumentation. For an expanded use of σύγκρισις within a larger work, see Philo, *Leg.Gaj.* 77ff.

the strictly historical discipline. Her emphasis that rhetorical theory must be combined with an examination of contemporary *praxis* is also salutary. In her own analysis, she attempts to give priority to the speeches of Dio Chrysostom and Aristides. In terms of points four and five, she shows that she has correctly understood that the classification of a speech or letter in terms of a rhetorical genre must be coupled with an analysis of the methodology specific to that genre in rhetorical theory. We shall examine how she does this shortly. Point five is also important for rhetorical genre analysis. As we have so far seen, there is a trend in rhetorical studies (helped along by the approach of G. A. Kennedy)[561] to isolate smaller units or chapters within the letters of the apostle Paul and to apply a rhetorical genre analysis to them. Mitchell quite rightly disputes the validity of this approach. In addition, she also rightly emphasises the need to pay attention to patristic commentaries and their use of rhetoric as an analytical tool (cf. 18-19). Interestingly, she is able to show the use of rhetorical terminology in the exegesis of both Chrysostom and Theodoret (although neither seem concerned with rhetorical genre analysis).

Her own use of rhetorical criticism is in terms of genre analysis of the entire epistle. She does not engage in textual rhetorical criticism, though she does not at all disparage it. It is simply not the focus of her study (see her conclusion.).

Mitchell begins by competently defining the deliberative genre in a four point characterisation (23ff):

1) a focus on future time as the subject of deliberation;
2) employment of a determined set of appeals or ends, the most distinctive of which is the advantageous (τὸ συμφέρον);
3) proof by example (παράδειγμα); and
4) appropriate subjects for deliberation, of which factionalism and concord are especially common.

All four elements are, according to her ensuing analysis, to be found in 1 *Ep.Cor.*.

It is at this point, however, that I begin to have questions about her thesis. For example, she quite properly argues that the concept of συμφέρον is one of the most important considerations for deliberative rhetoric, and even becomes a technical term in this context. The application to 1 *Ep.Cor.* is, however, suspicious. As she notes, συμφέρον was a common term in philosophy (esp. Stoicism) and religion as well as being a technical term for deliberative rhetoric. My question is whether Paul neces-

---

[561]   See chapter one, § 5.

sarily uses the term in a specifically rhetorical sense? 1 *Ep.Cor.* 6.12 and 10.23 do not seem to me to be used in the context of deliberative rhetoric (i.e., that the concept of συμφέρον supports the supposed proposition being argued). Even although one may parallel the question of whose advantage is to be sought (36, cf. 1 *Ep.Cor.* 10.23-33) with deliberative rhetoric, yet the question here still does not specifically revolve around what is ostensibly the thesis of the letter, namely, "let there be no divisions."[562] Συμφέρον in the first letter to the Corinthians appears only to be used with respect to side issues and not in respect of the main point (accepting for the sake of argument Mitchell's contention that 1 *Ep.Cor.* 1.10 is the *propositio*).

This aside, we come to the more important consideration as to how this letter may be interpreted as a coherent development of argumentation upon a single theme. When I began reading Mitchell's dissertation I was very interested to find out how she would show that this letter was a sustained argument for the supposed *propositio* in 1.10. This turned out to be a false expectation as, instead of showing it to be a sustained argument for concord, she rather seeks to define deliberative rhetoric in such a way that the relation between *propositio* and proof is loosened. This becomes clear in the excursus on "paraenesis and deliberative rhetoric" (50-53). Here a "bare bones distinction" (52) is given between the two. She states:

> "deliberative rhetoric contains advice about specific matters and incidents, whereas paraenesis is more general moral exhortation, which is of universal application" (52-53).

It is significant that Mitchell does not say that deliberative rhetoric is sustained argumentation for a proposition which concerns a specific matter or incident. Rather, she redefines it as "advice" about specific matters (pl.).[563] What she means is that any *one* deliberative writing may contain advice about various specific matters and inci-

---

[562] By the way, it seems to me that Mitchell's analysis of the development with respect to advantage in 1 *Ep.Cor.* 6.12-20 is not quite correct. She argues that Paul ends up by showing "the true sphere of advantage - the entire church community" (36). Paul does indeed show the Corinthians as a group of people brought together by the deity, with bodies that are considered temples of Christ. The Spirit of the deity (i.e., the Holy Spirit given from God through Christ) lives within the temples and so unites them to the deity. But all this rather argues that the συμφέρον they must be concerned with is not the συμφέρον of themselves (6.19b), nor so much that of the community (nowhere actually emphasised), but that of the Lord (6.13b). This of course undermines Mitchell's theory of a development in Paul's argument in this whole letter with respect to συμφέρον, namely, from advantage as self-interest to advantage as the interest of the community. For Mitchell: "In 6:13-20 Paul begins to lay the groundwork for his redefinition of τὸ συμφέρον which is at the heart of the entire argument in 1 Corinthians, in his effort to demonstrate to the Corinthians what their true best interests are" (35-36).
[563] The word "advice" itself can be a suitable translation for συμβουλή, but the word is rather too broad in meaning when attempting to define the nature of a rhetorical speech.

dents. This is clear when she adds (within the same context) that "1 Corinthians addresses itself to specific problems [my emphasis, R.D.A.] within the church community." Of course she appropriately adds that "if 1 Corinthians is a deliberative *argument*, then it should have a defined structure (τάξις)." But the question here is more whether that τάξις is a structure in terms of the sustained argumentation for a particular proposition.[564]

Ancient rhetorical theory is based on this presumption (when speaking of speeches, and when not using the term ἐπιδεικτικός in its broadest sense). An orator has a proposition which he wishes to prove. This was true originally of all three species of rhetoric. The argumentation is designed to persuade the audience of the proposition, *not* to give them various pieces of concrete advice that will help them to bring the proposition into effect in their lives as a community. And here we have a clear difference in the way examples are used in Paul (generally to support particular advice or exhortation), and in ancient rhetoric (to directly support a proposition).[565]

Mitchell returns to her characterisation of deliberative rhetoric on p.203 where she argues that the proof of deliberative speeches was often arranged topically as advice given on various subjects "affecting the audience's decision for future action." Although the handbooks on rhetorical theory do not really discuss this matter, she maintains that it is a clear trend in actual practice. Footnote 100 on p.203 contains alleged examples, which, because of the importance of this notion for her thesis, we will briefly review.

. The first citation is from Dio Chrysostom 38.3. She quotes the following from the *Loeb* translation, but inexplicably omits the word "other" (I have placed it in

---

[564] On p.62 (note 200) Mitchell identifies seven speeches on concord from Dio Chrysostom and Aristides which in her opinion are the closest to 1 *Ep.Cor.*. Not one of these seven speeches can be characterised as advice on various specific matters and incidents which serve to illustrate how concord may concretely be achieved!

[565] I leave here out of consideration the kind of speeches generally termed περὶ βασιλείας which often essentially consisted of nothing more than a series of precepts on how the king (or a particular king) should conduct himself throughout his reign, cf. Isoc. 2 (*ad Nicocles*). J. Klek (1919, *Symbuleutici*, 46-63) claims this as an example of deliberative rhetoric. It is true that Isocrates in describing this oration in 15.67-72 (*Antid.*) uses the verb συμβουλεύω. Nevertheless, he also makes it clear that this speech differs significantly from the norm, since instead of connected argumentation he has given separate pieces of counsel. Isocrates also uses the verb παραινέω in reference to this speech. The ancient ὑπόθεσις on it refers to it as παραινέσεις, although Photius appears to call it a συμβουλευτικὸς λόγος (*Bibl.* 487b M.). Klek's discussion of it as deliberative is related to his theory that deliberative rhetoric is derived from the παραίνεσις of poetical works such as Hesiod's *Opera et Dies*. He is even of the opinion that the form περὶ βασιλείας is related to deliberative rhetoric (37-38). T. C. Burgess (1902, *Literature*, 136), however, places its origin in epideictic rhetoric. In any event, 1 *Ep.Cor.* is clearly not related to this form, though there is a resemblance to the paraenetic sections of other letters in the Pauline corpus.

italics): "Well now, there are indeed some *other* things in your city which deserve correction (ἄλλα τινὰ παρ' ὑμῖν ἐπανορθώσεως ἄξια), and one after the other I shall apply my treatment to them." In context Dio is saying that whilst there are many minor matters he will eventually bring up with the Nicomedians, his subject for *this speech* is a matter of far greater importance, namely, concord with the Nicaeans (cf. 38.3-7). Dio is carefully building trust with his audience by defending the fact that he moves straight to an important matter (namely, concord with the Nicaeans, 38.6-7) instead of first testing the waters, as it were, by offering speeches of advice on lesser matters (38.3). Citation of this passage has nothing to do with a speech divided into various topical headings. The threefold *divisio* of this speech (38.8-9) is directly related to the *propositio* (that there must be concord with Nicaeans, 38.7): 1) the benefits of concord in general (38.10-20, cf. θέσις), 2) concord in this particular instance as most necessary and profitable (38.21-48), and 3) how to make concord last (38.48-51).

Mitchell next cites Isocrates 8.15 who in his *divisio* states: "I have come before you ... to make known the views I hold, first, regarding the proposals which have been put before you by the Prytaneis, and, second, regarding the other interests of the state." Isocrates' *propositio* which follows (8.16) is that Athens should make peace not only with the allies for whom the treaty proposed by the Prytaneis has been drawn up, but with all men, and then according to the terms of previous treaties. The proof (8.18-131) deals first briefly with the specific proposal (8.18-25) and then moves on to the second part of the *divisio*. But is this a discussion of various topics one by one? No, for what Isocrates referred to as περὶ τῶν ἄλλων τῶν τῆς πόλεως πραγμάτων at 8.15 are the facts that Athens must learn that τὴν μὲν ἡσυχίαν ὠφελιμωτέραν καὶ κερδαλεωτέραν εἶναι τῆς πολυπραγμοσύνης, τὴν δὲ δικαιοσύνην τῆς ἀδικίας, τὴν δὲ τῶν ἰδίων ἐπιμέλειαν τῆς τῶν ἀλλοτρίων ἐπιθυμίας (peace is more beneficial and profitable than meddlesomeness, righteousness than unrighteousness, and care for one's own things than desire for those of another). Isocrates means by this that Athens must not seek after empire any more, but turn to peace instead. He first treats this negatively with a general condemnation of Athenian practice (8.26-62) and then offers positive counsel, namely, that the Athenians must have no sea empire (8.63-115). He goes on to show that this is both just (8.67-69) and advantageous (8.70-115). The argument is wrapped up with a number of rhetorical questions. The *peroratio* (8.132-45) gives a review of the most pertinent points from the second part of his *divisio*. First the lessons from his negative description of Athenian practice: i) they must use good counsellors and not sycophants, ii) they must treat their allies as friends, and iii) they must ensure that they have a good name among the Hellenes. This is followed by a recapitulation of his main theme in the positive counsel, namely, that they should not go after empire anymore.

The speech forms a coherent unity of deliberative argument. There is no detailed regulation of various matters such as we find in 1 *Ep.Cor.*. The so-called "other matters" Isocrates deals with are directly related to the proposal of peace and are argued for in normal deliberative fashion, namely, by showing, primarily by means of examples, that the proposition is just and advantageous.

The third example is the seventh speech of (Ps.?) Demosthenes.[566] On the surface, this would seem to be a good choice for comparison with 1 *Ep.Cor.*. The speaker is reacting in his speech both to a letter from Philip of Macedon and to the (oral) speeches of his ambassadors. This parallels Paul's reaction to both the letter from the Corinthians and the various oral reports he received. Of course the main difference is that 1 *Ep.Cor.* is directed back to the Corinthians themselves, whereas this speech is addressed not to Philip but to the Athenian assembly. At the end of a short προοίμιον Ps.-Demosthenes gives a bipartite *divisio* which he does not stick to in the speech itself. The speech is in fact a point by point consideration and refutation of matters brought up in the letter of Philip. Nine separate issues are discussed. On the surface this seems much closer to 1 *Ep.Cor.* than any speech I have yet read. Yet all these points are intended to support Ps.-Demosthenes' proposed resolution (ἀπόκρισις) as both δικαίαν τ᾽ εἶναι καὶ συμφέρουσαν ὑμῖν (7.46). However, the speech breaks off (or ends?) before the resolution is presented. Given that the common conclusion of each point is that Philip's suggestion or interpretation is wrong and in fact devised against Athenian interests, one would expect the resolution to be along the lines of rejecting Philip's letter *in toto*.

Mitchell, therefore, fails to provide a good example of an extant speech that demonstrates her contention that deliberative speeches were often argued by giving concrete advice on various subjects. For this reason I can see little justification for her statement (205) that:

---

[566] Libanius (*Arg.D.* viii,618-20 F.), resting upon the work of other scholars, judged this work on stylistic grounds to be un-Demosthenic and perhaps a speech of Hegesippus. Photius (*Bibl.* 491a M.), who appears to have read Libanius, was not so sure. He was all too familiar with other authors whose works varied stylistically. It is worth mentioning that Dionysius of Halicarnassus (late first century BC) did not suspect the work of being spurious despite the fact that he recognised the different style (cf. *Dem.* 13).

"What many scholars have termed the "loosely connected string of topics" which we find in 1 Corinthians is no more loosely connected than other deliberative arguments which enter into complicated and multi-dimensional life situations which require advice."

The above is, perhaps, the most fundamental objection to the thesis as a whole.[567] Nevertheless, the details of her thesis also deserves some further comment.

In chapter three she attempts to relate all of Paul's various treatments of different issues to the central concept of concord in order to demonstrate that they function in support of the supposed proposition in 1.10. There is to some degree validity in this. It would seem that the issue of division in the church was a central line undergirding the development of Paul's thought in this letter. Such an hypothesis, at any rate, would seem to make sense of the fact that Paul chose to begin the letter (1 - 4) by dealing with the problem of divisions, and that the problem surfaces again in the letter from time to time (cf. 11.18ff; 12). But Mitchell's analysis does not address a central problem. Notwithstanding the fact that Paul gives extended ethical advice in regard to solving the particular problems (see comments above), he hardly ever relates these solutions to the supposed overarching problem of factionalism itself. A typical speech on concord would suggest that these particular problems are symptoms of lack of concord, or at least attempt to specifically relate them to the issue of concord in some way. Paul hardly does this at all throughout the entire letter.[568]

Mitchell is thus not always convincing in her attempt to relate the topics in Paul's letter to a central theme of concord. On pp.121ff, for example, she correctly shows that marriage, even for the ancients, was considered a vital component of the larger community group. Good marriages contribute to the concord of the political body and thus orators not infrequently used the concept of a good marriage as *examples* of how the larger community group should function. The problem is that Paul does not make any of these connections in his letter, neither does he use marriage as an example. Rather, he treats it as a topic deserving ethical regulation in and of itself. Chapter seven flows out of the condemnation of πορνεία at the end of chapter six. Is sexual union legitimate

---

[567] Already in 1896 C. F. G. Heinrici (1896, *Brief*, 31-32) had remarked: "Die verschiedenartigen Gegenstände, die Paulus zu erörtern hatte, sind nicht mit rhetorischer Kunst unter einander in Verbindung gebracht, sondern eine Frage wird nach der andern abgehandelt, wie das einem Geschäftsbriefe, der den persönlichen Verkehr zu ersetzen bestimmt ist und eine Reihe von persönlichen und sachlichen Fragen erledigen will, angemessen erscheint."

[568] Note that 11.2-16, for example, is an issue that Paul *resolves* by his own regulation, as elsewhere. Paul effectively says: "Don't be contentious, this is how it is!" cf. 14.37-38. Such a statement hardly belongs in a speech on concord. Mitchell's research on this point shows up a general weakness, (150f) namely, that she is too busy showing that particular terminology is very well at home in political contexts of division and concord, whilst she ignores the more specific context of the use of the words in Paul.

at all if we are temples of the Holy Spirit? Paul seems to have deliberately chosen this point in his argument to address something the Corinthians had written him about. Of course the undercurrent of divisions in Corinth is to be detected, and Mitchell rightly points to 7.15b (123). But the fact remains that *no* conclusions are drawn with respect to the basic issue of community concord. The supposed proposition (1.10) hardly plays a role. There is, perhaps, more point to what she says on p.125, namely, that "there is real advice here on specific concerns which divide the church community" that played a role in the division of the congregation into parties (so much is certainly implied by 8.1). But do speeches on concord do this? Even if *Paul* is doing this, he still doesn't identify the fact.[569]

As a final example, Mitchell's view that chapter fifteen is written as an extra argument against factionalism is very weak. She maintains that Paul "appeals to the resurrected life to minimize the importance of the present striving to supremacy within the community" (175). It is an "appeal to future life to urge concord in the present" (176). But unlike Aristid. *Or.* 23.75 (and the other passages she cites) Paul simply does not make the connection to factionalism or concord. Instead, Paul's own paraenetic conclusion is found in v.58, namely, that in view of the resurrection the Corinthians should be motivated to stand firm and abound in the work of the Lord, knowing that it is not in vain.[570] Had Paul written the chapter to deliberately furnish another argument against factionalism, then it is difficult to conceive that this application is not made in place of what he says in v.58.[571] It is clear from this chapter that for Paul the matter is, of itself, of the essence of faith. Mitchell does, however, add that "the major factional element in 1 *Ep.Cor.* 15 is that here Paul must respond to different views on the resurrection which various groups within the church hold" (176). This much is true, but we are still left with the fact that Paul does not place the emphasis here.

---

[569]   One is not always sure that Mitchell's emphasis is correct when she attempts to relate nearly all of Paul's argumentation to the central problem of concord. For example, she stresses (142) "one bread, one body" (1 *Ep.Cor.* 10), saying, "He urges the Corinthians to be united because their cultic participation in the same rites stresses their fundamental κοινωνία with the same deity and thus with one another as co-worshippers of that deity." Yet Paul's point is more that because they are unified with Christ in the sacramental meal, they cannot partake of the table of demons. I am not saying that Mitchell's point is not valid, but it is not the emphasis of the text.

[570]   Mitchell's comment that Paul turns here once again to the building metaphor which "is his positive counterpart to factionalism throughout the letter" (177), does not alter the situation.

[571]   Mitchell's treatment of v.58 as the epilogue of the speech as a whole seems to me unlikely in view of Paul's use of the περὶ δέ formula in 16.1. Although it is clear that Paul is wrapping up extra matters in chapter 16, nevertheless, there is no indication of a sharp break between 15.58 and 16.1. This is also an argument that weakens the common suggestion that the theme of resurrection is treated in chapter fifteen as the climax of the letter.

We may summarise the problem in this part of the thesis as follows: Her main purpose in chapter three of her book is to show that "the content of 1 *Ep.Cor.* is a series of arguments ultimately based in the subject of factionalism and concord, political entities appropriately treated by deliberative rhetoric" (65). She does not deny "that many other actual subjects are treated," but wants to show "how Paul's treatment of each of these subjects is rooted *by him* [italics hers] in the overriding concern for concord" (65n). Mitchell does show that Paul's series of arguments uses terminology that was often applied to situations of factionalism in the Graeco-Roman world. What she, however, does *not* show is that Paul's *arguments* themselves are deliberately directed to the goal of concord, or in her words, "rooted" by Paul in concord. To argue that certain terminology may be used (or even often is used) within a particular context or serving a particular goal is not enough to prove that Paul uses that terminology for that goal. Mitchell omits to mention the fact that Paul rarely makes a specific connection to the problem of factionalism in chapters five to sixteen. But in the orators Aristides and Dio Chrysostom, who serve as her models *par excellence*, such explicit connections are *always* made amidst their arguments.

> Mitchell's use of rhetorical theory (which is after all the focus of this book) is in places rather disappointing. It is clear that she has not really always properly understood the theoreticians or their relationship to rhetorical practice.
>
> On pp.198-99, for example, she argues that we should follow Aristotle's partition for deliberative speeches (namely, proposition and proof) without going into the Greek and Latin handbooks which distinguish between *propositio* and *divisio* etc.. According to Mitchell, "Aristotle's simplified description well fits the extant deliberative texts." Her reliance on Aristotle is probably responsible for the comment that "a statement of the course of action that is recommended to the audience is always required" (198-99). She is referring to a πρόθεσις.
>
> The problem I have with this is that the very seven speeches that serve her as the closest models for 1 *Ep.Cor.* (p.62 note 200) show that the situation is much more complex. Dio's 34th oration uses a *divisio*; 38 uses a *propositio* and *divisio*; 40 and 41 have neither; 42 has only a *propositio*. Aristid. *Or.* 23 has a *propositio*, 24 does not. Of course where neither *propositio* or *divisio* are present, the topic of discourse is either implied in the προοίμιον or at least in the whole context of the speech itself. But this is enough to show that Aristotle's approach does not do justice to the complexity of rhetorical practice.
>
> Note that Aristotle never really defines his πρόθεσις in any great detail; it just announces the subject matter. Perhaps this could be considered a generic term for *propositio* and *divisio*, etc., but I rather think that Aristotle means to say that προοίμια, whatever they contain, end up by stating what the speech is about, i.e., they encompass the πρόθεσις. And this is often true in practice, cf. [Arist.] *Rh.Al.* 29.2 who discusses the matter of the πρόθεσις within the section on προοίμια.
>
> On pp.200ff Mitchell confuses the nature of a διήγησις. She correctly notes that it may "set the stage for the situation which calls forth the advice," but then adds that it sometimes corrects mistaken impressions. She refers to D.Chr. 40.8-19 and 41.1-6. These passages, however, are not *narrative*, but rather a normal part of the προοίμιον, i.e., the removal of possible ill-feeling toward the speaker.

On p.86 Mitchell (like so many others as we have seen) mistakes προσωποποιΐα for "impersonation" and views 1 *Ep.Cor.* 1.12 as an example of this.[572]
These examples are perhaps evidence of the fact that whilst Mitchell has paid good attention to rhetorical practice and terminology, she has not paid adequate attention to the study of rhetorical theory.

Mitchell's general approach to 1 *Ep.Cor.* has recently been adopted (with minor modifications) by B. Witherington (1995, *Conflict*). Witherington accepts that the letter is "a lengthy discourse on concord" (75) and provides a similar analysis of the *partes orationis*. He also believes that the letter presents two important argumentative τόποι of deliberative rhetoric, namely, expediency and honour. In these respects the criticism already made of Mitchell's thesis, applies equally to Witherington.

Witherington, however, although following Mitchell in many respects, unfortunately rejects her stricture against applying the *partes orationis* to a portion of a letter (47n), e.g., for 1 *Ep.Cor.* 15 (291-92). He defends this application by stating that a letter could deal with a variety of subjects and a variety of argumentation. He is correct on that point, but that is still no valid argument for finding mini-speeches amidst a longer letter. We are confronted with a methodology estranged from practical acquaintance with contemporary orations.

1.3 Conclusion

Our review of the work of Mitchell has shown us that, unlike Paul's letters to the Galatians and Romans, the body of the first letter to the Corinthians cannot be analysed in terms of sustained rhetorical argumentation. It therefore bears little resemblance to a rhetorical speech. We must conclude that comprehensive rhetorical analysis of the argumentation of this letter is not feasible. It is, of course, possible to comment upon style, and also (in a restricted way) upon the argumentation of select portions of the letter (though without falling into the trap of interpreting them as mini-speeches), yet due to both the disjointed nature of such an endeavour and the limited scope of the application of rhetorical theory here we have foregone a detailed rhetorical analysis of 1 *Ep.Cor.*.

---

[572] This misinterpretation seems to arise from H. E. Butler's misleading translation in the *Loeb* edition of Quint. *Inst.* 9.2.30.

2 Paul's Outlook on Rhetoric: 1 *Ep.Cor.* 1 - 4

Although we have determined that the first letter to the Corinthians does not lend itself to rhetorical analysis in terms of sustained argument, there is still one aspect of this letter that deserves consideration. That is, the question as to whether Paul explicitly rejects rhetorical methodology in 1 *Ep.Cor.* 1 - 4. Amidst the recent upsurge in rhetorical analysis of Paul's letters, several studies have paid particular attention to this problem. The main concern is what Paul means when he characterises his preaching as:

οὐκ ἐν σοφίᾳ λόγου, ἵνα μὴ κενωθῇ ὁ σταυρὸς τοῦ Χριστοῦ (1.17)
οὐκ ἐν πειθοῖ[ς] σοφίας [λόγοις] ἀλλ᾽ ἐν ἀποδείξει πνεύματος καὶ δυνάμεως, ἵνα ἡ πίστις ὑμῶν
  μὴ ᾖ ἐν σοφίᾳ ἀνθρώπων ἀλλ᾽ ἐν δυνάμει θεοῦ (2.4-5)
οὐκ ἐν διδακτοῖς ἀνθρωπίνης σοφίας λόγοις ἀλλ᾽ ἐν διδακτοῖς πνεύματος (2.13)

Despite the general trend in recent scholarship to steer away from the more traditional interpretation of these passages which understood them in terms of a rejection of rhetoric, several recent studies have again sought to defend a rhetorical background.

M. Bünker's dissertation (1983, *Briefformular*), discussed above, deals with this question in a rather interesting way. He views 1 *Ep.Cor.* 2.1-5 as Paul's programmatic approach to rhetoric. Paul is not after bare persuasion (πειθὼ σοφίας) but a "Rede als Prozeß der Meinungsbildung und Überzeugung durch Beweise und Argumente" (49, cf. 38-39). This is Bünker's interpretation of ἀπόδειξις πνεύματος καὶ δυνάμεως. He regards the term ἀπόδειξις as used in a technical rhetorical sense, and thus it forms for him a proof of Paul's vision with respect to rhetoric (by no means totally negative). However, Bünker does not clarify how he interprets the genitives following.[573]

Certainly ἀπόδειξις is often used in a rhetorical sense in Greek literature, and given the use of πειθοῖ[ς] σοφίας [λόγοις] in the context, a rhetorical sense may be correct here. It ought to be noted, however, that there are at least two common nuances in this sense, "argument(ation)" which is Bünker's choice, and "proof." It should also

---

[573]   It should be noted that this interpretation is fairly common, cf. the influential commentaries of J. B. Lightfoot (18??, *Notes*, 173) and A. Robertson/ A. Plummer (1911, *Commentary*, 33-34). The genitive in this interpretation is usually (rather awkwardly) explained as a genitive of source or quality.
   It is unclear to me precisely what BAGD intends by the gloss "proof consisting in possession of the Spirit and power" (*ad verbum*) but they seem to want to see a parallel with Ph. *Vit.Mos.* 1.95 ἀπόδειξις διὰ σημείων καὶ τεράτων (as opposed to διὰ λόγων). Yet it is significant that Philo uses the preposition διά. Further, *none* of the citations given in BAGD include an example followed by a simple genitive. It is also difficult for me to understand why they state that this noun occurs "especially" in reference to the intervention of a divinity.

be noted that ἀπόδειξις in this rhetorical sense is normally followed by a genitive of the matter which is argued for (LSJ *s.v.* I.3). Thus ἀπόδειξις τινος = "proof of something" or "argument in proof of something."[574] Thus the most obvious way of taking the genitives would be objective, namely, a proof of (the) Spirit and power.[575] This would then be an indication of the pouring out of the Holy Spirit at the conversion of the Corinthians, most probably manifested by speaking in tongues (cf. *Act.Ap.* 10.44ff; 1 *Ep.Thess.* 1.5 and *Ep.Gal.* 3.2-5), and accompanied by miracles worked by Paul through the Holy Spirit (cf. *Ep.Rom.* 15.18-19; *Ep.Hebr.* 2.3-4; *Ev.Marc.* 16.20; *Act.Ap.* 4.29-30). Interpreted in this way, Paul may be giving the term ἀπόδειξις a twist by contrasting the persuasive power of words with the real tangible proof of the presence of the Holy Spirit. Thus, whatever Paul's actual approach towards rhetoric was, this passage cannot be viewed as a statement of his endorsement of argumentation by logical proof.

In this connection mention should be made of H. D. Betz' interesting article (1986) "The Problem of Rhetoric and Theology according to the Apostle Paul." With respect to the passage under discussion, Betz notes: "Here Paul clearly takes the side of the philosopher over against the orator, but his concerns are still different from those of the philosopher." The common complaint of philosophy against rhetoric was precisely the highlighting of mere persuasion versus the truth. But what distinguished Paul from the philosopher? Betz does not really tackle the problem of what Paul means by πνεῦμα καὶ δύναμις here. He does, however, state that Paul's terminology in the broader context is taken from the mystery religions ("it should be obvious to anyone who has read ancient literature connected with the mystery cults," 37). I am at this time unable to judge this remark, although I have my doubts. Yet is Paul really taking the side of the philosopher over against the orator here? The use of the noun σοφία makes this position rather difficult. Paul may be taking a combined swipe at both,[576] but we shall return to this question of Paul's use of σοφία below.

T. H. Lim (1987, "Words") noticed that this passage, if understood as a rejection of rhetoric, seems to pose an incongruity with the use of rhetorical devices by Paul.

---

[574] In addition to passages cited in LSJ, cf. J. *Ap.* 1.215; *AJ* 6.286; 14.218; 16.363; 17.106, 125; Ph. *Abr.* 61. The only exception in Josephus or Philo, is Ph. *Poster.C.* 167 λόγων ἀποδείξει "(by) argumentation using words." This last citation, if any, comes closest to the gloss supplied by BAGD (see footnote 573 above) yet they do not cite it.

[575] This is also the interpretation of the Greek church fathers, who, if they differed on their exact interpretation of πνεύμα, were agreed that δυνάμεις referred to miraculous activity, cf. Origen, Chrysostom, Theodoret, Theophylact as cited by H. A. W. Meyer, 1884, *Commentary*, 46.

[576] Cf. J. B. Lightfoot, 18??, *Notes*, 172.

Lim attempts to give what he calls a sociological interpretation of the text. He thus tries to understand the text against the background of the kind of preachers active in Corinth to whom Paul was opposed. These preachers he characterises (using the information contained in the second letter to the Corinthians) as men that took pay for their teaching as was common among the sophists of the second sophistic, and who also emphasised eloquence (for its own sake). Lim argues for a word-play on ἀπόδειξις in 1 *Ep.Cor.* 2.4, a technical term in rhetoric which Paul uses here *against* the art of rhetoric. He concludes that Paul is "refusing to adopt practices which are similar to those found among the Corinthian preachers. ... Paul is not rejecting rhetoric altogether, but that specific emphasis and practice of the Corinthian preachers to employ human wisdom of words in preaching" (147-48). In this way Lim claims to solve the apparent incongruity. Within the article itself there is, however, no explanation of what Paul actually means by ἀπόδειξις πνεύματος καὶ δυνάμεως.

Finally, we may briefly consider two published dissertations also devoted to this subject. Firstly, the work of S. M. Pogoloff who discusses Paul's relation to ancient rhetoric in *Logos and Sophia: The Rhetorical Situation of 1 Corinthians* (1992). Pogoloff's dissertation is an attempt to write a responsible yet imaginative descriptive narrative of the rhetorical situation of the first letter to the Corinthians. As such, the thrust of the book is not really related to rhetorical theory, although his analysis of the rhetorical milieu within which Paul worked and wrote, and his application of that to the particular (rhetorical) situation at Corinth (which provoked the letter and the manner in which it was written) is of interest. Pogoloff's interpretation of Paul's statements on rhetoric are thus intended to give support to the interesting, yet admittedly speculative, narrative forming the last few pages of the book. The opening chapters and his interpretation of certain texts where Paul appears to distance himself from rhetoric are, however, what concern us here.

Unlike others, Pogoloff strongly rejects the use of evidence from the period of the second sophistic. He takes as his starting point the admittedly difficult text of 1 *Ep.Cor.* 1.17 where Paul claims not to preach ἐν σοφίᾳ λόγου. What is meant here? Weiss had thought in terms of the arguments of philosophical wisdom dressed in rhetorical devices. Pogoloff believes that BAGD's gloss is essentially correct ("cleverness in speaking") and that Paul is in these chapters thinking about rhetoric and not philosophy at all. Misinterpretation of this fact is attributed by him to a disassociation of rhetoric from content as well as form. He spends a good portion of his dissertation detailing the revival of interest in rhetoric (both ancient and modern), and in showing how ancient rhetoric dealt with both form and content (which he describes in terms of style versus invention and argumentation). This is all ultimately argument to sustain his interpretation of these words in 1 *Ep.Cor.* 1.17. He correctly notes that the new movement in scholarship once again emphasises the aspect of invention and argumentation in rhetoric. He also regrets the confusion in much contemporary scholarship between ancient and modern rhetoric. He believes that both are necessary and does not therefore wish to restrict himself to ancient rhetoric alone, however he clearly sees the necessity of separating the two. Further, in terms of ancient rhetoric, Pogoloff speaks with praise of the work of Mitchell, at least in terms of her insistence that a study of rhetorical theory should be combined with contemporary practice.

In terms of his own description of the contemporary cultural world of the first century AD, Pogoloff disagrees that Paul is here rejecting some kind of mixed practice of philosophy and rhetoric (philosophy in rhetorical dress). He thus rejects the idea that Paul fails to distinguish between the two, or that the two were in his time often wedded as was *later* the case (according to Pogoloff) in the time of the second sophistic.[577] No, Paul is thinking of rhetoric, and rhetoric alone (defined in terms of both form and content). Pogoloff quotes with approval the words of D. L. Clark that "in the Greco-Roman schools education was almost exclusively education in rhetoric" (49).[578] Although he recognises that rhetorical "tertiary" education competed with philosophical schools, he characterises the latter as "a minority counter culture." The rivalry between

---

[577] Pogoloff admits the kind of incorporation of philosophy (among other things) in the thinking of men like Cicero and Quintilian, but he argues on the one hand that these are exceptional examples of highly qualified thinking men, and on the other hand that this is certainly not the same thing as Philostratus (*VS*) describes when he shows how the two professions were often combined in the period of the second sophistic. Pogoloff's arguments are a little exaggerated at this point, especially concerning the so-called second sophistic. He states that the second sophistic is a phenomenon dated a century later than Paul (65) and that therefore the kind of philosopher-rhetors Philostratus describes do not belong to this period. Philostratus begins his work on famous "sophists" by briefly discussing eight philosophers whom he also considers sophists because of their rhetorical renown. These must be the "philosopher-rhetors" to which Pogoloff refers. Far from being a second century AD phenomenon, the men Philostratus discusses are arranged in chronological order and date from the fourth century BC (Eudoxus of Cnidus) through to the late first century AD and just the beginning of the second century AD (Dio Chrysostom and Favorinus)! Philostratus' lengthy discussion of sophists proper is indeed concentrated upon famous rhetors from the second century AD, but several important names from the first century AD are also presented (e.g., Isaeus the Syrian, Nicetes of Smyrna, Scopelian). This is surely also what we would expect, given what we know of the "Asianist"/ Atticist controversy which continued in the first century AD. Pogoloff's statement that "we have no evidence that sophists who styled themselves as philosophers were present in Corinth" also needs to be tempered by Ps.-Dio Chrysostom 37 (the Corinthian speech) generally attributed to Favorinus (its relevance as background to 1 *Ep.Cor.* was already pointed out by E. Norden, 1898, *Kunstprosa*, 493n).

[578] *Rhetoric in Graeco-Roman Education* (New York: Columbia University, 1957) 65.

the two was won by rhetoric. In a reasonably succinct paragraph, Pogoloff outlines his view of the relationship between the two disciplines:

> The two approaches to education and life deeply affected each other, as outlined above. Yet never did philosophy become rhetoric or vice-versa, for their approaches were radically different. Rhetoric could so easily dominate the culture because it simply reflected the culture back to itself: the values which are found to be persuasive (including the value placed upon the mastery of language) were simply codified and mastered. Philosophy, on the other hand, always aimed to evaluate cultural norms by its own lights before accepting or rejecting them. Philosophers taught and even developed rhetorical theory, but only as a subject to scrutinize and employ for the sake of philosophical truth. (57)

As we have seen in our own brief synopsis of the clash between philosophy and rhetoric,[579] Pogoloff's insistence on holding the two disciplines separate is correct, as also his emphasis on the prevailing dominance of rhetoric. That the two disciplines were separate, however, does not mean that there were no rhetorical philosophers, in the sense of philosophers renowned for their ability in speech.[580]

Pogoloff provides a reasonably clear picture of the first century AD setting, though probably due to the confines of his dissertation this picture is built largely upon secondary sources. The conclusion of this portion of the dissertation is that "we must allow that he [*sc.* Paul in 1 *Ep.Cor.* 1.17] meant a cultured rhetor who could speak on any subject."

Pogoloff makes a fair case for the fact that σοφία and σοφός *could* refer to .rhetoric, explaining the scarcity of this word group in the rhetorical theorists because of the polemics against philosophy. But he really only cites one concrete use of this word group in a definite rhetorical context, namely, Isoc. 15.199-200.[581] He then sets out to show that rhetoric had a high social value attached to it. It was the pasttime and occupation not of slaves but of the aristocracy. The wisdom of rhetoric tended to support traditional aristocratic values.

He now sets out to solve the apparent paradox presented by 1 *Ep.Cor.* 1.17 and Paul's own alleged use of rhetoric. He rejects the proposal of Lim, and argues that Paul is not rejecting rhetoric *per se*, but the social value attached to it. Paul's rhetoric of the

---

[579] Chapter two, § 2.5.

[580] See also G. R. Stanton, 1973, "Sophists."

[581] That σοφία can be used of the art of rhetoric is clear not only from its general meaning of cleverness or skill, and its not uncommon collocation with τέχνη, but is also clear from a passage like Pl. *R.* 365d referring to πειθοῦς διδάσκαλοι σοφίαν δημηγορικήν τε καὶ δικανικὴν διδόντες. Mention should also be made of R. A. Horsley's article (1977, "Wisdom") which makes the same point with reference to wisdom literature and especially the works of Philo.

cross is a persuasion "about what is ordinarily unfit for contemplation," (120) namely, a crucified champion. Thus he is able to say with respect to 1.17 that: "To the Corinthians, Paul's preaching may have been persuasive, and thus "wise," but he reminds them that *he had used this speech* to draw the Corinthians into a world in which the "champion" is crucified." [italics mine, R.D.A.] (119)

In all this he makes much of a quotation from Sextus Empiricus, a Stoic philosopher from *c.* AD 200. Sextus (*M.* 2.43) asserts that some people thought that there were two kinds of rhetoric, the one refined and engaged in among wise men, the other used by lesser people. According to such people, typical attacks on rhetoric only apply to the kind of rhetoric used by lesser people.[582] Pogoloff puts this in his own words on p.125 by saying that Sextus reports "that rhetoric is often approved when it is refined and used by the wise, but criticized when used by less refined people." Several comments are, however, in order. First, Sextus does not say that this is "often" the case. Second, Sextus does not say that rhetoric was criticised when used by less refined people, but that lesser people used a different *kind* of rhetoric against which criticism arose. Third, Sextus does not say that such a division in terms of rhetoric existed, but only that some people make up such a distinction in order to avoid wholesale criticism against the art (τέχνη) of rhetoric. Fourth, there is the question as to which people in fact make this distinction. Sextus was not an original thinker, but one who merely summarised what others had already written. In the immediate context he is heavily dependent upon Plato's *Gorgias*. The idea (articulated just before our passage) that rhetoric would not be an art if it is not beneficial is taken from Socrates (*Grg.* 464bff), and the example of the pancratiast immediately following the passage is taken from Gorgias (*Grg.* 456d). I am, however, not able to say where Sextus derived the idea of a twofold art of rhetoric.

In general, Pogoloff's emphasis that Paul is only concerned with the social status of rhetoric, and not rhetoric (or some characterisation thereof) *per se* is not persuasive.

He seeks to bolster this interpretation (that Paul is only rejecting cultured rhetoric) by his exegesis of 1 *Ep.Cor.* 2.1-4. He is willing to accept BAGD's translation of 2.1 "I have not come as a superior person in speech or (human) wisdom," but

---

582   Sextus Empiricus continues, having just described the arguments against rhetoric made by the Platonists: τοσαῦτα μὲν οὖν καὶ τοῖς Ἀκαδημαϊκοῖς ἐν καταδρομῆς μέρει λέγεται περὶ ῥητορικῆς ὥστε εἰ μήτε τῷ ἔχοντι μήτε τοῖς πέλας ἐστὶν ὠφέλιμος, οὐκ ἂν εἴη τέχνη. ἀλλὰ πρὸς ταῦτα ἀπολογούμενοι τινὲς μέν φασιν ὅτι διττῆς οὔσης ῥητορικῆς, τῆς μὲν ἀστείας καὶ ἐν σοφοῖς τῆς δὲ ἐν μέσοις ἀνθρώποις, τὴν κατηγορίαν γεγονέναι οὐ τῆς ἀστείας ἀλλὰ τῆς τῶν μοχθηρῶν. τινὲς δὲ καὶ ὑποδείγμασι χρῶνται· There follows the example of the pancratiast who hits his father, which shows not that ἡ παγκρατιαστικὴ τέχνη is bad, but only that the person concerned had bad morals.

unfortunately misinterprets the point. He sees this as evidence that Paul is dealing not only with rhetoric but with "the superior social status of those who master it" (132, cf. 134). Yet the point of the text (and of BAGD's proposed translation) is that Paul is not superior (or a superior person) *in terms of speech or wisdom*, not that he does not have a superior social status *per se*. The problem is only worsened by his suggested alternative translation "when I came, I did not preach with the speech or wisdom of superiority [or excess]." Pogoloff defends this by arguing that κατά with the accusative may substitute for a genitive. This is true, but such a use of κατά is normally found in close connection with another noun. Furthermore, such a translation makes no sense here, for the genitives λόγου and σοφίας are then not really dependent on anything. To construe them with καταγγέλλω as Pogoloff apparently wishes is pretty far fetched. His translation would imply something like: [ἐν] τῷ καθ᾽ ὑπεροχὴν λόγῳ ἢ τῇ σοφίᾳ.583

Despite the above criticism, he does, however, show quite clearly that whilst ἀπόδειξις could be considered a term well at home in rhetoric, it was also not infrequently used over against rhetorical persuasion (137-40, cf. 133, 266). This must form a corrective to Lim's suggested word play upon ἀπόδειξις.

The second dissertation concerned with the interpretation of 1 *Ep.Cor.* 1 - 4 against the background of rhetoric is that of D. Litfin, *St Paul's Theology of Proclamation* (1994). Litfin seeks to understand Paul's statements as a rejection of rhetoric in favour of a straightforward placarding of the message of the cross of Christ. Like Pogoloff, he seeks to explain Paul's use of σοφία/ σοφός in terms of rhetoric. His description of rhetoric is, however, significantly different from Pogoloff. Litfin traces rhetoric from fifth century Athens onwards and seeks to show that by the first century AD rhetoric and philosophy were more or less synthesized. This is his most important argument to explain Paul's use of σοφία in connection with λόγος, understood as (philosophical) rhetoric. However, it is precisely on this point that Litfin's argumentation fails. Pogoloff (whose work was probably not available to him when writing) quite correctly stressed the continued separation of rhetoric and philosophy. Yet Litfin's analysis deserves some comment due to its more detailed nature.

His analysis of rhetoric in the first centuries BC and AD confines itself to Cicero and Quintilian. In line with his interest in σοφία, he highlights Cicero's (attempted) synthesis of philosophy and rhetoric and shows that Quintilian was also influenced by

---

583 It should be noted that Pogoloff does not always use rhetorical technical terms in the exact senses of the authorities he quotes, e.g., παρονομασία and ὁμοιόπτωτον p.106. For ὁμοιόπτωτον Pogoloff, for example, cites *Rhet.Her.* 4.28 but uses the definition of Quint. *Inst.* 9.3.78-80.

this. However, whilst he quite correctly appeals to both Cicero and Quintilian as masters of their trade, producing treatises of a quality rarely surpassed in antiquity, he fails to ask the all important question as to whether *this kind* of rhetorical theory was predominant in the Greek world of the first century AD. Although we lack any Greek treatises from this period, I have shown above that the kind of philosophical rhetoric found in Cicero's late treatises (under the influence of Aristotle) was *not* prevalent in school rhetoric, nor even among philosophers themselves. As we have shown above, the philosophical schools were on the decline towards the end of the first century BC and apart from Philo of Larissa and, perhaps, to some extent (in their own idiosyncratic way) the Stoics, philosophers had little interest in rhetoric and tended to oppose it (*contra* Litfin).

Related to this is Litfin's unjustified conclusion on p.123 that Greek audiences in the first century AD must have found it difficult to distinguish philosophers from sophists. Just because the word σοφία was frequently used by sophists does not mean that they would naturally be confused with philosophers! The two disciplines were generally kept quite separate. Popular philosophers frequently distinguished themselves quite distinctly by their apparel and manner. Parents knew the difference between hiring a rhetorical tutor for their children and hiring a philosopher! The professions were quite distinct and still frequently antagonistic to each other. The idealistic synthesis of a Cicero never really caught on in the Greek world.[584]

Litfin interprets Paul's statements in 1 *Ep.Cor.* 1.17 and 2.4-5 against the background of the dynamic of rhetoric. He means by this, the rhetor's skillful use of his crafts in inventing, arranging and stylising arguments in order to suit the given aspects of his rhetorical situation.[585] If a rhetor could use his skills to sway the audience in this way, then he had won his audience. Everything depended on *his* skill. On Litfin's reading of 1 *Ep.Cor.* 1.17: "Paul feared that operating according to the rhetor's dynamic would hinder the working of the Gospel, effectively voiding the cross's own power to create belief" (192).

We have already seen that his strongest argument that Paul is referring to rhetoric in these passages cannot hold, namely, the idea that the rhetorical theory of this period

---

[584] In addition, I fail to see that Philostr. *VS* 479-84 shows that he "struggled with the distinction" between philosophers and sophists. Philostratus provides some essentially correct notations on the kind of practical philosophical sophistry of the late fifth and fourth centuries BC. His *Vitae* is quite neatly divided into a short section dealing with eloquent philosophers, and the much more lengthy section dealing with sophists. Litfin's citations from Epictetus are likewise not to the point.

[585] In this respect, despite the differing characterisations of rhetoric in the first century AD, Pogoloff and Litfin are quite close to each other.

was a synthesis of philosophy and rhetoric. This brings us back to the question of Paul's use of σοφία and σοφός in the first four chapters of his first letter to the Corinthians. As Pogoloff had noted, these terms *can* be used of rhetoric (even outside of Philostratus), nevertheless, their use in terms of rhetorical theory is *not* common. This fact suggests that the *context* should clearly indicate whether rhetorical theory is meant. Now whilst Paul does speak of πειθοῖ λόγοι in 1 *Ep.Cor.* 2.4, there are several other indications that rhetoric (which Paul significantly never specifically names) is not meant.

There is first of all the fact that Paul speaks of σοφία in terms of content. The σοφία of the world is contrasted with the σοφία of God.[586] The world's wisdom cannot tolerate the idea of a crucified saviour. That is not wisdom, but stupidity. The word σοφία, therefore, does not refer to eloquence, nor does it refer to rhetorical εὕρεσις or τάξις (in Pogoloff's scheme of rhetoric as content as well as form). Paul's words are in fact quite deliberately generalised (cf. 1 *Ep.Cor.* 2.6 and 2.13, σοφία τοῦ αἰῶνος τούτου, διδακτοὶ ἀνθρωπίνης σοφίας λόγοι) and Paul probably didn't have any specific institution or group in mind. At most he is thinking of what Greeks in general consider to be wise or sensible, as over against Jews (1 *Ep.Cor.* 1.22).

Further, as suggested above[587], the contrast in 1 *Ep.Cor.* 2.4 is most probably between persuasive words of wisdom and a demonstration of the Spirit and power in the sense of wonderous spiritual gifts attending Paul's preaching.[588]

One should also note that Litfin's argument is based on the assumption that Paul's characterisation of his preaching in these chapters is a *defence* against accusations primarily from the Apollos party. This point, however, is also disputable in my view.[589] Paul nowhere in these chapters specifically indicates that he is responding to criticism of himself. Rather, the *use* he makes of the characterisation of his preaching suggests that this assumption is incorrect. Attention needs to be paid to the argumentative flow. Paul's concern in these chapters is quite clearly the party strife present in Corinth. This is the problem he lays out in 1 *Ep.Cor.* 1.10-12 and it is this problem to which he returns in 3.4 and 4.6ff. Why then the intervening characterisation of Paul's preaching over against human wisdom? To answer this question we must look to the *exemplary use* Paul makes of it in 1 *Ep.Cor.* 3.1-4. Paul here *applies* what he has said

---

[586] I accept Litfin's argumentation against those who read an early form of Gnosticism into 1 *Ep.Cor.* 2.6ff. Paul does not intend to speak of one kind of teaching for novices, and another for the mature.

[587] See p.240.

[588] Thus not, as Litfin, between rhetoric as means of persuasion and the Holy Spirit working in the hearts of the audience.

[589] For an interpretation similar to mine, see B. Witherington (1995, *Conflict*, 98-99).

of his preaching to the Corinthian situation. He has characterised his ministry as spiritual, but he proceeds to rebuke the Corinthians as carnal, that is, thinking in terms of human wisdom. Of course Paul does not mean to suggest that they have denied the validity of the cross as Litfin rightly shows from the presuppositions of the rhetorical questions in 1.13 (181-82). But Paul does consider that their party division is evidence of carnal human wisdom and not of the Holy Spirit (whose presence the Corinthians seem to have made much of). Paul's characterisation of his preaching is therefore outlined in order to rebuke a problem present among the Corinthians in general, not a criticism made by one party against Paul himself. We may surmise that Paul considered the arguments between the various parties to be symptomatic of human wisdom, however we know *nothing* of what divided the various parties.

In conclusion, Paul's characterisation of his own preaching in 1 *Ep.Cor.* 1 - 4 should not be interpreted against the specific background of Graeco-Roman rhetorical theory. These chapters say virtually nothing concerning Paul's views on rhetorical theory and practice.

VII. GENERAL CONCLUSIONS

1 Paul and Rhetorical Theory

Having looked at three letters of Paul from the perspective of ancient rhetorical theory and having analysed large portions of two of them in its light, it is now incumbent upon us to ask the rather more difficult question as to whether Paul consciously worked with rhetorical theory (or some aspect thereof) in mind. In order to provide some perspective to this question we must briefly consider his upbringing.

I do not believe that much can be made of the question of Paul's upbringing.[590] It would seem rather unlikely that Paul enjoyed a formal rhetorical training. Even if *Act.Ap.* 22.3 is interpreted to allow for a grammatical education in Tarsus (a city well known for its high standard of education, both philosophical and rhetorical, cf. Str. 14.5.13-15),[591] Paul probably attended a strict Jewish school (cf. *Act.Ap.* 23.6; *Ep.Phil.* 3.5). Even then, *if* such a Jewish school maintained a typical Greek form of grammatical education,[592] Paul, *at the most*, will have become acquainted with certain *progymnasmata*.[593] His Pharisaical upbringing in Jerusalem under Gamaliel *may* also have had Greek influences. We do not know.[594] But even then it seems highly unlikely that Paul received any formal training in rhetorical theory (cf. 2 *Ep.Cor.* 11.6 cited below). Where Paul speaks of his upbringing, he stresses its strict Jewish/ Pharisaical character (cf. *Act.Ap.* 22.3; 23.6; 26.4-5; *Ep.Phil.* 3.5). We ought also to remember that at some point Paul learnt the *trade* of tent-making.

---

[590] On this whole matter see M. Hengel, 1991, "Paulus," 212-39.

[591] On Tarsus, see also M. Hengel, *op. cit.*, 180-82 note 11. The interpretation of *Act.Ap.* 22.3 concerns the question as to whether the clause παρὰ τοὺς πόδας Γαμαλιήλ goes with the foregoing or the following clause. W. C. van Unnik has argued strongly for the latter, although his view has not been unanimously accepted (*Tarsus or Jerusalem: The City of Paul's Youth* [transl. G. Ogg; London: Epworth, 1962, first publ. in Dutch 1952]; cf. T. Schmeller, 1987, *Paulus*, 85-86; M. Hengel, *op. cit.* 217).

[592] This may be suggested by the fact that Paul appears to have written and spoken a reasonable level of Greek fluently.

[593] Note, however, that there is no direct evidence that Greek grammar schools (as opposed to Roman) incorporated the *progymnasmata* into their curriculum (see above, chapter two, § 3.3).

[594] The talmudic tradition that Gamaliel had 1,000 students in his house of whom 500 were instructed in Greek wisdom is attributed by Str.-B. 2.637 to Gamaliel II. (*c.* AD 90).

This leads us further to Paul's own characterisation of his literary abilities. We have already seen that not much can be made of the data in 1 *Ep.Cor.* 1 - 4. However, 2 *Ep.Cor.* 10 - 11 provides some important information. At 2 *Ep.Cor.* 10.10 Paul notes that his opponents claimed of him that: αἱ ἐπιστολαὶ βαρεῖαι καὶ ἰσχυραί, ἡ δὲ παρουσία τοῦ σώματος ἀσθενὴς καὶ ὁ λόγος ἐξουθενημένος. The contrast is clearly between his written and spoken word. Of course these words could admit of a variety of interpretations. The words βαρεῖαι καὶ ἰσχυραί are hardly used as rhetorical technical terms here. Relevant to their interpretation is Paul's own characterisation of his approach to the Corinthians in 2 *Ep.Cor.* 10.1 (cf. v.11) where he states that he is humble when in their presence, but bold towards them when absent. The adjectives βαρεῖαι καὶ ἰσχυραί thus refer most naturally to a boldness of tone contrasted with the weakness of his bodily presence. The weakness of his bodily presence, then, has reference to a humble, non-authoritative physical presence. The same consideration *may* apply to his "contemptible speech," although more may have been meant. At 2 *Ep.Cor.* 11.6 Paul further characterises himself as an ἰδιώτης τῷ λόγῳ, ἀλλ᾽ οὐ τῇ γνώσει.[595] Paul thus suggests that he had no formal training in public speaking. He does not, however, indicate which aspects of his speech *he* may have considered would have made this obvious. It may just have been his foreign accent (cf. Luc. *Nav.* 2), but more probably also the problem of grammatical slips (which must also have been obvious in his spoken language) and a general lack of literary sophistication (e.g., in terms of carefully crafted hypotactic, especially periodic, sentence construction). After all, Greek was *very possibly* a second language to Paul.

Whilst it seems clear that Paul not infrequently used someone to write down his letters for him (cf. *Ep.Rom.* 16.22; 1 *Ep.Cor.* 16.21; *Ep.Gal.* 6.11; etc.), the rough paratactic style and occasional grammatical anomalies do not suggest a professional secretary, at least they do not suggest the literary influence of such a secretary. Such passages as *Ep.Gal.* 2.4-6 suggest rather hasty dictation.[596] Of course, we cannot know for sure exactly how Paul used a secretary and the possibility that such a person may have influenced the style of one or more of Paul's letters must remain open.[597]

---

[595] Such a statement denigrating one's abilities in speaking was, of course, a rhetorical τόπος often associated with the προοίμιον (introduction of a speech), cf., for example, Cic. *Part.* 22; Quint. *Inst.* 4.1.8-9; Hermog. *Id.* 2.6 (p.346,18-20 R.). However, the low niveau of Paul's own language, and the criticism of it by his opponents (noted above), suggests that the statement should be taken seriously and not as rhetorical understatement.

[596] For the various methods of using a secretary in the ancient world, see E. R. Richards, 1991, *Secretary*.

[597] Such a possibility ought not to be overlooked in the question concerning the genuineness of the letters to the Ephesians and Colossians.

We turn now, albeit very briefly, to the evidence of the early church. It has not been the purpose of this book to examine the views of the church fathers on Paul's use of rhetorical theory in any dedicated way. Such a study remains an interesting desideratum. Many of these fathers were well trained in rhetorical theory and they would appear to have been in a much better situation to judge this question than we are today. We have already seen that here and there scholars have begun to pay attention to the church fathers on this point, and there is still much interesting work to be done. Long ago E. Norden provided a good summary of the church fathers' views on Paul's style generally,[598] and in the first section of this book we looked briefly at book four of Augustine's *de Doctrina Christiana* - the only more or less systematic account of rhetoric in the Bible extant from the early church. From these sources we can readily see that the church fathers generally viewed Paul's word choice and syntax as being on an unsophisticated level. Paul's self-characterisation in 2 *Ep.Cor.* 11.6 as an ἰδιώτης τῷ λόγῳ is frequently quoted. Norden also provides evidence that the church fathers struggled with many obscurities in Paul's letters. The absence of the important rhetorical virtue of σαφήνεια (clarity) was also apparent to them. However, we ought also to realise that the church fathers were distinctly apologetic when it came to speaking of the inspired Scriptures (cf. our discussion of Augustine). Such obscurity, whilst admitted, was frequently attributed to deliberate and pious motives (e.g., for the exercise of our minds, to keep pagans from learning the holy mysteries, etc.). Such reasoning, however, is not very convincing.

How then are we to judge Paul's style and relation to rhetorical theory? Several considerations seem to support the notion that Paul had no real contact with rhetorical theory as such.

Firstly, we have seen that rhetorical genres cannot properly be applied to the letters examined in this book.[599] In our conclusion to chapter two we saw that each rhetorical genre is coupled with distinct τόποι of argumentation. None of the letters examined show the use of such τόποι. Furthermore, none of these letters fit into a rhetorical scheme of *partes orationis*. Even if we exclude Paul's paraenetic sections from the picture, his writing does not give evidence of these divisions of a speech. Paul

---

[598]   1898, *Kunstprosa*, 501-506.
[599]   It should be noted that, despite the fact that only three letters of Paul have been discussed in this investigation, I have deliberately chosen three letters wherein one may have most expected a relationship to rhetorical theory.

never provides a *partitio* outlining his argumentation and hardly ever stops to direct his readers to the argumentative structure of his discourse (*Ep.Rom.* 3.9 being a noteworthy exception). The fact that we have been able to make some remarks drawn from the rhetorical theory connected with the *partes orationis* has more to do with the fact that most literary productions have a beginning, middle and an end, than that Paul was thinking in terms of a specifically rhetorical προοίμιον, πίστεις and ἐπίλογος.

Secondly, in terms of argumentation we may make some similar observations. It is not surprising that Paul uses παραδείγματα in his argumentation. After all, the use of examples is common to all literate societies. We have noted how Paul's παραδείγματα (examples) sometimes function differently than those in rhetorical theory. Of course, the largest difference is in Paul's use of Scripture citations, and the presumption of his own teaching authority. Much of Paul's "argumentation" is not defended. It is stated. In this respect we have more than once noted that Paul's discussions often come closer to "teaching" than "argumentation." Needless to say, we have discovered no evidence of carefully constructed ἐπιχειρήματα (rhetorical syllogisms). On the contrary, Paul's "argumentation" is frequently quite obscure, raising more questions than it supplies answers. It is not surprising that a scholar of the stature of E. Norden characterised Paul as a writer whom he found very difficult to understand.[600] Norden gave two reasons: i) that Paul's manner of argumentation is "fremdartig," and ii) that, as a whole, his style is "unhellenisch."

This leads us, in the third place, to the question of Paul's style. It is not my purpose to repeat here all the various stylistic observations made above on Paul's letters to the Romans and Galatians. A few points will suffice. In both the letters to the Galatians and to the Romans we have noticed a certain obscurity. We saw above that this obscurity did not escape the church fathers either. In discussing the style of the letters to the Romans and Galatians we noted that this obscurity transgresses one of the important virtues of style according to rhetorical theory, σαφήνεια.[601]

We have also seen that Paul's language is characterised by a paratactic style strongly influenced by the Semitic Greek of the Septuagint. It is at least possible, if not indeed very probable, that Paul's paratactic (as opposed to periodic or even certain forms of hypotactic) style had to do with the kind of Greek spoken by Jews generally.

---

[600] 1898, *Kunstprosa*, 499.
[601] It should be borne in mind that whilst Paul's style may, I believe, be characterised as obscure, this does not mean that the main thrust of what he has to say is not clear. Our analysis of the two letters in chapters four and five of this book shows that the essential points Paul wishes to make can be discerned. We are, of course, aided by the ability to compare Paul's letters with each other.

Their native Semitic language was paratactic by nature. Their basic religious textbook (the Old Testament), even in Greek translation, preserves this characteristic. It would be no wonder that periodising Greek or the use of subordinate participial constructions would not come naturally. Much of the apocrypha and pseudepigrapha also demonstrate this stylistic trait.[602]

Recently, J. Fairweather has provided a good sympathetic discussion of Paul's style.[603] She correctly notes how his style is not Atticising, nor γραφική (suited to writing), but rather ἀγωνιστική (suited to debate).[604] She also appropriately notes how Paul can make rather artful use of various rhetorical figures. The contrasts in Paul's style (between artful use of figures, and his "quasi-conversational approach") she attributes to the virtue of being able to "range through all the registers of style." Cic. *Orat.* 20-22; 56; 69f are referenced.[605] I am inclined to think that this pays Paul too much of a compliment. His style can range further, descending into plain solecism. Fairweather then asks why Paul restricted himself to the level of *koine* in which he writes (a level which earned him criticism by at least some in Corinth). She tenders a list of various possibilities, but it seems to me that the question may be phrased in the wrong way. Fairweather assumes that Paul had the ability to write better Greek but *chose* not to. This, to my mind, is not proven. The answer could equally be in the direction that Paul simply did his best to write reasonable Greek, but did not have the ability to write in a complex periodic style, nor possessed the vocabulary of the average philosopher or rhetorician. Much of his vocabulary and syntax (as Fairweather properly admits) must have been formed by the Septuagint, quite a contrast to Philo who did not let his use of the Septuagint affect his Greek prose. It seems to me (but this can only remain conjecture) that Paul strove to write what in his day was considered good Greek (though wishing to avoid sophistic excess). That he did not always succeed with his Greek is natural. He was well aware of his shortcomings (ἰδιώτης ἐν λόγῳ), being a man for whom Greek was probably a second language (even if learnt from an early age).[606] Yet

---

[602] I am, of course, not saying that *all* Jews spoke this kind of Greek. Well educated Jews such as Philo expressed themselves in a very sophisticated kind of Greek indeed.

[603] 1994, "Epistle," 229-36.

[604] She takes this point from a letter of D. A. Russell, *op. cit.*, 231-32. The terminology comes from Arist. *Rh.* 3.12.1ff.

[605] *Op. cit.*, 233.

[606] Anyone familiar with speakers of English as a second language will readily be able to think of parallel examples. Many Dutchmen are able to speak a very sophisticated level of English (being confronted with the language from early childhood, both at school, and at home via the television). Yet one is then often all the more jarred by the occasional grammatical or lexical slip in what for a native speaker is a very simple matter. I have to admit that even my own English suffers (I am a native speaker) by living in a Dutch environment and communicating in that language on a daily basis.

he also managed at times some rather striking passages (e.g., the last part of *Ep.Rom.* 8), and evidently could not resist a good word-play when one struck him (or did someone suggest them to him?).

Paul's penchant for word-play and stylised figures in general is remarkable, the more so for the fact that such playful figures tend to occur in serious emotional contexts. Of course it is not essential to have read rhetorical treatises on figures in order to be able to employ them. The use of tropes and figures is, once again, common to all literate societies.[607] In addition, as we have noted above in our comments on the style of the letters to the Romans and Galatians, the kind of use Paul makes of such figures was generally opposed by rhetorical theory, but it does reflect the popular style of the time (see the endnote to the select glossary). This quirk of style has not infrequently led scholars to compare Paul's style with "Asianism." E. Norden cautiously made such a comparison.[608] T. S. Duncan made the connection much more firmly.[609] But Fairweather, whilst noting certain affinities to Asianism, primarily in Paul's use of figures, also quite rightly points out that his syntax and word-choice are not at all similar to those authors most frequently categorised as Asianists.[610] We are, I think, better off viewing Paul's use of figures as a stylistic phenomenon common in the popular oratory of his day (whether of display or in the law courts). His own use of figures does not necessarily make him a contender for a particular stylistic "school."

One final consideration is pertinent when considering the relationship of Paul to rhetorical theory, namely, his possible use of technical rhetorical terms. It is primarily on this basis that Fairweather concludes that Paul was certainly not ignorant of "the classical art of rhetoric."[611] Fairweather isolates three terms used by Paul: ἀλληγορούμενα (*Ep.Gal.* 4.15); μακαρισμός (*Ep.Rom.* 4.6, 9) and μετασχηματίζω (1 *Ep.Cor.* 4.6). As argued above, Paul's use of the term μετασχηματίζω in the first letter to the Corinthians is not in the technical sense of the rhetorical treatises.[612] Although the term ἀλληγορέω in Galatians is used in a technical sense, we have shown

---

[607] Not even Paul's use of what may be considered more advanced figures such as προσωποποιία require this. It should be observed that in all the instances tentatively labelled προσωποποιία, Paul not once shows awareness that he is deliberately using such a figure. This is in stark contrast to the usage found in both philosophers and orators (see select glossary *s.v.*), who nearly always include an introductory statement to the effect that they are giving voice (φωνή) to their subject.
[608] 1898, *Kunstprosa*, 507.
[609] 1926, "Style." See above, chapter one, § 1.
[610] 1994, "Epistle," 229-36.
[611] *Op. cit.* 36.
[612] See above, pp.223-25.

that Paul, at that point, is not engaged in rhetorical ἀλληγορία. His use of the term comes from a tradition of allegorical interpretation not discussed in rhetorical theory.[613] This leaves only μακαρισμός, hardly a technical rhetorical term, even if it *might* be considered a technical term in literature. The absence of technical rhetorical terminology in Paul's letters can thus only support the notion that he had no direct knowledge of rhetorical theory.

2 Rhetorical Theory and Paul

If Paul probably had no knowledge of rhetorical theory, nor was directly influenced by the more specific methods of school rhetoric, what is the point of an analysis of his letters from this perspective?

In the first place, it is particularly important to set Paul's writings off against the background of the Graeco-Roman culture in which he lived and worked. Oratory was of fundamental importance in the Graeco-Roman world, not only in the courts, but ever increasingly as a form of entertainment, especially in connection with official functions. This importance is mirrored in the significant place given to rhetorical theory in "tertiary" education.[614] If rhetoric was so dominant in Graeco-Roman culture, then it is important for us to understand, as best as we can, the relationship between rhetorical theory and Paul. Even a negative result is important, and has consequences for both our view of Paul as well as the question as to the reception of his writings in the ancient world.

But is the result only negative? Not really. Even if Paul himself did not consciously think or write in rhetorical categories, his letters may still, with profit, be analysed in terms of relevant aspects of rhetorical theory. In this way, albeit in a limited respect, rhetorical theory can still inform our exegesis. After all, the rules and effects described in rhetorical theory often embody the general feelings and expectations in terms of language usage of the contemporary society, or at least an important segment of that society. In this way we are enabled to gain, at least partially, more of a *feeling* for the contemporary effects of various forms of argumentation and style. We are provided with a complex canon of rules and advice against which contemporary writings may be compared and contrasted.

---

[613] See above, pp.152-55.
[614] See chapter two, § 2.5.

One important caution ought to be borne in mind. Rhetorical theory was designed to help men *write* speeches, not, in the first place, to analyse them.[615] We need, therefore, to be careful in applying such theory retrogressively for the purposes of analysis. Many of the theorists themselves admitted that practice was often removed from theory. This consideration should highlight the need for a certain sobriety in our analysis, and also the need to couple our use of rhetorical theory with knowledge of contemporary rhetorical practice. But this does not mean that rhetorical theory ought to be ignored, not even for the purposes of considering the letters of the apostle Paul. If the reader has gained any insight from our rhetorical analysis of the letters to the Galatians and Romans, then the effort will not have been in vain.

3 Scholarly Trends

What then of the direction of recent Pauline scholarship concerned with rhetorical theory? Our review of recent scholarship on Paul's letters to the Galatians, Romans and first letter to the Corinthians with respect to ancient rhetorical theory has shown a rather mixed bag of contributions. The "new" approach is still young and it may be expected that mistakes will be made. Despite the fact that an historical rhetorical approach has often been mixed with its modern counterpart, we have observed a trend towards the separation of the two. Slowly on many scholars are beginning to recognise that, whilst each may have its relative merits, the two approaches ought not to be confused. Apart from these general considerations, recent scholarship has raised a number of more specific questions.

A fundamental consideration is one of appropriate sources. Several scholars have been content to rely upon summaries of rhetorical theory such as provided by H. Lausberg's *Handbuch* (1973). We have seen that this has its dangers, leading easily to misinterpretation of rhetorical theory. Yet, even when scholars have attempted to use ancient sources, few have stopped to address the question as to which treatises might be most appropriate. In chapter two we have addressed the problem of ancient rhetorical theory, in particular, the background and relevance of the various rhetorical treatises along with the question as to which parts of rhetorical theory might be of most relevance for application to the apostle Paul. There is no need to repeat in detail the conclusions arrived at there. We may, however, reiterate two problems which often sur-

---

[615] Of course tracts such as Demetr. *Eloc.* and D.H. *Comp.* also have the analysis of written documents in mind.

face in the recent literature, namely, the use of rhetorical genre classifications without regard to the particular arguments or τόποι specific to each, and the attempt to treat small segments of Paul's letters as if they could represent a whole speech in miniature.

Another serious problem in recent literature has been the not infrequent misinterpretation of primary sources. There would appear to be at least three major causes for this.[616] Firstly, the problem highlights the need to read these sources in their original languages. Translations may function as aids for those who do not read Greek or Latin quickly enough to be able to read a large portion of the surrounding context in a reasonable space of time, but nothing can substitute for the reading of the relevant passages in the original language. Secondly, there is the need to read rhetorical theory in conjunction with actual practice. It is a fact that sometimes the theoreticians are somewhat vague or ambiguous. Consultation of actual speeches can often help to give a much clearer idea of what was meant and put the theory in perspective. Thirdly, insufficient attention is generally given to the fact that the various theoreticians often employ the same terms in different ways. There was little standardisation of terminology before the second century AD, and especially before the first century BC. A reference work such as Lausberg's *Handbuch* can often be misleading in this regard. I have attempted to provide some help in terms of my *Glossary* (forthcoming).

It can readily be seen that the New Testament scholar wishing to apply ancient rhetorical theory to his field needs to prepared for some investment of time and effort. Yet it is to be hoped that this fact will not deter scholars from continuing research in this area. There is still much work to be done as New Testament scholarship matures into a more careful approach to the application of rhetorical theory. Despite the necessary restrictions and limitations to such application, there is still much to be gained from further study in this field. It is hoped that this book, despite its criticisms of recent scholarship, may serve to stimulate such continuing study in the relationship and application of ancient rhetorical theory to the letters of the apostle Paul.

---

[616] More obvious points such as the need to read the sources *in context* ought to be taken for granted.

Select Bibliography

Note that those reference works cited under the "List of Abbreviations" (pp.9-11) are not repeated here, nor are the editions and commentaries referenced in the bibliographical sections of chapter two unless elsewhere cited in abbreviated form.

Adamietz, J.
1966   *M. F. Quintiliani Institutionis Oratoriae Liber III: Mit einem Kommentar.* München: Wilhelm Funk.

Amir, Yehoshua
1973   Philo and the Bible. *Studia Philonica* 2:1-8.
1984   The Transference of Greek Allegories to Biblical Motifs in Philo. In *Nourished with Peace: Studies in Hellenistic Judaism in Memory of Samuel Sandmel.* F. E. Greenspahn, E. Hilgert, and B. L. Mack ed. Pp. 15-25. Chico, Calif.: Scholars Press.

Anderson, Bernhard W.
1974   The New Frontier of Rhetorical Criticism: A Tribute to James Muilenburg. In *Rhetorical Criticism: Essays in Honor of James Muilenburg.* Jared J. Jackson and Martin Kessler ed. Pp. ix-xviii. Pittsburgh Theological Monograph Series, no. 1. Pittsburgh, Pa.: The Pickwick Press.

Anderson, R. Dean
Forthcoming *Glossary of Greek Rhetorical Terms Connected to Methods of Argumentation and Figures from Anaximenes to Quintilian.*

Angermann, O.
1904   De Aristotele Rhetorum Auctore. Diss. Leipzig. Reprint in R. Stark ed., 1968, *Rhetorika: Schriften zur aristotelischen und hellenistischen Rhetorik.* Pp. 212-284. Olms Studien, no. 2. Hildesheim: Georg Olms.

Arieti, James A. and John M. Crossett
1985   *Longinus On the Sublime.* Translated with a commentary. Texts and Studies in Religion 21. New York: Edwin Mellen Press.

Arnim, H. von
1898   Sophistik, Rhetorik, Philosophie in ihrem Kampf um die Jugendbildung. Einleitung in *Leben und Werke des Dio von Prusa.* Pp. 4-114. Berlin: Weidmann.

Aune, David E.
1981   Review of H. D. Betz, *Galatians: A Commentary on Paul's Letter to the Churches of Galatia* (Hermeneia; Philadelphia: Fortress Press, 1979). *Religious Studies Review* 7:323-328.

Bachmann, Michael
1992   *Sünder oder Übertreter: Studien zur Argumentation in Gal 2,15ff.* Wissenschaftliche Untersuchungen zum Neuen Testament 59. Tübingen: J. C. B. Mohr.

Barwick, K.
1922   Die Gliederung der rhetorischen TEXNH und die Horazische Epistula ad Pisones. *Hermes* 57:1-62.
1936   Quintilians Stellung zu dem Problem sprachlicher Neuschöpfungen. *Philologus* N.F. 45:89-113.
1957   *Probleme der stoischen Sprachlehre und Rhetorik.* Abhandlungen der Sächsischen Akademie der Wissenschaften zu Leipzig: Philologisch-historische Klasse Bd. 49 Heft 3. Berlin: Akademie Verlag.

Beare, F. W.
1958-9 On the Interpretation of Romans VI. 17. *New Testament Studies* 5:206-210.

Berger, Klaus
    1977   *Exegese des Neuen Testaments: Neue Wege vom Text zur Auslegung*. Uni-Taschenbücher
              658. Heidelberg: Quelle & Meyer.
Betz, H. D.
    1975   The Literary Composition and Function of Paul's Letter to the Galatians. *New Testament
              Studies* 21:353-379.
    1979   *Galatians: A Commentary on Paul's Letter to the Churches in Galatia*. Philadelphia:
              Fortress Press.
    1986   The Problem of Rhetoric and Theology According to the Apostle Paul. In *L'apôtre Paul:
              Personnalité, Style et Conception Du Ministère*. A. Vanhoye ed. Pp. 16-48. Bibliotheca
              Ephemeridum Theologicarum Lovaniensium 73. Leuven: Leuven University Press.
    1988   *Der Galaterbrief: Ein Kommentar zum Brief des Apostels Paulus an die Gemeinden in
              Galatien*. Trans. Sibylle Ann. München: Chr. Kaiser.
Black, C. C. II.
    1989   Rhetorical Criticism and Biblical Interpretation. *The Expository Times* 100:252-258.
Black, D. A.
    1989   The Pauline Love Command: Structure, Style, and Ethics in Romans 12:9-21. *Filologia
              Neotestamentaria* 2:3-22.
Boll, F.
    1917-8   Zu Demetrius de elocutione. *Rheinisches Museum für Philologie* N.F. 72:25-33.
Bonner, S. F.
    1939   *The Literary Treatises of Dionysius of Halicarnassus: A Study in the Development of
              Critical Method*. Cambridge: University Press.
    1954   Roman Oratory. In *Fifty Years of Classical Scholarship*. Maurice Platnauer ed. Pp. 335-
              383. Oxford: Basil Blackwell.
    1966   Lucan and the Declamation Schools. *American Journal of Philology* 87:257-289.
    1977   *Education in Ancient Rome: From the Elder Cato to the Younger Pliny*. London:
              Methuen & Co..
Borgen, P.
    1984   Philo of Alexandria. In *Jewish Writings of the Second Temple Period*. Michael Stone ed.
              In *The Literature of the Jewish People in the Period of the Second Temple and the Tal-
              mud*. W. J. Burgers, H. Sysling, and P. J. Tomson ed. Pp. 233-282. Compendia Rerum
              Iudaicarum ad Novum Testamentum. Assen: Van Gorcum.
Bouwman, Gijs
    1980   *Paulus aan de romeinen: een retorische analyse van Rom 1-8*. Cahiers voor Levensver-
              dieping 32. Abdij Averbode: Werkgroep voor Levensverdieping.
Bowersock, G. W.
    1978   Historical Problems in Late Republican and Augustan Classicism. *Fondation Hardt*
              25:57-78.
Brooks, E. Jr.
    1970   *P. Rutilii Lupi de Figuris Sententiarum et Elocutionis*. Leiden: E. J. Brill.
Büchsel, F.
    1964   ἀλληγορέω. In *Theological Dictionary of the New Testament*. Gerhard Kittel ed. Trans.
              Geoffrey W. Bromiley. Vol. 1. Pp. 260-263. Reprint, 1979. Grand Rapids, Mich.: W.
              B. Eerdmans.
Bultmann, R.
    1910   *Der Stil der paulinischen Predigt und die kynisch-stoische Diatribe*. Reprint, 1984.
              Forschungen zur Religion und Literatur des Alten und Neuen Testaments 13. Göttingen:
              Vandenhoeck & Ruprecht.
Bund, E.
    1975   Testamentum. In *Der Kleine Pauly: Lexikon der Antike in Fünf Bänden*. Vol. 5. Pp. 619-
              628. Reprint, 1979. München: Deutscher Taschenbuch Verlag.
Bünker, M.
    1984   *Briefformular und rhetorische Disposition im 1 Korintherbrief*. Göttingen: Vandenhoeck
              & Ruprecht.

Burgess, Theodore C.
1902   Epideictic Literature. Pp. 89-261. The University of Chicago Studies in Classical Philology 3. Chicago: University Press.

Campbell, Douglas A.
1992   *The Rhetoric of Righteousness in Romans 3.21-26.* Journal for the Study of the New Testament Supplement Series 65. Sheffield, England: JSOT Press.

Caplan, H.
1954   *Cicero.* Vol. 1: *Ad C. Herennium de Ratione Dicendi.* LCL. London: Heinemann.

Christ, Wilhelm von
1920-4   *Geschichte der griechischen Literatur: zweiter Teil: Die nachklassische Periode der griechischen Literatur.* Mitwirker Otto Stählin. Bearbeitet von Wilhelm Schmid. 2 vols. Handbuch der klassischen Altertums-wissenschaft. München: C. H. Beck.

Clarke, M. L.
1951   The *Thesis* in the Roman Rhetorical Schools of the Republic. *The Classical Quarterly* 45:159-166.

Classen, C. Joachim
1993   St Paul's Epistles and Ancient Greek and Roman Rhetoric. In *Rhetoric and the New Testament: Essays from the 1992 Heidelberg Conference.* Stanley E. Porter and Thomas H. Olbricht ed. Pp. 265-291. Journal for the Study of the New Testament Supplement Series 90. Sheffield: JSOT Press.

1995   Zur rhetorischen Analyse der Paulusbriefe. *Zeitschrift für die neutestamentliche Wissenschaft* 86:120-121.

Colson, F. H.
1913   Τάξει in Papias: The Gospels and the Rhetorical Schools. *Journal of Theological Studies* 14:62-69.

1916   Μετεσχημάτισα I Cor. iv 6. *Journal of Theological Studies* 17:379-384.

1924   *M. Fabii Quintiliani Institutionis Oratoriae Liber I.* Cambridge: University Press.

Cope, E. M.
1867   *An Introduction to Aristotle's Rhetoric with Analysis, Notes and Appendices.* Reprint, 1970. Hildesheim: Georg Olms.

1877   *The Rhetoric of Aristotle with a Commentary.* Ed & commentary by Edward Meredith Cope. Revised & ed John Edwin Sandys. 3 vols. Reprint, n.d. Dubuque, Iowa: Wm. C. Brown.

Cosby, Michael R.
1991   Paul's Persuasive Language in Romans 5. In *Persuasive Artistry: Studies in New Testament Rhetoric in Honor of George A. Kennedy.* Duane F. Watson ed. Pp. 209-226. Journal for the Study of the New Testament Supplement Series 50. Sheffield: JSOT Press.

Cosgrove, Charles H.
1988a   Arguing Like a Mere Human Being: Galatians 3.15-18 in Rhetorical Perspective. *New Testament Studies* 34:536-549.

1988b   *The Cross and the Spirit: A Study in the Argument and Theology of Galatians.* Macon, Ga: Mercer.

Cranfield, C. E. B.
1975-9   *A Critical and Exegetical Commentary on the Epistle to the Romans.* The International Critical Commentary. Reprint, 1986-7. Edinburgh: T. & T. Clark.

Crönert, Wilhelm
1900   Der Epikureer Philonides. *Sitzungsberichte der königlich Preußischen Akademie der Wissenschaften zu Berlin* 942-959.

Crossett, John M., and James A. Arieti
[1975]   *The Dating of Longinus.* Studia Classica III. Pennsylvania: Department of Classics: Pennsylvania State University.

Davies, W. D.
1981   Review of H. D. Betz, *Galatians: A Commentary on Paul's Letter to the Churches of Galatia* (Hermeneia; Philadelphia: Fortress Press, 1979). *Religious Studies Review* 7:310-318.

Deissmann, G. Adolf
1895   Prolegomena zu den biblischen Briefen und Episteln. In *Bibelstudien*. Pp. 187-252.
         Reprint, 1977. Hildesheim: Georg Olms.
1923   *Licht vom Osten*. 4th ed. Tübingen: J. C. B. Mohr.
Dobschütz, E. von
1934   Zum Wortschatz und Stil des Römerbriefs. *Zeitschrift für die neutestamentliche Wissen-
         schaft* 33:51-66.
Donfried, Karl Paul
1974   False Presuppositions in the Study of Romans. *Catholic Biblical Quarterly* 36:332-358.
         Reprint, 1991, in *The Romans Debate*. Revised and Expanded Edition. Karl P. Donfried
         ed. Pp. 102-125. Peabody, Mass.: Hendrickson.
Dorandi, T.
1990   Per una ricomposizione dello scritto di Filodemo sulla Retorica. *Zeitschrift für
         Papyrologie und Epigraphik* 82:59-87.
Doty, William G.
1969   The Classification of Epistolary Literature. *The Catholic Biblical Quarterly* 31:183-199.
1973   *Letters in Primitive Christianity*. Guides to Biblical Scholarship. Reprint, 1983. Philadel-
         phia: Fortress Press.
Douglas, A. E.
1957   A Ciceronian Contribution to Rhetorical Theory. *Eranos* 55:18-26.
1973   The Intellectual Background of Cicero's Rhetorica: A Study in Method. In *Aufstieg und
         Niedergang der Römischen Welt*. Vol. I.3. Pp. 95-138. Berlin: de Gruyter.
Du Toit, A. B.
1989   Persuasion in Romans 1:1-17. *Biblische Zeitschrift* 33:192-209.
Duncan, Thomas Shearer
1926   The Style and Language of Saint Paul in His First Letter to the Corinthians. *Bibliotheca
         Sacra* 83:129-143.
Düring, I.
1950   Notes on the History of the Transmission of Aristotle's Writings. *Göteborgs Högskolas
         Årsskrift* 56:37-70.
1966   *Aristoteles: Darstellung und Interpretation seines Denkens*. Heidelberg: Carl Winter.
Elliott, Neil
1990   *The Rhetoric of Romans: Argumentative Constraint and Strategy and Paul's Dialogue
         with Judaism*. Journal for the Study of the New Testament Supplement Series 45. Shef-
         field: JSOT Press.
Ernesti, Io. Christ. Theoph.
1795   *Lexicon Technologiae Graecorum Rhetoricae*. Reprint, 1962. Hildesheim: Georg Olms.
Fairweather, Janet
1994   The Epistle to the Galatians and Classical Rhetoric. *Tyndale Bulletin* 45:1-38, 213-244.
Fiore, Benjamin
1985   "Covert Allusion" in 1 Corinthians 1-4. *Catholic Biblical Quarterly* 47:85-102.
Förster, R.
1927   Libanii Qui Feruntur Characteres Epistolici. In *Libanius: Opera*. Vol. 9. Pp. 1-47.
         BSGRT. Leipzig: B. G. Teubner.
Fortenbaugh, William W.
1992   Aristotle on Persuasion Through Character. *Rhetorica* 10:207-244.
1994   Theophrastus, the *Characters* and Rhetoric. In *Peripatetic Rhetoric After Aristotle*. Wil-
         liam W. Fortenbaugh and David C. Mirhady ed. Pp. 15-35. Rutgers University Studies
         in Classical Humanities VI. New Brunswick: Transaction Publishers.
Fraikin, Daniel
1986   The Rhetorical Function of the Jews in Romans. In *Anti-Judaism in Early Christianity*.
         Peter Richardson and David Granskou ed. Vol. 1: *Paul and the Gospels*. Pp. 91-105.
         Waterloo, Ontario: Wilfrid Laurier University Press.

Fritz, K. von
  1938   Philon 40). In *Pauly's Real-Encyclopädie der classischen Altertumswissenschaft*. Eds
              Georg Wissowa *et al*. Vol. 19.2. Pp. 2535-2544. Stuttgart: J. B. Metzler.
Fuhrmann, M.
  1964a   Review of "Hermagorae Temnitae Testimonia et Fragmenta," Collegit Dieter Matthes.
              Leipzig: B. G. Teubner 1962. *Gnomon* 36:146-149.
  1964b   *Untersuchungen zur Textgeschichte der pseudo-aristotelischen Alexander-Rhetorik (der
              Τέχνη des Anaximenes von Lampsakos)*. Akademie der Wissenschaften und der Literatur:
              Abhandlungen der geistes- und sozialwissenschaftlichen Klasse. Wiesbaden: Franz
              Steiner.
  1966   *Anaximenis Ars Rhetorica*. BSGRT. Leipzig: B. G. Teubner.
  1975   Caecilius III.2. In *Der Kleine Pauly: Lexikon der Antike in Fünf Bänden*. Vol. 1. Pp.
              988-989. Reprint, 1979. München: Deutscher Taschenbuch Verlag.
Fung, Ronald Y. K.
  1988   *The Epistle to the Galatians*. The New International Commentary on the New Testament.
              Grand Rapids, Mich.: W. B. Eerdmans.
Gaines, Robert N.
  1985   Philodemus on the Three Activities of Rhetorical Invention. *Rhetorica* 3:155-163.
Gelzer, Thomas
  1978   Klassizismus, Attizismus und Asianismus. *Fondation Hardt* 25:1-55.
Gill, Christopher
  1984   The *ethos/pathos* Distinction in Rhetorical and Literary Criticism. *Classical Quarterly*
              34:149-166.
Gilleland, Brady B.
  1961   The Date of Cicero's *Partitiones Oratoriae*. *Classical Philology* 56:29-32.
Giomini, R., and M. S. Celentano
  1980   Praefatio. In *C. Iulii Victoris: Ars Rhetorica*. Pp. v-xxxii. Leipzig: B. G. Teubner.
Glucker, John
  1978   *Antiochus and the Late Academy*. Hypomnemata 56. Göttingen: Vandenhoeck &
              Ruprecht.
Goldstein, J. A.
  1968   *The Letters of Demosthenes*. New York: Columbia University Press.
Granatelli, Rossella, ed.
  1991   *Apollodori Pergameni Ac Theodori Gadarei Testimonia et Fragmenta (accedunt Apol-
              lodoreorum Ac Theodoreorum Testimonia et Fragmenta)*. Roma, Italia: "L'Erma" Di
              Bretschneider.
Griffiths, J. G.
  1970   *Plutarch's de Iside et Osiride*. Ed with an introduction, translation and commentary.
              Wales: University of Wales Press.
Grimaldi, W. M. A.
  1972   *Studies in the Philosophy of Aristotle's Rhetoric*. Hermes: Zeitschrift für klassische
              Philologie: Einzelschriften, vol. 25. Wiesbaden: Franz Steiner.
  1980-8   *Aristotle, Rhetoric: A Commentary*. 2 vols. New York: Fordham University Press.
Groenewald, M.
  1977   Ein Fragment aus Theon, Progymnasmata. *Zeitschrift für Papyrologie und Epigraphik*
              24:23-24.
Grube, G. M. A.
  1961   *A Greek Critic, Demetrius on Style*. Toronto: University Press.
  1964   The Date of Demetrius *On Style*. *Phoenix* 18:294-302.
  1967   *How did the Greeks Look at Literature*. Lectures in Memory of Louise Taft Semple
              (second Series). Cincinnati: University Press.
Hall, Robert G.
  1987   The Rhetorical Outline for Galatians: A Reconsideration. *Journal of Biblical Literature*
              106:277-287.

1991   Historical Inference and Rhetorical Effect: Another Look at Galatians 1 and 2. In *Persuasive Artistry: Studies in New Testament Rhetoric in Honor of George A. Kennedy*. Duane F. Watson ed. Pp. 308-320. Journal for the Study of the New Testament Supplement Series 50. Sheffield: JSOT Press.

Hammond Bammel, C. P.
1981   Philocalia ix, Jerome, Epistle 121, and Origen's Exposition of Romans vii. *Journal of Theological Studies* N.S. 32:50-81.

Hansen, G. Walter
1989   *Abraham in Galatians: Epistolary and Rhetorical Contexts*. Journal for the Study of the New Testament Supplement Series 29. Sheffield: JSOT Press.

Harnisch, W.
1987   Einübung des Neuen Seins. *Zeitschrift für Theologie und Kirche* 84:279-296.

Hay, David M.
1979-80   Philo's References to Other Allegorists. *Studia Philonica* 6:41-75.

Heinemann, I.
1952   Die Allegoristik der hellenistischen Juden ausser Philon. *Mnemosyne* Series 4, 5:130-138.

Heinrici, C. F. Georg
1887   *Das zweite Sendschreiben des Apostel Paulus an die Korinthier*. Berlin: Wilhelm Hertz.
1896   *Der erste Brief an die Korinther*. Kritisch-exegetischer Kommentar über das Neue Testament. Göttingen: Vandenhoeck und Ruprecht.
1900   *Der zweite Brief an die Korinther*. Kritisch-exegetischer Kommentar über das Neue Testament. Göttingen: Vandenhoeck und Ruprecht.
1908   *Der litterarische Charakter der neutestamentlichen Schriften*. Leipzig: Dürr'schen Buchhandlung.

Hellholm, David
1993   Amplificatio in the Macro-structure of Romans. In *Rhetoric and the New Testament: Essays from the 1992 Heidelberg Conference*. Stanley E. Porter and Thomas H. Olbricht ed. Pp. 123-151. Journal for the Study of the New Testament Supplement Series 90. Sheffield: JSOT Press.

Hengel, Martin
1991   Der vorchristliche Paulus. In *Paulus und das antike Judentum*. Tübingen-Durham-Symposium im Gedenken an den 50. Todestag Adolf Schlatters. Martin Hengel and Ulrich Heckel ed. Pp. 177-293. Tübingen: J. C. B. Mohr.

Hester, James D.
1984   The Rhetorical Structure of Galatians 1:11-2:14. *Journal of Biblical Literature* 103:223-233.
1986   The Use and Influence of Rhetoric in Galatians 2:1-14. *Theologische Zeitschrift* 42:386-408.
1991   Placing the Blame: The Presence of Epideictic in Galatians 1 and 2. In *Persuasive Artistry: Studies in New Testament Rhetoric in Honor of George A. Kennedy*. Duane F. Watson ed. Pp. 281-307. Journal for the Study of the New Testament Supplement Series 50. Sheffield: JSOT Press.

Hinks, D. A. G.
1936   Tria Genera Causarum. *Classical Quarterly* 30:170-176.

Hock, Ronald F., and Edward N. O'Neil
1986   *The Chreia in Ancient Rhetoric*. Vol. 1: *The Progymnasmata*. Texts and Translations 27: Graeco-Roman Religion Series 9. Atlanta, Ga.: Scholars Press.

Holst, Hans
1925   *Die Wortspiele in Ciceros Reden*. Symbolae Osloenses Supplet. 1. Oslo: Somme & Co.

Horsley, R. A.
1977   Wisdom of Word and Words of Wisdom in Corinth. *Catholic Biblical Quarterly* 39:224-239.

Hubbell, Harry M.
1920 The Rhetorica of Philodemus: Translation and Commentary. In *Transactions of the Connecticut Academy of Arts of Sciences* 23:243-382.
Hübner, Hans
1984 Der Galaterbrief und das Verhältnis von antiker Rhetorik und Epistolographie. *Theologische Literaturzeitung* 109:241-250.
Hudson-Williams, H. L.
1954 Greek Orators and Rhetoric. In *Fifty Years of Classical Scholarship*. Maurice Platnauer ed. Pp. 193-213. Oxford: Basil Blackwell.
1967 Review of D. A. Russell (ed.) *Longinus on the Sublime* (Oxford: Clarendon, 1964) and (trans.) *On Sublimity* (Oxford: Clarendon Press, 1965). *Classical Review* 17:280-282.
Innes, D. C.
1972 Demetrius *On Style*: Introduction. In *Ancient Literary Criticism: The Principal Texts in New Translations*. D. A. Russell and M. Winterbottom ed. Pp. 171-173. Oxford: Clarendon Press.
1976 Review of R. Kassel, *Aristotelis Ars Rhetorica* (Berlin/ New York: de Gruyter, 1976). *Classical Review* 26:172-173.
1994 Period and Colon: Theory and Example in Demetrius and Longinus. In *Peripatetic Rhetoric After Aristotle*. W. W. Fortenbaugh and D. C. Mirhady ed. Pp. 36-53. Rutgers University Studies in Classical Humanities VI. New Brunswick: Transaction Publishers.
1995 Demetrius "On Style": Introduction. In *Aristotle*. Vol. 23. Pp. 311-342. LCL. Cambridge, Mass.: Harvard University Press.
Jennrich, Walter A.
1948-9 Classical Rhetoric in the New Testament. *The Classical Journal* 44:30-32.
Jewett, Robert
1982 Romans as an Ambassadorial Letter. *Interpretation* 36:5-20.
1991 Following the Argument of Romans. In *The Romans Debate*. Revised and Expanded Edition. Karl P. Donfried ed. Pp. 265-277. Peabody, Mass.: Hendrickson.
Joosen, Joseph
1941 *Beeldspraak bij den heiligen Basilius den Grote met een inleiding over de opvattingen van de Griekse en Romeinse auteurs aangaande beeldspraak*. Nijmegen: Dekker & Van de Vegt.
Kamp, D.
1968 Das Testament der Taharpaesis. *Zeitschrift für Papyrologie und Epigraphik* 2:81-150.
Kaster, R. A.
1995 *C. Suetonius Tranquillus: De Grammaticis et Rhetoribus*. Edited with a translation, introduction and commentary. Oxford: Clarendon Press.
Kennedy, George A.
1963 *The Art of Persuasion in Greece*. Princeton: University Press, and London: Routledge & Kegan Paul.
1968 The Rhetoric of Advocacy in Greece and Rome. *American Journal of Philology* 89:419-436.
1971 Review of M. Winterbottom, *Quintilian: Institutio Oratoria* (2 Vols; OCT; Oxford: University Press, 1970). *Journal of Roman Studies* 61:308-309.
1972 *The Art of Rhetoric in the Roman World 300 B.C.-A.D. 300*. Princeton, N.J.: University Press.
1983 *Greek Rhetoric Under Christian Emperors*. Princeton, N.J.: University Press.
1984 *New Testament Interpretation Through Rhetorical Criticism*. Chapel Hill: University of North Carolina Press.
1985 Review of W. M. A. Grimaldi, *Aristotle, Rhetoric I. A Commentary* (New York: Fordham University Press, 1980). *American Journal of Philology* 106:131-133.
1994 *A New History of Classical Rhetoric*. Princeton, N.J.: University Press.
Kirby, John T.
1987 The Syntax of Romans 5.12: A Rhetorical Approach. *New Testament Studies* 33:283-286.

Klek, Josephus
    1919   *Symbuleutici Qui Dicitur Sermonis Historiam Criticam Per Quatturo Saecula Continuatam.* Rhetorische Studien. Paderborna: Ferdinandi Schoeningh.

Koskenniemi, Heikki
    1956   *Studien zur Idee und Phraseologie des griechische Briefes bis 400 N. Chr.* Helsinki: Suomalainen Tiedeakatemia.

Kremer, Emil
    1907   *Über das rhetorische System des Dionys von Halikarnass.* Inaugural-Dissertation. Strassburg: M. Dumont Schauberg.

Kroll, Wilhelm
    1936   Das Epicheirema. *Sitzungsberichte* 216.2. Akademie der Wissenschaften in Wien: Philosophisch-historische Klasse.
    1940   Rhetorik. In *Pauly's Real-Encyclopädie der classischen Altertumswissenschaft.* Eds Georg Wissowa *et al.* Supplementband 7. Pp. 1039-1138. Stuttgart: J. B. Metzler.

Lampe, P.
    1990   Theological Wisdom and the 'Word About the Cross': The Rhetorical Scheme in 1 Corinthians 1-4. *Interpretation* 44:117-131.

Lausberg, Heinrich
    1960   *Handbuch der literarischen Rhetorik.* 2 vols. Reprint, 1973. München: Max Hueber.

Leeman, A. D.
    1993   De integratie van de retorica bij Cicero. *Lampas* 26:90-100.

Leeman, A. D., and A. C. Braet
    1987   *Klassieke retorica: haar inhoud, functie en betekenis.* Groningen: Wolters-Noordhoff/Forsten.

Leeman, A. D., H. Pinkster, H. L. W. Nelson, E. Rabbie, and J. Wisse
    1981-96   *M. Tullius Cicero, De Oratore Libri III: Kommentar.* 4 vols to date. Heidelberg: Carl Winter.

Leopold, J.
    1983   Rhetoric and Allegory. In *Two Treatises of Philo of Alexandria: A Commentary on de Gigantibus and Quod Deus Sit Immutabilis.* D. Winston, and J. Dillon. Pp. 155-170. Brown Judaic Studies 25. Chico, Calif.: Scholars Press.

Lightfoot, J. B.
    1865   *St. Paul's Epistle to the Galatians.* Revised. Reprint, 1993. Peabody, Mass.: Hendrickson.
    18??   *Notes on the Epistles of St. Paul.* Reprint, 1993. Peabody, Mass.: Hendrickson.

Litfin, Duane
    1994   *St Paul's Theology of Proclamation: 1 Corinthians 1-4 and Greco-Roman Rhetoric.* Society for New Testament Studies Monograph Series 79. Cambridge: University Press.

Longenecker, R. N.
    1990   *Galatians.* Word Biblical Commentary. Waco, Tex.: Word Books.

Lord, C.
    1986   On the Early History of the Aristotelian Corpus. *American Journal of Philology* 107:137-161.

Lossau, Manfred
    1976   Review of W. M. A. Grimaldi *Studies in the Philosophy of Aristotle's Rhetoric* (Hermes Einzelschriften 25; Wiesbaden: Steiner, 1972). *Gnomon* 48:13-18.

Lynch, J. P.
    1972   *Aristotle's School: A Study of a Greek Educational Institution.* Berkeley: University of California Press.

Macdowell, D. M.
    1970   Review of J. A. Goldstein, *The Letters of Demosthenes* (New York: Columbia University Press, 1968). *The Classical Review* 20:322-324.

Mack, Burton L.
    1990   *Rhetoric and the New Testament.* Minneapolis: Fortress Press.

Malherbe, Abraham J.
1988   *Ancient Epistolary Theorists*. Society of Biblical Literature Sources for Biblical Study 19. Atlanta, Ga.: Scholars Press.

Martin, Josef
1974   *Antike Rhetorik: Technik und Methode.* Handbuch der Altertumswissenschaft 2.3. München: C. H. Beck.

Matthes, Dieter
1958   Hermagoras von Temnos 1904 - 1955. *Lustrum* 3:58-214.

Mette, Hans Joachim
1986-7   Philon von Larisa und Antiochos von Askalon. *Lustrum* 28-29:9-63.

Meyer, Heinrich August Wilhelm
1884   *Meyer's Commentary on the New Testament.* Vol. 6: *Critical and Exegetical Handbook to the Epistles to the Corinthians.* Trans. D. Douglas Bannerman. Trans rev & ed William P. Dickson. Preface & notes by Talbot W. Chambers. Alpha Greek Library. Reprint, 1980. Winona Lake, IN: Alpha Publications.

Meyer, Paul W.
1981   Review of H. D. Betz, *Galatians: A Commentary on Paul's Letter to the Churches of Galatia* (Hermeneia; Philadelpiha: Fortress Press, 1979). *Religious Studies Review* 7:318-323.

Mitchell, Margaret M.
1991   *Paul and the Rhetoric of Reconciliation: An Exegetical Investigation of the Language and Composition of 1 Corinthians.* Hermeneutische Untersuchungen zur Theologie 28. Tübingen: J. C. B. Mohr.
1994   Rhetorical Shorthand in Pauline Argumentation: The Functions of 'the Gospel' in the Corinthian Correspondence. In *Gospel in Paul: Studies on Corinthians, Galatians and Romans for Richard N. Longenecker.* L. Ann Jervis and Peter Richardson ed. Pp. 63-88. Journal for the Study of the New Testament Supplement Series 108. Sheffield: Academic Press.

Momigliano, A.
1971   *The Development of Greek Biography.* Cambridge, Mass.: Harvard University Press.

Muilenburg, James
1969   Form Criticism and Beyond. *Journal of Biblical Literature* 88:1-18.

Nilsson, Martin P.
1955   *Die hellenistische Schule.* München: C. H. Beck.

Nock, Arthur Darby
1931   Kornutos. In *Pauly's Real-Encyclopädie der classischen Altertumswissenschaft.* Eds Georg Wissowa *et al.* Supplementband 5. Pp. 995-1005. Stuttgart: J. B. Metzler.
1972   Word-Coinage in Greek. In *Essays on Religion and the Ancient World.* Selected and ed with an introd by Zeph Stewart. Vol. 2. Pp. 642-652. Oxford: Clarendon Press.

Norden, Eduard
1898   *Die antike Kunstprosa: Vom vi Jahrhundert v. Chr. bis in die Zeit der Renaissance.* 2 vols. Reprint with Nachträge, 1915. 3d ed. Reprint, 1958. Darmstadt: Wissenschaftliche Buchgesellschaft.

Parker, D. C.
1989   Introduction. In *Philip Melanchthon: Paul's Letter to the Colossians.* Trans. D. C. Parker. Pp. 11-25. U.S.A.: Almond Press.

Perelman, Ch., and L. Olbrechts-Tyteca
1969   *The New Rhetoric: A Treatise on Argumentation.* Trans. John Wilkinson and Purcell Weaver. Notre Dame: University Press.

Pesch, Rudolf
1986   *Paulus ringt um die Lebensform der Kirche: Vier Briefe an die Gemeinde Gottes in Korinth: Paulus - neu gesehen.* Herderbücherei 1291. Freiburg: Herder.

Plank, K. A.
1987   *Paul and the Irony of Affliction.* Society of Biblical Literature Semeia Studies 17. Atlanta, Ga.: Scholars Press.

Pogoloff, Stephen M.
1992   *Logos and Sophia: The Rhetorical Situation of 1 Corinthians.* SBLDS 134. Atlanta, Ga.: Scholars Press.
Porter, Stanley E.
1993   The Theoretical Justification for Application of Rhetorical Categories to Pauline Epistolary Literature. In *Rhetoric and the New Testament: Essays from the 1992 Heidelberg Conference.* Stanley E. Porter and Thomas H. Olbricht ed. Pp. 100-122. Journal for the Study of the New Testament Supplement Series 90. Sheffield: JSOT Press.
Probst, Hermann
1991   *Paulus und der Brief: Die Rhetorik des antiken Briefes als Form der paulinischen Korintherkorrespondenz (1 Kor 8-10).* Wissenschaftliche Untersuchungen zum Neuen Testament 2. Reihe 45. Tübingen: J. C. B. Mohr.
Quasten, Johannes
1950   *Patrology.* 3 vols. Reprint, 1992, Westminster, Md.: Christian Classics.
Rabe, Hugo
1913   Praefatio. In *Hermogenis Opera.* Pp. i-xxviii. BSGRT. Leipzig: B. G. Teubner; reprint, Stuttgart, 1985.
Radermacher, L.
1899a   Eine Schrift über den Redner als Quelle Ciceros und Quintilians: Studien zur Geschichte der antiken Rhetorik III. *Rheinisches Museum für Philologie* N.F. 54:285-292.
1899b   Zu Isyllos von Epidauros. *Philologus* 58:314-316.
1901   *Demetrii Phalerei Qui Dicitur de Elocutione Libellus.* SWC. Leipzig: B. G. Teubner; reprint, Stuttgart, 1966.
1912   Harpokration 3). In *Pauly's Real-Encyclopädie der classischen Altertumswissenschaft.* Eds Georg Wissowa *et al.* Vol. 7.2. Pp. 2411-2412. Stuttgart: J. B. Metzler.
1917   Iulius 532). In *Pauly's Real-Encyclopädie der classischen Altertumswissenschaft.* Eds Georg Wissowa *et al.* Vol. 10.1. Pp. 872-879. Stuttgart: J. B. Metzler.
1929   Praefatio. In *Opusculorum Volumen Secundum.* In *Dionysii Halicarnasei Quae Exstant.* Pp. i-xxix. BSGRT. Leipzig: B. G. Teubner; reprint, Stuttgart, 1985.
1951   (ed.) *Artium scriptores: Reste der voraristotelischen Rhetorik.* Sitzungsberichte: Österreichische Akademie der Wissenschaften: Philosophisch-historische Klasse 227.3. Wien: Rudolf M. Rohrer.
Regenbogen, O.
1940   Theophrastos 3). In *Pauly's Real-Encyclopädie der classischen Altertumswissenschaft.* Eds Georg Wissowa *et al.* Supplementband 7. Pp. 1354-1562. Stuttgart: J. B. Metzler.
Reiling, J.
1988   Wisdom and the Spirit: An Exegesis of 1 Corinthians 2,6-16. In *Text and Testimony: Essays on New Testament and Apocryphal Literature in Honour of A. F. J. Klijn.* T. et al. Baarda ed. Pp. 200-211. Kampen: J. H. Kok.
Reinhardt, [Karl]
1913   Herakleitos 12). In *Pauly's Real-Encyclopädie der classischen Altertumswissenschaft.* Eds Georg Wissowa *et al.* Vol. 8. Pp. 508-510. Stuttgart: J. B. Metzler.
Richards, E. Randolph
1991   *The Secretary in the Letters of Paul.* Wissenschaftliche Untersuchungen zum Neuen Testament 2. Tübingen: J. C. B. Mohr.
Rist, J. M.
1964   Demetrius the Stylist and Artemon the Compiler. *Phoenix* 18:2-8.
Roberts, W. Rhys
1902   *Demetrius on Style: The Greek Text of Demetrius de Elocutione Edited After the Paris Manuscript.* Cambridge. Reprint, 1969. Hildesheim: Georg Olms.
1903a   Radermacher's "Demetrius de Elocutione." Review of "Demetrii Phalerei Qui Dicitur de Elocutione Libellus," Ed. L. Radermacher, Leipzig, B. G. Teubner, 1901. *The Classical Review* 17:210-217.
1903b   Roberts' "Demetrius de Elocutione": Reply to Dr. Rutherford. *The Classical Review* 17:128-134.

1909 Review of "Caecilii Calactini Fragmenta Collegit Ernestus Ofenloch" (Leipzig: Teubner, 1907) Pp.xl, 242. *Classical Review* 23:202-203.

1913 Greek and Latin in a Young University. *The Classical Review* 27:289-291.

1927 Demetrius' On Style. In *Aristotle*. Vol. 23. Pp. 257-487. LCL. London: Heinemann.

Robertson, Archibald, and Alfred Plummer

1911 *A Critical and Exegetical Commentary on the First Epistle of St. Paul to the Corinthians.* The International Critical Commentary. Reprint, 1986. Edinburgh: T & T Clark Ltd.

Roemer, Adolph

1924 *Die Homerexegese Aristarchs in ihren Grundzügen.* Studien zur Geschichte und Kultur des Altertums 13.2-3. Paderborn: Ferdinand Schöningh.

Rolfe, J. C.

1914 *Suetonius.* Vol. 2. LCL. London: Heinemann.

Rosenthal, Georg

1897 Ein vergessenes Theophrastfragment. *Hermes* 32:317-320.

Russell, D. A.

1964 *Longinus: On the Sublime.* Ed with introduction and commentary D. A. Russell. Oxford: Clarendon Press.

1981 Longinus Revisited. *Mnemosyne* 34:72-86.

1995 Longinus, *On the Sublime*: Introduction. In *Aristotle*. Vol. 23. Pp. 145-58. LCL. Cambridge, Mass.: Harvard University Press.

Russell, Walter B.

1993 Rhetorical Analysis of the Book of Galatians. *Bibliotheca Sacra* 150:341-358, 416-439.

Rutherford, W. G.

1903 Roberts' "Demetrius de Elocutione." Review of "Demetrius on Style The Greek text of Demetrius De Elocutione." Ed. W. R. Roberts, Cambridge University Press, 1902. *The Classical Review* 17:61-67.

Schenk, Wolfgang

1990 Korintherbriefe. In *Theologische Realenzyklopädie*. Vol. 19. Pp. 620-640. Berlin and New York: de Gruyter.

Schenkeveld, Dirk M.

1964 *Studies in Demetrius On Style.* Academisch Proefschrift, Vrije Universiteit te Amsterdam. Amsterdam: A. M. Hakkert.

1976 Review of W. M. A. Grimaldi *Studies in the Philosophy of Aristotle's Rhetoric* (Hermes Einzelschriften 25; Wiesbaden: Steiner, 1972). *Mnemosyne* 29:425-427.

Schissel, Otmar

1933 Die Einteilung der Chrie bei Quintilian. *Hermes* 68:245-248.

Schmeller, T.

1987 *Paulus und die "Diatribe": Eine vergleichende Stilinterpretation.* Neutestamentliche Abhandlungen N.F. 19. Munster: Aschendorff.

Schneider, J.

1971 σχῆμα, μετασχηματίζω. In *Theological Dictionary of the New Testament*. Gerhard Friedrich ed. Trans. Geoffrey W. Bromiley. Pp. 954-958. Reprint, 1980. Grand Rapids, Mich.: W. B. Eerdmans.

Schneider, Norbert

1970 *Die rhetorische Eigenart der paulinischen Antithese.* Hermeneutische Untersuchungen zur Theologie 11. Tübingen: J. C. B. Mohr.

Schoeni, Marc

1993 The Hyperbolic Sublime as a Master Trope in Romans. In *Rhetoric and the New Testament: Essays from the 1992 Heidelberg Conference.* Stanley E. Porter and Thomas H. Olbricht ed. Pp. 171-192. Journal for the Study of the New Testament Supplement Series 90. Sheffield: JSOT Press.

Schoon-Janssen, J.

1991 *Umstrittene "Apologien" in den Paulusbriefen: Studien zur rhetorischen Situation des 1. Thessalonicherbriefes, des Galaterbriefes und des Philipperbriefes.* Göttingen: Vandenhoeck & Ruprecht.

Schüssler Fiorenza, E.
    1987   Rhetorical Situation and Historical Reconstuction in 1 Corinthians. *New Testament Studies* 33:386-403.
Scroggs, Robin
    1976   Paul as Rhetorician: Two Homilies in Romans 1-11. In *Jews, Greeks and Christians: Religious Cultures in Late Antiquity: Essays in Honor of William David Davies*. Pp. 271-298. Leiden: E. J. Brill.
Shackleton Bailey, D. R.
    1965   *Cicero's Letters to Atticus*. Ed with commentary. Cambridge Classical Texts and Commentaries. Cambridge: University Press.
    1977   *Cicero: Epistulae Ad Familiares*. Ed with commentary. Cambridge: University Press.
Siegert, Folker
    1985   *Argumentation bei Paulus: gezeigt an Röm 9-11*. Wissenschaftliche Untersuchungen zum Neuen Testament. Tübingen: J. C. B. Mohr.
Sigountos, James G.
    1994   The Genre of 1 Corinthians 13. *New Testament Studies* 40:246-260.
Smit, Joop F. M.
    1984   Naar een nieuwe benadering van Paulus' brieven: de historische bewijsvoering in Gal. 3,1 - 4,11. *Tijdschrift Voor Theologie* 24:207-234.
    1985a   Paulus, de Galaten en het Judaisme: een narratieve analyse van Galaten 1-2. *Tijdschrift Voor Theologie* 25:337-362.
    1985b   "Hoe kun je de heidenen verplichten als Joden te leven?": Paulus en de Torah in Galaten 2,11-21. *Bijdragen* 46:118-140.
    1986   Redactie in de brief aan de Galaten. *Tijdschrift Voor Theologie* 26:113-144.
    1989a   De rangorde in de kerk: retorische analyse van 1 Kor. 12. *Tijdschrift Voor Theologie* 29:325-243.
    1989b   The Letter of Paul to the Galatians: A Deliberative Speech. *New Testament Studies* 35:1-26.
    1991   The Genre of 1 Corinthians 13 in the Light of Classical Rhetoric. *Novum Testamentum* 33:193-216.
    1993   Two Puzzles: 1 Corinthians 12.31 and 13.3: A Rhetorical Solution. *New Testament Studies* 39:246-264.
Snyman, A. H.
    1984   Style and Meaning in Romans 8:31-9. *Neotestamentica* 18:94-103.
    1986   Stilistese Tegnieke in Romeine 7:7-13. *Ned. Geref. Teologiese Tydskrif* 27:23-28.
    1988   Style and the Rhetorical Situation. *New Testament Studies* 34:218-231.
Solmsen, F.
    1931   Demetrios ΠΕΡΙ ΕΡΜΗΝΕΙΑΣ und sein peripatetisches Quellenmaterial. *Hermes* 66:241-267.
    1941   The Aristotelian Tradition in Ancient Rhetoric. First Published in *American Journal of Philology* 62:35-50, 169-190. Reprint, 1968, *Rhetorika: Schriften zur aristotelischen und hellenistischen Rhetorik*. Rudolf Stark ed. Pp. 312-349. Hildesheim: Georg Olms.
    1976   Review of W. M. A. Grimaldi *Studies in the Philosophy of Aristotle's Rhetoric* (Hermes Einzelschriften 25; Wiesbaden: Steiner, 1972). *Classical Philology* 71:174-178.
Staab, K.
    1933   *Pauluskommentare aus der griechischen Kirche aus Katenenhandschriften gesammelt*. Reprint, 1984. Münster: Aschendorff.
Stanley, Christopher D.
    1990   'Under a Curse': A Fresh Reading of Galatians 3.10-14. *New Testament Studies* 36:481-511.
Stanton, G. R.
    1973   Sophists and Philosophers: Problems of Classification. *American Journal of Philology* 94:350-364.

Stegemann, Willy
  1934a   Theodoros 39). In *Pauly's Real-Encyclopädie der classischen Altertumswissenschaft*. Eds Georg Wissowa *et al*. Vol. 5.2 zweite Reihe. Pp. 1847-1859. Stuttgart: J. B. Metzler.
  1934b   Theon 5). In *Pauly's Real-Encyclopädie der classischen Altertumswissenschaft*. Eds Georg Wissowa *et al*. Vol. 5.2 zweite Reihe. Pp. 2037-2054. Stuttgart: J. B. Metzler.
  1935   Neokles 6). In *Pauly's Real-Encyclopädie der classischen Altertumswissenschaft*. Eds Georg Wissowa *et al*. Vol. 16.2. Pp. 2416-2422. Stuttgart: J. B. Metzler.
Stirewalt, Martin Luther Jr.
  1991   The Form and Function of the Greek Letter-essay. In *The Romans Debate*. Rev and Expanded Ed. Karl P. Donfried ed. Pp. 147-171. Peabody, Mass.: Hendrickson.
Stowers, Stanley K.
  1981   *The Diatribe and Paul's Letter to the Romans*. SBLDS 57. Chico, Calif.: Scholars Press.
  1984   Paul's Dialogue with a Fellow Jew in Romans 3:1-9. *Catholic Biblical Quarterly* 46:707-722.
  1986   *Letter Writing in Greco-Roman Antiquity*. Library of Early Christianity. Philadelphia: The Westminster Press.
  1994   *A Rereading of Romans: Justice, Jews, & Gentiles*. New Haven & London: Yale University Press.
Strathmann, H.
  1967   μάρτυς κτλ.. In *Theological Dictionary of the New Testament*. Gerhard Kittel ed. Trans. Geoffrey W. Bromiley. Vol. 4. Pp. 474-514. Reprint, 1979. Grand Rapids, Mich.: W. B. Eerdmans.
Stroux, Johannes
  1912   *De Theophrasti Virtutibus Dicendi: Pars Prima*. Leipzig: B. G. Teubner.
Sykutris
  1931   Epistolographie. In *Pauly's Real-Encyclopädie der classischen Altertumswissenschaft*. Eds Georg Wissowa *et al*. Supplementband 5. Pp. 185-220. Stuttgart: J. B. Metzler.
Throm, Hermann
  1932   *Die Thesis: Ein Beitrag zu ihrer Entstehung und Geschichte*. Rhetorische Studien 17. Paderborn: Ferdinand Schöningh.
Tyrrell, R. Y. and C. C. Purser
  1885-1901 *The Correspondence of M. Tullius Cicero*. Ed with commentary. 7 vols. Dublin: Hodges, Foster and Figgis.
Ullman, B. L.
  1943   Review of Cicero: De Oratore, De Fato, Paradoxa Stoicorum, De Partitione Oratoriae. Translated by E. W. Sutton and H. Rackham (2 Vols; LCL; London: Heinemann, 1942). *Classical Philology* 38:262-265.
Usener, Hermann and Ludovicus Radermacher
  1904-1936 *Dionysius Halicarnaseus: Quae Exstant: Opuscula*. Vol. 5-6. BSGRT. Reprint, 1985. Stuttgart: B. G. Teubner.
Van Bruggen, J.
  1967   De oorsprong van de kerk te Rome. Rede. Kamper Bijdragen 3. Groningen: De Vuurbaak.
  1970   Het raadsel van Romeinen 16. Rede. Kamper Bijdragen 10. Groningen: De Vuurbaak.
  1973   *"Na veertien jaren": De datering van het in Galaten 2 genoemde overleg te Jeruzalem*. Ph. D. Diss. Kampen: J. H. Kok.
Van de Sandt, H.
  1988   1 Kor. 11,2-16 als een retorische eenheid. *Bijdrage* 49:410-425.
Van Eemeren, F. H., and R. Grootendorst
  1993   Klassieke invloeden in de moderne argumentatietheorie. *Lampas* 26:167-179.
Van Ophuijsen, Jan M.
  1994   Where Have the Topics Gone? In *Peripatetic Rhetoric After Aristotle*. W. W. Fortenbaugh and D. C. Mirhady ed. Pp. 131-73. Rutgers University Studies in Classical Humanities VI. New Brunswick: Transaction Publishers.

Van Unnik, W. C.
1970   Studies over de zogenaamde eerste brief van Clemens: 1. Het litteraire genre. *Mededelingen der Koninklijke Nederlandse Akademie van Wetenschappen, Afd. Letterkunde* N.S. 33(4):151-204. Amsterdam: N.V. Noord-Hollandsche Uitgevers Maatschappij.
1971   First Century A.D. Literary Culture and Early Christian Literature. *Nederlands Theologische Tijdschrift* 25:28-43.
Vorster, Johannes N.
1993   Strategies of Persuasion in Romans 1.16-17. In *Rhetoric and the New Testament: Essays from the 1992 Heidelberg Conference*. Porter Stanley E and Thomas H. Olbricht ed. Pp. 152-170. Journal for the Study of the New Testament Supplement Series 90. Sheffield: JSOT Press.
Vos, J. S.
1992   Die hermeneutische Antinomie bei Paulus (Galater 3.11-12; Römer 10.5-10). *New Testament Studies* 38:254-270.
Vouga, F.
1988   Zur rhetorischen Gattung des Galaterbriefes. *Zeitschrift für die neutestamentliche Wissenschaft* 79:291-292.
Watson, D. F.
1989   1 Corinthians 10:23-11:1 in the Light of Greco-Roman Rhetoric. *Journal of Biblical Literature* 108:301-318.
1992   Rhetorical Criticism. In *Dictionary of Jesus and the Gospels*. Joel B. Green, Scot McKnight, and I. Howard Marshall ed. Pp. 698-701. InterVarsity.
1993a   Paul's Rhetorical Strategy in 1 Corinthians 15. In *Rhetoric and the New Testament: Essays from the 1992 Heidelberg Conference*. Stanley E. Porter and Thomas H. Olbricht ed. Pp. 231-249. Journal for the Study of the New Testament Supplement Series 90. Sheffield: JSOT Press.
1993b   Review of Magaret M. Mitchell, *Paul and the Rhetoric of Reconciliation: An Exegetical Investigation of the Language and Composition of 1 Corinthians* (HUT 28). Tübingen, J. C. B. Mohr (Paul Siebeck), 1991. *Biblica* 74:291-294.
Wehrli, F.
1928   *Zur Geschichte der allegorischen Deutung Homers im Altertum*. Leipzig: Robert Noske.
Weidner, R.
1925   *Ciceros Verhältnis zur griechisch-römischen Schulrhetorik seiner Zeit*. Inaugural-Dissertation. Erlangen: Junge & Sohn.
Weiss, Johannes
1897   Beiträge zur Paulinischen Rhetorik. In *Theologische Studien. Herrn. Wirkl. Oberkonsistorialrath Professor D. Bernhard Weiss zu seinem 70. Geburtstage dargebracht*. C. R. Gregory and A. et al Harnack ed. Pp. 165-247. Göttingen: Vandenhoeck und Ruprecht.
Welsh, M. E.
1972   Review of *P. Rutilii Lupi De Figuris Sententiarum et Elocutionis*. Ed. with Prolegomena and Comm. by Edward Brooks Jr. Leiden: E. J. Brill 1970. *Gnomon* 44:776-780.
Wessner
1930   Marius 70) (C. Marius Victorinus). In *Pauly's Real-Encyclopädie der classischen Altertumswissenschaft*. Eds Georg Wissowa et al. Vol. 14.2. Pp. 1840-1848. Stuttgart: J. B. Metzler.
White, John L.
1971   Introductory Formulae in the Body of the Pauline Letter. *Journal of Biblical Literature* 90:91-97.
1981a   The Ancient Epistolography Group in Retrospect. *Semeia* 22:1-14.
1981b   The Greek Documentary Letter Tradition Third Century B.C.E. to Third Century C.E. *Semeia* 22:89-106.
1983   Saint Paul and the Apostolic Letter Tradition. *The Catholic Biblical Quarterly* 45:433-444.

Wierenga, Lambert
    1988   Paulus en de dwaze Galaten: aanzet tot een retorische beschrijving van Paulus' brief aan de Galaten. *Radix* 14:8-42.
Wilamowitz-Möllendorff, U. von
    1900   Asianismus und Atticismus. *Hermes* 35:1-52.
Wilcken, Ulrich, ed.
    1927   *Urkunden der Ptolemäerzeit.* Vol. 1b. Berlin: de Gruyter.
Winterbottom, Michael
    1964   Quintilian and the *Vir Bonus. Journal of Roman Studies* 54:90-97.
    1976   Review of S. Usher (transl.), *Dionysius of Halicarnassus, Critical Essays* (2 Vols; LCL; London: Heinemann, 1974-85). *The Classical Review* 26:173-174.
    1982a   Schoolroom and Courtroom. In *Rhetoric Revalued: Papers from the International Society for the History of Rhetoric.* Brian Vickers ed. Pp. 59-70. New York: Center for Medieval & Early Renaissance Studies.
    1982b   Cicero and the Silver Age. *Fondation Hardt: Entretiens* 28:237-274.
    1983   Review of A. D. Leeman, H. Pinkster, *M. Tullius Cicero, De Oratore Libri III* (vol. 1; Heidelberg: Carl Winter, 1981). *The Classical Review* 33:36-37.
    1986   Review of A. D. Leeman, H. Pinkster, H. L. W. Nelson, *M. Tullius Cicero, De Oratore Libri III* (vol. 2; Heidelberg: Carl Winter, 1985). *The Classical Review* 36:318.
    1991   Review of A. D. Leeman, H. Pinkster, E. Rabbie, *M. Tullius Cicero, De Oratore Libri III* (vol. 3; Heidelberg: Carl Winter, 1989). *The Classical Review* 41:64-66.
Wisse, Jakob
    1989   *Ethos and Pathos from Aristotle to Cicero.* Amsterdam: A. M. Hakkert.
    1994   *Welsprekendheid en filosofie bij Cicero: Studies en commentaar bij Cicero, De oratore 3,19-37a; 52-95.* Unpublished Dissertation, University of Amsterdam.
    1995   Greeks, Romans, and the Rise of Atticism. In *Greek Literary Theory After Aristotle: A Collection of Papers in Honour of D. M. Schenkeveld.* J. G. J. Abbenes, S. R. Slings, and I. Sluiter ed. Pp. 65-82. Amsterdam: VU University Press.
Witherington, Ben III
    1995   *Conflict & Community in Corinth: A Socio-rhetorical Commentary on 1 and 2 Corinthians.* Grand Rapids, Mich.: W. B. Eerdmans.
Wooten, Cecil
    1994   The Peripatetic Tradition in the Literary Essays of Dionysius of Halicarnassus. In *Peripatetic Rhetoric After Aristotle.* W. W. Fortenbaugh and D. C. Mirhady ed. Pp. 121-130. Rutgers University Studies in Classical Humanities VI. New Brunswick: Transaction Publishers.
Wuellner, W.
    1976   Paul's Rhetoric of Argumentation in Romans: An Alternative to the Donfried-Karris Debate Over Romans. *The Catholic Biblical Quarterly* 38:330-351. Reprint, 1991, in *The Romans Debate.* Revised and Expanded Edition. Karl P. Donfried ed. Pp. 128-146. Peabody, Mass.: Hendrickson.
    1979   Greek Rhetoric and Pauline Argumentation. In *Early Christian Literature and the Classical Intellectual Tradition.* In Honorem Robert M. Grant. Eds William R. Schoedel and Robert L. Wilken. Pp. 177-188. Théologie Historique 53. Paris: Éditions Beauchesne.
    1986   Paul as Pastor: The Function of Rhetorical Questions in First Corinthians. In *L'Apôtre Paul: Personalité, style et conception du ministère.* A. Vanhoye ed. Pp. 49-77. Bibliotheca Ephemeridum Theologicarum Iovaniensium. Leuven: University Press.
    1987   Where is Rhetorical Criticism Taking Us? *The Catholic Biblical Quarterly* 49:448-463.
Zwicker
    1913   Homonoia 1). In *Pauly's Real-Encyclopädie der classischen Altertumswissenschaft.* Eds Georg Wissowa *et al.* Vol. 8.2. Pp. 2265-2268. Stuttgart: J. B. Metzler.

Index of Ancient Works

Index of Modern Authors

Index of Greek Rhetorical Terms

Within italicised page references (where the relevant term is the main subject of attention) separate references are not made to footnotes. Possible synonyms are indicated in brackets and are only meant as a guide to seeking references. Note that where various terms are used in different ways, the indicated synonyms may not always be relevant.

Index of Latin Rhetorical Terms

Within italicised page references (where the relevant term is the main subject of attention) separate references are not made to footnotes. Possible synonyms are indicated in brackets and are only meant as a guide to seeking references. Note that where various terms are used in different ways, the indicated synonyms may not always be relevant.

Select Glossary of Greek Rhetorical Terms[1]

ἀλληγορία - **I.** Arist. *Rh.* 3.11.6-10, although not using this term, describes ἀλληγορία under the term τὸ προσεξαπατᾶν, i.e., temporary delusion. When something is described in oblique terms, whether by appropriate sayings (ἀποφθέγματα), riddles (τὰ εὖ ἠνιγμένα), puns (τὰ παρὰ γράμμα σκώματα) or ambiguity (ὁμωνυμία), there is a temporary delusion before the hearer realises what is really being said. Aristotle describes this as τὸ μὴ ὅ φησι λέγειν (*Rh.* 3.11.6) or λέγειν ἄλλως (*Rh.* 3.11.7, cf. ἀλλ-ηγορία). His discussion is subordinated to a consideration of what makes speech ἀστεῖον (cultured). Demetr. *Eloc.* 99-102 (cf. 151, 243, 282-86), using the term ἀλληγορία, explains that it is μεγαλεῖον especially when used as a threat. Instead of telling the truth straight out, one uses an ἀλληγορία and so is more fearful and threatening, although also more ambiguous. However, it should not become an αἴνιγμα to us.[2] Demetrius (§ 243) also uses the term τὰ σύμβολα (symbolic expressions) to refer to ἀλληγορία (as does, e.g., Corn. *ND* 35 and Ph. *Omn.Prob.Lib.* 82). At § 286 Demetrius suggests that ἀλληγορία is essentially poetical. Indeed, Heraclit. (first century AD) *All.* 5-6 discusses the use of ἀλληγορία in various poets, and Tryph. *Trop.* 1.3 cites a good example from Il. 19.222, cf. Ps.-Plu. *Vit.Hom.* 70.[3] Trypho (*Trop.* 1.4), like Demetrius, distinguishes the ἀλληγορία from the αἴνιγμα (defined as an expression whose meaning is hidden).

D.H. *Dem.* 5 (p.138,1-2 U.-R.) criticises Plato's use of ἀλληγορίαι. Theon *Prog.* ii, p.81,6-7 Sp. speaks of ἡ τῶν ἀποκεκρυμμένων ἱστοριῶν ἀλληγορία which detracts from the clarity of a διήγησις.

---

[1] The following is a modified selection from my *Glossary of Greek Rhetorical Terms connected to Methods of Argumentation and Figures from Anaximenes to Quintilian* (forthcoming). Note that the terms listed below *may* have more technical uses than indicated here. Only those uses pertinent to the discussion in this book have been included.

[2] Demetrius does not really contradict Aristotle at this point. Aristotle makes it quite clear that τὰ εὖ ἠνιγμένα are riddles which someone after a moment's thought perceives. Demetrius is warning against sayings which remain obscure to the audience. In this respect he agrees with what Aristotle says of the αἴνιγμα in *Po.* 22.5, a passage which cites the same example as Demetr. *Eloc.* 102, cf. Arist. *Rh.* 3.2.12.

[3] Both Heraclit. *All.* and Ps.-Plu. *Vit.Hom.* go on to argue that Homer deliberately spoke of philosophical doctrines using ἀλληγορία. This is of course rather far-fetched.

II. In a broader sense, the term ἀλληγορία could be used generically of a group of figures which say one thing but hint at another. Quint. *Inst.* 8.6.58 discusses the problematics of this definition.

Phld. *Rh.* 1.181 S. says that ἀλληγορίαι are normally divided into αἴνιγμα, παροιμία and εἰρωνεία, a division which seems to be reflected in *Rhet.Her.* 4.46 where *permutatio* (ἀλληγορία) is divided into, *similitudo* (using a string of metaphors), *argumentum* (a kind of dark periphrasis used to amplify or denigrate) and *contrarium* (calling something by opposite terms, cf. under εἰρωνεία). Philodemus adds that hereby several other related figures are passed by, e.g., ὁ γρῖφος and ὁ ἀστεϊσμός.

Cicero (*de Orat.* 3.166; *Orat.* 94, cf. *Att.* 2.20.3) speaks of ἀλληγορία in the sense of a string of metaphors (cf. Quint. *Inst.* 8.6.14).

Quint. *Inst.* 8.6.44-59 deals with the allegory in general, discussing under this term also αἴνιγμα, εἰρωνεία, σαρκασμός, ἀστεϊσμός, ἀντίφρασις, παροιμία and μυκτηρισμός. For use in jesting cf. Quint. *Inst.* 6.3.69.

III. The term ἀλληγορία was also used in reference to the interpretative method applied to the poets (especially Homer). It was used, for example, to show how they were really speaking about ethics or natural philosophy (in allegories). See the excursus on this method in chapter four, § 2.5, part two.

ἀναδίπλωσις - Demetr. *Eloc.* 66, 140, 267 understands this to mean the repetition of a particular word or phrase not necessarily in any fixed pattern. Whilst its primary characteristic is forcefulness (δεινότης), it can also provide μέγεθος and even χάρις. *Rhet.Her.* 4.38 (*conduplicatio*) defines it similarly and adds that it is used either for *amplificatio* or *commiseratio* and produces an emotional jab (compare here the figure *traductio* in *Rhet.Her.* 4.20 which is the elegant use of the same word several times in the same clause). Rut.Lup. 1.11 terms this emphatic repetition of a word or words ἐπανάληψις (cf. Quint. *Inst.* 8.3.50-51, who also uses the term ταυτολογία, and Quint. *Inst.* 9.3.28-29). It is mentioned at Cic. *de Orat.* 3.203 (= *Orat.* 135), 206 (= *Orat.* 137).

ἀνακοίνωσις - (Lat. *communicatio*) a figure whereby the speaker seems to consult with the audience or opponent, cf. Cic. *Orat.* 138 = *de Orat.* 3.204; Quint. *Inst.* 9.2.20-24. It may simply take the form of a short rhetorical question. The Greek term is first used by Iul.Rufin. 10 (early fourth century AD).[4]

---

[4] The only usage of this word recorded by LSJ is in the scholiast to Ar. *Pl.* 39. It is also found in Chrys. *serm.*2.1 *in Gen.* (4.652c).

ἀποστροφή - lit. "a turning away from" and thus in rhetoric, turning away from someone to address someone else specifically. [Longin.] 16.2-4 uses this term to describe the rhetorical use of an oath. Ps.-Longinus is concerned with a sublime use of this figure and thus gives an example from Demosthenes who turns to make an oath not to the gods but to those who fought in the battle at Marathon. He thus both deifies the former Greek victors and enables his audience to identify with them in the fight against Philip. Ps.-Longinus adds that one's timing and sense of placement need to be just right. Although under a different heading (that of shifts of person), this is again dealt with at § 27. *Rhet.Her.* 4.22 (*exclamatio*) notes that it is used to express grief or indignation and should be used sparingly when the importance of the subject requires it. It may be addressed to a person, city, place or object, cf. Quint. *Inst.* 9.2.26. Quint. *Inst.* 4.1.63-69 notes that many rhetoricians agree that it is inappropriate to the προοίμιον. Quintilian himself, however, argues (with examples) that it may sometimes be used here. It should generally not be used in the *narratio* (*Inst.* 4.2.103, 106-107), but may effectively be used in the *peroratio* (*Inst.* 6.1.3). The figure is mentioned at Cic. *de Orat.* 3.207 = *Orat.* 135 (*exclamatio*). See also Quint. *Inst.* 9.3.24-26.

Quint. *Inst.* 9.2.38-39 maintains that the term ἀποστροφή has a broader definition. It may denote any kind of utterance that diverts the attention of the audience from the topic in hand (contrast *Inst.* 4.1.63). In Cicero this seems to imply even the introduction of some kind of deliberate mistake, but his meaning remains very vague, cf. *de Orat.* 3.205 (*erroris inductio*) = *Orat.* 138 (*ut ab eo quod agitur avertat animos*).

διαίρεσις - Arist. *Rh.* 2.23.10 terms one of the (abstract) κοινοὶ τόποι, ἐκ διαιρέσεως. It occurs when several possibilities are listed and all but one are eliminated, cf. Cic. *Top.* 10, 33-34 (*enumeratio/ partitio*); *de Orat.* 2.165 (*partitio*). It is listed as a figure in *Rhet.Her.* 4.40-41 (*expeditio*) and a form of argumentation in Cic. *Inv.* 1.45 (*enumeratio*) with refutation at 1.84. Quintilian describes it as a form of *divisio* (*Inst.* 5.10.66-67, cf. 7.1.31-33). He notes that this form of argument is risky as it fails when but one alternative is omitted.

ἔμφασις - is used in the sense "hint" or "suggestion." This is related to ἔμφασις as an image or reflection, e.g., in a mirror. *Rhet.Her.* 4.67 (*significatio*) divides it into five kinds: i) by *exsuperatio* (ὑπερβολή) which increases a certain suspicion, ii) by ambiguity, i.e., use of a double meaning, iii) by a given consequence, i.e., when something is said which logically follows from something else, iv) by *abscisio* (ἀποσιώπησις), v) by laying a brief comparison beside the matter in dis-

cussion without comment, e.g., "Do not, Saturninus, rely too much on the popular mob - unavenged lie the Gracchi" (trans. Caplan). Quint. *Inst.* 9.3.67 is
unclear, but cf. 8.2.11; 8.4.26; 9.2.64. At *Inst.* 8.3.83-86 he discusses two
kinds: i) a word used which means more than it says, e.g., Od. 11.523 "the
Greeks <u>descended</u> into the wooden horse," the word "descended" showing at the
same time the size of the horse (further illustrated at Tryph. *Trop.* 2.2 and
[Corn.] *Rh.* 78); ii) a word deliberately omitted, either by stating that you omit to
say something, or by what is actually ἀποσιώπησις (which he admits). Demetr.
Eloc. 288-90 gives examples of both these kinds amidst a discussion on figured
speech (in the forceful style). Although he does not specifically term these examples ἐμφάσεις, yet he indicates in his introduction to the discussion (287) that ἔμφασις is an important aspect of his topic. Further see Demetr. *Eloc.* 57, 130-31,
171, 282-86, etc.. At § 286 he suggests that it is primarily poetical. Phld. *Rh.*
1.177 S., discussing the views of other rhetorical theorists, mentions ἔμφασις in
connection with the use of metaphors.[5] Ἔμφασις is further mentioned at Cic.
Orat. 139; *de Orat.* 3.202.

The use of ἔμφασις in terms of a word meaning more than it says can also be
used to produce wit, Cic. *de Orat.* 2.268; Quint. *Inst.* 6.3.69.

ἐνθύμημα - lit. "consideration." Compare ἐνθύμιον "scruple," ἐνθύμιον ποιεῖσθαί τι =
ἐνθυμέομαι, "have a scruple about."

For Aristotle's theory of the ἐνθύμημα see chapter two, § 1.2 above.

Demetrius' discussion of the ἐνθύμημα at *Eloc.* 30-32 is clearly related to the
Aristotelian tradition, although his material seems to have been drawn from an
intermediary source common to Quintilian (see below). Aristotle's theory has
been somewhat adapted. Demetrius defines an ἐνθύμημα as a kind of unfinished
syllogism that is found in two forms, namely, ἐκ μάχης λεγομένη and ἐν

---

5   At 1.176 (col. 17,14-17) he sets about mentioning at least three purposes of the metaphor according
to "some." However, the text breaks off after the mention of brevity and clarity. After two lines from
which no sense can be made, we encounter the second half of a sentence concerning what must be a comparison to the task of a poet. The genitive construction οὐ [μόν]ης τῆς τ[ὸ σαφὲς] ἐχούσης would appear
to have referred back to the noun ἔμφασις, as we may gather from the following sentence:
Πλανῶσ<ι>ν δ[ὲ] τῆς ἐμφάσεως ὡς οὔσης σαφηνεία[ς ἢ σ]υ[ντελοῦντος] τὴν ὑπ' αὐ[τῶν καλουμέ]νην
[ἐνέ]ργειαν το[ῦ μεταφέρειν δι]ὰ παντός (I have substituted ἐνέργειαν for Sudhaus' ἐνάργειαν). The
next sentence makes it clear that Philodemus is still speaking about proposed purposes for using metaphors. The otherwise unexpected introduction of the notion of ἔμφασις would suggest that the third purpose of the metaphor belonging to the sentence broken off at 1.176 (col. 17,17) is ἔμφασις.

ἀκολουθίας σχήματι.[6] Firstly, whilst Aristotle certainly permitted ἐνθυμήματα to exist in the form of unfinished syllogisms, he did not restrict them in this way. It is clear from his explanation as a whole that by ἐνθύμημα he generally meant a kind of syllogism in three parts (major and minor premises, and conclusion).[7] Secondly, on the surface Demetrius' two forms seem to correspond to Aristotle's demonstrative and refutative ἐνθυμήματα (cf. *Rh.* 2.22.14-17; 2.25.1; 2.26.3; 3.17.13). Demetrius does not explain them any further. Yet we have in Quint. *Inst.* 5.14.1-4 (cf. 5.14.24-26; 5.10.2; 9.2.106) an explanation of these forms clearly relying upon the same source. We learn there that these two forms are two quite specific forms of rhetorical syllogism, the one reasoning from consequences employing a simple proposition with a reason attached, the other employing contraries, i.e., using an antithetical form of reasoning showing the proposition to be in conflict with another consideration.[8] Quintilian goes on to add what seems to be another version of the second form, namely, when a reason is added to a proposition which is contrary or dissimilar to the point of the opposition. Quint. *Inst.* 5.10.2 (cf. 8.5.9-10) rightly notes that the term ἐνθύμημα was often restricted to this latter form (the former being denoted an ἐπιχείρημα). This represents a rhetorical definition of the ἐνθύμημα predating Aristotle.

Aristotle's definition of the ἐνθύμημα did not become standard within rhetorical circles. That is not to say that a kind of rhetorical syllogism was not further developed in rhetorical theory, but the rhetorical syllogism after Aristotle went under the term ἐπιχείρημα. The standard definition of an ἐνθύμημα in rhetorical theory remained what it had already been before Aristotle, namely, a short argument or consideration based on contraries.[9]

---

6   I accept here (following L. Radermacher [1901] and D. C. Innes [1995]) Finck's addition of ἤ in the text. The text thus reads: τὸ δ᾽ ἐνθύμημα διάνοιά τις ἤτοι ἐκ μάχης λεγομένη <ἤ> ἐν ἀκολουθίας σχήματι. The ἤ is surely required by the ἤτοι and the text represents a simple case of haplography. Furthermore, this addition brings the text into line with the interpretation in Quintilian (see below) clearly based upon the same source. Yet it should be noted that [Anon.] *Fig.* iii, p.111,25-26 Sp. (fourth century AD or later) gives evidence of a different interpretation: διάνοια γάρ ἐστι τὸ ἐνθύμημα ἐκ μάχης λεγομένη ἐν ἀκολουθίας σχήματι. The discussion in this treatise would appear to be based upon an already corrupted text of Demetrius.
7   See also W. M. A. Grimaldi, *Studies*, 87-91.
8   H. E. Butler (in the *Loeb* translation) consistently translates *ex consequentibus* as "from denial of consequents." The term "denial" does not come from the text, nor is it suggested by the underlying Greek (from Demetr. *Eloc.* 30) ἐν ἀκολουθίας σχήματι. It seems influenced by the explanatory note of A. Wolf (*Loeb* ed. vol. 2, p.524) who provides a dialectical interpretation of the two kinds of ἐνθυμήματα. I am not convinced that Quintilian had such a dialectical interpretation in mind. His own explanation does not seem to reflect this.
9   This fact seems not to have been noticed by W. M. A. Grimaldi who inappropriately cites Cic. *Top.* 56 as if it were dealing with the same matter as ἐνθύμημα in Aristotle's *Rhetoric* (*Studies*, 56).

This seems to be reflected in the definition provided by [Arist.] *Rh.Al.* 10 (cf. 5.1-4), namely, a short consideration as to whether any matters under discussion are in opposition to any of the τελικὰ κεφάλαια (e.g., δίκαιος, νόμιμος, συμφέρος, etc.) or their opposites, or the ἦθος τοῦ λέγοντος or ἔθος τῶν πραγμάτων. Such considerations, together with γνῶμαι, are used to conclude any line of argumentation (e.g., argumentation by εἰκότα or by παραδείγματα, cf. [Arist.] *Rh.Al.* 32.6, 8; 34.11; 35.12, 15f; 36.18). Cic. *Top.* 55-56 likewise argues that the ἐνθύμημα is a short proof from contraries used as a conclusion (example provided). The same kind of argument seems to be intended in *Rhet.Her.* 4.25-26 (cf. Quint. *Inst.* 5.10.2) where it is termed *contrarium*, e.g., "why should you think that one who is a faithless friend can be an honourable enemy?" He states that it ought to be one short sentence. It provides a forcible proof refuted only with difficulty, cf. Cic. *de Orat.* 3.207 (*contrarium*) which Quint. *Inst.* 9.3.90 appears to have interpreted in this sense (also using the term ἐναντιότης, cf. 9.2.106).

Of further interest is a comment in Quint. *Inst.* 12.10.51 where it is noted that some theorists considered the ἐνθύμημα as more fitting in a written speech, the παράδειγμα as more fitting in a spoken speech.

ἐπερώτησις - "rhetorical question." Concerning those questions left unanswered by the speaker, note the following: [Arist.] *Rh.Al.* 20.5 (the prefix προσ- is used at 20.1) lists it as a method of recapitulation (whether of parts or of the whole of a speech), as does Arist. *Rh.* 3.19.5 (ἐρώτησις). Similarly, *Rhet.Her.* 4.22 (*interrogatio*) suggests that it is best used as amplification when points against the adversaries have been summed up. The recommendation that ἐπερώτησις be used in recapitulation is most probably connected to the element of πάθος in its use (rhetorical theorists generally recommended the building up of πάθος in the ἐπίλογος). This is confirmed by Demetr. *Eloc.* 279 (τὸ ἐρωτῶντα τοὺς ἀκούοντας ἔνια λέγειν) who classifies it under the style δεινότης. He notes that the listener appears to be like someone under cross examination who has nothing to answer. It is thus a rhetorical question which expects no answer. Quint. *Inst.* 9.2.6-11 emphasises that such a question is not for gaining information but *instandi gratia* (insisting on our point/ threatening). It may also be used to invoke pity, admiration, etc. (i.e., other πάθη).

ἐπιμονή - "lingering." Demetr. *Eloc.* 280 appears to define it as a longer expression of the matter, i.e., dwelling on a point. He adds that it may greatly contribute to δεινότης. Hermog. *Id.* 1.11 (pp.285-86 R.) also characterises this figure as belonging especially to δεινότης. He states that one should use ἐπιμοναί when dealing with a particularly strong point, repeating it several times. He goes on to refer to a passage in Demosthenes and remarks that there the same thought is restated more than four times in the same place. Alex. *Fig.* 1.10 defines it as dwelling upon the same thought with αὔξησις. He gives several short examples. In this respect it may be noted that [Longin.] 12.2 uses this term to describe the effect of αὔξησις.

    Rhet.Her. 4.58 discusses *commoratio* which he explains in terms of dwelling long and often on the strongest point in the whole speech and often returning to it. This is somewhat different from ἐπιμονή proper, which designates lingering on the same point *in the same place*, cf. Cic. *de Orat.* 3.203. I am not aware of another Greek source which makes this distinction.

    The figure is mentioned at Cic. *Orat.* 137 = *de Orat.* 3.202.

ἐσχηματισμένος λόγος - "figured speech." In rhetorical theory the term "figure" (e.g., of speech) often had the same meaning as it has in English, but it could also refer to a more specific use of figures often referred to as ἐσχηματισμένος λόγος. In this case the term σχῆμα took on another connotation, best indicated by the definition of the cynic philosopher and rhetor Zoilos (fourth century BC): σχῆμά ἐστιν ἕτερον μὲν προσποιεῖσθαι, ἕτερον δὲ λέγειν (L. Radermacher, *Art. Script.* B XXXV *Fr.* 2). Demetr. *Eloc.* 287-98 notes that this more specific use of the term refers to the use of figures to hide or cover what one actually wants to say. It is a way of softening one's critique especially if that critique was to be presented to people high in authority. Two reasons for using figures in this way are given, ἀσφάλεια and εὐπρέπεια ("caution" and "propriety"). [Longin.] 17, however, warns against too obviously cloaking everything in figures in these situations as this arouses suspicion. One must use figures in such a way that they appear not to be figures. This is best achieved by ensuring that the figures are sublime for then their sublimity strikes one so much that the fact that a figure is used recedes into the background.[10] Quint. *Inst.* 9.2.65-107 discusses figured speech under three uses, caution (9.2.67-75), propriety (9.2.76-95), and charm (*venustas*, 9.2.96-107). The famous Asianist orator of the late first century AD, Scopelian, is said to have excelled in this kind of figured oratory (Philostr. *VS* 519), as are later orators. Two treatises probably to be dated to the early third

---

[10] The notion of concealing one's craft in speech-making was a general commonplace among the theorists. For a long list of references see Caplan's note to *Rhet.Her.* 4.10 (pp.250-51 Loeb ed.).

century AD (wrongly attributed to Dionysius of Halicarnassus, cf. Radermacher, pp.xxiii - xxiv, Teubner ed.) deal in detail with this kind of figured speech, [D.H.] *Rh.* 8 and 9, cf. [Hermog.] *Inv.* 4.13; Aps. *Prob.*. The treatises clearly presuppose earlier discussion (no longer extant), cf. *Rh.* 8.1.

μεταβολή - "change" or "reversal." Demetr. *Eloc.* 148-49 (under the γλαφυρά style) describes it as a kind of reversal of one's thought, or recantation. He gives two examples, the first involving the use of a more realistic description following a ὑπερβολή, the second involving the speaker/ author changing his intention (in this case whether or not to tell the reader the names of two dogs which the author has mentioned). The result of such a "correction" is to make the audience favourable (i.e., provide χάρις, cf. *gratia* in *Rhet.Her.* 4.36). This figure would seem equivalent to *correctio* (ἐπανόρθωσις, cf. [Iul.Rufin.] *Schem.L.* 17) as defined by *Rhet.Her.* 4.36 (cf. Cic. *Orat.* 135 = *de Orat.* 3.207 - *reprehensio*; *de Orat.* 203 - *correctio*). He notes that the initial use of the "incorrect" formulation helps to highlight the following "correction," and thus impresses the correct formulation upon the hearer. The examples provided show that initial statement does not have to be considered completely false, but that the *correctio* may only provide a different perception of the matter. Rut.Lup. 1.16 calls such a self-correction μετάνοια, cf. Quint. *Inst.* 9.2.17 (*emendatio*, a species of πρόληψις); 9.2.18 (*reprehensio*, a form of πρόληψις, being self-correction related to the meaning and propriety of one's words); 9.2.60 (*quasi paenitentia*); 9.3.89 (*correctio*). Compare also [Arist.] *Rh.Al.* 18.9 who advises that if in court the judges *en masse* make some kind of objection to you speaking, then you should rebuke yourself, not the judges (*vice versa* if it is only a minority of the judges).

It seems to have been common to employ a short apologising statement after the use of ὑπερβολή or an especially bold metaphor, cf. Arist. *Rh.* 3.7.9; Cic. *de Orat.* 3.165; Quint. *Inst.* 8.3.37.

παράδειγμα - "(concrete) example." [Arist.] *Rh.Al.* 8 states that examples are used to bolster arguments considered by the listeners to be improbable (cf. εἴκος and Cic. *Part.* 40). Examples can also be used to make an opponent's argument seem improbable. Although Anaximenes does not say so, he gives examples of παραδείγματα which show that they can also be used to reinforce an argument which may already be considered probable. Arist. *Rh.* 2.20 divides the παράδειγμα into two forms, namely, historical examples, and invented examples. Invented examples are further divided into the παραβολή (hypothetical example), and the λόγος (fable). He uses the term δημηγορικός to describe the λόγος, but notes that it is easier to find fables to support one's argument than historical examples (*Rh.* 2.20.7), cf. *s.v.* μῦθος. If no ἐνθυμήματα are available, then examples must be used *as proofs*, that is, they are to be put first and one's argument seems to be a proof by induction (cf. Cic. *Inv.* 1.51-56; *Top.* 42; Quint. *Inst.* 5.10.73). This requires the use of multiple examples, but is only rarely suitable to rhetoric. If ἐνθυμήματα are used then the function of examples becomes supporting testimony (μάρτυρες) which is placed after the main arguments (ἐνθυμήματα). In this case, only one example is necessary.[11] *Rhet.Her.* 2.46 briefly lists faults made in using examples. At 4.62 he suggests the same four purposes are possible as listed for the παραβολή, namely, embellishment, clarity, proof, or vividness. Cic. *Part.* 55 lists the use of *exempla* as a *locus* for *amplificatio* (αὔξησις). Cic. *Inv.* 1.49 briefly argues that examples are a subset of probable proofs. Use of examples is mentioned at Cic. *Orat.* 138 = *de Orat.* 3.205. Quintilian (*Inst.* 5.11.6-21), like Aristotle, discusses παραδείγματα in connection with comparisons and fables. Quint. *Inst.* 5.11.15-16 distinguishes between relating an example in-depth and merely referring to a (known) example. Quint. *Inst.* 12.10.51 notes that some theorists considered the ἐνθύμημα as more fitting in a written speech, and the παράδειγμα as more fitting in a spoken speech.

παρομολογία - "partial admission." The presentation of an equal or stronger argument after conceding some point to the opposition, Rut.Lup. 1.19. Quint. *Inst.* 9.2.99 denies that this is a figure, but compare *Inst.* 9.2.51 on *concessio* (a concession of something seemingly damaging to our case which serves to prove one's trust in the cause) and *confessio* (a confession of something innocuous by the person we are defending). *Confessio* is classified as a species of πρόληψις at *Inst.* 9.2.17.

παρρησία - *Rhet.Her.* 4.48-50 (*licentia*) defines it as reprehending someone to whom reverence is due. This may be smoothed over either by flattering the audience first, or by suggesting that they may not like what you are going to say, but truth, etc. compels you. The latter may be used effectively even when the speaker knows that the audience won't mind what he has to say, cf. Rut.Lup. 2.18. It is mentioned at Cic. *Orat.* 138 (*ut liberius quid audeat*) = *de Orat.* 3.205 (*vox quaedam libera atque etiam effrenatio augendi causa*). See also Quint. *Inst.* 9.2.27-29.

περίφρασις - the use of a phrase for a word, even a phrase that includes the word concerned, cf. *Rhet.Her.* 4.43 (*circumitio*) who gives as the motivation for its use

---

11   Contrast Plin. *Ep.* 2.20.9 who suggests that later theorists stipulated three examples to be necessary, although I am not aware of such a stipulation in the extant treatises, cf. Quint. *Inst.* 4.5.3.

ornandi ratio. [Longin.] 28-29 treats περίφρασις as an ornamental figure which engenders ὕψος, but warns that moderation is needed. Quint. *Inst.* 9.1.6 defines it as including the word concerned. At *Inst.* 8.6.59-61 he adds that it may be used to avoid explicitly mentioning something indecent, or for *ornatus*, but that excessive periphrasis is called περισσολογία (cf. D.H. *Dem.* 5 = *Pomp.* 2.5). D.H. *Amm.* 2, 4 provides examples from Thucydides.

προσωποποιΐα - Demetr. *Eloc.* 265-66 defines it as introducing a specific character (person or thing) and letting it speak. It is not to be confused with personification. *Rhet.Her.* 4.66 suggests that it is most beneficial in αὔξησις (cf. Cic. *Part.* 55), and appeals to pity (which are treated as a form of αὔξησις in Cic. *Part.* 57). Both these contexts belong to the ἐπίλογος in *Rhet.Her.* (cf. 2.47-50). In this respect Theon *Prog.* ii, p.117,30-32 Sp. also notes that it is especially suitable to the portrayal of characters and emotions (ἤθη and πάθη), two concepts frequently associated with the ἐπίλογος. See also Cic. *Orat.* 85 and Rut.Lup. 2.6.

Quint. *Inst.* 9.2.29-37 notes that this term sometimes also covers what others distinguish as διάλογος (*sermocinatio*, see *s.v.*), restricting προσωποποιΐα to fictitious persons or things. Yet in *Rhet.Her.* 4.65-66 where this very distinction is made, *conformatio* (the term in *Rhet.Her.* for προσωποποιΐα) may still refer to real persons who are nevertheless absent. Quintilian's own interpretation of the figure is rather broad and one is inclined to say that he sidetracks somewhat, e.g., at *Inst.* 9.2.36 where he refers to the possibility of introducing an imaginary objector. This is really another figure altogether (cf. *s.v.* ἐπερώτησις). Quintilian also notes that the speaker may not always be specifically introduced, but it is notable that his only example is from epic poetry (Verg. *A.* 2.29), and even here he adds that omission of notification of the speaker is itself another figure, namely, *detractio*. Quint. *Inst.* 4.1.28 (cf. 6.1.3, 25-27) recommends use of προσωποποιΐα in the ἐπίλογος, where (unlike the προοίμιον) free range can be given to the emotions, though at 4.1.69 he cites an example of its use in a προοίμιον from a lost speech of Cicero (cf. also D. 1.2). Cic. *Inv.* 1.99-100 suggests using it in the recapitulation of the ἐπίλογος as a way of varying presentation. His examples are of a lawgiver (dead person) or things (cf. Alex. *Fig.* 1.12). Cic. *Top.* 45 alludes to προσωποποιΐα and suggests that it is a device used by both orators *and* philosophers (cf. examples below). It is, however, to be avoided in the plain style (*Orat.* 85). It is further mentioned at Cic. *Orat.* 138 = *de Orat.* 3.205.

Προσωποποιΐα as a device is not only found in speeches. A particularly well-known example is to be found in Plato's dialogue *Crito* 50a - 54d. Socrates engages here in a dialogue with the laws. Plato seems to be deliberately playing upon how a rhetor might speak (cf. 50b). For good examples in the speeches of Cicero, see *Cael.* 33-34 (a dead person called up); *Catil.* 1.17-18, 27-29 (the *patria* speaks); *Planc.* 12-13 (the people speak - here the speech is interbroken with comment from Cicero himself). It also occurs in a philosophical dialogue, *Fin.* 4.61 (the pupils of Plato are called up). See further (the speaker is indicated in brackets) Pl. *Prt.* 361a-c (the *result* of a discussion); D. 1.2 (the present season); Bion Borys. *Fr.* 17 Kindstrand (poverty); Lucr. 3.931-62 (nature); Ph. *Cher.* 35-38 (vocations); cf. *Op.Mund.* 79 (nature); Plu. 2.1048f (life); Sen. *Ep.* 95.10 (philosophy); Arr. *Epict.* 3.1.23 (a choice example of some species); D.Chr. 45.5 (the noble man); Max.Tyr. 11.4 (the parts of the body, and, Asclepius); 17.3 (τέχνη); Babr. 71.5-10 (the sea).

Προσωποποιΐα was also taught as a progymnasmatic exercise, namely, the writing of a short speech in the style of some other (usually famous) person, cf. Quint. *Inst.* 3.8.49-54. Theon *Prog.* ii, pp.115-18 Sp. devotes a separate section to this but mainly discusses matters relating to appropriate language and possible forms of speech. He appears to suggest that this figure was commonly used in panegyric, protreptic and letters (*Prog.* ii, p.115,20-22 Sp.).[12] At *Prog.* ii, p.120,24-30 Sp. he shows (incidentally) that he includes διάλογος under προσωποποιΐα.

Later works on προγυμνάσματα distinguished between προσωποποιΐα referring to abstract concepts and ἠθοποιΐα referring to persons.

στάσις - a term used, mostly in connection with judicial rhetoric, to refer to the nature of the case to be argued. Whilst the details of στάσις theory vary among the rhetorical theorists, four στάσεις (or kinds of cases) were often identified: 1) στοχασμός, concerning the fact of the occurrence, e.g.; Did the accused actually committed the murder or not? 2) ὅρος, concerning the definition of the crime, e.g.; Did the accused commit the crime of sacrilege or the crime of theft when he stole sacred vessels from a private house? 3) ποιότης, concerning the quality of the crime, e.g.; Were there were mitigating circumstances that justified the

---

12   This seems to be what is meant by the words: ὑπὸ δὲ τοῦτο τὸ γένος τῆς γυμνασίας πίπτει καὶ τὸ τῶν πανηγυρικῶν λόγων εἶδος, καὶ τὸ τῶν προτρεπτικῶν, καὶ τὸ τῶν ἐπιστολικῶν. Alternatively Theon may be suggesting that this exercise embraced the writing (in another's name) of panegyric and protreptic (why not apotreptic?) speeches as well as letters.

crime? 4) μετάληψις, concerning procedural objections, e.g.; Has the accused been brought before the appropriate court?

τόπος (*locus*) - "place" or "source" where arguments may be found. The kind of τόποι contained in rhetorical treatises varies considerably. Sometimes a list of ready-made arguments are given which can be directly inserted into the appropriate place in a speech (e.g., standard arguments *pro* and *contra* the value of confessions extracted by torture). At other times a list of subjects is given upon which arguments may be based, e.g., sex, age, etc. (the idea being, for example, that certain crimes are more likely to be committed by a male than a female, or by a child than an adult). Another possibility is that a list of abstract argumentative patterns is given (e.g., argument by similarity, or by dissimilarity, etc.).

Τόποι were supplied in connection with many aspects of rhetorical theory, e.g., τόποι relevant to the various parts of a speech, or τόποι for the various στάσεις. The treatises frequently also make use of a distinction between specific and common τόποι. Κοινοὶ τόποι are, of course, more broadly applicable than specific τόποι, but the way in which they are more broadly applicable varies in the treatises (e.g., specific τόποι as ready-made arguments versus common τόποι as abstract argumentative patterns, or specific τόποι as arguments only suitable for one particular στάσις versus common τόποι as arguments suitable for any στάσις, etc.). Given the great variation in the treatment of τόποι, generalisations are difficult to make and each treatise must be carefully consulted for the way in which τόποι are used and distinguished in it.

See also chapter two, § 2.1.1 and § 5.

Endnote

D.H. *Dem.* 40 (p.217,7-13 U.-R.) in describing the γλαφυρὰ ἁρμονία notes that it makes use of those (poetic) figures which most move the crowds (τὰ κινητικώτατα τῶν ὄχλων). This comment would seem to give some indication of the popularity of artificial figures of speech among the kind of crowds that regularly attended orations in late first century BC Rome.[13] The figures listed in this category are: παρισώσεις, παρομοιώσεις, ἀντιθέσεις, παρονομασία, ἀντιστροφή, ἐπαναφορά, and ἄλλα πολλὰ τοιαῦτα ποιητικῆς καὶ μελικῆς λέξεως ὄργανα. They are elsewhere identified as Gorgianic figures, *Th.* 24.

---

[13] Such crowds (supposedly to hear orations in court) were to vanish later during imperial times (Tac. *Dial.* 39, cf. 19-20). The popularity of such artificial figures in first century BC Rome may be suitably compared with Gorgias' popularity in Athens some 400 years earlier.

Such figures are considered by Demetrius (*Eloc.* 27-29, 154, 247, 250) to be out of place in passages where forcefulness (δεινότης) is desired, or where emotion or characterisation is evoked (πάθη καὶ ἤθη). "Anger has no need of craft." Such figures may, however, produce charm (χάρις, § 29, 154) and dignified bombast (ὄγκος, § 247) and are said to work in conjunction with elevated vocabulary (μεγαληγορία, § 29). As such, they may be considered suitable to the μεγαλοπρεπής style (cf. § 77), and probably also to the γλαφυρά style (cf. § 154, and Dionysius above), although they are not explicitly mentioned in the discussion of either. Demetrius' considerations appear to be based upon an assessment of Aristotle's style.

Similar views are expressed by *Rhet.Her.* 4.32 who virtually restricts these figures to epideictic oratory (cf. Cic. *Part.* 72; Quint. *Inst.* 8.3.11-12), otherwise allowing only for a scattered use to brighten the style.

Cicero's approach to such figures is less negative. His comments are to be found in several places in the *Orator*, and are therefore probably bound up with his defence against the attack on his style by the proponents of a narrow Lysianic Atticism. Cic. *Orat.* 37-38 describes these kind of figures as most suitable to epideictic oratory (broadly defined so as to include history) where they are openly used (at § 65 far-fetched metaphors are also grouped with these figures and several other characteristics of sophistic oratory are mentioned). Use of such figures provides *concinnitas* and may even provide prose rhythm naturally, without deliberately aiming for such (cf. *Orat.* 164-67). Cicero notes that they are much less common in forensic oratory and even then are concealed (*Orat.* 38), although at *Orat.* 165 and 167 he provides two examples from his works which are hardly concealed (*Mil.* 10 and *Ver.* 4.115)! At *Orat.* 107 he cites a portion of an early speech containing such figures and notes that it gained great applause upon delivery (*S.Rosc.* 72).

Quintilian notes with disapproval how the kind of rhetorical display common in declamations found its way into the courts (cf. *Inst.* 4.3.2). He contrasts the concealed eloquence of former times with the ostentation (*iactatio*) in the courts of his own day (*Inst.* 4.1.9). The kind of bombast common in the courts and its hearty reception by the crowds is aptly described in *Inst.* 12.8.3 and more dramatically in Plin. *Ep.* 2.14. Yet the background here is somewhat different from the days of Dionysius of Halicarnassus, being influenced by the activity of the *delatores*.[14] Quintilian himself cautions that when strong emotions are called for, artificial figures are quite out of place (*Inst.* 9.3.100-102).

---

14   See M. Winterbottom, 1964, "Quintilian."